I0834658

America's History Retold

1400-2012 A.D.

Vol. 2.

Originating American Ways of Living and Working

Alfred de Grazia

AMERICA'S HISTORY RETOLD

1400 TO 2012 A.D.

Vol. 2

ORIGINATING AMERICAN WAYS OF LIVING AND WORKING

metron publications

ISBN: 978-1-60377-081-1

Library of Congress Number: 2011943961

METRON PUBLICATIONS

P.O. Box 1213 PRINCETON NJ 08540-1213

Cover by Metronax; photograph : Walt Whitman, by George C. Cox,

New York, April 15th, 1887.

I wish to thank my dedicated research assistant, tireless interlocutor, editor and beloved wife, Anne-Marie Hueber (Ami) for her help in writing this book; my always good-natured assistant Christoph Meyer-Rudolphi for his work on the layout and the illustrations; the Library of the University of Pennsylvania which opened its stacks to us; and the hospitality of the International House of the University of Pennsylavania which hosted us for several studious months

AMERICA'S HISTORY RETOLD
TABLE OF CONTENTS

VOLUME ONE:
CONQUESTS, COLONIALISM AND CONSTITUTIONS

VOLUME TWO: ORIGINATING AMERICAN WAYS OF LIVING AND WORKING

VOLUME THREE:
SHARING EARTH'S CULTURES AND POWERS

Revolution and Constitution - American Troop Assembly

Part Five

DIRECT DEMOCRACY

All tyranny needs to gain a foothold is for people
of good conscience to remain silent.
Thomas Jefferson

Much of what we shall talk about here relates to what
Jefferson believed. But he was too much of a gentleman and scholar,
even though a fine organizer, to be the
Front-runner of Direct Democracy.

This role can be consigned to Andrew Jackson, a brash rogue,
whose life typifies a large segment of the American mind and conduct,

from the beginning to now. We aim to set forth what direct democracy consisted of in sundry spheres of society and thought.

This is, moreover, a good place to remind ourselves of our strong interest in how the population trends on our scheme of values. Many changes occur in the period of direct democracy, especially with shifts in sectional political and federal power to the frontier margins of the West, North and South. The seats in Congress of the new States, with their cultural crudity and vast ambitions, soon numbered enough to put a man in contention for the presidency. Were the people of the United States now then better off than they had been at the start of the Revolution, in 1774 say, the last time we paid some systematic attention to their condition?

We have seen that from the earliest landings a very small number of men managed to get hold of well over half the power, wealth, reverence, and authoritative knowledge to be had, no matter what settlement we were talking about. We can call this the exponential (mal)distribution of values. We also noted that the development of cultures subordinate to the major Anglo-American culture did not produce lucky values-sharing peoples. Far from it. Here we are now fifty years after the Revolution, asking the same question. The answer is still a resounding "No".

But there may be a more interesting way of asking the question: perhaps it should be addressed from the other extreme: deprivation instead of fulfillment of values. Let us peruse the list of values attainable by humans in society and pitch them at the life conditions of the underprivileged. She (he) - or let us say "an American" - qualifies as severely deprived if described correctly in the following statements:

Indicators of Poor Welfare:

1.
Has been ill on the average at least 1 out of every 8 days of one's life.

2.
Has never had medical care better than a family member or neighbor could afford.

3.
Has been hungry at least one out of every 20 days of one's life on the average.

4.
Has never lived in a room of one's own for more than six months of one's life.

5.
Has few teeth left after the age of 32.

6.
Has died or nearly died of disease, malnutrition or extremes of temperature by the age of fifty.

7.
Has died or nearly died of violence or accident.

8.
Has never possessed more than two changes of clothes.

9.
Has never enjoyed a nutritious diet for over one month of the year during most of one's life.

10.
Has never been able to save more than a month's subsistence in a modest inn.

11.
Has never been able to give a dowry or gift to another person of the value of a horse.

12.
Has never felt that one was loved, cherished, and truly wanted by anyone.

Indicators of One's Weak Power:

13.
Has never been able to decide matters for anyone outside of one's immediate younger siblings or one's children.

14.
Has never particularly been helped by the authorities or police.

15.
Has not served involuntarily as a slave, soldier, sailor, worker, servant, spouse, or in another capacity for more than one-twentieth of one's life.

16.
Has voted on less than 20 occasions for a public officer in one's life.

17.
Has not held office in a group of any kind on more than three occasions in one's life.

18.
Has belonged to no more than two voluntary groups or associations in the course of one's life.

19.
Has experienced forty or more occasions when one was physically bullied by persons outside of the family, whether in authority or not.

20.
Has rarely dared to express in public an opinion contrary to one adopted or prevalent among the authorities or other opinion leaders around one.

21
Has been denied in nine cases out of ten due process of law (as presently construed by the Supreme Court) in all the externally handled troubles one has had in life.

22.
Has considered oneself to be low-class or discriminated against.

Indicators of Retarded Culture:

23.
Has not been taught to read, write, and figure.

24.
Has belonged to no organized church for more than ten years, counting childhood.

25.
Has acquired nothing but the barest of skills, like ditch-digging, chopping, fighting, sewing, and primitive cooking.

26.
Has never visited a museum of art, natural history or technology, nor a professionally presented concert or theatrical performance.

27.
Has not traveled beyond the nearest town, except twice to larger more distant towns, nor lived within a mile of a century-old culture-government-business complex for more than five years.

28.
Has learned nothing but a few sayings and myths about history and civilization, except for some stories from the Bible.

———

We might reasonably declare that a person who scored "yes" on practically all of these statements was extremely deprived. We might reasonably believe that few people would be zero-scorers, that is, with 100% yes-answers. This is probably not correct.
One can argue over the meaning of the indicators;
still, it would not be surprising if one out of ten Americans would have scored zero - winning a lousy deprivation score of 28 affirmatives - in every generation from 1600 at least up to 1822, say.

We might expect one out of every three Americans from earliest times up to 1822 to have scored 15 or more, and two out of three to have scored 10 or more, which is still an index score of heavy deprivation. As to what will have happened after 1822, that remains to be seen. But we had better not expect too much.

Napoleon Bonaparte selling the vast Louisiana Territory to the USA

Chapter Twenty-two

Jefferson's Time

You would imagine that the changeover from opinionated Federalists to stubborn agrarian Democratic-Republicans would be a crisis for a new Republic, the world's largest, and the fourth largest nation in land mass, especially following upon an internal crisis in which thousands of politicians were calling each other crooks and traitors, particularly, too, inasmuch as it was a violent country where every year thousands died in brawls, riots, massacres, and brutal bondage.

Not to mention that the election just held for the President had resulted in a tie vote of the Electoral College and underhanded machinations to deprive the incoming President of his Office. And, too, the opponent in the tie, one Aaron Burr, was about as smart and unscrupulous a Patriot as you could hope to find, quite capable of recruiting a gang of thugs, as he would reveal later, to take over the unattended White House.

For President John Adams, outgoing, did not wait to be jovially ushered away or rudely thrown out. He simply departed town, much relieved. And Thomas Jefferson dropped in. To my recollection, the only country in history where this sort of behavior has occurred has been Switzerland, where, according to one rumor, the incoming and outgoing Presidents shook hands and left on different trolley cars. It was one of the greatest days in the history of the United States, March 4, 1801.

Since the Constitution implied some kind of ceremony upon taking office, Jefferson went over to the Senate Chamber, where one of his numerous political foes, who had just been appointed days before under tricky circumstances to be Chief Justice of the Supreme Court, John Marshall, that is, asked him to take the oath of office - him, Jefferson, who did not believe in the intervention of the Lord and much less the Bible in such matters. He so swore.

Perhaps all potential conspirators were temporarily exhausted. Or, more likely, they were conspiring at their home bases impossibly far from the scene of action, a blessing of the Federal system. Even had any group come to Washington, they would have had little chance of finding board and room. The town was small and its houses transparent, except for the grandiloquent Capitol and manorial White House. Anyhow, the ceremony ended, Jefferson went off to dinner. And the Congressmen, too, dispersed to the several taverns of the town and to their lodgings. It was the rude Republican Rome of Cato the Elder, some imagined. (But the Romans lived near their work.) Jefferson looked upon the White House as an immense *harem*.

Major Pierre l'Enfant had designed the Capital. He had been a volunteer in the Revolution. He laid out Paterson, New Jersey. In Washington, he laid out a large grid of streets. He pasted upon it a network of diagonal boulevards; he provided a large avenue with the Executive mansion at one end and the Congressional Capitol at the other end of it: both were genial ideas. The Potomac River flowed not far away, upstream from Mount Vernon. In fact there were streams here, there, and everywhere, and, if not, then mud.

Surveyor George Washington had selected the site. Virginia and Maryland bordered the District of Columbia, and as the town of Washington grew under the negligent eye of its master, the Congress, it became rather more of the slave culture than any other. It is curious that there was no battle over giving the nation's capital to the slave cause. In the secret deal between the "North" and "South" to exchange in effect money for location, this may have been a second implied assurance.

Many "insiders" and common folk anticipated that Jefferson would "clean house" once in office. Maybe he would have. Actually he did not. He hired surprisingly few supporters, allies, family, and friends to government positions, none of which were under civil service tenure rules and most of whom would not be for another century and more.

But rumor had it that another deal had been made when the shocking situation dawned upon Congress: Jefferson and Burr had each 73, the same number of electoral votes, while Adams gained 65, and, speaketh the "greatest design ever spun off by the mind of man", the candidate with a majority of the votes should become President, and, in case of a tie, the House of Representatives, with each State delegation voting as a single State with one vote, would determine by majority the winner. It seemed that Burr, who knew right well that he was supposed to be Vice-President, if anything, was going to let the "red-baiters" of the Federalist party vote against Jefferson.

But Hamilton hated Burr more than he disliked Jefferson, and suddenly discovered new virtues in the man he had been denouncing scurrilously just recently. It might have been he or a clever idea on Jefferson's side that sent an informer to the Federalists confiding that Jefferson would not only uphold the Hamiltonian fiscal system but would not fire every Federalist on the payroll. Jefferson was chosen by the House.

As you might imagine, one of the first items of business was to change the manner of electing the President, so as to make sure that a candidate who was running for the office of President was not also running for the office of Vice President, and vice versa. This Twelfth Amendment passed in time for the next Presidential election. The Electoral College still would not work well, but that is a long and boring story to come.

Meanwhile, the pretentiously bucolic Jefferson, who welcomed distinguished foreigners in sloppy attire, but who drank better wines than practically anybody in America and dined upon the culinary creations of a French chef, set about continuing the Revolution that he was always talking about. Almost nothing of the sort occurred. His Inaugural speech proclaimed that we were all Republicans, all Federalists, as if nothing had been happening and politics were a great spoof. It was a useful spoof, a myth of unanimity. A second myth was in the same speech, and it was also essentially fine: that this nation was unique in that every man would meet invasions of the public order as his personal concern.

What did happen usually contradicted his theory of the Constitution, or was bad for the country. He advertised the belief in minimal government: *"That government is best that governs least"*. This foolish and impossible notion has been forever an American favorite. It is not only impossible in the face of the realities of winning politics and resolving issues thrust upon one. It is also an invitation to greedy and destructive special interests to take over the role of government in their sphere.

Preferable might be the operating principle that the government is best that is so flexible as to increase or decrease its governance in accord with the changing state of wickedness in the halls and nooks and corners of society.

Flexibility to expand or contract as required:
such is the more important mechanism
of "good government".

Jefferson believed that all the money needed to run the Federal government could come from moderate tariffs (if not smuggled in) and from the sale of lands owned by the government, although procured by hornswoggling Indians. He went on a saving spree - he, of all people, who still owed personally large sums of money and would be turned out of his house for debt in the end - and began paring the debt that had been so cleverly built up into a useful tool of fiscal management by Hamilton. He was helped in this by a Swiss-born American, naturally: Albert Gallatin, one of those Republicans whose appointments pleased the Federalists. The Bank of the United States continued to prosper in the hands of his enemies and various British investors.
Jefferson ran the army and the navy down to practically nothing, during a time when foes were sharking about the Seven Seas and Britain was hovering about in the Northwest, and Spain, under French influence much of the time, was considering whether or not to close down the Mississippi River to Americans.

Even the Bey of Tripoli felt his oats and decided to ask more in the way of tribute from the United States than ordinarily had been forthcoming annually since 1786.
He wanted $300,000 next time around and in 1801, when the payment seemed unlikely, he declared war on the United States. Since the shipping at risk was in the Mediterranean, Jefferson sent several boats to teach the Bey a lesson. But a frigate ran aground, its crew taken prisoner and the boat burned by the Algerians. After a year, in faint echo of what would happen in Iran when the U.S. was Super-Power of the World, Jefferson paid over $60,000 as ransom and the crew was released.

Jefferson also opposed the extension of judicial power through the Supreme Court and its growing national network of district and circuit courts. He seems not to have appreciated that the exceedingly dangerous interposition and nullification proceedings of which he was author several years before might have destroyed the new Republic, and that a Supreme Court with the power to declare national laws unconstitutional would have probably voided the Alien and Sedition Acts.

He did little about his views, save growl, whereas he might have
mustered his Congressional majorities and
undo the lame-duck judiciary law of the Federalists;
in fact, he helped cut back the number of justices to the old number
of five, instead of going ahead and packing the court
as he might have done, if he had any idea of what he
should expect the packed court to do.
(So that the later case of Franklin Roosevelt is not comparable.)

In his second Inaugural Address (he won a second term easily), he
exulted in that no farmer, laborer, or mechanic ever saw a tax-gatherer.
They did not see internal improvements either. And very few
of the civilized amenities that Jefferson so admired in France.
Most shippers avoided customs and saw as little of tax-gatherers as possible,
an habitual dodge for Americans to this day.
His Embargo Act, when it came, should have
won a medal for asininity.

It began with his British enemies.
They were fighting a quarter-century war, first against the
French Republic, then against the French Empire. They were
repeatedly defeated on land, so preferred the sea,
where they did very well, Nelson at Trafalgar
representing the peak achievement.

However, their fleet needed wretched bodies, so they stopped American ships and took about ten thousand of them over a decade of time, of which only 1,000 turned out to be true deserters (desertion being the pretext for the impressment). Too, their fleet blockaded as much of the European Coast and West Indies as possible to prevent any traffic with the French. And American ships were informed that they must have permission from the British before proceeding to the Continent, even with innocent cargoes.

But when Napoleon learned that many American ships were getting permits in English ports before proceeding to the continent, he ordered their taking, according to the rules of his so-called Continental System, which was designed to counter the British Orders in Council. This meant basically that all shipping had to serve two masters before reaching its consignees.

Then, in 1807, the British bombarded and boarded an American ship, the *Chesapeake;* several men were killed and wounded and several were impressed, so that when the vessel returned to port, a hullabaloo carried around the country, and Federalists (whose merchants seemed to get along somehow under any circumstances) cried for war.

Jefferson remained peaceable, but committed the Embargo Act. That is, with a bill out of Congress (under the most dubious and loose un-Republican Constitutional warrant that an embargo was a regulation of commerce), he forbade all American trade with France and Britain. This folly endured for fifteen months. Evasion of the law was epidemic. (Napoleon foxily caught American vessels entering forbidden places and let it be said that he was only helping America to enforce its laws.)

Now let us have more of the good of Jefferson. We already know that he composed the Declaration of Independence, but are not sure that it was an honest document and are sure that it was great propaganda, and needed. We know, too, that he had been Governor of Virginia, Ambassador to France, performing with distinction, that he was a fine build-it-yourself architect who put up his mansion and designed the University of Virginia's earliest structures. He also prompted the State of Virginia into a full tolerance of the various religions present and prospective in the Republic, notwithstanding considerable opposition from Anglicans and others who continued to struggle against disestablishmentarianism.

More than an aesthete - unique among United States Presidents - he was an intellectual - almost unique among U.S. Presidents, read in several languages, had friends in several countries. He could have been a Lorenzo de' Medici or Frederick II of Prussia or Prime Minister Johann-Wolfgang von Goethe of Weimar had he the cultural base to support him. His correspondence was voluminous and highly literate.

He used his competence and energy as a writer to more than compensate for his poor performance as a public speaker. The first mass democratic party system in the world was an outgrowth of his endless epistolarianism. Neither rains, nor snows, nor perilous waves that erased many a good letter could dismay his pen.

He held pomp and protocol in contempt. He was an egalitarian as far as he could be one while espousing the doctrine of merit - two practically contradictory positions unless you coin the phrase "equality of opportunity". And this is precisely what Jefferson wanted and expounded continually. It was to be a classless society, where individuals might rise to their just level of work and recognition. He looked about the fast-developing world, saw there industry and cities, and shrank from them.

The happy life, the ideal society, was to be next to nature; the independent yeoman (farmer, peasant) would join with kindred souls in a participatory democracy. There, all possible decisions would be made as close to the heart of the problem as possible by people who knew one another. He hoped that America could get what it needed in the way of manufactured goods from the wage slaves of Europe, in exchange for their raw materials and foodstuffs. He felt no guilt regarding the political circumstances of women, because he felt that their tender breasts should not suffer the blows of power politics.

His affections for women were genuine; no one accused him of sexual harassment. He was the intended victim of blackmail for "incorrect relations" with a neighbor's wife. The fabulous story has Hamilton first being blackmailed by a wicked drunken journalist for adultery, admitting it in order to avoid a worse charge of financial corruption. The journalist had been briefed by a henchman of Jefferson, none other than President-to-be James Monroe. But allies of Hamilton trumped up a trial and conviction of the journalist, who was helped, but not enough, by Jefferson; he was the source of the story and other stories of Jefferson's sexual adventures. Jefferson became President and, helping to pay the man's fine and pull wires, got him released. The journalist, drunk, slipped into a flooded gutter and drowned. (No, I doubt that anybody pushed him.)

Jefferson's relationship with his wife remained affectionate

throughout their lives together. His adulterous affair
with a Frenchwoman was practically *comme il faut* in France.
More interesting is his love affair with Sally Hemings,
his slave, who was actually half-sister to Jefferson's wife,
whom Jefferson did not and could not legally marry,
though she bore him children, as did his legal wife.
Nor could he claim the infants legally as his own,
without admitting to a crime. The long-time liaison
has still its consequences in that both Black "Jeffersons"
and White "Jeffersons" can lay claim to such honors as Monticello,
their ancestral home, and now a national foundation, affords.
Although a historian in 1997 won a literary prize
partly for covering up nicely the love affair,
a comparison of the DNA of the two branches
in 1998 confirmed that Jefferson was ancestor to both.

The Jefferson household was one of the convivial households
of the slave culture, if you had to be a slave. People of all colors
ran around the place as if they belonged there.
And they were bought and sold, beaten up, and
otherwise treated ambivalently by a man who,
after all, was inconsistent, headstrong, and mean
in politics, too.

One of the Jefferson black offshoots, it developed,
did not carry his telltale DNA chromosome ,
revealing thus an illegitimate liaison by the
lady of a later Jeffersonian.

But as the Good Book says, "It's a wise man
who knows his father". So one should not gamble
on the DNA of all the White Jeffersonians.
Nor, for that matter, on the DNA ancestry
of thee and me.

When he came to write about Africans and Caucasians,
Jefferson gave a good account of himself as a
rudimentary anthropologist and psychologist,
trying to be just, but with hints of prejudice, including a
major, yet reserved, "finding" that, unlike the slave of

Socrates' parable who could understand the Pythagorean theorem in Geometry when dialectically explained, Africans could not do so well (or passably) in mathematics as Europeans.

Many years earlier, Jefferson had tried to get the Virginia Assembly to bring slavery to an end, and failed, though not by much. But then, why did he not free more of his slaves? Because they would have a worse life? Because his creditors would not have allowed it? And when the time came in 1808, he promptly, on January 1, carried out the Constitutional directive to ban the slave trade.

Then why did not Jefferson exert his great influence and power to put teeth into the law, to provide an agency for its strict enforcement? For he must have known that his countrymen were the world's worst smugglers. In fact, an estimated 300,000 slaves were smuggled into the United States between 1808 and 1860, an awful fact, that people who approve of smuggling on principle might ponder. And with the costs of non-compliance to the law, the price and monetary value of slaves went up.

Not everything went wrong for Jefferson in foreign affairs. Napoleon promised the Spanish government that he would put a Spanish prince and spouse on the throne ruling over a few square miles of land in Italy called Tuscany in exchange for the vast area from the Mississippi River to the borders of the Far West, and the Spaniards snapped up the offer. Then, Napoleon, not bothering to give the Spanish anything, instructed Talleyrand to ask the Americans whether they wished to buy it, the great Louisiana Territory. When he heard this news from Paris, Jefferson - everyone says - searched his soul, and decided only then that he might evade his convictions on the subject of a strict construction of the Constitution, and hastened a second envoy to Paris to reinforce the first. The price: $15 millions.

The envoys did not cavil. They mentioned boundaries, a map, and Talleyrand told them that they had an excellent deal and they should not worry about a million acres here and there,
like where did Texas belong, and
where did the Northwest fit into the scheme?
The Senate, filled with strict constructionists,
contradicted its own views in a jiffy.
Louisiana became American.

As to why Talleyrand and Napoleon acted as they did, it may have been to put the huge territory in American, rather than Spanish or British, hands; America would not trouble them. Besides, Americans were already rafting across the big river; French settlers were few, and Napoleon needed all potential settlers as cannon fodder for his Grand Imperial Army that was already battling around the continent. Anyhow, like almost all Europeans of wealth, culture, and power, the French leaders regarded the Americas as a perennial sideshow.
The acquisition was genuine, despite its informality.
Every once in the while a French voice is raised to claim that
the U.S. never paid the 15 million dollars,
but no one has threatened to take Louisiana back.

Inspired by the new acquisition, particularly as to the vagueness of its boundaries, American gangs began to invade Florida, particularly from the East bank of the Mississippi to the present-day Panhandle. The area stretched up to touch present-day Mississippi and Alabama, which had come into the United States with the Pinckney Treaty of 1795. All of this was hot, humid, lowland, predestined, it would appear, for planters to grow cotton with slave labor. Actually, the irregular invasion and occupation could be called the West Florida Rebellion. Once more, the Spanish government acceded to aggression, and a face-saving deal was struck to legitimize the acquisition.

Meanwhile as part of this stupendous expansiveness, an expedition , called the Lewis-Clark Expedition for its leaders, was despatched by Jefferson, even before the Louisiana offer came up, to go as far West as possible and report back what they found. They had a wonderful trip, were led, in a Hollywood romantic touch, by a young Indian squaw with a worthless husband, a good part of the way across the High Plains. They achieved the mouth of the Columbia River.

They might have put up a settlement there - British, Russian, Spanish, Americans and other types of traders and trappers were roundabout - and this would have firmed up the American claim to the Oregon territory that was made upon their return. Or a settlement could have been despatched. For the region was not ignored. The Russians were down from Alaska with solid claims. The British had docked in the estuaries and traded, and put in claims. The tenacious and redoubtable MacKenzie had been up and down and across Canada with a vision on behalf of the British Empire second to none.

Still, further South, the trail of Lewis and Clark and that, too, of Lieutenant Pike, whose company had covered a good part of the near West before it was arrested and taken into custody by Spanish troops and ushered out, were observed by mountain men and traders and fugitives, so that, before long, more stable pioneers began to make the trek Northwest.

About the time that Lewis and Clark were told to go West, Aaron Burr was making plans for the West himself, and shortly was to send a great American "West". Burr was the son of a President of Princeton University, a Colonel in the War of Independence, a handsome New York political figure of consequence, and a rich lawyer.
He was projected upon the national scene in 1796, you will recall, when Jefferson of Virginia and Burr of New York came close to beating the Federalist ticket, and you will recall, too, that he and Jefferson tied in the Electoral College count for President, as head of the Federalist ticket, and, as was right and proper, Jefferson won out, not without the aid of Alexander Hamilton, also a New Yorker.
I repeat myself because these injuries at the hands of Hamilton, no matter how deserved, were not forgotten.

But Hamilton, ever nasty in verbalistics, would not get off his back. When Burr got involved in something called the "Essex Junto", which was a feeble attempt by last-ditch Federalists to disjoin New England from the Union, Burr was wondering about adding New York to the disjuncture. Hamilton would have believed so even were it untrue. That was not all. Burr, still Vice-President, decided to offer himself as a candidate for Governor of New York and lost out in the preliminaries. Hamilton delivered himself profusely of defamatory language in the course of events, and received finally from Burr a challenge to duel. Duels were banned in New York, but they might cross the Hudson River and duel at Weehawken, for example. They did so.

Depending upon how much you hate the one and like the other, you can believe how high was Hamilton's pistol when he shot first. After he missed, Burr fired and mortally wounded Hamilton. At which point a perfectly justifiable volume could be written on the "If..then" pattern. If Burr had also missed, would Hamilton have become President, and would Burr lead a group of Northern States out from the Union? ..etc.

Burr lost a certain esteem, to be sure, but one must remember that Hamilton had a great many enemies and Burr was a charming man. Burr had the nerve to resume his office as Vice President and gavelled the Senate into order when it convened. But then, hardly in the good graces of Jeffersonian Republicans or the Federalists, he was soon without a job and still thinking big. So he journeyed West and joined up with a General Wilkinson, a man of questionable Revolutionary War conduct, who was in the pay of the Spaniards as a spy. He persuaded Wilkinson that they should set up a separate Republic in the West, and began to recruit men for his army. Wilkinson betrayed him in a letter to Jefferson and a warrant of arrest went out on Burr.

He was soon captured and brought to trial before a U.S. circuit court on a charge of treason, the same court over which John Marshall, Chief Justice of the Supreme Court, and foe of Jefferson, was presiding. But who could find *"two witnesses to the overt act"* of treason, as the Constitution required for conviction?

Jefferson went out of his way to find evidence against Burr, promising a pardon to conspirators who turned state's evidence, and was sure there was plenty to convict him in an ordinary court of law. Questionable conduct, his, but, then, Marshall was seen to be dining out with the defense, including the defendant, for which today he would be impeached and probably convicted of malfeasance. Marshall subpoenaed the President to appear in court with relevant documents, but Jefferson, referring to the independence of the executive branch, claimed the privilege of refusal.

The two men reversed their roles. Jefferson, strict constructionist, would have overlooked the explicit language of the Constitution. Marshall, broad constructionist, referred to the express letter of the law, becoming a strict constructionist: no two eye-witnesses, no conviction.

Burr went free. He returned to New York, practiced law, lived as well as he could, but too lavishly for his purse. His cherished daughter was married to a Carolinian, and on her way to visit her father, her boat disappeared in a storm. Burr would go down to the Battery and look out to sea on occasion, hoping for a glimpse of the missing ship. He enjoyed for many years the affections of a woman-about-town. He was divorced for adultery in his eighties, but no matter, for he was not alone. It was men like him who gave New York City a bad name.

Some of the work of Mr. John Marshall, C.J. seemed to be of lesser importance than treason. Not long after Jefferson became President, and Marshall Chief Justice, a minor official named Marbury came into court pleading that he been denied his commission to a job in the court system; he knew that Adams had signed the commission, along with many others, in the last moments of his presidency, but through an oversight, his, Marbury's, commission had not been delivered, and, what was more, the new Secretary of State, one James Madison, refused to let him have it. The Judiciary Act of 1789, argued Marbury, allowed him to come before the Supreme Court and get from it a writ of mandamus, which would direct the Secretary of State to hand over the appointment.

The panel of justices pondered the case, then Chief Justice Marshall wrote up the decision, the judgement, the opinion of the Court, the other justices concurring, in the case of *Marbury vs. Madison.* Yes, said the Court, Marbury's facts were right, but the Constitution expressly gave the Court the right to hear cases as a court of first instance, that is, gave it an original jurisdiction, only in cases involving foreign officials. All other cases had to come to it on appeal from lower courts. Therefore, said Marshall, the broad constructionist, the Constitution forbids us to take on this case and the section of the Judiciary Act of 1789 that says otherwise is unconstitutional, null and void.

The elegance and irony of the incident are remarkable. Poor Marbury, the Federalist, was out of luck, the Federalist Court decided. The law ushered through by his party, the Federalist Party, was unconstitutional. The Court was sworn to uphold in its judgements the Constitution. It could do nothing else. And the principle of Judicial Review of the constitutionality of actions of all branches and all actions of all federal officers was thereby practically established. The very insignificance of the substance of the case, along with its involuted reasoning prevented Congress, public opinion, and the people on the street from becoming angrily aroused.

Here was the beginning of the most powerful judiciary in the world. The Supreme Court became much more powerful in the years to come; often its legislative powers exceeded those of Congress, and its executive powers those of the Presidency.

Judges could be impeached, but only for high crimes and misdemeanors and then by elaborate trials by the Senate to achieve convictions. It happened twice in Jefferson's time, with no effect on the power of the Court. The one case dealt with a Pickering who was not only often drunk on duty, but prone to obscene language, and furthermore, to all appearances, insane. He was impeached and convicted and removed. A second case, Justice Chase, involved a Federalist of loudly voiced, scandalous opinions of persons and ideas with which he disagreed. He was not convicted, and, this action having failed, future attempts to get at the Court's personnel and sense of power were few and far between.

Thomas Jefferson must be bid adieu, as he leaves office and retires to Monticello, not a little disgusted with his experience and relieved at getting out of Washington. It is just as well that he did not write a treatise on his theories of government. They would be contradictory, whereas as they found their way into policy documents, they appeared over the years as superb and useful to all kinds of people, ranging from Southern Bourbons to New York communists.

He was basically a nice guy, which means that he did not engage in duels, massacres, denials of widows and orphans, hatreds of common people anywhere in the world, and promises of the apocalypse. (It is surprising how many famous leaders are discharged from a decent respect by these criteria.)

His idea of democracy and the republic, as distinct from a systematic theory on the subjects, was individualistic, cooperative, participatory, and because there was no way to get unanimity in the short run, it was majoritarian. (We shall not ask when, if ever, a majority government is possible, except when we mean by the term a way for settling a tally of voices.) He resisted Franklin's democratic pragmatism, wrongly, for Franklin was quite ready to be idealistic when other people were ready.

Far from becoming conservative with age, Jefferson stuck to his extreme democratic views. He thought (1816) that every biological generation, certainly every social generation, should have the right to, and actually should, redo the Constitution. Writing Baron von Humboldt in 1817, he declared,

"*.. The* lex majoris partis *is the fundamental law of every society of individuals of equal rights; to consider the will of the society enounced by the majority of a single vote, as sacred as if unanimous, is the first of all lessons in importance".*

The genial Baron, having suffered the worst jungles of the world, could tolerate such tangled nonsense with aplomb.

Jefferson could not stomach the *realpolitik* of his close collaborator James Madison, who thought of society as composed of a variety of interests that had to be compromised. He detested Hamilton's preference for a republic governed by and for the wealthy and powerful. By implication and some hard evidence, he felt somewhat the same about ideas of George Washington and John Adams.

He was an indigenous civilized
and cultivated American
when this category of person was not numerous enough
to appear in any sampling
no matter how large.
His influence was broad and vague.
Bycontrast, around Boston now, a small
and sharp influence was growing
out of the Unitarian movement.
Started up in England by Theophilus
Lindsay (need we be amazed that
at the very first gathering in London,
Benjamin Franklin dropped by?),
the Unitarians came around to
discounting the literal truth of the
Scriptures and the Holy Trinity, and
proposing the radical notion that the Deity was a God of love,
holding - to quote the leader of the sect in America,
Ellery Channing – that the God who
"regards us with displeasure before we have acquired
power to understand our duties and reflect on our actions" is no God
at all, and the true God is "*infinitely good, kind, benevolent... good in*
disposition as well as in act, good not to a few but to all".

The Puritan outlook was reversed. So was the revivalist. God wanted humans to become educated adults, not caterwauling children born again and again, after sin upon sin, fall upon fall. Love for God and Humankind reciprocating. The few Unitarians would have disproportionately large influence upon American theology, education, science, and literature. Were persons like Channing and Jefferson in charge, there would never have been a Civil War.
Neither was a typical American.

Jefferson was grand in displaying merit and democratic feelings simultaneously. Wherever he went, whenever he wrote, he spoke frankly, and as a result was a great and rare teacher of the public - at a time when the Second Awakening in religion was resulting in sadistic and masochistic orgies, intemperate outbursts worse than anything in politics, but in the name of God hence ignored and forgiven and even embraced by historians and civic leaders since then - at a time when, according to most foreign expert observers, the country was peopled by semi-savages of high ambitions and low tastes.

He remained thoroughly loyal to his country
despite his being so *outré*, of such a tiny minority.
Moreover, at the same time, he secured a majority
of his countrymen to the general cause of benevolent democracy -
a phenomenon of the first instance in America.

CAPTURE AND BURNING OF WASHINGTON BY THE BRITISH, IN 1814.

Chapter Twenty-three

The War of 1812

War, opined ancient Greek philosopher Heraclitus, is the greatest teacher of man. One lesson, however, it has not taught to man: he should not go to war.
English opinion was shocked that the United States should declare war against Britain. An English editor declared the War Message to Congress of President Madison to be
"the most labored ,peevish, canting, petulant, querulous, and weak effusion, that ever issued from a man

assuming the character of a statesman and the President, or elective quadrennial King, of a professedly Republican country".

Mere weeks before the Declaration of War, England had revoked the Orders in Council that had appeared to so outrage the Americans, but the word had not gotten through. One may ask, why could not legislation be passed canceling the Declaration? That's not the way history happens: other reasons and pretexts were available.

The War, when it came, had absurdly large territorial dimensions; it was preceded by acts of war and would be succeeded by them. The War was a continuation of the troubles that Jefferson had suffered with France and Britain. Both countries wanted American trade for themselves but not for the enemy, and they were in desperate conflict. England desired no war, but it would pay any price to stop the delivery of raw materials to the armies and allies of Napoleon. The French Republic, on its side, fighting the great powers of Europe, had the same reasons as Kaiser Germany and Hitler Germany a century later for blocking American shipments to Great Britain.

That is, given the principle of freedom of the high seas, accepted in the recently developing law of nations, the United States could have gone to war with both countries, and there was a thin range of opinion that advocated this action. At the moment, however, there appeared to be more of an argument for going to war with Britain than with France.

America had endeavored to avoid war and punish both countries by its embargo on all shipping abroad, which was unenforceable and opposed by the North especially. Now, in Madison's administration, it experimented with an embargo aimed at both England and France, but not at other countries, with the proviso that the embargo would be lifted in the event that either or both of these countries ceased its depredations against American shipping. This "Non-Intercourse Act" was still persuant to the policy of "peaceful coercion".

The British Minister, perhaps maliciously, informed the American Secretary of State that Britain would comply,

and the embargo against Britain was lifted.
But his report proved false.
Next, Congress cleverly reversed the order of things and enacted legislation that allowed trade with the warring powers, but promised to reward either power, would it drop its restrictions, by imposing a non-intercourse policy upon the other power.

Napoleon's government took the next step by informing the Americans that the Berlin and Milan decrees interrupting their trade were revoked. Hearing this, Madison interdicted trade with Britain. But France had asked for more - not only restoration of trade, but the actual Revocation of the British Orders in Council, which were blocking theoretically all American shipping from possibly ending up in French-allied hands.

This was beyond American capabilities, but Madison still kept the restraints upon Britain.
The War party grew stronger.
Possibly Madison reckoned with the fact that his re-election depended upon the nomination and campaigning of the caucus of Congressional Members of the Democratic-Republican Party.

On June 1, Madison asked for War on four grounds: impressments, harassment of commerce off the American coastline, the use of blockades falsely to plunder American commerce, and the total blockade of commerce implied in the Orders in Council.
Congress declared war against Britain.
On June 16, the British government announced the revocation of the Orders in Council. On ships that passed in the night, there went benightedly the Declaration of War and the Revocation of the Orders.

A few months before the Declaration of War, two-thirds of the House appeared to be committed to peace. When the war vote came, 79 to 49 for war, the votes for the declaration could be readily traced in a giant crescent that started in New Hampshire and swept down around the frontier areas until it turned at the lower South to reach the sea again above Florida. These seem hardly to be regions under the British guns.

So historians have been hard put to find appropriate and sufficient, rational or material reasons, for bellicosity.

The New England interests that should have been most bellicose before the event were not the actual provokers of War. They were supplying many of the necessities of the West Indies, regardless of nationality. They were evading the laws of all and sundry countries that restricted shipping. To the price of the next shipment of goods would be apportioned losses sustained on the last shipment. No one knows the extent of smuggling and running of the blockades, American, British, and French. The restraints were obviously not destroying Northern foreign trade. The oceans are very wide. Even the Straits of Gibraltar and the English Channel were too wide to police fully.

With the damaging interplay of the French and British navies, privateers and merchant fleets, there was all the more room around the world for the Americans to trade - China, India, the Mediterranean, and South America. One may think of the situation as comparable to the Prohibition era in America in the 1920's when the final legalization of whiskey in 1933 took the charges of the smugglers and gave them over to the government as tax payments, and smugglers escalated into the now legitimate alcohol traffic, building up such enormous multinational concerns as the Canadian, Schenley liquor-based conglomerate of the Bronfman family.

The issue of impressment of seamen from American ships was admittedly painful. It reflected upon the dignity of the new nation. The British captains refused to recognize naturalized Americans of British origin, and were prone to make many mistakes that took a long time to admit and rectify, meanwhile profiting them.

Commercial troubles assailed the Southern plantations; their markets were smaller, prices received lower. Many there blamed the British blockade for the reduced demand for staples of the South. Southern Congressmen generally voted for war.

The South and West were driven by wild dreamers. In the very first decade of the nineteenth century could be heard

cries from those quarters that only in 1845
would be given the term "manifest destiny". The
extremists visualized the whole North American Continent and
Caribbean as desirable, logical, possible, even inevitable, and therefore
legitimate annexations of the United States.

Look to the North, they would say. There is nothing but a thin line of
Canadians, hardly worthy of respect, being Loyalists and Frenchmen.
We need both sides of the St. Lawrence. We need, because they are so
much like us, New Brunswick, Nova Scotia, Upper Maine. We need
Quebec and the full Great Lakes to prevent ourselves from being
attacked by the British and their Indian allies.

Look to the West. There we need to protect ourselves from the
Indians, backed by the British, and beyond that by the Spaniards who
are allies now of the British.

And the same goes for the South: Florida East and West to the
Mississippi. We need to protect our commerce on the Mississippi. We
cannot have Spanish threats overhanging the delta region.

And why should we not be thinking of the fate of our Mexican
neighbors, who are intermittently but persistently engaged
in a struggle for liberation from the Spanish yoke?

As for the Caribbean, there we have the Spanish and British Islands,
where our plantation system is compatible and ideologically
akin to the people there, not to their masters in Europe.

War with England would justify all-out war against the Indians and
aggression against the Spaniards.

It may appear bizarre, but at this very early date, this second-rate
nation had a great many people with untrammeled imaginations.

Typically in such cases, where the offenses only with difficulty justify
the risks and losses of war, paranoid rumors circulate and are believed.
Injuries are exaggerated. Dreams become realities. Americans who had
led the demand for War, especially the group called "War Hawks" in
the Congress, believed in the impossible -

that Canada and the Eastern provinces could be won,
that the Indians might be forever routed westward,
that the Spanish would retire from the Continent,
that the British Army and Navy would be sent flying,
that American shipping would take over the Seven Seas,
that after the British would come the turn of the French,
etc.

So enthusiastic were the Hawks that Henry Clay of Kentucky resigned his Senate seat to be chosen Speaker of the House of Representatives partly in order to pursue the cause of war in what was then the more important chamber of Congress. Naturally, he expected in return to be elected President.

As America went to war, the Grand Army of the French Republic was assembling for its ill-fated march deep into Russia, ending at Moscow in freezing weather with a cold welcome from the few Russians to be found there. After a horrible retreat in the depths of winter under the guns of Russian guerrillas, the Army's remnants reached safety. The one episode cost France more casualties than the War of 1812 produced on the part of British, Indian and American forces. The cost to the Russian forces and civilians was enormous as well.

Only the Indians lost heavily in the War of 1812; their alliances with Britain aroused aggression along the frontier that speeded up their vast gradual retreat into the West. The ruin of Napoleon's power and the decline of France began at Moscow. In April of 1814 Napoleon surrendered, and the British could turn more attention to waging war on land and sea in America.

American land forces were negligible, 6,700 badly trained and badly-led men, with of course many thousands of militiamen of the States in the same poor condition. Naval forces included a score of ships. Most were bottled up by British blockade. New England was allowed leeway in trade with the outer world, for the British could see there a considerable sentiment for peace and even cooperation with themselves, though the enemy.

American land strategy called for the conquest of Canada. Three task forces were engendered. One was to invade Canada via Detroit, another along the Niagara River, and a third along Lake Champlain toward Montreal. The British disposed of some 16,000 men in Canada, newly arrived from overseas. They were ample for the occasion.

The 2000 Americans at Detroit stayed put, underwent siege, and surrendered prematurely to a British General who used the psychological warfare trick of parading seemingly large numbers of Redcoats and Redskins before the frightened eyes of the Americans.

On the Niagara Front, hundreds of American soldiers managed to seize commanding positions on the Canadian side, but withdrew when the New York State militiamen who were supposed to reinforce them refused to budge, claiming that their obligation to fight stopped at the borders of the State.

The Easternmost Army set off from Plattsburgh, New York, but once again, having arrived at the border of Canada, the New York militia declined to go farther.

Thus, the campaigns to conquer Canada ended ridiculously. The town of Newark in Canada was burned to the ground, it should be noted, for later reference, when the British burned Buffalo and turned their attention to Washington, D.C.

There, the British landed an army forty miles from Washington, at Benedict, Maryland, and marched on the Capital. Madison had sent out a call for 95,000 militiamen to defend the place. Only 7,000 volunteered. Still, the Americans had a larger force than the British, but this melted away in the early phases of firing, and on August 24, 1814, the British entered the Capital.

The government fled to Virginia and watched, while the British set fire to all government buildings except one, the Patent Office. The next day violent storms attacked the town and the British withdrew to prepare for an assault upon Baltimore, fourth largest American city. However, they were repelled in a duel of cannon, and decided not to land a force against an entrenched and larger American army. Here was a genuine victory for the Americans.

Around the same time, a British Army of 15,000 was descending along the shores of Lake Champlain, accompanied by a fleet of boats upon which the task force commander placed great reliance. It appears that he had sufficient forces to capture Plattsburgh even without the help of his fleet. That his reliance was misplaced soon became evident, for the fleet soon engaged a vigorously combative American flotilla, led by Commodore Thomas Macdonough, that completely destroyed it.
The British Army made little further progress.

On the high seas, American defeats and victories occurred. And immediately following the war, Captain Stephen Decatur was sent on a punitive expedition into the Mediterranean, where he extracted from the rulers of the semi-piratical states of Algiers, Tunis, and Tripoli promises to not molest commerce and to
free American prisoners .

Three years after the war began, and a couple of weeks after the Peace Treaty was signed at Ghent in Belgium, the British suffered a bitter defeat at New Orleans, but the War was not renewed.
Preliminaries to the Battle of New Orleans were colorful.
The Americans might have lost the battle, if General Andrew Jackson's men had not been able to round up arms from the area,
because the supplier entrusted with a consignment
of rifles and ammunition delayed deliberately,
possibly engaged in speculations with a premonition of peace,
or possibly paid to delay delivery by British agents;
patriotism was still one of the cheaper commodities and
weaker motives of many Americans.

A contingent of Kentucky militiamen arrived, only a few of them carrying rifles. Jackson cursed and declared that he had never before seen Kentuckians without a pack of cards, a bottle of whiskey, and a rifle. But probably the poor Kentucky boys had shrewdly left their family gun at home and had gone to Louisiana to win one for themselves. The price of cotton in the neighborhood jumped from 6 to 16 cents a pound.

Jackson played his cards right, using cotton bales to protect his entrenchments against balls, shot, and bullets, and effectively

assimilating to his ranks several state and territorial militias coming from far and wide, free African-Americans and Creole Francophones, planters, gangsters and pirates.
General Sir Edward Pakenham, the British Commander, descending in fine order from his fleet and with leisurely preparations, seemed to undervalue the element of time in combat operations. When he led his troops on the ascent to the American positions, he was only pursuing the tactic that would win the Battle of Waterloo for his brother-in-law, Lord Wellington, next year. As the British neared, the cowering Americans arose in their trenches to deliver fire. They killed him and over a thousand of his men, not to mention wounding twice that many. Prompt counterattack, quick pursuit and annihilation were not part of the military doctrine of the U.S.Army of the day, so the American forces dispersed and got drunk.

As for what was changed by the Battle of New Orleans and the War, historians are hard put to find much of importance. If the British had won the battle, no doubt, peace treaty or no, they would have loitered indefinitely in the vicinity, and the unwritten understandings behind the written treaty would have been interpreted less favorably for the Americans.

Too, Andrew Jackson would have given up his brevet as Major General and returned to his slave-worked plantation in Tennessee. He had a substantial military record even beforehand, won or his campaign against the Creek Indians in Georgia, from which victory he had ridden directly to New Orleans.

The provisions of the Treaty of Ghent solved none of the problems "causing" the war, at least not on paper. Both sides, more so the British, dropped territorial and indemnity demands. Commissions were set up to discuss issues for future resolution, prisoners were to be exchanged, and that was all.

For lack of rational justification and apparent effect, some have termed the War a "Second War of Independence". In its literal meaning, the appellation is inappropriate. Psychologically, as a second stage of separation from the parent, it makes more sense. France could have been equally the enemy, but the psychic separation from the French had no historical meaning to most Americans.

Indeed it had little meaning, with reference to the English, within the Federalist core of New England, who were already "healed". They were strongly anti-Napoleonic, and their ties with England had been increasingly numerous and sympathetic, formed in education, visits, trade partnerships, and consumer fashions. The women of New England thought that they "knew" the women of England.

The frontiersmen were more likely to be Scots-Irish or other ethnic groups hostile as a matter of course to Englishmen. They were less settled, more taken up with evangelical religious cults, more emotionally deprived and uncontrolled. They could be cured in some of this through additional aggression against the authority of Great Britain, a Second War of Independence. Irish Catholics and some Protestants fled to America after the Rebellion of 1798, and their influence was particularly noticeable in the press, which, some complained, had fallen into the hands of Irishmen. They were vigorously Anglophobic and were sometimes accused of being insufficiently Americanized and of carrying their homeland's struggle with them to the United States. The same accusation, usually with a considerable measure of justification, was to accompany the course of British-American relations down to the present.

Notably, major American myth and symbolism erupted from the War. *"Orleans Saved and Peace Concluded!!"* went the headlines and a collective amnesia set in that placed the Battle of New Orleans in time before the Peace, as of course it was in reality, in the time frame on the spot. For all American schoolchildren of the future, for whom the timing could not be juxtaposed, the Battle became a marvelous joke, an extra kick in the pants to confirm that a victorious Treaty had been won.

"Immortal lines" of the post-war period included those of Oliver Perry, commanding the American flotilla that defeated the British on Lake Erie: "*We have met the enemy and they are ours*!" The U.S. frigate *Constitution* became a legendary vessel, whose lines and fittings were seared into popular memory amid tales of cannon, carnage, and heroism. (The ship's surgeon's log in 1811, before the sailors became heroes, noted syphilis and gonorrhea as the most common ailments coming to his attention.)

The poetic stanzas of the national anthem were composed during the English bombardment of Fort McHenry, that commanded the port of Baltimore (and put to the music of an old English drinking song later, and made the national Anthem even later). The slogan later to be adopted for the country, and to be placed incongruously on U.S. currency appears here, "*In God we trust*".

Uncle Sam, the cartoon image of the United States, began as a fat man, not the tall, top-hatted, flag-dressed later figure, in the War. The nickname was derived from a man, Sam Wilson, who supplied meat to the United States Army, stamping it "*U.S*"., but when a United States Army's inspector asked what the initials meant, he was told that they were for "*Uncle Sam*".

A sinister precedent for the Union's Unity also came out of the War, the Hartford Convention. Called by the Massachusetts legislature, delegates from five states convened in December of 1814.
They talked of secession from the Union, they almost repeated Madison's Virginia Resolutions of 1798,
but concluded with a mixed bag of seven proposed constitutional amendments, including:
abolition of the 3/5 clause in Congressional apportionment giving partial credit for slaves in apportioning Congress,
barring foreign-born from federal office,
limiting the tenure of Presidents to one term, and
making declarations of war more difficult.

South Carolina could point to the Convention later on when it proposed to nullify an Act of Congress, and it became a stock rebuttal against Northern unionist arguments before the Civil War.

The Monroe Doctrine carried little weight at its inception in 1823. Yet in 1912, President Taft could declare: "The day is not far distant when three Stars and Stripes at three equidistant points will mark our territory, one at the North Pole, one at the Panama Canal, the third at the South Pole. The whole hemisphere will be ours in fact as, by virtue of our superiority of race, it is already ours morally."

Chapter Twenty-four

Governance without Power

Presidents between Jefferson and Lincoln were no great shakes. There were twelve of them. I refer to the men as they conducted their office, not the rest of their lives. Perhaps we should list them all in order, just once: James Madison 1809-17; James Monroe 1817-25; John Quincy Adams 1825-29; Andrew Jackson 1829-39; Martin Van Buren 1837-41; William Henry Harrison 1841; John Tyler 1841-5; James K. Polk 1845-49; Zachary Taylor 1849-50; Willard Fillmore 1850-53; Franklin Pierce 1853-7; and James Buchanan 1857-61. The average term of office was slightly over 4 years.

James Madison and John Quincy Adams looked best on paper, but performed at low average effectiveness. Several had done remarkable work before entering the White House; here, besides Madison and Adams, might be named Van Buren. Others - Taylor, Tyler, Harrison, Fillmore, and Buchanan amounted to little, one way or the other. Jackson had done both good and evil before his arrival at the White House. Most of them as President scarcely outshine the Indian leaders of that generation such as - Pontiac, Tecumseh, Black Hawk, Osceola, Minigret, Kanehamata, Sacajaweha.

If you were to compare them scrupulously with their political opponents, you would be hard put to claim any superiority on their behalf. The same would be true if you compared them with the numerous Vice-Presidents and vice-Presidential candidates and governors who came to the fore. Put another way, it is most unlikely that American history without them would be significantly changed. Again an exception might be Jackson; American history might have profited from his defeat.

James K. Polk, a smart Tennessee lawyer and politician, emulated well Jackson's wrong positions on money, tariffs, banks, Indians, and slavery. He outdid his master in aggressive expansionism, favoring the South and hastening the crisis of North against South. His was the Oregon boundary settlement with England, a poor deal for the USA. His was the war with Mexico, coldly and falsely promoted so as to provoke the struggling Mexican government into defensive actions that would seem to excuse a declaration of war. His tactics and those of Mussolini in Ethiopia and Hitler's against Poland a century later were practically the same. Yet, as with Jackson, numerous historians have begun to call him one of the several "great Presidents" - showing how hard up they are to locate great Presidents.

None received the votes of over a third of the adult population.

(Eighteen would be a proper age for voting although it never became such; I argue thus because by then half the population had lost one or both parents and was on its own, and had long since begun adult work and assumed adult responsibilities and vices.) The better Presidents had no military experience: Madison, J. Q. Adams. The worst were elected in large part because of their military experience: Jackson, Harrison, and Taylor. None of them as President initiated or engineered legislation or great projects of positive value and enduring importance.

Political leaders more glittering than the Presidents were to be found, even in politics: Henry Clay, who led the House of Representatives, accomplished domestic peace-keeping compromises, and failed in several attempts to be elected President; Daniel Webster was also a great political performer, sometimes to be found on the side of the angels; Sam Houston, who led Texas' independence struggle, and its entrance into the Union, but failed in his attempt to preserve it for the Union; Brigham Young who headed the Mormons on their way West and ruled them afterwards; John Fremont, explorer, swashbuckler, and politician; and Tecumseh, although he could be considered either a heroic resistance leader or a visionary and futile rebel.

What a shame that in his time or earlier, or even later, the opportunity was not seized by Congress to invite capable Indians to set up Territories and apply for Statehood: the Iroquois, the Algonquin, the Cherokee, the Seminole, the Pueblo, *et al* - they could all have founded proper States and fitted them into the Union under the Constitution well - perhaps with a refreshing originality.

Some heroes are recalled differently from one age to another: Admiral Matthew Perry, who opened up Japan to world trade and modernity, may not have done the world - or Japan - a great favor; his ship's guns may have taught the Japanese not to treat ship-wrecked American sailors badly, but sent them on their way to treating a billion people cruelly less than a century later.

There were also remarkable men who ended up doing major wrong, Aaron Burr, for instance, or John Calhoun (not for his secessionist views but for defending slavery). Should John Brown, the fanatic anti-slavery insurrectionist, be included here? He massacred innocent people as a terrorist object lesson. Americans have little to learn from Russian anarchists and Middle Eastern religious extremists about terrorism as a political weapon. Terror was the principal instrument against African-Americans for centuries. The 1995 Oklahoma City explosion that brought down the Federal building and killed and injured hundreds was the work of clean-cut, ex-soldier-boys, "100% American", native-born, Midwest "heartland", super-patriots.

Other men may outshine the politicos of the times: poets, artists, educators, intellectuals, scientists, inventors, and writers. Religious leaders as well: the Unitarian sect took hold and the Catholics dug in solidly. It was the age which may be finally best remembered for producing independent intellectuals such as Ralph Waldo Emerson and David Thoreau The development was not sensed alone in and around Boston, for New York City, Philadelphia and Charleston experienced, too, the birthing of intellectual and cultural sets.

There were of course a great many unsung heroes, else the nation would not have budged. I would not debate that the thousand or so top elite individuals of the country in the various spheres were not exceeded in competence, moral worth, and contributions to society by the next fifty thousand individuals as such: probably these were the backbone of the Republic and its cultural and technological progress: as Americans say, "Somebody must be doing something right!". They are remembered almost entirely in monographs, thousands of which have been published, but all together their sales and readers would not equal the books sold and read about half a dozen Presidents.

Americans typically created and worshiped heroes of all kinds in every field. Fame was the veritable life-blood of popular democracy. Yet here we say that the famous leaders were not at all typically great of mind or soul or skill. We have to introduce by way of explanation two ideas or concepts, first that the popular mind needs heroes but only a few of them; for too many will not be known enough to create the widespread and even national need for instant mass recognition.

Furthermore, in the kind of country it was, America afforded extensive liberty to a great many persons, and these accomplished a great deal by their own right, in their own interest, and displayed much courage, ambition, improvisation, endurance, organizing ability, whether occasioned by compensation, promises of favors, or voluntariness. So that in every field of endeavor there were many, rather than only several men of consequence, and the country bustled at every corner with people exploiting the land and each other. Historiography cannot name and discuss all of these individuals and cannot indeed even find them and describe them as they entered life, did their life's work, and departed.

Like others, I speak here and there of utopias.
But the individualism of Americans was also
utopian; nowhere ever did millions of people,
unfortunately almost entirely male,
set themselves up, isolated, with the explicit aim
of living happy alone, free, a law unto oneself.
If they followed Aristotle's dictum -
that to live outside of society,
one had to be a god or a beast -
they saw themselves as gods, not beasts.

So history contributes to the regrettable fallacious conception of the popular mind, that of the great hero moving large events. Certainly history can teach the absurdity of the heroic conception of history. It must do so, to relate what happened and what was said to have happened. It must not go so far, however, as to destroy the inspiration afforded by role models. Parents, leaders, gods: they are psychologically and functionally related; history-writing should provide a proper framework for their appreciation as it moves along: teach this, not that, because....

In the end, we may have better citizenry and leaders, ultimate goals of our historiography.

The picture of America in the early nineteenth century after the War with England gives us a generation that is acting rather in line with history thus far: land speculation, Indian riddance, quarrels over slavery now focusing upon the eligibility of territories for statehood, raising or lowering tariffs, the fate of a National Bank of the United States, endless continental expansion, economic booms and busts. Newer developments entered the picture, making it not so dull. Catholic Irish immigration on a large scale began; German immigration renewed, both Catholic and Protestant. With their arrival, a disgusting nativism rose in strength.

Aggressive warfare stripped newly independent Mexico first of Texas, then of a huge territory up to and including California. A threefold revolution in scale, organization, and mechanics occurred in the fields of agriculture, transportation and industry. A movement to organize labor into unions began. Japan was coaxed and coerced into opening up trade with the outside world. The field of constitutional law moved in the direction of nationalism, then retreated somewhat under a pro-slavery influence. Romanticism in thought and literature came out of Europe and struck Enlightenment ideas hard, contributing to a new school called Transcendentalism and a variety of original writers. It combined with the native American constitutionalism to foster a great many utopian communities. These new developments are all subjects of chapters to come. Let us here give brief attention to some international events.

An army led by Andrew Jackson, we may recall, had defeated the Creek Indians prior to his going to New Orleans to set up the defense against the British there. He had forced the Creeks to give up most of their land, that was promptly taken over by the slave culture. The Seminole Indians of Florida, who some claim were separatists from the Creeks and others claim as a distinctive culture, were clashing with border Whites in Southern Georgia. Andrew Jackson was called in again to chastise them, and what was named the Seminole War took place in 1819. The Americans defeated some Seminoles and their Afro-American allies, hanged several alleged conspirators against the United States, and raided all of the Spanish settlements from St. Augustine to Pensacola. In all of these adventures, Jackson was hyper-aggressive, behaved with uncontrolled temper, and exceeded his authority.

The Spanish government was upset by his invasion of Florida. The American government, in this case Secretary of War John Calhoun, was angered, too, but John Quincy Adams, who was negotiating with Spain on a boundary line defining the Louisiana purchase, was secretly pleased to bring pressure to bear upon Spain, tending to make Spain realize how short-lived must be its remaining tenure in the Floridas.

The formula came about. For assuming claims of $5 millions, the United States would receive all of Florida. The Louisiana territory was more clearly defined so as to run along the Sabine River, jump up to the Red River, and move along there to the Arkansas River; then, where the Arkansas had its source, at the 42nd parallel of latitude, it would strike directly to the Pacific Coast at what would be the Northern boundary of California.

The Seminoles had again to be defeated in a second war of the 1830's because they refused to cooperate in their own dreadful expulsion to the trans-Mississippi west.

The Oregon country came into play in these years. Four countries were involved at first, Russia, Spain, Britain and the USA, all claiming some or all of the territory. Spain bowed out in 1819 of any claims North of the 42nd parallel. The Russians sought the coastline as far South as the 51st parallel, which came within the American definition of the area, and Secretary of State Adams in 1823 informed the Russian government of America's disinclination to permit any further European colonial settlement in America. The Russians withdrew their challenge, having too many irons in the fire elsewhere. They agreed to confine themselves to claims above the line of 54 degrees, 40 minutes North Latitude. That left the British and the Americans arguing over Oregon, until they agreed to at least temporary joint occupancy.

❖❖❖

The idea of America for the Americans was fetching. Within living memory of the American Declaration of Independence, all of Spanish America had liberated itself and divided into young nations, except Cuba, Puerto Rico and Santo Domingo. But in 1823, Ferdinand VII of Spain was restored to his throne as absolute monarch by the French, now also under a monarchy and a far cry from the French Revolution. Reports were circulating that the French hoped also to restore to Ferdinand his American Empire and thus obtain a measure of suzerainty for themselves there. Britain's foreign minister, George Canning, thought he might get America to join him in warning the Continental European powers against intervention in the Americas.

Secretary of State Adams counseled against joining England in the maneuver, but suggested America make a pronouncement on its own, knowing full well that the British were unlikely to stand by if other powers intervened in Latin America, and furthermore would be likely to use a joint proclamation to interfere with American designs on the Southwest.

Thereupon, President Monroe, in his annual address to Congress on the state of the nation, enunciated what came to be famous as the Monroe Doctrine. He asserted that the Americas were not to be subject to further European colonization, that the political systems of Europe were different enough from the American republican system to be dangerous to America's peace and safety if introduced in the Americas, that America would not disturb still-existing European colonies, and that the United States would stay out of European wars and domestic arrangements.

The Monroe Doctrine did not set international circles afire. It carried no force in international law, as the non-legislative pronouncement of the executive branch of the American government, and as at most the unilateral position of the United States. It took what amounted to an imperialist position with regard to the Americas: this vast hemisphere was to be America's domain. The brazen claim had roots, gigantically enlarged, in the insularism of England, for

it was tied into the proclamation of isolationism,
America's form of insularism.

The United States did not, moreover, pledge itself to abstain from forcible intervention in the internal and external affairs of the Americas. It was in this light that the Monroe Doctrine grew to be of large importance in the minds of Americans; and millions of American schoolchildren would thrill to the idea of their country standing as defender of the Americas against the world that would recapture it; they were made quite ready to fight in the name of the Doctrine.

General Jackson slays the Monster Bankers

Chapter Twenty-five

"Jacksonian Democracy"

Far too many American schoolchildren have been taught that Andrew Jackson was a great man because he killed many Indians and British. Others, scholars with minds of schoolboys, have found in him the qualities of a great democrat, a revolutionary against the moneyed and aristocratic interests of the country. He leads the list of "strong"

Presidents that is often advanced, usually to the detriment of the incumbent of the moment.

His childhood excites sympathy, for his father died before his birth and two brothers were killed by British soldiers in the Revolution. His mother had to work as a housekeeper. But childhood misfortune cradles many a criminal, as well as many a saint. His grandfather left him a small fortune at the age of fifteen. He was of a slaveholding household, and in due course bought and kept slaves until his death.

He was by far the least educated of the Presidents up to his time in office. He was a land agent and speculator very early in life and became a lawyer. He had more than his share of the ordinary male vices of the time. Once he killed his opponent in a duel, waiting to shoot until the man had used up his bullet first. Whatever he did, it must be said, he did with fierce determination. His temper would frequently explode. He was rash and impulsive. He was not introspective; he would be what a psychiatrist might call an extroverted rage type. And while at it, the psychiatrist would also call Jackson a borderline schizophrenic, because of his inconsistencies of thought and behavior and relationships. He became rich. He became a general in the Tennessee militia.

He came from Scots-Irish stock, which might have been cited first, in explaining his character, the first President to be such and symbolizing the coming of age of this large group of the population who had gone destitute to America and had been blamed with some reason for a century of troublemaking on the frontiers. He was not a religious man.
He became Senator from Tennessee after his Indian and New Orleans adventures, but he was not a legislator, never framed a piece of legislation. He was "a man of the people" - whatever that means.

He helped measurably to destroy the most Europeanized and stable of the Indian nations, the Creeks and the Cherokees, and to drive the Seminoles and escaped free Africans into the interior swamps of Florida and to compel the Spanish to sell the territory to the United States, all so that land-greedy and earth-ravishing Southern Whites could seize more land and, if profitable to do so, bring in slaves to work it.

He had ideas that were stupid and destructive in most areas that they touched upon: race relations, human rights, currency and banking, government administration, land settlement, and public works and transportation. His position on the tariff issue labored with contradictions. He is to be praised for his strong position in the face of states rights' advocates attempts at nullification of federal law and secession from the Union. He may not have been constitutionally correct on these or on other issues, and he may have driven the country closer to Civil War.

Still, if one agrees that a single nation was better than a Northern and a Southern nation, he must be seen as striving forcefully toward that end. One must commend him for his famous toast, amidst agitated states rightists at a Jefferson Day banquet, for having lifted his glass to exclaim, *"One Union - It must be preserved!"* At the same time, one must appreciate that the man giving the toast really wanted this Union so that people like himself could roam up and down the nation, in command of a populist majority, doing whatever they pleased.

Jackson was eliminated in his first run for the Presidency. It was 1824. Four candidates were in the field. He and John Quincy Adams were close in popular vote and electoral votes, both falling well short of a majority of the Electoral College. The House of Representatives had to decide. Henry Clay, Speaker of the House and himself a candidate running a poor third, pulled his votes over to Adams, defeating Jackson. There was an uproar over his tactic, accusations of a "deal" , seemingly confirmed after Adam's inauguration, when Clay was named Secretary of State.

Adams presented the nation with what we would today regard as an ideal program for the Republic, but it brought him nothing but defeat after defeat in the Congress, and defeat in the next election. He called in his inaugural address for measures that would distinguish a President even today: a national University; investment in scientific research and development; and a national network of roads, bridges, and canals; among others.

The election of 1828 found Jackson primed for office. He won easily in the popular vote and in the Electoral College. Jackson invited everybody to the White House reception following his inauguration. A great many came, all too many, many of the "boys in the back room" class, and descriptions of the event have ever since sent shivers down the backs of respectable hostesses. He was a widower of two years, so he might forgivably escape the grounds behind a tipsy human screen when the gathering became unbearably noisy and unruly.

His wife Rachel, some say and he said, had died partly from shame at the campaign slurs directed at them because, unaware that her divorce had not been valid, the couple had "lived in sin" (legally construed) until the matter was straightened out. Obviously there was fully at work then the sleazy slurring element that had come in at the very beginning with the Puritans from Britain and Germany, and had been paralleled by Jackson's Presbyterian forebears, and exists, and prospers to this day. There was also the expectation now that the tactics and propaganda of political campaigning need stop at nothing; all was fair in war and politics.

Jackson had a bad cold and could hardly be heard as he delivered his inaugural speech. It had some original passages, atypical of the genre. The passage that foretold the most trouble read nicely, generously. It said, in effect, anybody could be President, or if not that, the next best place. The duties of public office were such that an ordinary person of intelligence was qualified to handle them. Men too long in office grew indifferent to the public interest and failed to discharge their duties. *"As few impediments as possible should exist to the free operation of the public will".*

Scholars have calculated the damage in his administration. He replaced under a quarter of all the persons he might have fired and replaced. They do not include the many cronies and followers for whom he created jobs and placed in jobs that turned up as a result of his policies. Or the jobs that his appointees could fill and did fill with small fry.
Too, the need for dedicated and experienced diplomats to aid, control, and inform the rush of American interests overseas was frustrated by Jacksonian spoils system policies. There resulted mediocre, often corrupt, American representation abroad for the balance of the century.

It is no accident that he turned to a man quite unlike himself as his confidante and successor, a man from already "wicked old New York", a professional politician insofar as such existed in those days, Martin Van Buren, a Dutch descendent of seven generations - without a single intermarriage, he would boast - a clever son of a tavern owner who also owned slaves where slaves were practically non-existent.

And this man Jackson preferred to a man who was one of the most keen in the nation, from his own culture but much higher in its class structure, who was a nationalist and should have been kept on that track instead of being driven into the states-rights camp, John Calhoun, who was his Vice-President, and had at one time as Secretary of War had the temerity to think of removing Jackson from command of the Army in Georgia for going on a rampage in Spanish Florida, invading, shooting and hanging without due process of law. (Behaving rather like the Mexican Revolutionary chieftain, Pancho Villa, a century later, but then President Woodrow Wilson would react by invading Mexico.)

Jackson did not finally discover Calhoun's attempt at discipline until so informed when he was President, and - irony always - the man who had saved his post and thus ultimately made him President was his political foe, then President J.Q. Adams, whom his campaign managers later smeared as nobody could smear until Joe McCarthy appeared on the scene 125 years later. Learning that Calhoun had in 1819 called his conduct into question, Jackson now instituted an exchange of communications, the termination of which left little doubt in anyone's mind that Calhoun would not be Vice-President next time around. Nor was he.

But Calhoun, presiding over the Senate, made another mistake. When President Jackson nominated Martin Van Buren to be Minister to England, the Senate presented itself evenly divided for confirmation. Calhoun had the deciding vote. He could not resist the urge to put both men down. He exulted. He cast his ballot against the nomination. When the next election rolled around, Calhoun returned perforce to South Carolina and States Rights. Van Buren was called from his interim appointment in England to receive plaudits from his home state and the nomination as Vice-President under Jackson. There was little problem in electing the duo this time.

Calhoun, who at one point would try to do anything to save the union provided he could also save the slave culture, get low tariffs, etc., now turned his genius into composing a finely wrought thesis on nullification and states rights. Its argument will be summarized later. But we cannot postpone telling what happened under Jackson because we are still almost a generation away from the Civil War crisis of states rights.

The issue was the tariff. Jefferson believed in charging for goods brought into the country at rates merely sufficient for obtaining revenues to run the government. He sought to keep both tariffs and governmental expenditures low. This was good Democratic-Republican Party doctrine. However, the party had slipped in a Federalist direction and the Northerners had succumbed to Hamiltonian policy, so that the tariff had risen higher and higher. It became indubitably and deliberately a protective tariff. It kept the goods of the industrial countries of Europe from being sold freely in America while these same countries were buying - or so it was hoped - great amounts of the South's staple crops, especially cotton.

Would they not be unable to buy from the South if they could not sell to the USA what they produced? The Southern argument was logical and probably true. There were, we hasten to add, other reasons for shifts in world trade. Other countries besides the United States were producing cotton in increasing quantities and all else that the South produced. Furthermore, why could not the South sell well to the North, whose increasing industrial work force could sell them the manufactured goods that they needed.

One would have to analyze the character of the middlemen here to give a straight answer. There was a large body of agents, middlemen between South and Europe as between South and North and these were in competition too, and eager that their particular kind of tariff should succeed. So they were manipulating their principals, as agents will usually do, given the chance.

Yet why had the Carolinians settled upon nullification as a tactic? As Daniel Webster had pointed out in a set of debates with Haynes in the Senate two years earlier, the Supreme Court had designated itself determiner of what was and what was not constitutional. Why not let the Court decide? Anyhow, the Union was sacred and could not be fractured, claimed Webster. Many politicians did not agree with Webster on this point, certainly not the states-rights people, who had watched Chief Justice Marshall's long nationalist career with annoyance. The Court would very likely declare the act of nullification unconstitutional.

Following his re-election, Jackson and his congressional associates made some concessions to the South by lowering tariffs. This was not enough for the South Carolina legislature, after four years of the "abominable tariff" schedule of 1828. The State was suffering in this decade a frightening drainage of population and low prices on its agricultural exports. To find work, to locate better land after ruining what they had, to adventure in the wide open spaces, to live in a more egalitarian society - such were the motives of the migrants. The legislature called a convention to declare the tariff legislation of 1828 and 1832 unconstitutional, null, and void; this it did. It further forbade the collection of said tariff charges.

Jackson responded with typical vigor; he loved a good fight.
He announced that he would enforce the nation's laws.
He mustered the Army for an invasion of the State,
and did send troops quietly to Federal forts there;
he sent revenue cutters down to block any exports
or imports whose tariffs had not been paid.
He issued a fine Proclamation on December 10, 1832,
and obtained a Force Bill from Congress authorizing him
to employ violence if necessary in execution of the laws.
(Presumably he had this power anyway, but thought he
should have the reassurance and commitment from Congress.)
Next Henry Clay, still at work compromising, got
Congress to cut key tariffs greatly over several years, the
cotton goods tariff by half.

Frightened, mollified, lacking support from other states, but still prideful, the legislature rescinded the nullification of the tariff laws, then proceeded to nullify the Force Bill as being unconstitutional. This hardly provoked anger since force was no longer forthcoming. Still, there it was, nullification, a dormant but not dead issue. Jackson's threats were directed at the politicians of the slave areas, where force was the best understood instrument of power. Where Jackson's heart was located was displayed in 1835, when he voiced approval of a Charleston riot against opponents of slavery and against the anti-slavery propaganda that was being sent through the post-office for delivery to points within the State. He expressed the wish that he might bar anti-slavery materials from the mails.

Decades before Jackson, during his tenure, and decades after him, the States were democratizing their political structures to the best of their knowledge, and the world became aware of America as a thoroughly democratic country (always forgetting the slave culture or dismissing it as exceptional to the real America). But what the American people and the world believed to be an historical fact, that America was a pure democracy, was far from the truth.

In the first place, the word "democracy" is as close to a meaningless word as popular and political discussion affords. It conveys several definitions that not only are separate but also contradictory, and yet so stuck in many minds as to irritate them when the meanings are extracted. Nevertheless, it must be said that democracy means equality of all in respect to all; it means conducting business by a majority vote, or a plurality vote, or by forcing a consensus, or by unanimity; it means equality of opportunity to rise above one's fellows, but not among the resulting unequal achievers; it means anarchism or extreme individualism. It means a widespread official proclamation of doctrines, usually to no great effect.

Harking to the pandemonium surrounding the word in America in the

first half of the nineteenth century, one detects especially the strains of individualism and equality of manners;
a person can seek his interest and way of life without bother by others;
one man's conduct is as respectable as any other man's.
Neither of these was very true.
They reduced to the right of every man to do what he pleased and could get away with, and the right to deny shame for the way he was behaving. The refusal of special privileges for anybody (above the privileges and birth position already enjoyed) was as far into a philosophy of democracy as most moved.
Unfortunately, in practice, this included,
besides a demand for the right to vote and such like,
a suspicion of anyone or any group pursuing the arts, intellectual subjects, and uncommon behaviors.
In this large period of United States history,
democracy was low-brow.

Most Americans believed that they were on their way to the blessed state of democracy. The people in their voluntary associations, and State after State, introduced populist devices into their organization and rules. The Federal Government was less active and, in any event, was affected by transference of practices; thus, if the suffrage for a State's elections was widened, the same electorate would be entitled to vote for federal representatives. Inasmuch as the Federal government was spending little and doing less, Washington, D.C. - even with all the battles and wars of the ante-Civil War period - was less the concern and regard of most people,
especially the three per cent who were politically active,
than their local and state governments.

The suffrage was widened almost everywhere to the level of universal White manhood suffrage, including, in some States, aliens (to get them to settle down locally).
Where officers had been appointed or indirectly elected before,
they now became directly elected by popular vote,
governors and State officials, for example. Practically every officer of significance and many insignificant ones, on the local and State levels, and whether a new post or an old one,
became popularly elective.

The Electoral College, supposed to be a great filter of public sentiments, lost layers of the filtering system with the advent, first, of state, then of national conventions, to nominate Presidential candidates, then, with turning over election of the Presidential electors to popular vote, binding electors in fact, if not in law, to vote as they had promised for the President and his favorite for Vice-President.

Tenure of office was shortened in many places, so that Jefferson's dictum that *"where annual elections end, tyranny begins"* was translated into endless election campaigning for next year's election. There was a movement to tighten even the controls that short tenure would supposedly provide by declaring that elected officials must take instructions from their constituents, an impossible idea to put into practice, but one to which all, including Lincoln, had to pay lip service.

Nor did this mean simply the right to petition the Congress (or the government), which the Constitution provided. It meant that somehow people would find a consensus or at least a majority on all issues of significance and that this would be adequate for instructing legislators on how to vote (amendments, legal language, committee reworking, and compromises notwithstanding).

Devices for ensuring popular "representation" were impressive - the farther away from the scene, the more impressive, as the abundance of compliments from radical democrats like Jeremy Bentham and Karl Marx abroad would reveal. But first to be realized is that the laws commanded only a fraction of people's behavior, and government in that half-century was so limited a band of the social spectrum, that it could not affect deeply other determinants of the distribution of desiderata of life.

Furthermore there were countervailing agencies, the most important of which was the political party. The political party in America, built up to ensure majorities, consensus, and unanimity, was drawing sustenance and growth hormones from anti-democratic sources. It became a way of making a government beset by

innumerable "democratic measures and devices",
which was becoming impossible,
possible - by integrating offices and policies.

Additionally, fraud was as pervasive under the new
direct democracy as it was in the preceding centuries.
The secrecy of the polls was still not all guaranteed.
The floating vote was enormous.
In Michigan up to the edge of the Civil War,
perhaps the hottest issue concerned requiring qualified persons
to register ahead of time in order to be allowed to vote.
The collector of federal revenues at Detroit and along a
stretch of 900 miles of lake coast
had his men hire "Kanuck voters" as watchers for
smugglers at $60 per year, provided that on election day
they would cross into the USA and
vote in Michigan for his party.

The railroads had to be built by thousands of laborers,
and these men were harbored in camps,
and they could be induced by whiskey and money to go
to any voting place, swear they were citizens and vote.

Finally we return to the "spoils system" as a democratic device
that ended by being an oligarchic one.
It was democratic in one of the senses of the term,
in that more people got a chance
to have a government job,
and the elected officers could appoint more people to
government payrolls and honorary commissions, thus bringing
government, even the least political and measly clerical or labor job,
closer to the people.

It worked out oligarchically, in that this system
of fighting off bureaucracy fell prey to the oligarchic tendencies
of the political party. The jobs were filled by the band of
politicians in control of the party and offices. Once given a job,
the free and independent voter became a party henchman and hireling,
though paid out of the government treasury.

The spoils system enervated the solid nationalism that had come,
and would come again with a permanent federal bureaucracy.
Meanwhile, the cause of sectionalism was forwarded by the
strong sentimental ties and bonds of life-style between
the state and local elected and appointed political class
and the federal class, whose offices depended upon local ties.

Jackson rode roughshod over the Supreme Court and Congress,
as he did over private individuals and institutions
and his own branch of government.
When the Court decided against the State of Georgia,
in a case regarding the disposition of Indian rights, he showed no
disposition to assist the Court in having its judgement enforced.
He exclaimed: it's your decree, now enforce it yourself.

He also picked up the Presidential veto power,
hitherto employed rarely (9 times in all) and for defensive purposes,
and used it twelve times to frustrate the majority of Congress.
The veto now began its career as a major weapon of Presidential power,
and ended by practically constituting the Presidency as a
Third House of Congress.

Finally, he disposed of the deposits held by the
Bank of the United States by placing them in favored banks
of Democratic-Republican partisan persuasion -
state banks, often fraudulent and prone to bankruptcy
He had a paranoid obsession about the Bank.
It symbolized the ascendency of the Eastern financial elite;
it was that of course, but also much more, a most useful
device for keeping the country's financial system in order.
While the state banks ran amok, issuing paper money,
lending freely, and speculating wildly with depositors' funds,
Jackson was hotly promoting metal money -
the result was fiscal chaos, panic, depression.
Picturing him who ruined the currency on the modern
$20 bill is an ironic twist of history.

Jackson was as close to a crowd leader of a mobocracy

as America would ever have. He ran up a heavy urban workers' vote as well as capturing the poorer rural votes.
Yet we cannot find in his record much that would prove him the representative of either city or countryside workers.
As they would say a century later about President Eisenhower:
"No one likes him, except the people".
Thus proceeded "Jacksonian democracy".

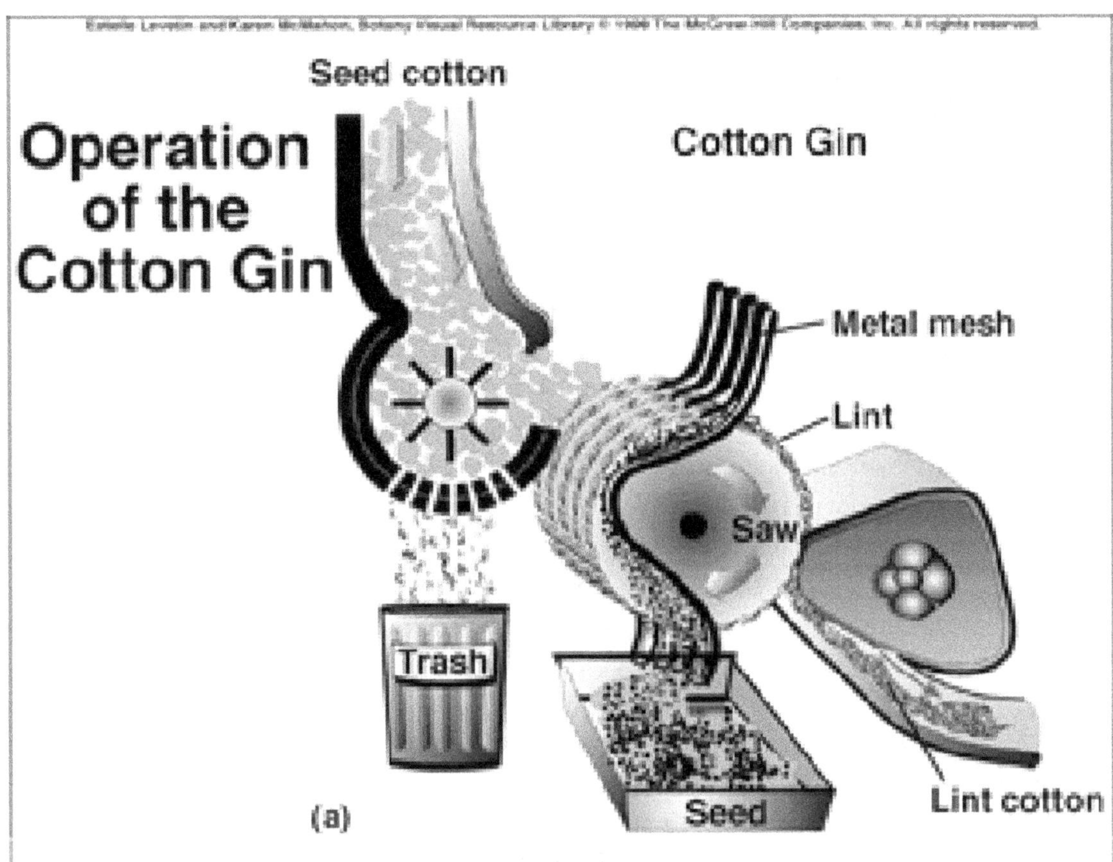

Operation of the first Cotton Gin invented by Eli Whitney

Chapter Twenty-six

Settlement and Infrastructure

The development of America had little patience for the South and Washington, D.C., once the country was into the nineteenth century. The Capital was a dismal and uncomfortable hangout for politicians and placemen. The Southern system, once it had leapt forward with the Yankee inventor's cotton gin, hardly changed over the sixty years until Secession: the same crops, the same exhaustive soil practices, the same slavery, the same application of these to the West as far as the slave owners could betake themselves. Its population was steadily declining in relation to the North. Its industries lagged. Still, because of the two-seat equality of States in the Senate, and because politics as a way of life appealed more to Southerners than to Northerners, the South was well represented in national affairs.

Eleven out of sixteen Presidents up to and including Lincoln were Southerners by birth or culture. Yet constructive participation in the creation of the modern age came entirely from the North. This phenomenon was to continue because the South was its own worst enemy. As it had become addicted earlier to whiskey and tobacco, the South fell prey to its cotton crop. In the eighteenth century cotton had been in great demand everywhere, but was difficult to comb because of its tight seeds. When a long-staple variety was bred, it could be combed readily, but could not stand higher terrain than tidewaters country.

In 1792, Eli Whitney, recently graduated from Yale, was visiting a schoolmate in Georgia and, after hearing that seed-picking averaged a pound per day, he labored for ten days and came up with a cotton en-GIN-e that could de-seed ten times the amount. With a few improvements, such as fixing pins on a drum, the cotton gin was capable of twenty times the prior productivity.

Substantially the South was fixed for life.
Cotton bales piled up on the wharves of New Orleans,
now the greatest export point of the country. Cotton fields devoured
the old Eastern South and moved ever Southwestward.
They afforded a cash crop, but the need for cash seemed endless
and the land, which seemed endless, too, was progressively exhausted
until modern chemistry brought in cheap fertilizers just
before the stroke of midnight.

In the North, machines were changing agriculture also.
The plow, thousands of years old, suddenly acquired
well-tempered iron blades, then steel ones.
A Virginian, Cyrus McCormick developed a reaper.
He moved to Chicago where he prospered mightily.
Next came mowers, and then threshers, until the

individual farm family could handle three times as many acres
as it could before, provided it could
pay for the machines and maintain them in good repair.

The exploitative industries were getting into full swing.
The lumber industry was gnawing its way out of New England
and New York into Michigan and Wisconsin. Hardwood forests
were vanishing in the East, and with them their ecology.

Fur trade had provided over a third of the exports of
New York and Pennsylvania before the turn of the century,
but now it had gone West, all the way to the Pacific coast in fact,
even before the acquisition of these territories.
John Jacob Astor, a young German immigrant, set up
a string of trappers and trading posts, dealing with
typical unscrupulousness and using Mafiosi muscle on the
Indians and independent traders. His fortune founded a family
conglomerate, that was to be in finance, merchandising, and real estate.
Its extensive tenement holdings in the slums of New York City
were a favorite target of early social reformers,
justifiably so.

Mining was coming into its own as a miracle fortune producer,
coal and iron of Pennsylvania, copper of Michigan
(where Indians had dug, aeons before), lead from Missouri,
and gold and silver in a number of places, mostly West
of the Mississippi. Natural water power and steam engines
provided energy that supplemented human digging and hauling.
Explosives were used, although hard to handle until the
invention of dynamite late in the century.

One after another, exhausted and abandoned mines
came to dot the topography of America.
It would be a century before public notice was taken of the
degeneration of river and soil systems occurring from the
very start. Early European visitors to these areas commented on how
avid for land Americans were, and yet how little they cared for it.

Conditions in the mines were unspeakably bad, of course.
Labor was casual and treated with stalag hospitality;

the death and injury rates were sky-high, but untallied.
As did the farmers, the mine-owners, to get workers,
dipped into the human tide that ebbed and flowed around
the great country, while generally moving westward. Often mines
would become the focal point for larger settlements by providing
employment, a stimulus to trade by the needs of the mine staff, and
some semblance of law and order.
When a mine would fail, its town would despair and shrink.

In 1802 the U.S. Corps of Engineers was
established and located at West Point, where it eventually
became an elite corps to which many of the best students aspired.
The Academy of the Army itself, as well as the Corps,
was modeled quite along French lines, a wise choice,
emulating the top engineering school of the world, the
École Polytechnique. Ever afterwards, public
construction in America related to the Corps;
much of it was the work of the Corps - roads, bridges,
harbors, drainage, dams, flood control -
all in all a wide variety of projects,
until the Corps became politically powerful,
dealing with Congressmen, exchanging favors and projects,
also advising forcibly the state and local governments on their
infrastructural needs and possibilities and budgets.

In retrospect, it is evident that the Corps became
megalo-minded, seeking big costly developmental
projects, and paid little attention to the upcoming crises of the
environment. They made of the Missouri River, it's been said,
a plumbing system, with six dams and reservoirs
upstream and a shaped straightened deep channel downstream,
destroying wetlands now cherished and giving
passage to barges now few in number. The Corps'
task lately was changed to deconstruction and rewetting.

In wartime, the Corps of Engineers would supply a critical branch of
the Army services; in peacetime it was the most active element of the
military. In fact, the Corps history shows very well how an army

component can work usefully at all times, and on occasion, as in the Civilian Conservation Corps of the Great Depression, the Army did organize civilian projects for employing the youth of the country.

The enormous American military system could have slid readily into full-time employment in transformed roles at high priority civilian tasks, upon the collapse of the Soviet Union, had Congress and the Presidency reconceptualized the new world, and provided due initiative. Instead, reduction in the war function was ill-conceived as a problem of how to fire a great many people despite the many pressures to keep thousands of smoothly functioning units on the job with the same military roles.

Providing and supporting a single job whose product is sold outside a community - that is, exported - will support a couple of jobs within the community and several dependents A single mine hiring thirty men will support a settlement of a couple of hundred persons. And as with mines, so with construction projects of roads and turnpikes (toll roads), canals, bridges and railroads.

There is a progression to be observed in the settlement of an area by European Americans moving from the Atlantic coast. First come the fur and gadget traders, mountain men, escaped felons, prospectors, all living at the lowest level of subsistence, often hanging out, when allowed, on the fringes of Indian villages or in settlements occupied by French or Hispanic or British or even, as in San Francisco, near Fort Ross, that was bought by the Swiss immigrant Sutter from a Russian company, his Russian predecessors. These fringe-men will supply information to newcomers, and if they do not rob them, may help them.

The newcomers are usually regarded as the pioneers, even though, wherever they go - upper New England, Florida, the Great Lakes region, the Mississippi valley, Texas and the Southwest and the West Coast, they encounter Indian tribes, both settled into villages and nomadic, French settlements like Kaskaskia on the Mississippi River in Illinois or the impressive city of New Orleans, Spanish settlements in Florida, and all over the Southwest and in California.

Still, Kaskaskia in the 1790's appeared to a French traveler as a settlement of savages in dismal huts, clothed in breech-clouts, more prodigal and reckless by far than the Indians roundabout, and given to gambling and fighting in Virginia frontier style - no holds barred, eye-gouging a specialty.
A French priest, not so dauntless as some of his forbears, departed finally in fear lest some zealous Protestant in the new lot come for him with a scalping knife.
The first wave of Easterners, that is to say, had arrived.

Revise, therefore, the Hollywood and textbook image of the population moving along a vast front Westward and Southward in blissful ignorance of what would befall pioneers, and encountering a vast nothingness of nature; they usually bumped into a human culture the equal of their own, but less of it, of course.

The first pioneers on the trail of the wild men would hope to have some piece of paper filed somewhere to a claim on the land, or at best a title from the faraway state title office. There were all degrees of entitlement to be found, including the shoot-out. Squatting was a form of title. The squatter might ordinarily expect that whoever came with a better title would lop off a piece of the land just to appease him and have him around. We are talking here about many millions of acres, large parts of every state and territory in the final summation. The weakness of land title in the United States is proverbial; one cannot go very far back without discovering some egregious error or incident, and in the beginning, the whole, of course, was based upon forceful seizure.

Meanwhile the pioneer, relieved to see the first denizens slump off with the Indians, would be building a sod house or log cabin or shack of sawed boards, with a dirt floor. He would use the outdoors for a toilet or build a seat over a hole for reflective contemplation while eliminating. He would plant seeds for fruit trees and build a garden fence of rails and boughs. He would turn up two or three acres of the sixty or more that he claimed to own. He would slash underbrush, cut trees and burn stumps. He might assemble an ill-assorted group of animals. And he would wait for a purchaser to come along. If he could, he would sell his property for enough cash and goods to move on in better style than he had enjoyed on arrival.

The next man, who might or might not have a woman and even children, would have at least a start on life in the new area and be furnished with knowledge of his neighbors, the wild life, waters, and directions to the nearest sources of supplies and the nearest market for selling any surplus that he might put aside for cash sale or trade. That is, he would receive more than just land; he would receive some kind of legal claim, improved land, fittings and animals, and a short orientation course.

Usually such a farmer, for that we can now call him, came in association with several others - kin, old neighbors, a church group, army buddies. With luck there might be some French, Spanish or friendly Indians within a few miles. If not, a village might well grow up shortly. Unlike the Old Country farmer or the New England and Northern East Coast farmer, his family would live not in a village but at a considerable distance from the nearest neighbor. Yet, if a person had a skill, it would be put to use - a woman of experience would be called on to assist in childbirth, a man who knew how to throw up a house would be called to take charge of an instant construction or cabin-raising, and so forth.

Somewhere in the area there would be a crossroads, and here a general store and trading point would be set up, soon to be followed by a hardware store, saloon, lawyer's office, a grain dealer, a barber or even a printer to purvey news, and a blacksmith, the whole characteristically American in that the stores lined themselves up along a street, the inevitable "Main Street".

Preachers, schoolteachers, and back-packing peddlers would call at isolated houses beyond the settlements. Often the process of settlement would be precipitated by several neighbors, who would plot a developmental area where their lands joined, and promote it as a settlement location. Often, too, speculators and promoters would lay out lots in an area, draw pretty pictures of them, and sell them far and wide. Second-story facades, as in a Hollywood Western movie, were often constructed as a hopeful sign, and to lend a loftiness to the drab rows of stores. Failures were as numerous as successes, in every aspect of the process of settlement. Frequently frauds mingled with failures, so that it was hard to tell foolish mistake from moral delinquency.

Whether in the country or in a village, family housing would be about the same. Larger towns and cities would carry West their models from the East. Little from Europe was tried directly in the West. Folk housing pertained to three, some say four, styles corresponding to the triple belts of culture from North to South. New Englanders built from frame, and developed clapboards. They built two-rooms deep, in two stories, with a central chimney. Later came a central hall with chimneys at both ends. Still later came a story-and-a-half with a central chimney. Then in the nineteenth came a two-story house with a gable on top and side- wings.

The pluralist culture of the Mid-Atlantic and its western extensions had the log cabin, often expanded, sometimes to form a double cabin with a corridor between them. The other form was a two-story frame or brick rectangle with gables at both ends. There were also New York Dutch styles, often lending a porch to other American forms as well. The Chesapeake Bay region imitated the English cottage with end chimneys and a front porch. Out of Louisiana came the Creole house with paired front doors and an inset porch. The chimney was centrally located. The large plantation homes adapted a Roman-Greek style, usually in brick.

No fully American design was invented, no wooden wigwams until the hamburger age. A method of putting up houses fast was developed in the 1830's, approaching prefabricated housing of a century later.

A new abundance and cheapness of nails and lumber invited this
response to the mobility and immediacy of American needs.
A house could be set up or disassembled in a few days
with a crew of men, a lot of boards and wood shingles
for the roof, all done with saws, hammers, and nails.
These "basket-houses" were not flimsy, and cut costs by two-thirds.
They were more common and authentically American than log cabins.

Cheap and abundant lumber and nails, the saw and the hammer:
there's the winning American combination of the age.
The "balloon-frame" house was a common type -
a light frame of studs and frames nailed together.

American towns, even off Main Street, acquired a typical and distinctive look or air, a *je ne sais quoi,* with their generous lots and elms and chestnut trees. They carried straight across the country, entangling themselves with some additional central European elements in the North and Spanish elements from the South until the whole began to reverse itself in a variety of ranch houses, colonials, Cape Cods, and truly modern (rare) homes and office buildings in the twentieth century.

A booming invasion of Southern Ohio, Indiana and Illinois, and also of the Mississippi Valley, occurred in the first decades of the nineteenth century. After the defeat of the Indians in the Battle of Fallen Timbers in 1794 reassured people that they might move into the Ohio Valley, a wide-scale occupation began. It was struck by a price and money panic in 1819. In the early 1830's a recession set in, banks began to fail, money became scarce, many farms and villages were abandoned; it seemed that everyone owed money that they could not repay. The recession plunged into depression, from which the country did not recover until 1845.

Humanity would flow through, trying, failing, looking for better chances. A cadre would be left behind in charge. These would usually be the more successful in one way or another, the more committed, the exhausted. Often a town would shrink from an initial boom and remain with a few of the original inhabitants; these would become the elite of the town, boastful historians, scrutinizers of all new faces to try to hold some and send others on their way.

A single memorial generation was sufficient for this process to begin and mature, yet to hear people talk, it seemed as if the place were some ancient Rhineland village or a Stratford-on-Avon, draped on a bluff of the Mississippi River.

The Southern portions of the above-mentioned states of the Midwest, beginning with Southern Pennsylvania and going straight across the Mississippi River and as far as Colorado were usually of Southern culture, of the type of the family of Abraham Lincoln. Very few escaped anonymity and poverty, however. The Northern belt of settlements did better, bringing with them more steadfast farmers, who were better capitalized through connections in Philadelphia, New York and Boston.

Quincy, Illinois, perched upon the Mississippi River, was one of the successful new towns, although from its (re)founding in 1825 by a John Wood, who rode West from New York in 1818 and built a substantial home in 1835, to the early decades of the 1900's, a score of architectural styles graced the homes of the well-to-do, who profited from a three-generation-long 3000-boat annual traffic, carrying goods from the whole world and taking wood, livestock, and cereals back down the River; styles ranging from Mr. Wood's Greek Revival mansion (Southern fashion) through the Palladian to Frank Lloyd Wright's "prairie modern". In the East End of town every U.S.-adapted European period and style of over a century of time lent its model. After traveling extensively, one bachelor erected an Islamic culture-schmeer, from minaret to harem, overlooking the Father of Waters.

A direct German immigration of the mid-1800's built a neighborhood of small two-room and four-room brick houses, still occupied today. Shacks abounded. Frame houses came and went, as did most immigrants and residents of the town, as did the steamboats. Still, half a century was and has been a respectable average time of thriving for an American town. The rest has been prologue and epilogue, brutally cut short or nostalgically and indefinitely prolonged. There always remained much babbitry and know-how, both, in towns like Quincy.

The White population that stayed managed fairly well, drawing upon a rich agricultural region and special manufactures.

There settled into these hundreds of towns all over the Midwest a new elite. They were the cadres that continued to lose their populations, but hung on and prospered. The top of the social pyramid had a degree of proud constancy, but the total base of the pyramid was being continuously renewed, 70% more or less, even as fast as 50% per year. They remind one of the U.S. Army cadres of World War II, regular Army volunteers, holdovers used to train the mass of recruits streaming into the camps. Or of teachers handling one grade of children after another.

The elite followers celebrated and honored each other and wrote their histories and did their best to get *hoi polloi* to join in the masquerade even if *en passant*. They assured that the local media, their media, recorded the veneration emanating from the passing crowd, as if these had remained in place like themselves, and tried to make the throng of ordinary cooperative "extras" appear to be more or less everywhere part of a permanent scenario, their lower class base.

Thus functioned "high society" in America.
The process formed swiftly.
In one memorial generation, 1833 to 1898,
Chicago, typically, grew a social and industrial elite
that presented and represented itself as
having been in place since times immemorial.
And, *mirabile dictu*, was able to surround itself
with a mass of country folk and immigrants,
wave after wave, who saluted them in passing through,
cheering internally *ad astra per aspera*!

People followed roads, and roads people. In the initial phase, there were the ancient Indian paths, far more extensive than acknowledged by the latecomers. Hiawatha and Tecumseh, on their evangelical journeys, centuries apart, to unite the Indian nations, traveled rapidly and knowing full well where they were going and whom they would be encountering - just as well, shall we say, as the preachers and peddlers of the mid-nineteenth century. The Wilderness Road, first publicized by the doughty scout Daniel Boone in 1795, as I mentioned earlier, soon began to carry Virginians through the mountains into Kentucky and Tennessee.

It was a path, then a practically impassible road, then with the efforts of one local group after another, a cart-traversable road with bridges and well-marked fords, then in places a turnpike charging a fee, and so on until stage coaches could manage the whole journey in exchanges at a going speed of perhaps six miles an hour. The second great road was the National Road, that carried one from Baltimore through Pennsylvania, Ohio, Indiana, to Vandalia, Illinois, thence to St.Louis, Missouri.

Waterways were many, beginning with the St. Lawrence on the North that, with portages, could direct a person ultimately to Lake Huron, where from Detroit one could go overland to Chicago. Better than this route, one could in the late thirties go by boat up the Hudson River, transfer to the Erie Canal for a 350-mile ride, and thence proceed via Lake Erie west.

Governor De Witt Clinton of New York worked assiduously for years to finance and build the Erie Canal, and, once its success was publicized, every area wanted its own canal; 3000 miles of them, mostly in the North and Midwest, were built by mid-century. It was possible theoretically to go by water from New York to New Orleans, but the busy coastwise sea lane connecting the two cities was greatly preferred.

Swift packets were also available for the Atlantic crossing, several times a week from New York, a score of lines running between other American seaboard cities and Europe. Early in the century, they were square-rigged sailing vessels; in some places the American-designed clipper ship was stream-lined and tall-masted with a rigging set for speed. This boat for twenty years stupefied everyone with its velocity in voyages around the world, carrying a good proportion of the adventurers of the California gold fields, with their supplies and support personnel, male and female. The clipper was especially good at bringing back oriental tea that was still fresh. However, steamships, tried out in England and elsewhere for more than a century, finally took workable form for trans-Atlantic voyages and dispossessed most sailships. But this would only occur in the sixties and seventies.

Steamboats moved onto the Mississippi River and its tributaries very early. The flat-bottomed paddle-steamers were well designed to avoid the bars and rocks of the shallow rivers. Their boilers often blew up in their captains' enthusiasm for speed, killing and maiming crew members and unlucky passengers. Irish stokers were sometimes employed because their deaths would cost nothing, while a slave was expensive. (But this may have been a report spread by Irishmen who would risk death for a job involving travel.)

Soon a great many locomotives would need their Irish firemen. A threat to boats and canals, a shaper of the topography of use as against nature, a front-runner for coal and iron mines against water power: such was the railroad. By the fifties, railroads had far outstripped in mileage the canals of the country. They began only several years after the first railroads of England (1825) and the Continent, with the Baltimore and Ohio Railroad, 1830, reaching the Ohio River but only in 1852. Needless to say, most devices and designs were pirated.

The Americans, with great distances to travel, built track and locomotives feverishly. Their locomotives were lighter and less durable than the British, cultural symptoms of a country where nothing was thought to last long. They were also made to run fast to make up for the long distances, and powerful, to climb long, steep grades.

For those who look at maps of the American railroad networks of several successive decades, the pace of building appears to have been most rapid. The fact is, however, that for many years the federal government turned its fiscal hindside to all forms of transportation. From Jefferson onwards, most politicians in Washington held the belief, as long as was permissible, that local governments, states and private companies should build turnpikes, canals, and railroads. The dominant political aggregations believed in minimal expenditures and activity in Washington.

So railroad construction was actually constrained in America. (In Europe, by contrast, the central governments were active in every way from the beginning, ending up with thoroughly socialized, and generally efficient systems.)

But then, every financial device was exercised, other than federal participation. A common form for a railroad to take would be the corporation, privately organized, with some private money and liberal distribution of shares to politicians for little or nothing, which company would then receive extremely liberal charters that would permit them every freedom except grand larceny (which was understood to be present without saying), with loans from cities and state governments, with guarantees against being taxed for a period of time, and with grants of land along their proposed right-of-way, including not only the necessary land but large swatches of land on the sides of the tracts, such that a railroad could go into the business of selling land, plotting settlements, building hotels, and setting up shops and industries.

The increasing use of machinery and the availability of the means of transporting crops permitted sections of the agricultural economy to go onto a cash basis, borrowing money, investing it in machines and freight charges, and collecting it from the sales. Of course, middle men came into the picture. There had to be men who built grain elevators to hold crops for shipment on order. Commodity speculators came into being who bought and sold crops at all dates forward, sight unseen. These made the market. But, too, the market made them. And the market was in the Northern cities and Europe. (The South was self-sufficient in practically all foods, despite its concentration upon tobacco, cotton, and whiskey.)

Here and now the American farmers re-experienced
the fate of farmers everywhere.
It seemed that every good year was more than matched
by a bad year for the crops.
The farmer had to pay interest on his
machines and other purchases
that he had no cash to pay for. He
appeared to be forever in debt,
the question continually posing itself

whether his total assets of land and buildings
and machines did not add up to his debt..
But this was determined, like the market for his crops,
by factors beyond his control, the money supply and interest rates.

It is mistaken to review the history of farming as though farming were an ordinarily prosperous occupation. The American farmer, North, South, East, and West, has always been more of a financial failure than a success. Where he appears to have succeeded it has been due to subsidies paid to him indirectly or in hidden form by the government. The great majority of American farmers have failed and left the land, beginning with the Pilgrims and the Jamestown settlers and coming down to present times. The farmer could really only survive and prosper when he behaved as a subsistence farmer, to whom cash was a luxury.

In the whole of New England, farming became, first, a misery, and then an avocation. Instead of the eldest son being favored with the farm, he escaped, and the youngest son was stuck with it. In this ante-Bellum period, New Englanders streamed West, abandoning their farms to poor relatives, handymen and city cousins. When they reached the rich undisturbed prairies, they bathed in a paradise of *"unshorn fields, boundless and beautiful, for which the speech of England has no name, the prairies"*. So wrote Poet William Cullen Bryant in 1865.

Yet, by then, most prairie was shorn, and the rest would go in the following memorial generation; in the late 1900's patches of prairie flowers and grasses and their animal companions were being laboriously restored in small part by conservationists.

The question then arises, if this is true
- and it will have to be studied later on –
has not farming in America from the very beginning been
viewed in a totally illusory fashion,
the dream of agricultural riches
based upon cheap land initially stripped from barbarians?
The riches came out of the farms,
and were spread far and wide, not excluding
the agricultural sector;

still most farmers had to be forever on the edge
of bankruptcy, if not this year, then next year was the year to go bust.

Moreover, at least half the farmers, so-called, of America
never nor now deserved that appellation.
"Poor country-folk" is perhaps the most exact neutral
term for them; derogatory names given them
were and continue to be numerous. They lived a
marginal existence away from the growing cities
until the time came for most of them to
descend upon the cities, as individuals continually,
but sometimes in waves of migrants. In 1880
25% of farmers were tenants, in 1900 35%, with
sharecropping in the South and cash rents North.

Street scene of an American City Slum in the mid-19th Century

Chapter Twenty-seven

Industrial and Urban Frontiers

Cities had to begin somehow. The early towns of America were boat landings, road terminals, warehouses, trading agencies for domestic and foreign imports and exports, rendezvous for property exchanges and sales. They were commercial and trading centers with the same artisanal shops than villages had, but in greater numbers. They would in some cases start out as forts, as Chicago did with Fort Dearborn. Or the military would add its weight to the scene later on.

All towns of consequence required access to the sea or a navigable river. There were ocean cities like New York, Bay Cities like Philadelphia and Providence, river cities like Cincinnati and Louisville, and lake cities like Chicago and Milwaukee. Later transportation forms - the railroad, the automobile and the airplane - would tend to create their own kind of city. Power sources had to work in tandem, first water, then coal, oil, electricity, nuclear power. Abundant water was always needed, even if not for generating power.

The towns of the first half of the nineteenth century grew fast with the coming of the European industrial revolution to America. Whereas New York alone had over 100,000 residents in 1820, eight cities exceeded that number in 1860, and many more had climbed above the 25,000 mark. By then New York City numbered over a million persons. All nations congregated in the City, wrote Poet Walt Whitman, a Brooklyn boy. By 1860 it handled two-thirds of the nation's imports and one-third of its exports. America's urban growth was exponential and would continue on the same upward curve until the end of the 1900's. By the end of the 1800's America was more urban than rural.

With its abundant land and mineral resources to occupy the population, American cities would not have grown so rapidly were it not for the development of the factory system and the specialization within the cities of certain functions and production processes. That is, Americans were aware to a degree from the beginning that it would be nicer to decentralize manufacturing, and held up before all eyes as horrible examples London and Birmingham. But "birds of a feather flock together", and "misery loves company", so manufacturers went where the cheap labor pools, the pre-existing dock and road facilities were, to the neighborhoods of the managerial and entrepreneurial and capitalist class, but especially where people like themselves were already working, even if only in small shops. Once begun, only major forces would re-route and transfer industrial centers.

Cincinnati bounded forward in the early nineteenth century, its population rapidly turning over, its founders, Revolutionary War

veterans, mostly disappeared. One group of its settlers, African-Americans, never increased by much; it averaged several percent of the people; it was periodically expelled from the town, like lepers. Yet the city's developmental energy increased exponentially, with a great change from a native Protestantism and British foreign population to a majority of Catholic Irish and German (both Catholic and Protestant) immigrant population in 1850,
never to return to its former Protestant condition.

Catholics were subject to vicious discrimination and abuse. But they held together. The Irish particularly were bellicose, while the Germans were persistent and busy bees, so that when the Protestants wished away the combative Irish they encountered the stubborn Germans and were back where they started. They passed an ordinance to have a Protestant Bible read in the public schools and the Catholics insisted that the Catholic children be given the Catholic Bible. (Neither thought that the Federal Constitution afforded any
protection against reading any Bible in the public schools.
This was a century into the future.}

At the same time a vigorous Jewish element accompanied the German immigration and set up trading and manufacturing facilities for the region. (By now there were Jewish congregations in every state of the Union; there were, besides, a growing number of free-thinkers and non-sectarians of Jewish origin.) In 1841 Cincinnati, the "Queen City" was the world's largest pork market, with a $3 million market in meatpacking, mostly pork, and a $1 million product in butchering (in German towns traditionally butchering was a Jewish special occupation; the tradition was ultimately dissipated in America); ready to wear clothing was produced to the amount of $1.2 millions (the Jewish tailor was also proverbial in Germany, and persisted in American business, bringing in the largest competitors to the old New England interests).

Between $800,000 and $400,000
originated from each of food and flour processing,
furniture, foundry castings, steamboat-building,
printing and publishing, boots and shoes, and housing.
The next decade trebled the growth of the top ten industries
and of all industries of the city.

The ingenuity of its entrepreneurs was considerable, in pork by-products such as soap and candles for example. One can observe even in the skeletal statistics the operation of fevered imaginations, fully captivated by capitalist expansionism and product development.

Returning in time and place to New England, we review the prototypical textile industry as it springs forward. It begins with the theft of English machine designs by Samuel Slater, who takes them within his brain storage to America to sell in 1789. It starts up soon with nine children on the job. So go the precedents. By the War of 1812, hundreds of textile factories were at work.

Water power was used at first; a half century later stationary steam engines fired by abundant coal could do better. The principle of the steam engine had been discovered much earlier by a French Huguenot, Denis Papin, who had fled to England, where he invented a pressure cooker, and then to Hessen. By the beginning of the nineteenth century inventors all over the western world, including America, were trying out steam-driven vehicles on waters and roads. Not much later, a Frenchman invented the de Rivas steam automobile.

Water power would be generated wherever rivers and streams rushed off, along the whole length of the Appalachian Mountains. Still the textile industry had grown in New England and stayed for another century before moving South, and much of it stayed on anyhow. Inertial factors work unceasingly against unforced change in industrial processes as in every aspect of life. New England was lucky, too, in that female labor was perfectly suitable to factory work in textile mills, poor, quick, docile, and often abandoned by their boy friends headed West. With cheap factory goods becoming generally available, girls were not worth their keep in a household economy.

Children were welcome in the factories, too.

Somehow, the factory owners managed to get twelve hours
of work a day six days a week from these young things,
and a certain group of high-minded capitalists and
intellectuals, transcendentalists and Unitarians among them
(usually connected with Harvard University)
created a "Lowell System" at Lowell, Massachusetts,
an experiment that they were so pleased with
as to boast about it, and they were touted
all over the Country as philanthropists.
Mostly it consisted of giving the workers a dormitory bed
to keep them out of trouble, providing uplifting lectures
to the drowsy girls, and seeing that they got to bed and
arose from bed at the right times.

Unfortunately for all of America at the time and
ever since, the farm was taken as a model for the shop,
the Puritan father as the model for the owner.
If a person worked on the farm every daylight hour,
so should he or she work in the factory. If there should be no recourse
from the will and word of the father, so should it be with the boss.
These were happy days, in between firings and layoffs,
earning less than a dollar a day,
breathing the fumes of engines and lint of rags, for
children of the promised land of early modernity.
Lowell within a decade, with many well-wishers,
became an appalling city of many mills.

Lowell's premier creative genius, painter James Whistler,
caught something there (1834-55),
but went abroad to Europe to live, work and die.
The story was to be repeated everywhere a city grew up in
America. All who hoped that its promising experiment would be
copied elsewhere got their wish.

What caused this outburst of industrial energies,
these far-reaching innovations, this new civilization?
The reasons in America are probably much the same
as they were in Europe. One had to be prepared

religiously for hard work, for daily suffering,
and treat them as good, at least for others.
Religious ministers had to believe so for their parishioners.

The traditional settled society had to be shot full of holes.
So it was even in old New England,
where irreligion had taken over, preserving
only the convenient social doctrine, and the population was moving
out and around, save for the tenacious rich nucleus.
Turnover of the Boston population averaged
40% annually in the 1850's.
The rich had money earned from shipping, with all that implies of
smuggling, the slave trade, and immigrant transport,
and their derivative, banking.

The natives had mechanical skills and could tend and repair machines.
They learned quickly to make new ones.
It is the machine-making-machine that separates the
burgeoning from the passive machine culture.
There was no aristocracy built upon ancient history, which
could pour contempt upon the busy-ness of the capitalist industrial
class. There were the large natural resources of the
country, a good part controlled by New Englanders,
even if the region itself contained little mineral wealth,
and its land and forests were disappearing.
Behind the bent back of every machine-tender was
the specter of an Irish or German replacement.
It would not be long before the good people of Lowell and Boston
would stand by in amazement to watch the Lowell girls go on strike.

Skilled crafts organized into unions now in every town and city in
the country, seizing monopoly powers over jobs, as in medieval times.
This was against the American creed of laissez-faire, but crafts
unions managed to continue in this manner until the government,
not the capitalists, fractured the monopolies
in favor of the disemployed.

Crafts unions continued to enjoy the highest wages and best work
conditions , and fought off attempts of outsiders, regardless of skills,
who were attempting to take up the trade. Catholics could not gain

admission to unions dominated by Freemasons and natives. Italians
could barely eke out memberships here and there until they forced
their way in through violence and politics -
and, of course, skill was something of a factor.

Jews could hardly ever obtain a union card,
were told off flatly, and so sent their wives and daughters
into the sweat shops while they peddled
whatever could be bought and resold,
then set up their own enterprises,
until finally as builders and employers,
they were sitting opposite the union agents in determining
who would work for whom at what wages and
under what circumstances.

Now what was happening in Cincinnati?
There, in 1811, 38 different trades
were represented in the shops. In 1819, a year
when most businesses began to fail owing to
a bank panic and steep recession throughout America,
55 trades were practiced. By 1826
there were 76 different trades.
Factories were still few. The masters met to control
prices, review practices and exert controls over apprentices.
It was a high-wage city, the skilled worker earning
three to five times the national average daily wage.
The word did not take long to get around,
immigrants and Southerners would enter, and there would
soon be a nativist, anti-Catholic, and unionizing feeling erupting.

The one-dollar-a day wage for a mature semi-skilled worker was
standard in America for a hundred years, the 1800's. Real wages
declined in the 1830's. The bottom 50% of the population of the city
held 8.1% of the wealth in 1838, even less than the 9.8% it held in
1817. This was the Golden West of the times.
It was soon the turn of St. Louis and Chicago.

The population of Chicago jumped from practically zero

in 1803 to 100,000 thirty years later.
Its early garrison and people were mostly killed by their escort
of Indians and hostile Indians while trekking to Detroit
to escape precisely this fate when the War of 1812 was announced;
perhaps the Indians felt insulted by their desertion.
But soon their ilk were back and the Indians gone West,
so that Chicagoans could begin a way of life that was a source
of uncomplimentary astonishment to visitors
from abroad thereafter.

Most people then as now labored to keep body and soul together.
A letter from a German immigrant, once well-to-do in
Hamburg, now working in Cincinnati,
tells of having to send his young son to work in order
to save something to build a shelter for his family and old age.
(The old were usually destitute all around America
in the lower 1800's, the happy days of Tom Sawyer,
one of the best-selling books in the old Soviet Union,
itself another collective victim of American myth,
just as Americans and West Europeans became suckers for
"Gone with the Wind" mythology.)

If material inequality was great before the Revolution, where we speak of 1% of the people owning 30% to 60% of all assets, and most people owning practically nothing, the situation only worsened during the Jeffersonian and Jacksonian periods of direct democracy, whether rural or urban sectors are considered. By 1828, 78% of New York City assets were owned by a few merchants, bankers, brokers, auctioneers, manufacturers and attorneys - and idlers.

The rate of intermarriage among the rich was high,
more in Boston than in New York, probably more than ever after.
Moreover, in New York City, Brooklyn, Philadelphia and Boston,
some 81% to 95% of the richest people
were children of rich or eminent people;
only 2% to 3% came from humble circumstances.
Between 1828 and 1850,
an age of social fluidity in the minds of most students,
almost no rich person became significantly poorer,
perhaps only one in fifty of them.

Officials of the reformist Empress Catherine the Great of Russia
responded to her well-intentioned desire to see how her people were
doing in the empire by building a set of facade villages along the royal
road to deceive her. American mythology has operated in the same
way, or, to use a doubly delusory analogy, like the rows of giant
billboards that ran along the sides of American highways in the first
part of the twentieth century.
Americans became thoroughly hoaxed about country and city.
Rural slums surrounding and infiltrating most countryside were ignored.
The rural slum was a life-style, even as the frontier, amusing, to be admired.
The city slum was a threat to the adjacent superior class.

. The rich had their grounds for complaint, but all too often
they were directly involved in the problems on a day-to-day basis,
neglecting the government in its most important respects,
caring not at all about the welfare of the people.
It did not take the good citizens of Boston long
before adjudging the Irish immigrants, possibly the most pitiable
group that ever came "voluntarily" to America,
the Haitian boat people notwithstanding,
as criminally insane, helpless drunk automatons of the Pope.

All that history really shows is that the Irish picked themselves up
off the floor when they arrived in America,
behaved as they thought free citizens of a republic should behave,
tried to get work, any job,
go to church, marry, have children, and
acquire the vicious prejudices of their predecessors as soon as possible.

I speak not alone of men, but also of priests and women.
The Irish immigration had this astounding feature. It was
composed as much and more of women than of men. Tens of
thousands of women came over and worked at the most menial tasks
and scraped together enough to send for a man of the family to come
along or a sister and maybe later a dependent parent.

There had nothing like this in all the history of the world: an immigration of single independent women, with here and there a man, and then, too, the priest who made it all possible, because the priest stood as their moral authority, and he was pledged to watch over them and ward off evil, to help them, though he be half-literate himself, to assert a right, and post a letter to Erin, and to ward off the advances of the boy of the house where they worked as domestics.

The priest took his pennies from them, for we speak of women who earned a dollar a week and their keep, and with these and what he could get from the men and the Germans down the road and secret friends and politicians, the priest somehow managed to put together a construction deal for a church. Soon the church went up, and the Protestants and Freemasons ground their teeth,
just as the priest knew they would.

The Irish immigrants were luckier than others in one respect;
at the cost of total national humiliation,
they had been forced to learn English and in part
abandon their Celtic tongue, as had the Welsh and lowland Scots.
But now in the New World, this gave them an entry,
though their accent was scorned, and Irish jokes
were the quintessential ethnic jokes.
They had an advantage over the Germans and others from abroad.
They could move rapidly into jobs and politics.

New England science and secularism had gained over Puritanism, and now regarded most religions, including Catholicism, as superstitious belief systems congenial to domestic help. The transcendentalists and Unitarians were filing into a softer establishment in New England. Meanwhile the distaff side of New England and mid-Atlantic households were losing their female servants to the Lowell plan or with a "Westward, Ho!"
So, breasting gusts of crankiness and abuse,
the Irish servant-girl made her way.

The English fared better, and found America less traumatic.
They had less interest in politics, with less to gain personally, but they were favorably impressed by the ease of the suffrage after

witnessing the battle of half a century to accomplish a moderate suffrage reform in England in 1832. Fewer now were from the most downtrodden classes. They were readier to take advantage of some of the better living conditions to be expected in America. They were familiar with the disgusting conditions of life in the cities of the Industrial Revolution.

The German immigration of the period before the Civil War was perhaps the most balanced in American history. It contained a surprisingly large number of professional, highly skilled, economically competent, and artistic individuals (composer Richard Wagner, a genius of the century, wanted to immigrate to Chicago when he was in political trouble and financially broke around 1850). Nevertheless, the best is none too good: accounts of the arrival of immigrant ships in Philadelphia are disgusting. One report tells us that redemptioners were many and those who had not paid their fare beforehand had to be sold on the dock to wealthy farmers; batches of a score of children were sold, and separated from their parents for years.

Because they were so well established in several sites of the country East and West, and set themselves up even in a new area near San Antonio in Texas, and because they were coming in increasing numbers, and because they felt qualified to constitute a society unto themselves, a movement developed to organize a given territory of German culture and apply for admission as a state or autonomous nation. Northern Missouri with St. Louis as Capital was suggested by some of the ethnarchs.

However, Germans were of different nations; Germany would not be united until 1870. Moreover there were both religious and cultural differences among them. Too, so many Germans were becoming assimilated so rapidly and successfully to American society in such separated parts of the country, that the movement halted. German ethnicity found some independent expression in a large Turnverein movement, associations for the expression and development of Germany culture in America that prospered for over a century before gradually petering out, partly because of the cosmopolitanizing of American society in general, where facets of German culture were admired.

❖❖❖

The lot of the Catholic Irish now was in several ways worse than the first immigrants to America in Virginia and New England. It was probably the worst of any group in American history, the African-American aside. Although they were not degraded persons, criminals, or dissenters, they were on the verge of starvation, after being thoroughly subjected and culturally deprived by a foreign power - England. Their death rate in passage was extremely high. The landscape and inhabitants upon arrival were more hostile than in the time of the Indians.

The first settlers made enemies of the Indians; the Irish were received by the descendants of their Puritan enemies, most notably in New England. These were Americans, true, but generally firmly anti-Catholic, and related to those who had invaded Ireland and had imposed a totally new population upon the Northern part of the country, while distributing to Protestant Englishmen the choicest estates of the rest of Ireland. The Irish had been treated worse than the British colonists of pre-Revolutionary America. Rarely had the American had to observe the obsequies to the English official that the Irish were forced to perform.

The Irish girls, the Irish priests and the Irish laborers who came over were poignantly aware of all of this. That they did not know all about how to handle their problems in the New World is to say that they were like all the other immigrants from the beginning. Human beings destined to repeat all the faults of their own plus those of their enemies in a new combination, the Irish did not come to America to aid and convert the Americans whom they found on arrival. They came, like the rest, perceiving the best chance of survival in a cruel world.

A passage from the report of Edward Jarvis, a path-breaking statistician and social pathologist, both unknown professions then, marks the relationship between insanity, poverty and ethnicity. He inquired of the physicians and hospital and prison personnel of Massachusetts and elsewhere about cases of insanity known to them (control over the term "insanity" rested merely upon institutionalizing of the insane if poor, or confinement at home for mental reasons.) Some 1400 cases were reported from 800 returns; his was the best study of the nineteenth century concerning mental disturbances in America.

He found more insanity among the poor, that he ascribed to their life conditions in part, but also to their genetic constitutions - weak, ill health, etc. Then he could show a significant, but basically questionable difference in the rates of the Irish and the natives, 1 case per 368 persons as against 1 per 445.

More important is his framing of the concept of immigrant shock. He considered that the habit and conditions of the Irish poor in this country operated more unfavorably upon their mental health, and produced a larger number of the insane in relation to their numbers than was to be found among the native poor. Being in a strange land and among strange men and things, meeting with customs and surrounded by circumstances widely different from all their previous experience, ignorant of the precise state of affairs here, and lacking education and flexibility by which they could adapt themselves to their new and unwonted position, they necessarily formed many impracticable schemes, and endeavored to accomplish them by unsuitable means. Of course, disappointment usually succeeded their efforts. Their lives were filled with doubts; harrowing anxiety troubled them, and they were cursed with frequent mental, and probably physical, suffering.

He further ascribes to the Irish a *"greater irritability; they are more readily disturbed when they find themselves at variance with the circumstances about them"*. Their insanity also comes, he says, *"from intemperance, to which the Irish seem to be peculiarly prone, and much to that exaltation which comes from increased prosperity"*. Jarvis, partly because he was pressured to distort his findings and explanations to arbitrate against the immigrants and poor, let himself advance uncalled-for remarks.

Using a report about Blacks and Whites, based upon the 1840 census, and prepared by the Federal government, comparing insanity rates among free Blacks, slaves, and Whites, Jarvis found that the figures made out free Blacks to have six times the insanity of the Whites and eleven times that of slaves. He thereupon investigated further, and found the census-takers scandalously erroneous. But the data were seized upon by Senator John Calhoun of South Carolina for his pro-slavery propaganda. Jarvis protested, to little avail.

In a population so mobile and flustered as the American, rates of mental disorder (depending upon where you draw the line) reach to over 50%, until the question inserts itself as to whether the normal are simply stunned. More of this in the next chapter, for here we should take the opportunity to look into the high rate of crowd violence in this period.

Peddlers of the bucolic life often point to violent urban disorders as one more proof of rural superiority, notwithstanding the fact that many of the worst civil disorders in history (including ours) have originated in the countryside, and the best place for a rural agitator or crook to pursue his career is by going to a town or city.

You have to gather a crowd in order to riot, and it is not so easy to do so in the country. Crimes of family violence, child abuse, incest, alcoholism, and evasion of laws - to mention a few categories - were invariably more rural than urban. There is nothing persuasive to show that violence itself, personal infliction of forceful injury or threat of same, is less common in the country than in the city, relative to population and frequency of human interaction. Aside from innumerable unregistered killings, maiming, and bullies, in isolated circumstances, the same occurred, were even provided for, in every rural district by a tavern and roadhouse where gathered the toughs to talk, drink, argue, plot against the public order, and fight.

The panorama of violence in the growing towns and cities was lurid and bloody, but it had been part of the picture of colonial life. The nuclear elements of the infamous gangs, the North End Mob and the South End Mob, and others less historically durable, formed in the latter part of the 1600's, graduated to full stature in the 1700's, and proceeded unchecked in the 1800's. The Liberty Boys were of higher status, bringing together unskilled dock workers, skilled artisans, shopkeepers and other activists in repeated riots against the British and colonial authorities in Charleston, New York, Philadelphia, and Newport as well as Boston. Their agitators and leaders became heroes in later schoolbooks, names like Samuel Adams and John Hancock of Boston and Thomson of Philadelphia.

The period between 1820 and 1860 saw the heaviest and most frequent urban violence that America has ever seen. Baltimore had twelve serious riots, New York eight, Boston and Cincinnati four. In one riot in Louisville, involving nativist Protestants and German-Americans, 20 were killed, hundreds wounded. Between 1834 and 1844, more than 200 sizeable gang wars occurred in New York City. (The roaring Chicago of the 1920's was a mewing kitten by contrast.)These included labor riots, election riots, anti-African riots, anti-abolitionist riots, anti-Catholic and anti-foreigners riots, some of these propelled by more than one motive and all of them driven by a fundamentally insecure social order and a distraught threatened population.

The tension was always sensed; the immigrants were fairly well aware of the situation that they were moving into. One boat from Germany in 1852 unloaded its immigrants in Boston, who were then marched through the town to the railroad train station that was to carry them to the Midwest, preceded by a banner proclaiming, "Hail Columbia, Land of the Free. We Will be No Burden to Massachusetts".

In the fifties, 90% of all immigrants from continental Europe originated in the Germanies. Farmers suffered from economic depression, the technological revolution was reducing industrial jobs, and political repression was general. They came especially from the South where agents were most active. Official propaganda in Prussia and Saxony denounced emigration, stressing the economic problems and rank nativism to be encountered in America.

Once arrived, German radicals became active. They led parades against the Kansas-Nebraska Act for its permitting an extension of slavery; Stephen A. Douglas, its proponent, was burned in effigy (his special legislation to build the Illinois Central railroad to run from Chicago to Mobile gave them work, however, for German construction crews often labored on the roadbed). They agitated, as did the Irish, against anti-liquor and anti-saloon legislation.

In 1856, half the German language press in the United States was controlled by free-thinkers, rationalists, atheists, and refugee rebels of the 1848 uprisings in Germany. Almost all of this literature was lost to the American tradition. Condemned, untranslated, it disappeared with its creators, who were easily the largest group of non-institutional intelligentsia in America. By this time most of the Germans came to America as free men, without passage money to pay back and with a few dollars in their pockets. In the forties and fifties clashes between Germans and Irish were common, with the Irish as the aggressors in most cases. Competition for jobs was almost always the precipitating cause.

Even the aesthetic could arouse collective violence. In 1849 on Astor Place in New York, rivalry between the fans of the English actor Macready and the America actor Forrest transformed itself into an anti-aristocratic and anti-English riot that left 22 persons dead. The riotous pattern persisted, its description to be continued in later pages, as a feature of the wretchedness of American life for most of it inhabitants. In New York at this time, the average wage hovered at less than a dollar a day, should work be available. Of its population of 500,000 in 1840, 200,000 were declared to live in utter and hopeless distress.

A silly nun of the Ursuline convent in Charlestown, Massachusetts ran away and asked for protection, then reconsidered and returned. Rumor soon had it that she was forced back. A posted notice exclaimed: "*To Arms!! To Arms!! Ye brave and free. The avenging sword unshield!! Leave not one stone upon another of that curst Nunnery that prostitutes female virtue and liberty under the garb of holy Religion. When Bonaparte opened the Nunneries in Europe he found scores of infant skulls!!!!!*"

The mob gathered and attacked. The several nuns (the returned one by now in delirious frenzy), sixty children, and several sick and infirm, managed to escape between assault waves. The convent, an adjoining library, a bishop's lodge, and farm house and barn were all ransacked, looted and put to the torch.

Prominent citizens stood about. No one interceded by word or deed. To some Congregationalists the riot would punish not only Catholics but Unitarian parents who had entered their children in the school. The year was 1832. Evangelistic pietism working in tandem with a strenuous new nationalism captured the native working class and made of the advancing 1800's an untidy unruly introduction to modern urbanism.

From the end of the Revolutionary War to the panic of 1819, about 250,000 European immigrants landed in America. The rate doubled in each of the next two decades. The 1840's brought in 1.7 millions and the 1850's 2.6 millions. Never again would immigrants constitute so large a part of the total population. By 1860 immigrants in the population included 1.6 million Irish (almost entirely Catholic), 1.2 million Germanophones from the various Germanic nations, and 588,000 Britishers (largely English).

Not only the poorer immigrants but their upper ranks as well - professionals, engineers, *et al.* - could count on being insulted by persons of every level of society, or at least upon being patronized: *"Coming to America was the smartest thing you ever did"*, and having their speech mocked or every little distinction from the most local habits jeered, told *"You start at the bottom like everybody else"*, and asked incredulously *"What kind of a name is that?"*

It is a wonder that the American States, in the name of anti-popery, republicanism, democracy, and the right to a job, did not use the now thoroughly established direct democratic political rights to legislate a halt to immigration, especially the Catholic.
A large number of signs around the country declared,
we want no foreigners here, keep moving!
That was one way to preserve local workers
from foreign competition.

But the States felt that they would be interfering with foreign commerce, a federal prerogative, if they acted. The federal government wanted the West settled and the Democratic-Republican

Party was getting many needed voters from the new immigrants. The heavy Irish vote for Andrew Jackson in the election of 1828 turned the tide in New York and defeated John Quincy Adams there and, in consequence, for the Presidency.

Besides many local politicians were already becoming dependent upon the Irish vote, or felt that they must appease the newcomers. When the vote was restricted, it had been of no help to immigrants, who were practically all poor and therefore unqualified. Now however, every man had a vote once he had spent five years in the country so as to become a citizen (unless he was one of the great many illegal voters passed through the polling place by election managers.)

On the female side,
the native daughters of New England and elsewhere
had snubbed themselves out of the kitchens and bedrooms
of the well-to-do employers,
in an instant caste action against the
oncoming Irish domestics.
The householders wanted badly the young
Irish woman who would work
sixteen hours a day for her bed, board
and a dollar a week.
The industrial employers felt the same way;
they were interested in an oversupply of labor at all times.
Irish women next
moved into the factories in large numbers.

Considerable agitation for political action occurred from the 1920's onwards, led by Protestant groups.
An American Party did organize
and with a convention of 13 states
put up local and state candidates in
1954 and a Presidential candidate in 1856.
They were called "Know-Nothings"
because they pretended to secrecy about their doings.
They urged the exclusion of Catholics
and foreign-born from public office

and the extension of citizenship residence from five to twenty-one years. They made little progress nationally, but their considerable membership moved over into the Republican Party of Abraham Lincoln.

American workers were not so stupid as to deny in principle the advantages accruing to a well-organized and politicized union work force. The "Labor Party" formed by Philadelphia artisans in 1828 was the world's first. As many as fifty newspapers espousing the cause of labor appeared and, mostly, disappeared. They took strong positions on meaningful issues: public education, imprisonment for debt, freer access to the judicial system, opposition to child labor, female labor, and foreign labor - all of these last three groups deemed competitive to native male White workers.

Too, they urged that the courts and legislatures cease their attempts to treat all labor organizations as conspiracies to deprive employers of their property. They were also against monopolies and to the banking control of the economy; both, they felt, held down wages and restricted economic growth.

The new worker movements won many elections for local offices, sending off some of the old elite and even the new businessmen in politics. But soon the business interests were back and after them came the age of the professional politician, who effectively barred the further visible presence of labor in urban politics; but this happened in the late century.

The cross-pressures against labor organizations were too strong. The motive of solidarity of the workers of a given skill in a given factory or city - say carpenters - could not go far and expand widely because of the countervailing forces of religious ethnic and racial differences among workers, the desire of so many workers to move to another area, the continuous oncoming immigration, the hostility of courts who ruled early against even the right to strike in some cases, and the erratic job markets accompanying business cycles.
For the same reasons, class consciousness was an impossible development, despite the extreme maldistribution of wealth.

Nor should one neglect the strength of the egalitarian ideology that would discourage people, whatever their actual share of the wealth and respect of the nation, from claiming publicly the existence of a class society. There were heroes and heroines, a considerable number of them in New England, some in New York City, not so many elsewhere. Horace Mann turned from a directly political career, significantly, to become an unelected civic reformer:

"The mobs, the riots, the burnings, the lynchings, perpetrated by men of the present day are perpetrated because of their vicious or defective education when children".

So he said as he began his work in public education.

Western Fronteer life in the 1880s: a crew of surveyors receiving friends in S. Dakota..

Chapter Twenty-eight

Character and Speech

We are midway in the so-called *ante-bellum* period, the decades before the Civil War, "Huckleberry Finn Time". We talk about American character earlier and later, but, following the stretching of the country, and in the period of direct democracy, the people require another sketch. Urbanism now plays this character against the backdrop of cities. A large Catholic population has entered the mix; by 1860, it will be the largest religious denomination. Still, another century would pass before the voters brought in a Catholic President.

Character is the unique way in which a person deals with the outer world. Speech is part of character. Therefore, all who use the same language must have much in common as characters. Even so, many aspects of character can be or must be approached by different routes - by observation of behavior, by testimony - introspection and what intimates and strangers say.

We aim to find typicalities, enduring general behavioral and attitudinal patterns, which, when noted, and especially if noted along with certain other patterns, would justify declaring that the person is behaving like a typical American. A trait may be mental, intellectual, a conduct, preference, taste, mood, or set of manners; it may relate to other traits or to all of these. Note that one trait may be typical, but another, opposite to it, just as typical. It is typical of an American to be laughing all too often; typical, also, to be a perpetual grouch. When a particular group or section is exceptional, we shall allude to it. Also typicality does not mean everyone, nor necessarily a majority, but always means "commonly found in the population".

American traits, around 1833, might be listed in several ways, not alone to the number of sixty-four, as here I have done. If it were possible, we should retroject the traits in 33-year intervals back to 1472, and project them to the year 2000, 16 socio-generations in all, or 530 years.

In "Huckleberry Finn time":

Americans were exhibiting strong individualism, a sense of living for themselves, a jealous regard for their personal interests, a seeking for personal gratification.

They were highly mobile, moving it would appear by some inner urge at the slightest pretext. Historian George Bancroft said that *"America is composed of separate, free, and constantly moving atoms, ever in reciprocal action".*

They appeared very often to be dissatisfied with the way things were going around them, and seemed to be suffering or tolerating other people rather than enjoying them.

They were attracted by group expressions of a chiliastic nature, especially in the religious sphere, but often in social, fraternal, political and ethnic gatherings. Frequently they acted in ways contrary to their normal behavior, exhorting themselves, one another and the Lord or some other object.

They often engaged in self-justification, as if how they were behaving ought not and could not go unchallenged.

Americans were very often hypocritical, as for instance saying they were religious but acting quite materialistically; or denying any interest in sex but secretly pursuing sexual fantasies and adventures; or claiming to be peace-loving, but working toward conflict and violence. The truly hypocritical person is sincere, unconscious of his-her two-faced character.

Americans formed volunteer groupings readily to do a great many things. They were a nation of joiners. They associated together with slight pretext, and in every sphere of life, from religion to knitting circle and *kaffeeklatsch*. Much praise has been given people for acting so, especially in regard to the rural way of life.

The ruralites were frightfully interdependent, as much as they sought to be otherwise. As soon as they could obtain cash and purchase what they wanted, they dismissed this excessive mutual dependence, except for stark emergencies, posses, natural disasters, visiting, holidays, social cake-bakes and Church on Sunday.

Alexis de Tocqueville in the justly famous record of his travels in America in the year 1831 admires what he believed to be universal associationism and cooperation, but he may not have noticed that the same minority of inhabitants were doing all the associating and the rest were out on their own as much as possible; besides he came from a country of villages, France, where administrative and infrastructural services had been set up for a long time. He was properly amazed.)

Tocqueville also pointed to an urge to uniformity among Americans. This started with the first break-outs of the impressed and young, and came with the desire for equality, but as a demand, we must stress, uniformity reacts against individualism and freedom, such that "free and equal" are often a contradiction in terms.

We also remark that the demand for uniformity produces rapid assimilation and denies equality to persons who are different: so the dog turns to bite its tail.

❖

Americans were verbally committed to equality in all affairs, the most vocal among these being often the very persons who were behaving contrariwise, putting down people, showing racial and religious biases, and espousing rugged individualism. The word "fairness" was always in the air. Equality of manners was often demanded so as to protect one's own manners, that were felt to be gauche.

Americans sought for and were producing a homogeneous culture. They expected and hoped that everyone would talk the same, behave the same and share the tastes of all others sooner or later, the sooner the better.

They believed that "the people" were always right and only wished they might know what people were thinking so that they could agree with them.

Racism and to a lesser extent xenophobia were widespread in thought and action. Maltreatment of immigrants began with the second boat to arrive.

They were obviously interested in all kinds of

schemes for self-improvement and improvised many for themselves.

They exhibited a ready sociability and congeniality that would carry them through encounters with strangers and strange places, and would be maintained, even when false, to carry one through a potentially difficult situation.

Materialism was strong, even alongside the willingness to believe in magic and anomalies and religious miracles of mind.

It was a careless materialism, not minding the loss of objects procured. America was always littered with discarded, lost, useless, wasted, or surplus material. Yet people sought to acquire material things endlessly.

Americans were quick to improvise solutions to material problems, in fixing broken things or in building a dam over a stream. They did not wait for the proper agency to come along. They invented and adopted cures of all kinds.

Typical was a cultural barbarism and a pride in it, a rejection of intellectuality, or, at best, a lack of interest in intellectual matters. (One pauses to contemplate the enormous harm that Tom Sawyer's detestation of school did to millions of children compelled by the schools themselves, suicidally, to read the book of his adventures.)

The resort to violence was more common and accepted in America than in any other country of the world at that time. It had been for two hundred years. It would be for the next century and a half, too.

The American typically was un-historical and amnesiac about his own ancestors. An African-American knows that he is originally from Africa, but rarely from which of the highly distinctive major cultures from Sierra Leone down to Angola, and far into the interior; but of course, one was practically forced to forget. Indians usually have to call upon expert informants to recall a few of their traditions and vocabulary. Here again, destroy a nation, destroy its history. German-Americans have half of them forgotten which of a hundred German nations their ancestors came from.

Genealogy was cultivated by a few pretentious ladies of means in order to impose a class system upon a distracted and uncaring people. Tradition was easy to sacrifice. Traditions were continually improvised; *"Let's make this a tradition"*.

Americans were short-sighted in their outlook and habits, going broke often, not planning ahead or for their future or their children, unsaving, building and manufacturing with an eye to replaceability or abandonment. Bankruptcies were frequent and regarded lightly.

They were wasteful of resources of nature, society, and personal property. They could be easily aroused over questions of property rights but would lose interest in the property, when it was no longer a bone of contention. They were unused to owning much, and therefore would not take care of it properly; but, when showered with things, they held them in little esteem.(This was more typical of Anglos, Celtics, Indians, and Blacks than of Germanics.)

Faced with pressing needs of the moment and religious beliefs that the Millennium was near at hand, they were hasty and careless about their resources, excusing themselves on the belief that it did not matter, given Millennial expectations. This lessened with the Catholic influx.

They liked scientific ideas and the march of science and were inventive. The Yankees were especially so, and the trait lost its productivity as it went West, remaining strong in the Northeast and near Midwest.

The people were observably restless and kept busy at one thing or another, often overly busy, and watched the passage of time nervously, but not so much in the West and much less in the South.

They denounced social classes and didn't believe these

amounted to much in determining a person's life. They believed in equality of opportunity. There was in fact and for various reasons only a weak class system, witness:

*

Federalism separated the state peoples from one another.

*

The rate of disintegration of families was high.

*

There was rapid technological, occupational change.

*

A strong ideology of equality and equal opportunity and advancement by merit existed.

*

Basic cultural-religious differences existed among potential members of the same class, e.g. Quakers, planters, Jews, manufacturers, Catholics, Freemasons, Baptists.

*

Sect and commune had stronger appeals.

*

African-Americans and Indian-Americans were already distinct from the general population along caste lines.

*

The colonial class system was broken up by the civil strife of the Revolution.

*

There were few "class" schools, Harvard and William and Mary being two of them, along with several grammar schools.

*

Self-help, volunteerism, self-education, and pragmatism undermined social classes.

*

Alcoholism affected the lives of a great many Americans from beginning to end.

*

Aggressiveness was also a very common trait, found in the far reaches of wealth as much as among the poorest. It contained elements of egalitarianism, getting one's share, and also was the syndrome of the "go-getter" and the tough competitor in games, business and politics.

*

Generosity was common, even typical, both in the giving of material things and in the acknowledgment of the worth of others as individuals.

*

Ambition was widely applauded and expected and practiced.

*

Acquisitiveness was ordinary conduct and was applauded.

*

Practicality and pragmatism were widespread working principles. What was effective was right and good. They wanted "know-how", and books and lessons on how to do everything, from the taming of bees to human relations management (not yet called that).

*

Social irresponsibility was the rule of conduct and even of thought among very many. "It's none of my business" was acceptable as excuse, and hardly any verbal or practical sanction attached to the evasion of civic or social responsibility.

*

Prudery was general. Even the roughest manners as well as the most polished manners kept sexual references and physiological functions to a minimum in conversation. Few would speak of common practices such as resorting to houses of prostitution.

*

Laughter and good humor came readily to Americans, more and more so in the so-called democratic period than before.

*

The concealment of identity was common, concealment of one's antecedents, concealment of one's family life in the past and of one's relatives.

*

The typical American would be regarded as vulgar in speech and manners and simplistic in ideas within his corresponding group in Europe.

*

Americans tended to unlawfulness and disregard of authorities, but not to the extent of uprooting the structure of their governments. They spoke against corruption but usually took part in it if it was not "too bad".

*

They were quick to pass rules and laws on every subject imaginable, while claiming that they were free and while breaking rules continually. Perhaps the contradiction in this behavior is that there are two sides always contending, each making rules for the other and breaking the other's rules, or that half the Americans love rules, the other half to break them, or perhaps there is true ambivalence, with the same persons liking to make and to break rules, like a child who repeatedly builds a tower of blocks in order to knock it down.

*

They were inclined to philanthropy, were big tippers wherever they went, gave to charity and to voluntary groups more often than Europeans at home.

*

They thought America was self-sufficient, a virgin nation, it should not involve itself with other nations.

*

They had a passion for novelty. They were neotropic. The popular literature was sure to publish reports of anything new, whether in science, gadgetry, health, customs, ideas.

*

A belief in progress was general. Every day things got a little better and pretty soon would be a lot better: so people thought and were given to believe from all the media. Faith in the future was general.

*

They were hopeful, were suckers for panaceas, and given over to wishful thinking, even while practical.

*

They were optimistic, believed that there was a cure for everything , which must only be found.

*

They believed in education, and in this period colleges were being founded every month somewhere in the vast domain, usually by New Englanders or their descendants..

*

They believed in the righteousness of the Christian religion though they might not practice it. If back-sliding, they would be rather proud of it.

(A typical humble deviant might be Huckleberry Finn, Mark Twain's creation. A spirited vagabond, taken up into a respectable lady's household, Huck fled because too many mannered demands, including religious observances, were made upon him. The villagers searched for him, tossing bread upon the waters, supposing this act to bring a corpse to the surface. Huck grabbed and ate the floating bread, and reckoned that the prayers of the widow and parson had been answered in that the bread did find him. So their prayers worked; prayers did work for the right kind of folk, he figured... *"There's something in it when a body like the widow or the parson prays, but it won't work for me"*. The unconscious operations of the Puritan ethic are manifest: Prayers work for those already blessed and predestined to be saved; *"To those who have shall be given"*.)

*

They had lost their pre-Revolutionary respect for the aged. They practiced a cult of youth, believing the country was young, the young had it good in America and that they might be young forever (even while the age of death averaged in the early fifties for men and women).

*

Americans generally had a weak sense of family. No comparable large culture of the age gave its members less dogged family attachments and less of an extended family. In the 1800's, for example, the practice of primogeniture broke down completely, and inheritance proceeded with the changeable will of the parents.

*

They had only a meager interest in cuisine, ate enormous amounts of corn and pork.

So, to conclude, given these sixty-four indicators, we had in this period of American history and in conformity with conditions in the beginning and shaping the conditions of the future, an extroverted, novelty-seeking, hopeful, self-concerned, instable character, who was active, aggressive and congenial, and capable of extraordinary voluntary exertions for limited periods of time.

Ideally we should now retroject and project these traits.
They would be charted, each of the 64,
as they occur in each generation back,
say, to the year 1470 and up to the
year 2000, in proportion to their presence in the
population over a period of 19 generations.

In each political-social generation of 33 years,
the profile of each of the 64 traits would change somewhat;
never could it be said, whether at the beginning or in 1833
or in the generations thereafter, that all or no
Americans thought or behaved so. At the least we would
need to introduce several qualifiers, such as the following,
to designate more or less what proportion of the population
exhibited the trait (not even taking the care to say whether the
individual had much or little of the trait):

Prevalent = P = 75-100% of the Americans
Majority = M = 45-75%
Typical = T = 15-45%
Unusual = U = 5-15%
Rare = R = 1-5%

This can hardly be done, even as a quick and
dirty research job. Historiography is not peanuts.
One may be forgiven if it is understood that a well-designed study
along these lines would occupy some twenty professional
expert-years in order to fill in the 64 x 17 cells
that would be required as the study design proceeded,
and, even then, the raw data would probably
be only 25% satisfactory for creating
valid measured judgements out of it.

A less expensive alternative would be to employ the
Delphic Panel: that is, locate an expert on
every trait and every period
(64 traits x 13 generations) and
ask them to draw upon their many years of study to
make a judgement and score each item.
Study-design research and meetings would have to be

conducted to be sure that standardized judgements are being made, and the study could be cut back by 80% then to the equivalent of four expert-years.

Incidentally, if this kind of methodology were applied wherever feasible in historiography, a catching-up to American history would require thousands of man-years. Thus, for instance, a scientific inquiry into the abilities and characters of presidential candidates might take anywhere from 10 to 200 professional years; yet, equally important would be similar studies of at least a random sample (it would have to be large because of the federal system) of the thousands of Congressmen, the tens of thousands of state legislators and all those who contended with them and were their managers and confidantes. Did someone say, "Historiography ain't peanuts."?

Then we would proceed with the history of the economy, the culture of welfare, all the systems of data that stand behind in more or less rough parallelism to the beliefs and conduct, etc.

A budget of several billion dollars and half the twenty-first century would be taken up with such projects - and worthily so. Hopefully this kind of labor would help to obtain good government; that would be worth thousands of billions of dollars. Furthermore, nowadays the future of the world is a matter of American public policy, and even a few corrections of policies, and some good instead of bad decisions, would cover neatly the gamble of several billions for historical research.

Is there a typical character that you could call "the good American"? Possibly there is. One may at this juncture, when the history of the country has been only partially written, move from one item in the list above to the next item, putting together those traits that one would like to see in a person, and then ask oneself whether he has ever encountered that ideal person. It is possible to descend the list, asking whether the trait could be applied to another nationality at various times in history or today, such as the English or the Mexican or the German. Such a procedure might not show who is good or bad, but it would indicate whether the American was (and may still be) different from other nationalities.

This author's comparison of Americans and English of the Period 1810 to 1860 shows a sharing of only 11 typicalities out of the above listed half-hundred traits. These are English alone. If the Isles Celtics were taken together - Welsh, North Borderers (a kind of English), Scots, Scots-Irish, and Irish Catholics, who in all numbered probably a quarter of the American population - and considered in place in the Old Country, they would probably demonstrate twice or more as many typicalities of the American character as the English. This author's comparison of American and French typicalities gave an even division of the shared and disparate.

The results point dramatically to a typical American, or, better, a constellation of American types, clarifying what many have sensed but few have discovered: Americans verged early toward a Celtic Norm, all the more so since it was compatible with the Indian and African components of the nation.

We did not include in the typicalities above the fact that Americans were speaking a modified form of the English language of the most typical kind, that of the greater London area. The American language was developing at a moderately rapid pace from the beginnings of settlement, rebuffed now and then by a King's English revival in presumptuously literary quarters, only to resume its differentiation. Inasmuch as language and character are interactive determinants, our statements about language should support rather than contradict what

has been said about character.
The South was more capable of producing new language and new popular culture to express its character during these times, with the especial contributions of the African-American sector. Dancing and music were scarcely the forte of New England, nor were they especially produced in the pluralist Atlantic culture or the frontier. It was exciting enough that people might occasionally dance, let alone invent music and dances. There was a large territorial grouping where only the beginnings, or more exactly the remnants, of old folk cultures were noticeable, among the Germans, and, soon, other continental groups, supplemented by visits from Europe of performing artists, the principal source of artistic stimulation.

The country was of two minds respecting the development of the American language. There were those who, having recovered from anti-British Revolutionary sentiment, wished to keep the English and American languages tied together as closely as possible. Lawyers (who memorized Blackstone's *Commentaries* on the English common law), medical men, and merchants were particularly intent upon the retention of English.

There also were those who felt that long isolation had already created a somewhat different language and that this ought to be allowed to take its course; the population, having learned to speak and write in many different ways ought to be allowed to keep their ways, and even add to them when naturally educed. Noah Webster, a lexicographer who took upon himself the heavy task of arbiter of the American language (and who did such an impressive job of it that to this day large corporations are suing one another over the right to use his name on their dictionaries), did himself go through a period first of Americanization of the English language ,
and then an Anglicizing of the American language,
leaving matters upon his demise rather as they were before,
but in neater form. He fell in line with the
crusade against abominable spelling, a failing of
some of the nation's high leaders - but, then, too, a failing of
English intellectuals and men of affairs as well,
until a late date, mainly because
the King did not prescribe under penalty the King's English,
and Oxford might not tell Cambridge how to vocalize.

Many effects were amusing. The frontier folk and African did most to invent words and freak out the English syntax and idiom. At this time, the late 1830's, the world's most widely known word came into being, "O.K.". "O.K." has the welcome attributes of conveying a positive attitude in an egalitarian agreeable way, without the slightest demeaning sense of other words for the affirmative. It suggests understanding rather than affirmation alone.
It suggests camaraderie.

And lexicographers have spent the century and half between then and now arguing its origins, the most commonly accepted etymology explaining that Andrew Jackson could not spell, and would mark a document that he approved, "Oll Korrect". This is very likely a Federalist smear. More suggestive is a claim that the Choctaw Indian language contained the word "oke" for "it is". Indeed that syllable is found throughout the world, often with sacred connections. The *langue d'oc* is the language of Southern France that says "oc" for "yes". The term has an almost incantative and liturgical connotation.

Most likely the word derives from the Irish pagan Celtic god, Ok, or Og, whose ancient vigorous celebration, with copious libations, was banned by the Church but persisted anyhow. The public notice given O.K. coincides with the arrival of the Irish in large numbers in New York and Boston, and the graffiti OK (no punctuation, but, precisely then, a fad for acronyms struck the Northeast) is first remarked on the side of whiskey barrels on wagons accompanying Irishmen parading through the streets in election campaigns and fiestas. Everybody was decidedly OK under the circumstances.

And the several meanings conveyed did their part to pull the world together when American empire swelled to its greatest extent in the late twentieth century. It is speakable and hearable in all languages.

At the time many new English words, especially scientific, slang and vernacular, were flowing across the Atlantic to America, but beginning also then a reverse flow commenced that was to acquire tsunami proportions in the mid-1900's. Words from remote areas of England in some cases were hand-carried to America without merging first into proper English. There were words from the Scots, the Irish, the French, several Indian nations, the German, the Spanish, and the African languages, while pretentious orators and ministers larded their speeches with mellifluous and resounding syntactically complicated words of Latin and Greek roots to give American speech its discombobulated and heterogeneous character. (Italian, except for musical terms, and Yiddish words and constructions, came in later.) Midwestern Americans who used often the word "lousy" for all kinds of dislikables, had picked it up from the German "laus", (louse), which was also a mutant of most varied applications.

Boasting and bragging became a form of literature in America, reaching a peak now then. The Davy Crockett cycle was famous, his stories, his deeds, his humor, his self-depreciation in the very excess of self-praise; there were more of these. And Americans were reputed everywhere in the world to be boasters.

Where did this come from? It might have developed from people, without control by authorities, who needed to boast because they felt intensely insecure about their origins and circumstances of life.

It could come from the lonely mammal male yammering his superiority to the winds hoping for a female listener somewhere. And also rejecting women, who are not there to be rejected. (For the insistence of little American boys upon their dislike of girls and independence from women is unlike the messages conveyed by little boys elsewhere. The English upper class boy was trained to avoid intimacies, but this is not the same feeling.)

Boasting was a frontier speciality to begin with, and we are therefore bound to imagine the origins of boasting in the Indian practice of braves dancing about and shouting of their prowess and deeds. This is noted early so that the frontier-prone Scots-Irish cannot be pinned for it, but the practice needs a conveyor to the larger culture and they served well to that end.

American character became ever more typically playful,

with large exceptions.
Abroad, therefore they were often regarded as juvenile.
Peer emulation, too: "Entering upon the spirit of the occasion".
"Is this a personal fight, or can anyone get in on it?" .
The universal success of American popular culture begins with children,
and extends to those adults to be found in foreign countries who,
in their own culture are often jestingly called "the American".
Much to the chagrin of the "serious" "fundamentalist" and such types.

Whence originated the American sense of humor?
Probably more often than not the most typical humor arose from the
pluralist borderlands running between North and South..
Here there were few authorities to admonish them to
act less childishly and be more grave, to boast less.
Loose Anglicans, secularists, aristocrats, cavaliers.
English were disposed often to be role-players, poseurs, and frauds,
possibly emanating from noble pretensions and commerce.
Also Jews from central Europe (sometimes via Britain)
–jesters, clowns, magicians, carnivals, wits, irony, mockers
(note nickname or slur-name, Mockies).
Then, importantly, oppressed blacks, needing to sublimate their tragedy,
but with a direct African inheritance of smiling and laughing,
then as outsiders looking in upon the foolishness of white society.

Hispanics were resentful and macho, hence too earnest.
So, too, American Indians.
The Irish "Mackerels" (cheap fish on Friday Catholics)
or Micks – from "Mc") importing often a sneering and
ridiculing habit reflecting low self-esteem,
too often butts of humor themselves,
in the old world, fed bitter jesting. Italian and Hungarian,
with ineffaceable humor, had no trouble becoming typical.
French, mostly dedicated Protestants and Canadien Catholic
to begin with: but southern Louisiana loosened up the type.
Germans, Swiss, Scandinavians, Scots,
Puritans, Chinese, Japanese, Vietnamese
did not catch on readily. Non-Jewish, ex-communist
post-WWII East Europeans tended often toward
the melancholic, hence dark humor.

The American character also seduced its own type from abroad,
selected them - "Like attracts like".
Once here for a while, most people Americanized.
After magicians, vaudeville and minstrels, comic
cartoons and situation comedies on TV became highly
popular among all but most intellectuals and grouches.

Americans usually felt dissatisfied with an exchange of last names,
and had to be recalled to the functions of last names for
respect, authorities, and registration, while first names
became sectionally segregated, so that you could use his or her
given name as one indicator of whether a person was a
White or Black Southerner, a Pluralist, a New England
or a frontier type.

The period was one for continuing the modification of names
sometimes to conform to peculiar American general
pronunciation or spelling practice. The absence of records
and illiteracy helped variegate names.

The process began early, in the "Old Country".
The name "Shakespeare" was spelled 83 ways
in his own times. "Mainwaring" had to accommodate
131 varieties. Writing and spelling were
poor, records unkept. Diversification
sped up in America. In the 1790 First
U.S. Census "Kennedy" and "McLaughlin" counted
each 32 spellings, Campbell 27.
"Mac's" were lopped off Scottish and Irish names.
Most long Welsh names went on acquiring English surrogates.
German Schmidts often became Smiths as well,
Müllers Millers, etc. König could be read
Koenig, Konig, Kenig, Kayng, or King.
There is no Eisenhower in Germany.

One of 100 Americans by 1920 had arrived at "Smith",
and in 1995, its top standing remained at just that.

By 2000 A.D. some 100,000 different
American family-names were to be found.
The top ten, loaded with un-British un-English types,
were "Smith, Johnson, Williams, Jones, Brown,
Davis, Miller, Wilson, Moore, and Taylor".
The number of female first names was about 4000,
topping with "Mary, Patricia, Linda, and Barbara".
while male naming lagged at some 1200,
"James. John, Robert, and Michael" leading off.

With last names, a reducing factor was always
present, but in the twentieth century,
a highly differentiated immigration brought in
a multitude of new names from hitherto exotic countries.
The Korean "Kim" leaped up. "Lee" climbed
with the aid of Chinese not from Virginia.

In 1928 some 66 million people had
English and Welsh surnames, of which 41 million were
traceable to the Old Country, 7 million
were of Blacks, and 17.2 million
represented adaptations or adoptions in America.
Thus about one-third of the people with
English surnames were hardly of English ancestry.

Then there were the Scots who acquired altered
names in the Old Country, though also after arrival.
The clans were old but the membership often young,
like joining a fraternity or club or gang.
The MacGregor Clan was so full of gangsters and ruffians that
in 1603 the name itself was barred to
everyone on pain of death, whereupon thousands
took to "MacDonald".

Given names generally followed religious and regional
patterns and moved in cycles and with fads.
"John" has been the favorite, via the Bible,
the Greek, the French "Jean", the Teutonic "Johann",
and royal characters. But the more Anglican "James" ("Jim") edged him
into second place by 1994. Mary, "Mother of Jesus,"

and favorite among queens, together with "Maria" outshined
its nearest competitor three-to-one.
But any odd candidate could compete,
as in the New York Marathon race -
whether a famous person like "Franklin",
a flower ("Lily"), or a virtue ("Temperance").

Indians took on double names, one translating the other,
or were dubbed with names by other Americans.
African names were almost entirely lost in
favor of given first names of Anglo-American,
natural, or Biblical origins, then, upon emancipation,
retained the surname of the former owner, a practice that has
since bothered many African-Americans
who would have preferred their original African name
or some African name. The practice was reversed,
mistakenly in many cases by the use of Islamic
names by the Black Islam Nationalist movement in the
twentieth century, and in some fewer cases
more authentically African ones by intellectuals,
entertainers and social reformers, leading to a
probability that at some point there might occur a
wholesale exchange of largely British and many
French and Spanish names for African names,
either based on some evidence of the African nation of
personal origin or by translation into an African tongue.
This would emulate the Indian trend.
So long as the dominant political class could express
its power by, on the one hand, scorning a "slave name" that
it could pronounce, while jeering at an African name
it was refusing to learn to pronounce,
the Afro-American, like the Indian, and like many another
"ethnic", was caught in a "no-win" bind.

African-Puerto Ricans, Haitians, South Louisianan, and other
Americans of African origin without the Anglo experience would
probably not turn in their Spanish or French names so often.
These lacked the sinister quality of the British names.
Later waves of change simplified to American speech and
orthography various Polish and other Slavic names,

also Greek and Armenian names.
In some "difficult" cases names were quite altered:
Rostenkowski sometimes to Ross or Rosten,
Agnopoulos ("Lamb's Son", cf. British "Lamson") to Agnew.
In many instances Jewish names were altered,
both to simplify and to evade possible anti-semitism,
Cohen to Cole, and Levinsky to Levin or LeVine, Rose, Harris, and Stein, etc. In Italian names, the last vowel might occasionally be dropped as Martini, Martin; Martelli, Martell; adding also phonetic changes, Vincenzo, Vincent: Giuliani, Julian. Changes of Spanish names have been rare, and logically, as a result of demographic changes of the past century, more and more
American names became Hispanic.

The end result was a horde of names found only in the United States and names from other languages that have seemed to proliferate here. Coming out of every country were surnames that became peculiarly American. Moreover, almost all names acquired an American pronunciation that would not be readily understood in the Old Country. This includes many British names. "Daugherty" is spelled and pronounced several ways. Van der Pohl can be Vanderpool. Mullen is French from "moulin, mill", although it might seem a variant of the Irish Mullins. Morley was Moor-lea. Some Tagliaferro's of Southern planter origin pronounce their name "Tollifer" while persevering with the original spelling. At least six countries furnished the basic material for the name "Johnson".

All in all, it may be said here, because the subject will not recur in later pages, it came about that today perhaps nine out of ten Americans have a full name that is not to be found in any other country in the world, or that does not reflect their principal ancestry, or that is pronounced differently when encountered elsewhere. At the same time, Americans, reversing a long-time movement to carry formal titles and surnames into social discourse, no matter what the social class involved, began in the 1960's to prefer first names, to be called Jimmy and Jane rather than Carter, Rumpelstilskin and Johnson. (Politely, the New York Times had moved into calling everyone without noble or professional title, even if nitwit or criminal, "Mr." or "Ms.")

First-name usage was not solely egalitarian vulgarism; it was a denial of differences, a shame of the unpronounceable, a vote for freedom of name against family and status, a search for a buddy, and for universal cordiality.

Place names in America were usually Indian because the Indians were the only ones who knew their way around, and they were not to be overlooked. Thousands of places - -paths, towns, springs, mountains - kept their Indian names or were given them. The process continued all across the country. In Louisiana French names outnumbered the Indian and maintained themselves. French names were kept for very many places of the old Northwest and Louisiana Territory. So, too, Spanish names dominated Southwest and West Coast locations and roads, and some were added fancifully.

Admirers of the famous and rich were more than ready with new names: Marietta, Ohio, for the unfortunately and wrongly guillotined Marie Antoinette, Queen of France, or Dauphin County, Pennsylvania for the French "Prince of Wales", etc. Virginia goes for Elizabeth, the "Virgin Queen", meaning *in fondo* that she took no husband. English cities were honored (or disgraced) by namesakes in America: New London, *et al.* Bismarck, North Dakota, was settled during the days of the Prussian "Iron Chancellor", by Germanophiles not within his grasp.
Not to mention New England.

Names full of promise that went unfulfilled dotted the land, like Paris, Tennessee. Great cities might begin humbly: Chicago, the "wild onion" of the dunes around Fort Dearborn. Hundreds of place names in the South have been traced back to Africa.

African sources have to be credited for a great many words of the language, more than the Indians or Spanish. The 11-word sentence, *"Buckaroo guy he goose her diggin dirt fer yams an goobers"*, holds 7 African words and three dialect usages and 1 proper word "her". (It is not a direct quotation in the vernacular.) Africans, probably Bantu, profited from their relative isolation and low status on the offshore islands and lowlands of the South Atlantic Coast to produce Gullah, a distinctive Anglo-African language, the only natural language to originate in America, or at least it is more indigenous than Pennsylvania Dutch.

African-American "soul food" is made up of the cheapest greens and animal offal, once pretentiously abhorred, now chic in some upper class circles, Black and White. Some African culinary exotica ultimately vanished. An old-timer of the Sea Islands told an interviewer, *"They ate funny kine uh food, roas wile locus an mushruhm an tanyan root. It lak elephant-eah and taase lak Arish potatuh".* In this case, but also generally with dialectical Afro-American speech and Gullah, at work is not an inability to master the major American language forms, but an adaptation of Niger-Congo tongues, following their rules of grammar and pronunciation, to the new language.

Indeed, every people that has ever come to America has produced this highly interesting linguistic phenomenon; it amounts to bringing in a peculiar form of whatever basic language was spoken, including numerous types of English, and adjusting this system to the peculiar form of the American language where the group has settled. The process ensuing, which accepts and rejects, and combines with several American language variants, and invents and continues to evolve, is almost entirely unconscious.

Only a few linguistic environments in America have been able to discipline significantly a tongue: a private socially pretentious school, a narrow special military unit, a specialized occupation with a tight *esprit de corps*, a small cult, and an isolated locality.

The New Orleans area became also a center of African-American culture: it was hospitable to voodoo, a Dahomean religious cult, well-developed also in Haiti and the Caribbean, and for folklore and aesthetics of Bantu origin. Bantu influence was heavy in South Carolina and Louisiana, but enjoyed also a wide dissemination around the South. The authorities of the larger culture were of course interested mainly in the extirpation of African language and practices, but were captivated at the same time, as in warfare one comes to resemble the enemy.

Writing and literature in America remained fairly constant and continuously changing in all major sections of the country. Speech varied from section to section. The Yankee speech with its nasality, dryness and high pitch moved from New England and Upstate New York along the Great Lakes line going West - Northern Ohio, Indiana, Illinois, Michigan and Wisconsin –and continued right on to the Northern Great Plains, then to Washington and Oregon. A related Delaware Bay speech moved through Pennsylvania, and struck out westwards to the Pacific Coast.

The coastal Southern speech forms - drawling, softly enunciated, the most singable - were bred in the Chesapeake Bay region and moved through Virginia down to Florida and the Gulf of Mexico. Meanwhile, the uplands Southern speech pattern - high inflected, both nasal and throaty, slightly drawling, slow-spoken - grew up in Appalachia, moved along the Southern border states across the Mississippi into the Hispanic Southwest, including originally Southern California.

The egalitarian period witnessed the wide-scale increase of nationalistic sentiments and a heavy production of national symbols. At times the elite of the South were alarmed at the enthusiastic adoption of national symbols, for in every enhancement of nationalism or federalism was an implication of lowered state loyalties.

The South was learning too that even the frontiersmen who were of Southern origin were acquiring Federalist habits of thought. The basic cause was evident, but nothing could be done about it: new states were being formed with a paltry history, a mixed bag of people, a total dependence upon the federal government, a set of boundaries drawn more by a Jeffersonian geometrician than by an ecologist and anthropologist.

The great body of people yearned for a union with all the trimmings, flags, songs, legends, and mottoes and these were forthcoming in this period. The flag, that had been evolving, was adopted according to its present design and principles only in 1818, when thirteen stripes and as many stars as states became the norm. The poem composed by Francis Scott Key at and after the siege of Baltimore, and put to the music of an English drinking song, became the national anthem only during the Civil War.

There were other songs and poems about, and glorifying patriotism, by the likes of Oliver Wendell Holmes, Joseph Rodman Drake, Julia Ward Howe, and John Greenleaf Whittier. (The same process, incidentally, was occurring in Europe, even more rapidly and with larger historical and cultural resources, for wherever the gospel of democracy was carried - everywhere in those days - a mass direct democratic feeling was aroused that required far more symbolism of nation-*plus*-people than the old regimes afforded.) Washington, long venerated, was given the company of Jefferson and others. The Fourth of July speech became a fixture of every annual assemblage in every public place of the country. Then selected orators would give forth, all hardly modifying the litany that follows: to give a proper Independence Day oration you must -

a. Recite the history of America's founding in the colonial era.
b. Show how the Hand of God interposed Itself at every stage.
c. Reveal fully the American love of liberty.
d. Detail the oppression suffered under the British.
e. Announce the earth-shaking events that began the Revolution.
f. Glorify the heroic fighters of the Revolution and its Leaders.
g. Stress how, by emulating their virtues, all problems today can be solved.
h. Point to the amazing progress of the Republic since Independence.
I. Express our unbounded loyalty to the nation.
j. Conclude with the prophecy of a great future for America.

On this day the Liberty Bell in Philadelphia would be tolled (It cracked and was silenced in 1835.) It was not rung for the celebration of the signing of the Declaration of Independence, as legend would have it. Nor was it called the Liberty Bell until long afterwards, and then by African-Americans in reference to their own need for liberty. Legends of the bell and other American symbols and figures were contained in a fulsome work by George Lippard published in 1847 (The same George Lippard whose "smutty" play was banned from the Philadelphia stage.)

One may wonder whether the seizure upon symbols by so practical a group as the Americans may not have accelerated the growth of the advertising industry in the United Sates. This vast realm of enterprise had its origins early. British soldiers besieging Breed's Hill received well-composed appeals in print from a rebel press, urging them to recognize their common bond and not to press the battle, a very early instance of psychological warfare.

A stalwart pioneer here as in numerous areas was Benjamin Franklin. He used a number of icons - boats, horses, etc. He could not stand a simple ad appearing in his newspaper, especially when his brother's product was concerned, and wrote a fitting recommendation and announcement for his super-fine soap.

Newspapers were built up on advertisements, notices, political payments, and, to a degree, news. The million or so potential readers of 1820 might be reached by one of over 500 newspapers. Their ads were at first directed largely to the well-to-do, but then democratized.

America was destined to be a gigantic bulletin board from the start. Since people moved about in vast numbers - the National Road was a continuous stream of traffic - notices were profitably posted everywhere.
A nation of bouncing atoms, a nation of strangers, a people hungry for consumer goods, for quick-cures, for ways of making money, for influencing people in large numbers: there was every reason for the success of the new medium.

Decision-making at a Puritan town-meeting…

Part Six

EXPANSION AND INTEGRATION

This land is your land, and this land is my land, sure, but the world is run by those who never listen to music anyway.
BOB DYLAN

This section is about land and more land -
from whom it was taken by the United States, when and how.
Once again, we go about the boring job of tallying acreage,
so many million here, so many million there.
(See the map below concerning expansion.)

Once more we advise against gloating over the
conquests achieved by already
the world's largest Republic.
If one says that the United States
as a whole grew ever richer and more productive
and powerful, he must ask himself
how a few beggars with hand tools

and several years of food
supplied from abroad could have done the job.

One answer seems ever more plain:
The United States was capitalized on land
(taken by one or another means from the Indians,
or whoever else claimed it). One has to think of land as an
increasingly valuable asset from the time of its acquisition,
readily convertible into other assets,
as a form of currency.

Americans were over-capitalized on land.
It took over three for them to realize that
they had been living off their capital.
The land offered up food, the forests game.
The offshore fisheries, lakes and rivers cast up fish unending.
The forests provided timber for millions of homes
all types of construction, and supplied fuel for
warmth and industry for centuries.

The land was granted or bartered or sold at a pittance,
to railroad companies, farmers, veterans, speculators, immigrants, schools,
states, counties, towns, cities, special districts of all kinds.
The land was used to back up borrowings of funds.
The land was asked to give up its mineral resources:
coal, silver, gold, lead, copper, oil, and
precious, semi-precious and just plain stone.
Land did all this, most generously.

A large proportion of all the products of the land -
minerals, timber, plants and animals -
were exported abroad for cash to buy consumer and producer goods.
In modern history, perhaps only Russia had been so well capitalized.
But it was as gross an aggressor in
conquering Siberia and the nations on its fringes.
Nor was its large population worse off than the American,
all in all. Sounding strange to myth-duped ears are
reports that Czarist capitalism was modernizing rapidly.
However, Americans were taught by their God
how to capitalize their bonanza to the utmost,

while Russia turned communist, bureaucratic, and atheist.
Being a madly free republic helped the U.S. greatly.

What is the morality of seizing other peoples' lands,
developing them in accord with your own standards?
Millions of Americans asked themselves this question,
not once, but dozens of times.
Does life become a little less worthwhile,
when one realizes or believes that one is heir to gigantic
thefts, rapine, compulsory contracts, and phony purchases?
Should history assume the task of condemning long afterwards
actions scarcely sensed to be wicked by the actors?
Yes, why not - if it educates us now?
Should the historian, in that case, give credit,
where credit is overdue, to historical actors?
Yes, doubly so.

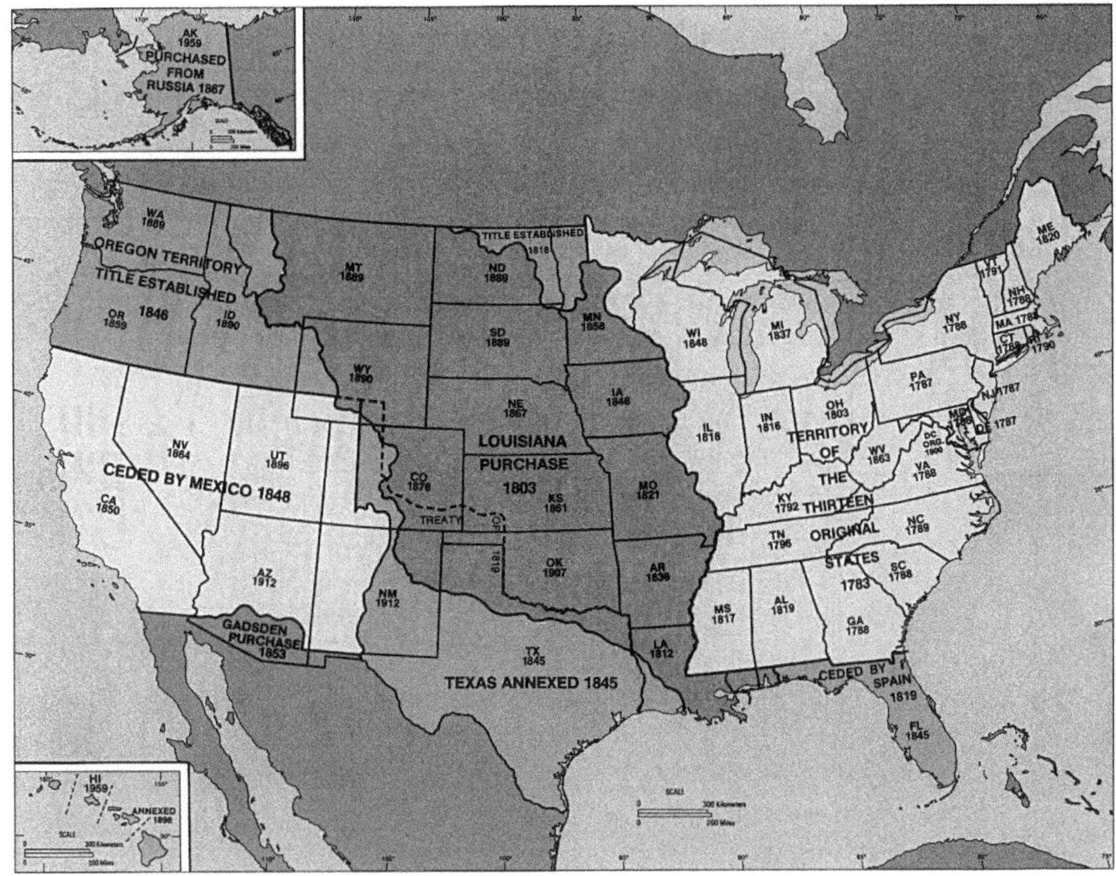

Growth of a Nation

Chapter Twenty-nine

International Transactions

Like George Washington, President Harrison caught his death of cold. He did so on his Inauguration Day and did not survive the ensuing plague of office-seekers. The usual quarrels over the national bank and tariffs occupied his successor, John Tyler, who would not be domineered by Henry Clay's Congressional capers.
He accomplished little.

Relations with Britain were as bad as usual, when a well-disposed Prime Minister sent to America a Lord Ashburton to dicker with Daniel Webster, now Secretary of State, and the two sent skimming back and forth across the table chunks of territory the size of England, Switzerland, the Netherlands or Portugal.

The Maine boundary was settled; it was a good deal for Britain; the natural boundary seemed more properly to include New Brunswick. But perhaps the two gentlemen wished to keep the French-Canadians all on the British side. (In a century or so the Francophones would be hopping the border to settle and proliferate in New England.)

The boundary line between Lake Superior and Lake-of-the-Woods was also agreed upon, a simple straight line that by a stroke of luck put inside the States the great Minnesota Mesabi Iron Range to come.

The idea of "manifest destiny" meant more than horizontal expansion to some people. The phenomenon "filibusters" acquired its name from sundry adventurers who combined here and there to expand or capture pieces of territory, recently liberated from or still pertaining to the weakening Spanish imperial domain. A group calling itself Knights of the Golden Circle claimed 65,000 members pledged to liberate the whole of the Caribbean on behalf of the slave culture. The Civil War cut short its expansionist efforts.

A William Walker sailed with a gang of self-styled "Immortals" on news of a Nicaraguan Civil War in 1855. He espoused many causes, some good, like the abolition of slavery and the rights of women. He claimed to have taken over the seat of government in Managua, whereupon President Franklin Pierce recognized his regime. He got mixed up with American businessmen, and especially the robber baron, Cornelius Vanderbilt. Soon thereafter, Walker was run out of office by a combination of Vanderbilt and British interests in the country. Eventually he was executed by firing squad in Honduras.

Other filibusterers with a Cuban penchant were aching to "liberate" the Pearl of the Antilles on behalf of the slave culture. When President

Pierce, ever hopeful, told American Ambassador Soulé to offer Spain $130 millions, the Spanish government ushered him out the door.

Piqued, Soulé then got together in Ostend with the American ambassadors to Britain and France. The trio composed a manifesto which they leaked to the media, declaring that only *"stubborn pride and a false sense of honor"* motivated note to sell the Island, and in such case, it would *"seriously endanger our internal peace and existence of our cherished Union"*. Thus, *"then, by every law, human and divine, we shall be justified in wresting it from Spain"*.

Instead of delivering the ambassadors to the custody of the insane asylum recently set up in Massachusetts, the first in the nation, Pierce merely disavowed them, following an uproar of opinion.

Yankee traders harbored in the most esoteric and exotic ports of the world in the ante-bellum decades. After them came the flagged gunboats. Like Pocohontas, Indian trinkets, Squanto, *et al.* their cultural items and living specimens were carried back as cultural exchanges. The exchange worked both ways. Trade flourished when nations were prosperous; economic cycles matched between Europe and America; when English merchant houses and banks failed, so did the American.

When Germans immigrated (a form of cultural exchange) they found the same economic recession here that drove them to leave Germany. The progress of republican revolutions and constitutional revolutions in Europe sent thousands of emissaries to the United States, depressed and poor, some of them accomplished and skilled.

The American Revolution and Constitution made their way steadily as cultural transfers to Latin America. If the Revolutionaries of the United States had not in effect set up the ruling class of Canada and the Maritime Provinces when it expelled the Loyalists, Canada would have probably revolted and become a republic along with the rest. (Actually Brazil performed the novel turn of hiring a member of the Portuguese royal family to head its independent government, but after some years subsided into a regular republic along U.S. federal lines.)

Inventions moved back and forth. Americans carried many innovations to the Orient and South America, many of them received from Europe of course. There was a considerable traffic in pirated literary works and inventions, mostly to America, the cheapest form of import imaginable - next to the immigrant, who paid to be taken from his domicile. Aesthetic imports were also heavy, and cost next to nothing. In short the culture of the Old World, as fast as it could be transported, and of the Orient as well, journeyed to the New World. If it were not for the ghastly sight of the new immigrants, the docking of a boat from Europe would bring a cargo of valuable cheap thrills.

Nor should it be overlooked that America was becoming once again big news in the Old World, not only for its political and diplomatic or commercial news that the upper classes enjoyed, but for once there was news throughout Europe of the lower classes, the masses of people, who would hear all about their own kind living other styles of life in strange circumstances. Just as the Age of Discoveries flooded the European mind with stories of the New World, so did the age of Immigration, first in Latin America but then even more forcibly in poly-national North America.

We have yet to study in depth the enormity of the impact of the American experience on the changes occurring in Europe from the British Isles to the Russian steppes and Anatolia. The perspectives of the European masses changed greatly in the nineteenth century, owing in good part to the influences flowing back from America through people-to-people communications as well as through the exchange of goods and devices and political designs for the elites.

America was a haven for political refugees, New York especially, though not nearly so much as London and Paris. In reverse, there were political and religious refugees from some of the Latin American revolutions in the same cities and in Madrid and Lisbon. America could be proud that practically its only refugees were expatriates in England, France, and Italy from philistinism.

The Far East was known to Catholic missionaries from the sixteenth century onwards, preceded by men-o-war and followed by traders. The Chinese Emperor and his mandarins were of two minds about foreign trade, let it in or keep it out, and finally allowed it at selected points. The American boats entered through Canton alone beginning in 1785. The ports of entry were increased to four by the Treaty of Wanghsia in 1844, conditions the equal of those granted the most favored nation.

By the same treaty, drafted by Secretary of State Daniel Webster, the USA was afforded extraterritoriality, the right to create a little nook in the port city where Americans would be subject to their own laws, not the Chinese. America obtained eleven additional ports of ingress fourteen years later and the right to travel throughout China. Missionaries were already hammering at the gates and soon poured in, so that China was paramount among targets of Protestant proselytizers.

The USA was by no means the largest trader in China. But, by the end of the century, Secretary of State John Hay would be striving for an Open" Door" policy, disallowing any discrimination against any nation's traders. Great Britain was still by far the most aggressive and successful operator in the region, with a new colony at Hongkong emerging from victory in the Opium War of 1839-42, a disgraceful episode in British history, amounting to forcing a nation to aggravate its hard drug problems, to stay hooked so that British traders could gain the means of taking rich goods out of China; the British even got the right to set Chinese tariff duties. Lessons like this the victims long remember.

Japan was meanwhile closed to American trade, and did not hasten to return shipwrecked sailors. In response to this offensive posture, an armed intervention seemed called for - after all, figured the Yankees, what are we paying taxes for? One day in July of 1853, there appeared before the startled eyes of the Japanese, engaged at their usual business around Tokyo harbor, a flotilla of eight gunboats. Its commander let the Japanese shogunate of Tokugawa, dominant political elite of the country, know that he was sending a note to the Emperor.

Negotiations followed. and by the Treaty of Kanagawa the next year, America gained representation in Japan, promises of improved treatment of castaways, and visiting privileges. Commercial relations set in several years later. In 1860 a Japanese diplomatic mission viewed for the first time the interior of a western nation, and retired before the shot and shell could more deeply impress them.

The Oregon territory was also subject of international dispute at this time. Russia pulled out, we know already, and so Spain, but how to get rid of Britain? There were many who wanted to fight Britain again, crying "54.40 or fight" this being the Northernmost boundary-latitude of the American claim. But the line that had already been traversing the continent from East to West was just too tempting to the logic of large empty spaces. The American negotiators gave in to it. They thought that the Mexican War would be enough to handle. America could have used a Lord North or Talleyrand, a diplomat who knew how to give away *other* people's claims.

Alaska, the next stage, was a horror story from the standpoint of the indigenes and, if humanitarianism for the plight of the Indian people had been common currency, the United states might have insisted then and there that the Russians get out. The great Russian Empire, unlike the British Empire, whose containment Secretary of State John Quincy Adams believed to be the major object of American foreign policy, was not uncontainable. It would have been easy enough to enforce the directive, since Russian capabilities were centered some thousands of miles away.

Any American flotilla that showed up would have contributed to the resuscitation of the whale, seal, otter and furry critters that the Russians were obliging the natives to kill as fast as possible. Like their Southern counterparts, the Russians used alcohol as a currency and the Alaskans, America's future citizens, became vodka-sodden well in advance of the Alaska Purchase of 1865. At least the Americans could not blame *this* tragedy upon themselves.

A continual hullabaloo was raised over how high tariffs should be, and there are those who go so far as to say that they great struggle in America was between the protectionists and the free traders, the North and the South, the merchant and the farmers. It requires no proof of great importance to the country whether the tariff was high or low; chances are that it made no difference.

Still men must wage politics, and a trivium will do - the existence of the holy trinity, the seduction of a woman, the theft of a donkey, the chance shots of a stupid patrol boat - to ignite a war. The tariff struggle did not cause the expansionism or even affect much the bloating of U.S. territory.

One would have to admit that the United States was dedicated to expansion, if this were the full story, but it is less than the half, the rest of which concerns Mexico, at least for another memorial generation. What motives underlay this eager expansionism by a people who had so much land to till and mine that all of Europe could be fitted into it, all the European peoples, for that matter?

There are, pursuing a conventional kind of explanation, the economic reasons of trade. Go out unto the world and profit thereby. Admittedly this was a great good of the modern nation. It could encompass and organize the energies to do this job well.

Was it the fault of the Slave Culture that drove its gallant leaders into dreaming of the conquest of far off places where the cotton fields far away would be forever fertile? That would hardly account for Oregon, Alaska, California, Alaska and places yet to come in the next delirious period of American expansionism.

Was it the human needs of Americans abroad, the shipwrecked sailors who needed consuls to rescue them and ship them home, the travelers who were stranded and uncertain in strange lands, the bureaucrats who fantasized ministries and consulates and assistant consuls in every city of the world? Hardly. But here one must consider the enormous evangelical dynamism contained within the United States.

Could the churches with their endless missionary energies never fully satisfied domestically have prompted and pushed the advocates of manifest destiny and given them the moral courage that they needed to do their utmost? Yes, here was a strong reasons for moving out into the world. The profiteers needed justification for a presence everywhere; the missionaries could provide it.

But it was also a case of the missionaries finding not only sustenance in the traders but also continual supporters of their far-flung missions. Every sect in America wanted to proselytize the heathen. Never mind that it had been such failure - who would admit it? - among the Indians. Nothing a missionary could dream of would be so comfortable as proselytizing in India or China or even in the few places in South America or Europe where you might be permitted - servants, a fine cuisine, polite pagans.

Is there a disease that could be called spatial megalomania? Many distinguished foreign observers and a great many common people everywhere marked the American mania for expansion as a reprehensible religious hypocrisy, which explains the economic expansion, the western expansion, the Mexican aggressions, etc. (not that the world's nations were innocent of the trait, particularly when it extrudes from nationalism, but, then, they would not normally consider the beam in their own eye when seeing the mote in the eye of another).

There is something called agoraphilia, the irrepressible desire to keep moving away from the center in which you were born. To escape from the inhospitable womb of mother and motherland, from the good and bad neighbors, to conquer land simply by putting one's feet upon it, often finding this enough, viz., *"Oh, yes, I've been there too"*. That such a disease was the basic motive for all the aggression of a great people in achieving its natural limits could not even be imagined, much less accepted by Americans; and the New Englanders, doing it their way, scorned the footloose West-bound, while the Westerners, doing it their way, contemned the house-bound Easterner. And the military scorned the pacifists, and vice versa.

There is yet a point to be made about this that supersedes all the rest. The people of the United States have always believed that they were peaceful and unaggressive. The word "isolationist" has been used by them to describe themselves and has been employed by others who listen to such twaddle. Actually, the Americans have never been isolationist. They have held to two other positions, which, sliding over one another like two films, gave a unified false impression.

America from its rebirth at the instance of European invaders has been a society immensely involved with the outside world, with the Indian nations by the score, who themselves tried vainly to become united enough to act in internal proceedings, and then with any single nation that approached its shores, then with individuals by the millions from every country of the world, then with all countries of the world that would get in its way. The United States has been an integral member of the world order from its seeding time onwards.

Its claim that has been called isolationism is a warning in fact of its own weakness as a popular democracy: the United States was too decentralized, unintegrated, full of popular and elite passions and partisanship, to be able to promise anything to any nation or group of nations. Its promises were not to be relied on. Its policies were capable of instant change.

The problem was beyond *raison d'état.* The isolationism of America was a kind of helpless exclamation to warn others away. It is the child, grown adolescent, become adult, and even old, saying, in ashamed knowledge of oneself,

"Do not believe me when I say yes,
because tomorrow, I insist, I may be driven to say no.
I cannot help myself".

The Alamo, Davy Crockett's last sunrise by Mark Churms

Chapter Thirty

The Hispanic Southwest and Texas

When the Mexicans won their independence from Spain, in the year 1821, their domain included the present American states of Texas, New Mexico, Arizona, California, Nevada, Colorado in part, and Utah. They numbered about 25,000 in this vast region and their neighbors were some 100,000 Indians, some of whom were Catholics, most of whom were of the rites of the many tribal nations.

The region was dry, its distances great. its topography often rugged, its soil generally infertile. (Actually, North of the region, the land that came from the Louisiana Purchase was also dry; all seventeen present-day American states West of the North-South line of the Missouri River are arid or semi-arid all or in part.)

The areas of principal Hispanic settlement were along the upper Rio Grande at El Paso, along the lower Rio Grande, near the upper Gila River, in middle and Northern New Mexico especially around Taos and Santa Fe, and around San Francisco and the lower part of California. The modern points of Santa Fe, Nogales, San Antonio, El Paso, San Diego, Los Angeles, Monterey, San José and San Francisco were alive and thriving.

The Pueblo peoples were long settled and had been in a state of relative decline as integrated societies by the nineteenth century. They were surrounded by Navaho, who had been nomadic, but had now settled down with a culture developed partly by borrowing Pueblo elements. Around many Indian and Mexican villages and farms circled nomadic Apaches. Little effort went into subduing them. They were now masters of horsemanship and firearms. Subjection would have been impossible without a large infusion of cavalry supported by a much larger resident population.

This came not from Mexico, but from the East, the United States. Meanwhile the Apaches governed *de facto* a territory the size of France with perhaps 10,000 people of their tribe. The Pima-Papago Indians had, like the Pueblo and Apache, endured Spanish rule for three hundred years before the invaders from the East appeared. Like the other Indians, they would at long intervals rebel, and then, once put down, return to their traditional ways. Agriculture was ingeniously suited to the dry and hot land. It had a long pre-history, probably as long as that of Middle East farming.

The 300 years, however, had introduced Spanish and Catholic culture into Indian life. The Spanish had adapted readily to the modest and appropriate Indian agriculture, adding the horse, some iron tools, wagons and a few new types of seed. They were careful to maintain the old irrigation system employed by the Indians and accommodated Spanish law, which regulated ownership among individuals to water rights as against communal modes of rationing. They were closer together and now became integrated, but were distinct from the water distribution system brought from the East.

Eastern law allowed only riparian rights; if a farmer did not own the well or hole or bank of a river, he held no rights to water and had to buy them from the owner. In the Hispanic system that came to be adopted in most places, the rights were governed by the community and parceled out in accord with the priority of the possessor and the amount seasonally available. Such was the "beneficial use" or appropriation system as opposed to the riparian rights system.

Most Pueblos professed Christianity. A number of Catholic missions had been established in what became American territory. The Jesuits and Franciscan monks operated them. Distanced far from one another, they acted as community centers for a growing number of Mexican-Indians and pure Indians. A few of these were taught in mission schools, a few became acolytes, a few ventured to make their fortunes in Chihuahua, which was the city to the South from which trade radiated into the region, or even in Mexico City, much farther South and the largest city in North America until the nineteenth century industrial revolution matured in the East. (In the late twentieth century it became again the largest city in North America.)

Land ownership was generally in small plots associated with villages, but very large tracts were given or sold to individuals. The missions were dispossessed of their property after the revolution, when the Mexican revolutionary government pursued a policy of anti-clericalism, and their lands also ended in the hands of great landlords.

Many of the rich families had much the same reputation as the planters of the East; they lived for horses, rodeos, gambling, and feasting. On their ranches a cowboy culture developed. It was from the Mexican gaucho that the American cowboy assumed his habits, skills, and something of his character. The uniform was Mexican: hat, chaps, spurs, lariat and saddle, down to the cinch *(cincha)* belly banding the saddle, that became a dozen common American extensions used ever after by people who had rarely been near a horse - the "dead cinch" being, for instance, a sure bet. Also Mexican were the cowboy yells.

The cowboy culture had also Southern roots, from Eastern Louisiana; many Africans were cowboys in those earlier times and kept up the tradition farther West.

Herds of cattle and sheep roamed on the usually desiccated plains from one watering place to another. The rivers, with marked exception - the Colorado, Rio Grande, Nueces, and Gila particularly - dried at the end of summer, to wait for the rains of winter and the mountain snows of spring to melt; furthermore, their flow from one year to another was and is erratic. It was discovered that ranging livestock was about the only occupation suited to the land, beyond a few specially endowed areas.

The famous East-West routes-to-be were known to Indians, Spanish, Mexicans, French and a few Americans by the beginning of the nineteenth century. The first regular use of a route from American territory to a significant Mexican settlement came with the opening of the Santa Fe Trail by Mexican-American traders in search of an outlet to the Northeast. It linked the bend of the Missouri River where now stands Kansas City, by way of the Arkansas River, to the Upper Colorado River.

Another point of contact had been initially set up by French traders at Taos, New Mexico. San Miguel del Bado had achieved contact with Eastern trading wagons. Taos workers built Bent's Fort on the Arkansas river. Soon the monopoly of Chihuahua of trade with the Southwest interior was broken and Santa Fe caravans might proceed all the way to St.Louis. Thereupon, regardless of borders, Americans ventured as far South as Zacatecas, and in the end the goods of this huge interior country were competed for by the port cities of New York, New Orleans and Vera Cruz (Mexico).

By the 1830's aggressive American commercial dealers had a new route to follow. Hispanic traders had marked a new so-called "Old Spanish Trail" that took them from New Mexico in a giant U-turn Northwest (through Utah) and South through the San Bernardino

Mountains (Cajon Pass) into California. For decades, California mules and horses were driven all the way to Missouri, with exchanges on the way there to add New Mexico woolen goods.

Actually commerce and settlement and development could have proceeded well, conducted by the United States and Mexico without war and eternal grudges. But this was not to be. The authority of the United States entered upon the great Southwest, "The Golden West", the "Arid West", *via* three acquisitions that came after the Louisiana Purchase: the Annexation of Texas of 1845; the Mexican Cession of 1848; and the Gadsden Purchase of 1853. The last of these was simply a boundary straightening deal involving a small payment to the always cash-needy Mexican government (welcome, then, although the same land would cost billions of dollars today).

The Texas story occupies us for the balance of this chapter, the Mexican war in the next.

The father of Stephen F. Austin of Missouri got an enormous land grant from the Spanish authorities of Mexico, and Stephen could employ it in liberated Mexico. He started a colony on the Brazos River just as Mexico was achieving independence in 1921 and before long had persuaded 2000

people from the East to settle in. Other impresarios were offered similar deals to bring in immigrants by the State of Coahuila-Texas. Eastern Texas had good cotton land, so that before long thousands of cotton planters had come in. One thousand slaves had entered at the same time.

Mexicans became alarmed at the influx and tried to stop it, bringing up troops to police the border, but the effort was no more successful than the recent efforts to prevent illegal Mexican immigrants going the opposite way. Soon there were ten times as many American immigrants as there were Mexicans in the area.

Among them was a man named Sam Houston, or Paul Samuel Houston as he had renamed himself, an attorney of Nacogdoces.

Houston is a man worth knowing. He is a top contender for the most remarkable man in American history. He was a Mexican citizen. He also had been and probably still was a Cherokee citizen named Oo-Tse-Tee Ardee-Tah-Skee, meaning "The Big Drunk". He had been solely an American citizen, a citizen of Tennessee, and had been born in Virginia.

In his teens he had left his widowed mother (now in Tennessee) with her nine other children to go live with the Cherokees, where he was adopted by Chief Oo-Loo-Te-Ka. In 1812, at 19, he decided to open a school in the nearby White community, then gave it up after a year to join the Army, carrying a heavy drinking habit with him.

He fought against the Creeks, and at the battle of Horseshoe Bend was shot in the groin while charging the enemy. He also was shot in the leg by a barbed arrow that was jerked out, and then in the renewed attack caught two more bullets. The commander, Andrew Jackson, was so impressed by his impetuous courage that he would take his side for the rest of his life.

As token of his esteem, Jackson helped him become a lawyer, a Congressman from Tennessee, and then Governor of the State. He married while Governor, but his wife deserted him for her family within months of the ceremony. Some say that she loved another man, others that he was an impossibly jealous drunk. Many years later she was quoted as having called him demented, insanely jealous, while another reported that she was repelled by the running sore in his thigh.

He was so dismayed that he resigned as Governor and rejoined his Cherokee father at the Indian camp about 100 miles from the Texas border. There he was often dead drunk, and sometimes engaged in the liquor and general trade. He married an Indian in a traditional ceremony. He went to Washington to appeal the case of the Cherokees and, dressed in his Indian clothing, pleaded with Jackson for relief.

He then attacked a Congressman who had denounced him and was tried by the House of Representatives. Appearing before the House drunk, he asked for respect for "the rights of American citizens". He was reprimanded and left for home, and, shortly, for Texas, bearing credentials from Andrew Jackson.
At Nacogdoches, he not only became a Mexican citizen, but also was converted to Roman Catholicism. He conspired on behalf of the "Texians" for independence. The Committee on Vigilance and Safety appointed him their military commander. When a convention of March 4, 1836 declared for Texan independence, he was chosen to be the Commander-in-Chief of the Armies of the Republic of Texas. This and a lot of recruiting effort brought him a rag-tag army of some 800 men. They were a rainbow of ethnic and social types, including Mexicans.

But if this was riff, then the Army of the Republic of Mexico under Dictator Antonio Lopez de Santa Anna was raff, crowded with convicts and homeless men. But it was larger. It was encamped by the San Jacinto River, when Houston's army practically blundered upon it. Houston of course ordered a charge and, shouting *"Remember the Alamo!"* sent the disrupted enemy flying in a matter of minutes. The men became instant heroes of Texas. Their commander suffered a severe leg wound.

The legendary Alamo affair had witnessed to begin with a large collection of Texan and other adventurers, like Davy Crockett, holed up in an old Spanish mission built in 1718 and housing Indians. They proclaimed the independence of Texas and awaited the consequences. It was February 23, 1836 when the army of Dictator Santa Anna marched up. The Texans repelled its attacks for twelve days, but in a final assault all of the remaining Alamo defenders lost their lives. (The wounded were despatched by order of Santa Anna.)

The commander, William Travis, was crazed from drinking mercury, then the therapy-of-choice for syphilis. His co-commander, Jim Bowie, who had been smuggling slaves and fighting Indians, had cached in a hole on the Mission grounds a hoard of gold and silver that he had stolen from Apaches whom he had murdered, so he was loath to leave, and was sick anyhow. Crockett tried to surrender, but failed.

It is with such tidbits from modern historical research that the Hispanics of the area, angered at a century and a half of racism and subjection by Anglos, argued away recently the protests of the Daughters of the Republic of Texas, who have guarded the site as a patriotic shrine. The reformers and reconstructionists of history wished to reconstruct the Alamo Mission.

Santa Anna was captured at San Jacinto. He signed a declaration of the Independence of Texas and was released. The Mexican Congress reassembled from its disbanding by Santa Anna, and denounced the action, but no one paid any attention to it. The Texans wrote a Constitution and elected Houston as President of Texas. Besides the United States, both France and Britain, sensing cheaper cotton, recognized Texas as a sovereign nation.

Houston now presented a petition on the part of the new Republic to be annexed to the United States. Friendship or no, Jackson was not of a mind to fight a war with Mexico at the moment, and the opposition to another slave territory and state was strong in Congress and the nation. President Van Buren also evaded the issue of annexation. President Tyler, next at bat, asked his Secretary of State, John Calhoun, to put the treaty of annexation before the Senate. Opposition was heavy, nor was it soothed with a leaked letter of Calhoun explaining the wonders another slave state would do for the Union. The bill failed.

Next in line was President Polk, a man full of expansionist sentiments. He was well-educated and had lengthy political experience, including two terms as Governor of Tennessee. After his election, during the "Lame Duck" Congress that preceded his inauguration, Tyler and the expansionists took liberties with the Constitution and long practice: they introduced a joint resolution in Congress (practically the same as a normal bill) offering to admit Texas as a State, were it to apply. (Treaties, we recall, required a two-thirds approval in the Senate.) Tyler signed the resolution as soon as it passed through both houses by simple majorities, 27-25 in the Senate, 120-98 in the House.

Even the immense and free acquisition, gratifying to the nation's expansionists, had to buck against an increasingly stubborn and growing free-state sentiment. Texas voters ratified the proposal and on December 29, 1845 became citizens of the State of Texas and the United States of America.

Sam Houston meanwhile had married for the third time, now to a young woman named Margaret Lea. She was full of the Bible and converted him to Baptism. She cured him of drunkenness, wrote poetry, underwent the removal of a breast cancer without anaesthesia, and proceeded withal to bear him eight children.

After annexation, he became a U.S. Senator and tried to become a Presidential candidate of the American (Know-Nothing) Party, attacking Whigs, Democrats, and Republicans.
His Senate seat was withdrawn by the legislature.
But he had two big acts left.
In 1859 he ran for Governor and was elected once more.

In the crisis of secession, he contended for the Union. He refused the Confederate oath, but also turned down President Lincoln's request that he take command of Union forces in Texas. He was forced from office by the Texas Secession Convention.
He died two years later.

Following upon Statehood, the young giant Texas went after more of Mexico. It also extended its economic and cultural influence into Oklahoma, Eastern Louisiana, New Mexico and Arizona. Its people came from several cultures that stamped various sections of the State. In the far South and upper West Rio Grande, Hispanic Catholic culture prevailed. In the far East sprang up a cotton culture of Blacks and White, sharing much the same way of life but set apart as castes. Their lands were soon eroded, and the people became even poorer than they were when they entered. In the

1850's 90% of the people of Texas
lived in this area composing 2/5 of the state;
75% of the White population
owned only 15% of the wealth.
The many African-Americans, of course, owned zilch.

Catholic and Lutheran Europeans, Germans, pushed in from the Gulf coast to settle on a group of hills in middle Texas. Midwestern Protestants came down from Illinois, Missouri, Iowa and points in between to people the Panhandle that was ultimately patched on to Texas.

A large number infiltrated from the states of Tennessee, Arkansas, and Missouri to lend a border Southern White complexion to the state as a whole. They promptly formed the poorest 21 counties of Texas and stayed that way, despite heavy emigration westward. The area remained, in effect, part of Appalachia (It is spooky to recall the theory of *Chapter One* that these hills of Texas are a distant geological continuation of the Appalachians so far away). The same group pushed West and ultimately colored New Mexico, Arizona and Southern California, though not so much as Texas.

It is well to allude once again to the expansive propensity of the poor Southerners: they had nothing to lose by moving; they did not build neat farms usually and enrich themselves from the environment at hand or the goods to be imported; they achieved a subsistence standard and looked around for new country; they would move even when the difference between what they had and what they might expect was small.

But they were also at the same time romantic dreamers. Territorially, although not in numbers, wealth, or creativity, their culture came to characterize in some part half the area of the continental United States. In the late twentieth century, you could drive all over the United States listening to their country music and Bible sermons on the radio.

From every point of the compass, the phenomenon of the Texas cattlemen put in an appearance. They collected beasts, for some years the rather scrawny and tough-eating longhorns, hired gauchos and cowboys, and bought and fought for pasture and range. Small fortunes were made and lost continuously in the risky business of the wide-open spaces. They dealt in hides and beef. Their richest markets were in the growing Northern cities. They tried every desperate measure to walk or transport their animals North and East.

The metals and minerals, the petroleum, would come later; meanwhile life was grim for the vast majority of Texans - Indian, Hispanic, African, or Anglo (the term used for everyone of full European descent, whether an original Texan or a newcomer). Without exception, Texas was ruled by an oligarchy of rich Anglos of several ethnic strains. Later on, populists would be elected to office, invariably in the pay of the cattle, real estate, and oil interests.

Finally, a process of assimilation of other elements to power and wealth, and therefore dignity, began - first under the New Deal, then, after World War II, at a faster yet still vastly frustrating pace. A great influx of technical, academic and industrial families from the North heightened and broadened the change in culture. The native Anglos themselves altered their own perspectives. The word "Anglo" was disappearing: an American, a Texan, yes, but not an Anglo.

Lyndon Johnson, a schoolteacher and politician wheeler-and-dealer, before becoming President by accident of an assassination, would exemplify the worst of the traditional Texas Anglo - were it not for his late conversion to the cause of the poor and oppressed of the nation.

So far as the Mexican War is concerned, it simply crystallized the initial peculiar forces of Texas, as Sam Houston himself had discovered in the end.

Called "Big Drunk" by his Indian wife and Tribe,
Sam Houston was a vigorous and competent military commander
and later served as Governor of Texas.
He dissented on breaking the Union.

Chapter Thirty-one

The Mexican War

President Polk had no intention of letting the Mexicans off the hook. He was either less frightened or less kind to them than to the British, or was it because he was a slaveholder? He had settled upon the British a goodly part of the wonderful, free, well-watered and well-settled territory of Oregon, whose American pioneers were ready, with considerable Northern sentiment in their favor, to fight for the disputed land.

Soon enough, now that the sheen had rubbed off the fur trade, the Russians might retire and there might come a land juncture with an American Alaska, the whole Pacific Coast, no less! Whereupon Canada would collapse into itself until it should become totally annexed by the United States, hopefully by peaceful means, assimilating both Canadiens and Royalists in due course. (This Author can yak Expansionist as well as the next jingo!) There was no hurry about the Mexican lands; they were ripening on the vine.

The Texans were bellicose and would trespass willy-nilly.
Their story version went like this:
John Quincy Adams had given away part of the
Louisiana Purchase when, in his treaty with Spain,
he had agreed to its boundaries. On the South,
the Rio Grande should have been the boundary line
and on the West, a North-South line more or less
following the continental divide.
President Polk agreed.

In truth Polk wanted more, ultimately California and all that lay between. He wrote the American consul in San Francisco, telling him that, although the United States would not openly support an independence movement of Californians, he would recognize an independent nation of California - preliminary to annexing it, of course.

He ordered the American Army under General Zachary Taylor to move beyond the Nueces River, which practically every expert and politician except himself and the Texans considered to be the boundary of the United States, so as to take up positions 150 miles to the South on the Rio Grande. The Mexican population was astonished to see the American troops. Several bloody incidents occurred. Fearful of "ethnic cleansing", those who could, fled across the Rio Grande.

Polk was preparing a message to Congress, putting forward various rationalizations for declaring war against Mexico,

when the best kind of excuse was afforded:
Mexican troops had attacked an American detachment North of the Rio Grande, and killed or captured them all.

A call for thousands of militia went to the governors of Texas and Louisiana, and Taylor sent a message to Polk saying that *"Hostilities may now be considered as commenced"*.
Polk had already pen in hand, concocting arguments for going to war, like: Mexico owes us money for damages to American citizens; and, Mexico has refused to receive my negotiator John Slidell who was sent to buy up disputed lands. But now he could declare that Mexico had *"invaded our territory and shed American blood upon American soil"*. He had the gall to exclaim that *"the cup of forbearance has been exhausted"*.

Congress promptly panicked and voted for war, 174-14 in the House, 40-2 in the Senate.
The debates were negligible. Opponents of the war felt that they could not raise their voices. Congressman Joshua Giddings of Ohio was one of a half-dozen who stuck it out, refusing to vote appropriations for the troops, declaring that he would have no part *"in the murder of Mexicans upon their own soil, or in robbing them of their country"*.

It must be said that Congress was sobered up when Polk began to ask for money to carry on the War. Then the real debate on the merits of War and expansion could be heard. Feeding the flames was the eternally bobbing-up rider, the "Wilmot Proviso", practically sure death for a money bill, since it forbade using any funds to buy land in which slavery would be allowed. (At this point in our history, both the Senate and the House were fairly evenly divided between representatives from the slave and from the free states.)

Walt Whitman, the poet, rationalized the war, but poet James Russell Lowell spoke out against it, and wondered why relations with the slave states could not be severed. Henry Thoreau then wrote his famous essay in favor of civil disobedience and went to jail for a night (until his friends bailed him out - no Socrates he)

rather than pay taxes that would go to support the war.
The Anti-Slavery Society also denounced the War.
The press was gung-ho for conquest and expansion.

It mattered not to Americans that their country could not properly use the vast lands that it already possessed. They wanted more, even without end, to hear some versions of the expansionist dream. John O'Sullivan, who coined the famous term in 1845, had said it was

*"our manifest destiny to overspread the continent
allotted by Providence
for the free development of our
yearly multiplying millions".*

The expansionist ideology took several forms. The sane propositions dealt straight-out with the profits of land-grabbing, precious metals, trade, and communications from coast to coast. They were, of course, morally impermissible. The insane ones, morally more permissible in American and some European minds, dealt with providential mission, "laws" of national development, social duties, will of God, the rightness of "Anglo-Saxon" rule over inferior peoples, and the desire to extend the benefits of American liberty to peoples everywhere. Very few talked of the costs in blood, destruction, and permanent hatred. Not to mention delusion and wickedness.

Over 100,000 men were enlisted as volunteers in the American armed forces, some thousands of them for longer terms as regulars, including sailor and marines. At first, half were foreigners. (As usual, a promise of land was made, and an immediate cash payment to keep a family alive.)

The discipline, training, and conduct of the men were on the whole bad. Many decided after a while that they had made a mistake; desertions were at the high rate of 5% in the field; several mutinies were aborted; insubordination was normal. One sizable group of deserters, Irish Catholics, thought they might find a better life on the Catholic premises of Old Mexico, but they were captured hobnobbing with Mexican troops and shot offhand.

For the most part the Americans fought more savagely than the Mexican troops, who outnumbered them generally but could complain also of bad leadership, non-exploding ammunition, and outmoded guns. Of the factors in morale, only the American food, often rotten, was worse. Disease and accidents and friendly fire accounted for more casualties than the actual fighting, which went to make this war, and most other American conflicts, the more disgusting for those who were near or into it.

The armed forces clashed in large and small engagements, all bloody and for real. Taylor's Army won two victories North of the river and then crossed the Rio Grande to occupy the town of Matamoros. He marched upon Monterrey and took it after a brief siege. There he had been joined by a column that had come from Santa Fe via El Paso.

Damage to civilian property was great. A number of civilians were killed. A large amount of killing, rape and looting was reported by Mexican and religious sources, and by shocked American officers and men. None of this was to be unusual; it occurred wherever armies were engaged. Not alone in this war, as we have learned from the colonial, Indian, and Revolutionary wars; but more would occur, in wars to come.

Taylor had already given up his best troops, on orders from President Polk, to reinforce General Winfield Scott in a new strategy: to land an army near Vera Cruz, take the town, and from there march up the highway to Mexico City. Taylor, who was a stout-hearted man, instead of standing in place, advanced Southward, there to encounter before long General Santa Anna, Houston's old foe.

It seems that Santa Anna proposed to President Polk that he be allowed to enter Mexico from his exile and ride to Mexico City, where he would set up matters for a settlement in which America would pay Mexico money in return for much territory. Instead, Santa Anna's genius was once more recognized by his countrymen: he was named President, and he led an army hastily North to strike at Taylor. The two armies fought to a stand-off at Buena Vista, and the front stabilized. Taylor went home on leave.

Scott's army met Santa Anna and the Mexican army at Cerro Gordo, where the Americans evaded a trap and won the field, taking many prisoners and much booty. Next the important town of Puebla was captured. Time out was called, because here one-third of the American Army disappeared, their periods of enlistment ended.

After several months, his forces doubled to 7,000 men by reinforcements, Scott resumed his invasion and, although losing contact with his base, was able to outflank the Eastern defenses of the City and, in several sharp clashes, conquered it. The National Palace, the "Halls of Montezuma", flew the Stars and Stripes. Santa Anna resigned and again left the country. Polk's emissary, Nicholas Trist, appeared on the scene to negotiate a peace treaty, but could find no one with whom to deal. Polk, impatient with him, dismissed him, but by the time Trist received his letter of recall, the Mexican Congress named an interim government and appointed commissioners to deal with him. So he went ahead anyway, sending an explanatory report back to Polk, who just became angrier.

However, from Guadelupe Hidalgo village, there emerged in January a treaty by that name, signed on February 2, 1848, whereby Mexico gave up all claims to all of its lands North of the Rio Grande, including besides the greatly expanded Texas, the territories of New Mexico (which included the now Arizona) and California. The United States was to pay Mexico $15 millions and to assume no more than $3.5 millions of claims of American citizens against Mexico.

Nothing was said about the destruction of Mexican towns,
or deaths and injuries to Mexican citizens.
They had simply gotten in the way.
Polk accepted the Treaty, so did the Senate.
The fleet that had been blockading the Mexican Pacific ports
was disengaged, and American forces cleared out of
what was left of Mexico that summer.
There seemed nothing much that General Taylor and General Scott
could do anymore, unless it was to run for President.
So they did.

A juvenile flag led the small motley bands that took over California

Chapter Thirty-two

California

California was a world in itself. As large as Italy, a country that it resembles significantly, in length, with a spine of mountains often covered with snow, adjoining the sea, troubled with earthquakes, and endowed with a Mediterranean climate that merges into a Northern less-warm climate, there was a latent promise that California would grow to the population of Italy. Whether they would be as comfortable, well-fed, picturesquely distributed, socially adjusted, and cultured - all this would be asking too much.

The natural regions of California confronting the human species were the hot Southern coastal area, the interior South Mohave desert merging into the Arizona desert, the central coast running from above Santa Barbara to North of San Francisco (Marin County) and then the Northern Coast Area (the Modoc), while, along the center of the state, South to North, after leaving the Southern desert, one found a Central Valley, highly fertile if its water supply were stored and controlled. The central coast was settled first, and it was not until the twentieth century that the Southern areas and central valleys came into their own. The North is still remarkably wild in appearance.

Actually the history of California - Indian, of course, but also the European - is as old as the history of the Eastern colonial states. It did not get sucked into the central vortex until its gold was exposed in 1849. Also the great population rush into the state did not begin until the 1920's. There is a Golden Age of the "Golden State" stuck in its history somewhere, but prying it out is difficult. There was always some deficiency.

Even, in the very beginning, the Indian tribes of California belonged to the least civilized tier of Indian nations. (*Nota bene:* civilized does not mean perforce happy: in the lovely setting and benign climate of Inverness Bay there dwelt a tribe by an endless source of oysters, whose void shells grew into hills from which one could have an ever-prettier vantage point to view the oyster beds as one ate oysters. I imagine that they were happy.)

As a hint of what grew to be a monstrous problem for later Californians, the region did not present adequate water supplies for even a modest population until one arrived above San Francisco. Irrigation would have worked elsewhere, but, as I said, the Indians of California... etc.

The Spanish government had sent a fleet to warn away Russian intrusions into Northern California late in the 1700's, and had constructed a fort at San Francisco. Traders of several nationalities were already there, including the Russians of Russian Hill. The Presidio got its start then. American boats appeared from time to time to purchase hides and tallow from the ranchers or their agents. They would sell or exchange what they had brought from the East or

Spanish America or the Orient.

Also in the late 1700's Father Junipero Serra and his Franciscan followers proceeded to build a chain of missions beginning at San Diego and ending at San Francisco. The missions acquired and worked large tracts of land with Indian help. The Indians in many cases acquired skills as farmers and artisans, but, too, they often might justifiably feel that they were really serfs. The architecture and method of construction of the missions would serve as a model for a great many structures to be built in California and elsewhere in the West for two centuries.

There were not half a hundred large ranches in the State but they owned most of the private land and operated much on the style of the Southern planter, compete with arrogance and imperiousness. They were reinforced by a number of additional land grantees, beneficiaries of an 1824 law of the new Mexican republic. Ever avaricious for labor, these oligarchs inveigled the government in 1833 to confiscate the missions and expel the Franciscans, to free the Indians from obligations to the church, to privatize and dispose of the lands. Seven hundred huge ranchos resulted from the confiscation of church lands and the freed Indians were promptly subjected to the brutal and harrowing conditions of serfdom on the *rancho grande.*

In 1846 there were an estimated eight to twelve thousand Hispanics, about 800 Americans, and some thousands of Indians in California. The Americans were shipping agents, traders, trappers, ranchers, adventurers, mariners, outlaws, and employees of Spanish interests. The Spanish capital was at Monterey down the coast a ways from San Francisco.

Into this scene stalked John Fremont, politician, explorer, author, and adventurer. He had moved around most of the West from his base in Missouri. He appeared now in California as leader of a band of sixty men who to all appearances were mountain men, but whom he referred to as his exploring party. He was ordered out of Spanish territory by the governor and left apparently for Oregon.

Another group of Hispanics and Americans then took over the office of the government in Sonoma, and declared the independence of California (with the Texas case in mind). They raised a flag with a bear emblazoned upon it.

Neither the Republic nor the Bear lasted long, because news of the Mexican-American War arrived and an American fleet appeared and landed marines. The Mexican authorities escaped to the South. A Commodore Stockton appeared and pronounced himself Governor of California and Commander-in-Chief of whatever armed forces might be available; he could at least count on his fleet.
Fremont had reappeared and was designated Commander-in-Chief of Northern California. Next, Santa Barbara and Los Angeles were occupied.

Meanwhile, Stephen Kearney, with an Army brevet, left Fort Bent and took the Santa Fe trail to Sante Fe, arriving on the heels of the Governor of New Mexico. He now decided to march with a large company to California. On the trail, he met Fremont's favorite scout, Kit Carson, also a man with a large Eastern public, and learned from Carson of the occupation of California.

He sent part of his force South, and continued westward. Upon arrival in the San Diego area, he discovered that a popular revolt had restored the Mexicans to power in Los Angeles. So he joined up with the Commodore's forces and together they overcame the Loyalists, and restored American control. The date was January 13 of 1847.

An interested observer of the excitement was a certain John A. Sutter, a Swiss-American who had been a trader in Missouri and Oregon before setting up shop in the Sacramento area. He had obtained from the Mexican government a permit to construct a utopian village of New Helvetia (usually called Sutter's Fort) for Swiss immigrants, whom he proposed to obtain. All sorts of people found his Swiss village attractive, and it was soon filled. It later became the city of Sacramento. He owned much land, including a stretch up-river that proved to carry gold.

The area around became the scene of the greatest gold rush known yet to history. It was an arena of wild greed, theft and murder. Yet men thought and acted to set up rules of fair play, of trial and judgement. The Puritan ethic was dug out of the recesses of the mind. The philosopher, Josiah Royce was there in 1849, and long afterwards wrote, *"In the air,..the invisible net of social duties hung, and descending, enmeshed irresistibly all these gay and careless fortune-hunters even while they boasted of their freedom".* In these transient communities - there had been and would be thousands of them around the country, the consensus among the people seemed to be that good law was self-evident, that the law was there to be discovered, that the law was in the Bible, and that the law was in every man's heart.

Perhaps this should be regarded as the code of the good vigilantes. California was the largest most enduring center for vigilantism, particularly San Francisco, where the "best men" of the community were volunteer members of the committee to maintain order in the midst of chaos. Vigilantism was needed - there can be little question - in circumstances where public authority was absent or non-existent, a crime has been committed, and the culprit was sure to get beyond the reach of any law very soon.

Many thousands of men left their homes and jobs around the country to board ships that circumnavigated South America or ride whatever combination of land vehicles was possible, in order to arrive at the gold fields before all the gold was gone. For most, the gold never panned out. For a few it did. Largest profits were made by men like Sutter who sold panning equipment, picks and shovels and grub to the prospectors. An estimated 100,000 immigrants descended upon the region, with the usual representation of New England "school teachers", and most of them stayed, having no home or job elsewhere.

Californians were most eager to become a territory and then a state. They had now to deal with a Mexican war hero, General Zachary Taylor, for he had wasted no time in running for the presidency and getting elected. He cannily advised them to apply directly for admission as a state, by-passing the status of territory. They did so and within a year Congress had granted statehood.

Many Southerners were unnerved at the procedure, particularly since Taylor was himself a slave-holder. They would have felt even worse if they could have foreseen that California's Central Valley would become the richest cotton-growing area in the world.

The North and West are supposed by many to have been creatures of the railroads, that, without them, they would have remained frontiers. Actually they were rapidly filling up without a single railroad, and should probably have continued to do so. Even the Civil War did nothing to staunch the flow of humanity and animals. The terrible War might as well have not been happening.

Besides the old trails that now carried streams of wagons, pack animals, pushcarts, and plodders, there were regular clipper ships between East and West coasts; both the Panamanian portage route and the around-Cape Horn route were heavily employed. In 1858 a stagecoach between East and West entered service, the Butterfield and Overland Express.

Several years later Wells-Fargo Company unleashed the Pony Express to carry mail expensively, but it lasted only eighteen months, except in the mythology of childhood, because telegraph lines were posted across the nation and, when they were not cut by Indians or varmints, they could provide instant communication from coast to coast. By 1860 50,000 miles of wire were humming.

But there was no stopping the railroad in the imagination of continental expansionists. It stormed along on the rails snorting of manifest destiny. The transcontinental railroad company that was blocked by Southern Congressmen before the Civil War was able to begin work promptly, war or no war.

Union Pacific Railroad Company promoters received a Congressional charter (note the use of a Congressional power - unexpressed in the Constitution - to charter corporations for transportation and to subsidize them); they were given the right of way for the track, free cutting of timber and mining of minerals occurring on any public land useful in competing their job, and ten square miles of land along the right of way for every mile of track laid, a generous grant soon to be doubled.

Moreover, Congress agreed to award the Union Pacific thousands of dollars for every mile built. They were to begin in Nebraska and proceed to the California border. Similar terms were given the Central Pacific to begin in California and connect up with the UP. In May 1869 the connection was made near Ogden, Utah. Other companies entered the game, and soon several lines crossed the nation.

A few men made millions of dollars knowing little of railroading. They even grafted huge amounts, making contracts with themselves to supply materials to themselves at large profits, and selling stocks and bonds to the public at fraudulently inflated prices.

A great many Chinese and Irish and other ethnic and native laborers knowing little of railroading worked for wages that in many cases covered the cost of bringing a loved one from the Old Country. Many workers died from accidents, violence, or disease. Every milestone could be called a gravestone.

Chicago soon became the busiest railroad center in the world, just as three political generations later it would house the busiest airport in the world. The Atchison, Topeka, and Santa Fe and the other trains could now stop along the way and pick up the hordes of cattle driven on the hoof to the railhead, and the beasts could ride rapidly in discomfort for the rest of their short unhappy lives.

But the age of the great cattle drives was nearing an end. Not because of the railroads alone, reaching out to wherever the herds were gathered; in 1874 the first barbed wire appeared. Soon everyone could fence out cattle, and did.

The railroad bosses could do much more. They could make deals with foreign agents to round up immigrants and transport them to a point on the right of way, where the railroaders could sell them land and supply all of their needs at a profit. They could charge ruinous prices for carrying goods and animals, if they pleased. They could pass up a disfavored location in order to stop at a favored location. There were more of such tricks.

A great many people - passengers, workers, farmers, suppliers, towns and villages, stockholders - were cheated, discriminated against, driven out of business; but the railroads grew at a tremendous speed, laying more track than could be found in all of Europe. It was the American way: make haste, get the job done, tolerate no interference, lay the costs on others, hope for a large profit, live it up - on your private train.

Actually, most railroad inventions were European, even down to the standard gauge tracks, 4 feet, 8.5 inches, which descended from the axle span of Roman war chariots via wagon wheels, via English rail tracks, via imported English builders. American locomotives were faster and less durable than their European counterparts; they had more crashes, and more workers were killed and disabled, 30,000 brakemen a year at the prideful height of railroading. But men gloried to be railroaders, even when engaged in the violent strikes that sometimes occurred. The glamour lasted for a hundred years, until about 1947 and the age of the airplane.

Scholars have lately pointed out that the West was always a land of urban centers, with never more than a few people in between. Salt Lake City, Kansas City, and San Francisco come to mind. In 1847 San Francisco was a quiet Hispanic village of 500 persons, yet by 1880 contained 233,000 residents, one of the top-ranking cities of the nation. It had a wealthy elite living in palatial homes. A pioneering group of merchants built up the city and led it in all of its various voluntary and governmental institutions through the 1850's after which a more general elite infiltrated.

A separate Chinese population and merchant leadership also developed. Japanese tended more to farm labor, numbering half the total working the land by 1909. They organized themselves into oligarchic work groups that brought them the best conditions of any farm workers in the nation, a total adapted collective life. A young immigrant, George Shima, came to control by 1913 85% of the California potato crop.

Only about 15% of California adult males were domiciled with wives in 1852. By 1880 the sex ratio was even. Obviously, with such a seven-to-one in-migration rate, women of all kinds were skipping into the state in search of mates.

No more than one percent of the population constituted a recognized elite. Among these were already national figures of wealth and power: Charles Crocker, Leland Stanford, Colles Huntington, Mark Hopkins - all of the railroads; James Fair, James Flood, William O'Brien, and John Mackay - all miners. The major part of the early elite was otherwise composed of merchants and industrialists. A political generation later capitalists, company executives, politicians real estate dealers and professional men had taken over half the top rankings.

The elite was open, by contrast with the Boston and Charleston (pre-Civil War) elites. Although Jews were present to the number of 7% of the population, they were much more evident in the elite, where they constituted about 20% of the total listings. Several of the top Jews such as Levi Strauss - he of the canvas pants - were in the Christian rather than the Jewish list of addresses, suggesting perhaps that they were asked to choose which list to belong to and opted out of the Jewish ranks. Yet anti-semitism was part of the City's heritage, too, and not until a century later were the last Clubs to lose their Christians-only designation.

As the city grew large, rich, and productive, the lot of the working class changed not at all. The rich who ruled the city did not save their incomes but spent lavishly in consumption. When Dennis Kearney extended the proscription list of his workingman's party to include, besides the Chinese, the rich, capitalists, manufacturers and importers, the rich formed a vigilante Committee of Safety, armed with the latest weapons and aided by mercenaries. The mostly unarmed gangs of workers disbanded under the threat. Despite all the glamour attendant upon its location and supposed opportunities to get rich quick, after the first merchants had their two decades, the city afforded no more chances to rise economically, and therefore otherwise, except to a degree in politics, than any Northern city in the East. Indeed, one scholar theorizes that the activities of the Vigilance Committees over three decades indicates a large sense of frustration among the old and aspiring merchant class who had lost their pre-eminence.

Racial and ethnic animosities were strong throughout, and anti-semitic and anti-Catholic discrimination continuous until after World War II. Breakthroughs were made infrequently, by individuals among the German-Jews, by persons such as the banker A.P.Giannini who had been born in Italy and founded the Bank of Italy that became later the largest bank in the country, the Bank of America, and by attorney-politicians and leading professionals and professors.

Amadeo Peter Giannini, in fact, would offer stiff competition to John Jacob Astor, John D. Rockefeller, J.P. Morgan and the like for the all-American entrepreneurial crown: He began farm labor at 13 for an adoptive father, became a well-to-do produce dealer, opened his bank, then, spurred on by the Earthquake, took to the road literally with wagonloads of cash to lend to disaster-stricken farmers and ranchers. His policy of lending to the small farmer and businessman, his method of extending banking by setting up branches wherever the demand existed - finally moving beyond California - usually in the face of opposition by local banks, large conservative banks, state bank regulators and later federal officials - became universal practices in America a half-century later.

His bank financed much of the growth of the Hollywood film industry. He disbursed shares and assets as he aged, never direction, and when he died, a mythical figure, he left an estate of under half a million dollars. It may be remarked that the fathers both of Giannini and a second "California's greatest son" of the next generation, Governor and Chief Justice of the United States Supreme Court Earl Warren, were murdered by maddened workmen on the job, when the sons were mere boys.

The beautiful city of San Francisco attracted a culture of poor artists and musicians, of a rewarding, remarkable Chinatown and Little Italy, of close relations with exotic Pacific peoples, of Jewish-endowed public institutions, and finally a quickly superior quasi-democratic university at Berkeley across the Bay and another one, of less consequence, Stanford University, at Palo Alto, so that, in the face of rather weak competition, it could boast of being at the top among American cities in life-style, and in popular and sophisticated culture.

The Oregon Trail

Chapter Thirty-three

North and West

No one in the world has had as many chances as the American to draw the boundaries of autonomous political jurisdictions with due regard for geographical, economic, and cultural considerations. Most of the chances were muffed. The shapes of the original thirteen colonies were pointless enough. Compare Rhode Island with New York. Too, New Jersey, Maryland and Delaware. There is hardly a reasonable boundary line from North to South.

Of course, we know that there was already a perception that the small states might be asked to rectify themselves out of existence if they did not guard their borders; so they insisted upon inserting a clause in the Constitution that forbade any change in state boundaries without the consent of the states involved. On the western side of the original Thirteen States, however, it may be said that the ridges of the Alleghenies justify the lines in some cases.

Then begin the combinations of rectangles and rivers, and even these become more meaningless when the rivers out West become less influential. When Jefferson said that a revolution every generation may be a good thing, he should explicitly have added that a change of boundaries every generation might also be good. This would allow for demographic and economic changes. (But not until the age of computers - actually not until after the traumatic experience of bearing the info-behemoth through the year 2000 - will we have been able to change all the millions of dependent records to conform immediately to the new lines.)

The same absurdity is present in the boundaries of the several thousand counties of the country. And the situation respecting cities is as bad and has worse consequences because of the enormous inefficiencies generated by the clash of dozens of jurisdictions within a given metropolitan area. I say this as I look at the map of the Northern and Western states, and, too, at the metropolitan regions of the East and Midwest.

We know how the pieces were acquired. In fact, we now know how all of the continental United States was acquired. Puerto Rico, Hawaii, the little islands, and Alaska can be dealt with later. We know that five early new states lined up along the Ohio River, Kentucky (1792), Ohio (1803), Indiana (1816), Illinois (1818), and Tennessee (1796), which wedged itself in to where the Ohio enters the Mississippi River. The states of Alabama and Mississippi stand up above the Gulf of Mexico. It is not at all clear why Florida (1845) should have been left with its Panhandle running below Georgia and Alabama (1819), although its history tells why. Louisiana (1812) sits compactly in part below Mississippi (1817), reasonably in view of the ecological and ethnic makeup of the huge delta, but then shoots up to a straight line boundary with Arkansas (1836). Why? No good reason.

All the way to Canada we find these straight lines, with Missouri (1821), Iowa (1846), and Minnesota (1858). Back across the "Father of Waters" we find straight lines separating Wisconsin (1848) from Illinois, and Indiana and Ohio from Michigan (1847).
For no good reason, Michigan leaps across Lake Michigan to form an enclave that distinguishes itself from Wisconsin by a squiggly line. The business of this area is definitely to the South in Wisconsin and Illinois, except where governmental decree forces it to cross the Lake into the real Michigan to pay taxes and receive state salaries and benefits.

A second tier of states is drawn about Texas (1845). The first block has an unreasonable panhandle, and was designed to box in some Indian tribes that had been conveyed on death marches from the East. It became Oklahoma ultimately (1875) with shrunken Indian nations included. Above Oklahoma, big trouble begins: Kansas territory (1854; statehood 1861), where slavers occupy the South and Free Soilers the North. A line is drawn and the solution seems to appear, Nebraska Territory (1854, statehood 1867), that, said the Southerners, could be made free, if Kansas were to be a slave state.
Never, said John Brown and many others.

Above Nebraska a straight line is drawn, and to the North the Dakota territories (1861), soon to be sliced in half into North Dakota (l889) and South Dakota (1889). Much of this is Indian country, supposedly reserved for the Sioux nation and others.

We step to the West and we come upon the remaining eleven states, all of them affected by rectangularism. The first tier from South to North holds New Mexico (1863, statehood 1912), Colorado (1861, statehood 1876), Wyoming (1863, statehood 1890) and Montana (1864, statehood 1889). The second tier contains Arizona (1863, statehood 1912), Utah (1868, statehood 1896) and Nevada (1864) side by side, then Idaho (1863, statehood 1890), with its panhandle pointing up to Canada). Only the Pacific Coast trio is left, California (1850), Oregon (1859), and Washington (1863, statehood 1889).

Territories, we note, waited varying lengths of time

before gaining statehood; California waited not at all, Utah until 1896, Arizona for 60 years; the time taken had nothing to do with preparation or tutelage, but to national political issues, such as sectionalism, slavery, party affiliation in the territory, the practice of polygamy (Utah), ethnicism, jockeying for patronage and command of resources.

The Old Northwest is the term used for the territory North of the Ohio River and East of the Mississippi that was legally turned over to the United States in 1783. It was larger than France. It was mostly rolling prairie, heavily forested, with pine barrens in Michigan and large flat grassy plains in Illinois. In 1785 the Confederation Congress ordered it surveyed, and two years later gave it governmental form. Squatters were ordered out; some left, most did not. Veterans were awarded land. Speculative and settlement companies bought large tracts.

Pioneers and settlers came, or were coaxed in. By 1810 Ohio held 230,000 people. By 1815, the number was 400,000. (The effect of the 1812 War was small.) It was definitely a pluralist culture, ranging from Kentuckians to New Englanders, and holding a great many European newcomers. One commentator refers to "almost a migratory furor" in New England in 1815. The Ohio migration proceeded to Indiana and thence into Illinois. It would soon cross the Mississippi River into Iowa.

Travelers give us a fair impression of rural Ohio: roads extremely rough, land fertile but hilly, tall trees, log cabins, "ugly women", many ragged, unschooled children, no sign of industry, ample grain, fat horses, lots of whiskey, plums and peaches, deer, wild turkey, vicious hogs, no building stone, no school, ague, sick milk, frequent flooding. Settling fanned out from the river banks, ten miles, thirty, fifty, until it met people fanning out from another river or a Great Lake shore.

Conventions in the several new states to draw up constitutions were hardly exertions of imagination and planning.

The federal constitution was the safe model, which could readily win approval by Congress. Snippets from older state constitutions were patched in, if admired and necessary. Easier to amend than the federal constitution, they became longer and longer as the generations passed.

The Framers believed that they had solved the currency problem by putting it in the hands of the Federal government. But not enough species, banknotes and credit for expansion of the economy was provided. Everyone wanted species, but the National Bank, until it was closed down, and then after reconstitution in 1817, and the Eastern banks, generally wanted it too, partly because their European correspondents insisted upon cash. The relatively more secured banks would not deal with the debtors and other banks without receiving some species as least in any transaction. By 1818 all species was sucked out of the West. Gold and silver coins were cut into pieces, into bits, which were used for smaller transactions.

The old as well as new states let individuals and syndicates set up banks. Indiana and Michigan set up true State Banks. Indiana's system consisted of ten branches of equal weight. Private banks multiplied. All printed their own bank notes, containing promises to pay the bearer in species or other bank notes. Someone said in 1816 that a bank would be set up at every church, every smithy, every tavern. In retrospect, the disastrous chaos of banking produced a great many people who learned something about the role of money in the economy, a college of hard knocks. It was, wrote one newspaper, *"a jubilee of swindlers and the Saturnalia of non-specie paying banks"*.

Early state government was simple, as were the people who ran it. In Indiana's first year it borrowed $25,000 to pay off a small debt left over from its territorial prior existence and pay its expenses. By 1823 its treasury showed a balance of $33,661. It levied a tax on non-residents that had to be cleverly contrived to avoid the ban on discrimination against citizens of other states. A smaller tax affected residents' land, at a minuscule flat rate, which allowed the rich to pay hardly more than the poor.

There seemed to be nothing to spend money on, until an urge to help counties improve roads was felt, and a means of constructing canals came about. Soon, Illinois and the other states' finances were complicated by schemes to sell land from here and there, to borrow money here, lend money there, tax this one, toll that one, pay this one in land, that one in concessions - all to get the hundreds of thousands of dollars needed for the smaller and then larger waterways. The counties were administrative agents of the state, and were usually delinquent in handing over receipts on time.

Corruption was common in the Old Northwest, but, until the sums of money and notes moving through the account books became large and the public till could be robbed directly, the typical bribe occurred in the exchange of favors, the lending of facilities to legislators and officials, and the payment of cash purchases in notes of wavering value. Differences existed among the States, some of it attributable more to ethnic and religious differences. Corruption was less common in areas where the German and Scandinavian Lutheran presence was not only numerous in proportion to total inhabitants, but also influential in the government. It was more common where the Southern Protestant presence was heavy.

Scandinavians began to arrive in significant numbers in the 40's and usually headed for jobs at large construction projects or into the Northernmost regions of Michigan, Wisconsin, and Minnesota, whence they, like the Germans, wended westward from one generation to the next.

Some of the people who were employed and kept ranches and cereal fields in the far Midwest region stayed. Some of the farmers moved in who had failed farther East, usually of Scandinavian and German stock, but with a representation of settlers of Slavic culture. Inevitably more farmers of the West failed, or endured incessant hardship, than prospered. Land was cheap enough to suck in would-be farmers from as far off as Latvia; but livestock, wagons, tools, horses, fences and most other items were costly enough to bring failure, and when the survivors or their replacements were confronted with the second wave of technological invasion in the form of mechanical equipment of all kinds, for pumping water, plowing, seeding, harvesting, threshing, and transporting, the ranks of the farmers were once more reduced to a few by their costs.

The gyrations of the commodities markets took their toll regularly, also. As did natural disaster: tornadoes, wind and hail storms, early freezes, floods, plagues of locusts, dust storms and drought. The vast far Midwest and the high plains down to Texas have been among the toughest farming and ranching regions of the world; and much of the region has been damaged by excessive exploitation and poor conservation practices. Luckily the surplus population could move quickly elsewhere; in India and China, the millions died, because of over-population without outlet for the reckless breeding, but basically their soil and climate were superior to the American.

We might delineate the other subcultures of the West in relation to the state boundaries, but we need say only a word of their substance. From Montana down through Colorado a cattle and mining culture. In New Mexico and Arizona, wherever possible, Anglos especially, but also Hispanics, ran cattle. The Southern part of New Mexico became culturally Texan; Texans moved straight through, the Southern hill type especially, until arriving in California, where they helped constitute, with many Chicanos, Mexican-Americans, prairie Northerners, and pluralist Easterners, a Southern Pacific Coast cosmopolitan sub-culture.

Early Hispanic culture persisted with the Indians of Northern New Mexico and Arizona, a high coolish area, fairly isolated, until they were joined by a Northern chic crowd in considerable numbers in the twentieth century. Nevada was virtually empty until some Basque and Italian herders occupied the pastures and grazed sheep; some large landholders introduced also the cowboy culture. Mines were developed there of value, and the gambling industry mined tourists, beginning in the 1920's, when Californians in numbers would be able to visit.

There was no real break naturally between California and Oregon, only an end to the Spanish claim. So Southern Oregon blends with Northern California and then moves up into the Willamette valley, a highly fertile region that invited early settlers from the Midwest, who were in many cases descended from New England - Upper New York Yankee culture.

To the North depends Washington State, that is not naturally distinguishable from Oregon until it arrives at the Puget Sound region. Moving Eastward, one encounters the interior Spokane region, much drier, and South of this the Columbia River region of Washington and Oregon. Fish, timber, and orcharding were original major occupations, and remained important through the industrialization that brought aircraft industry and frozen foods processing industry to the region.

Commercial netting of fish began on the Columbia River in 1823, well before most "pioneers" arrived. By 1883, Chinook salmon were being taken and canned at 55 canneries.
By 1890, one memorial generation from the beginning, and when the American frontier was said to have just ended, the Chinook salmon had been practically extincted.
The catch and canning of other species continued apace until the "New" Northwest became piscatorially exhausted.
A considerable dam for producing hydro-electric power and controlling flooding was first built in 1933, so dams did not cause depletion of fish stocks.
They simply assured that the species could not recover even if all fishing were to halt.

We note how cleanly the ruler swept across all of these tiers West of the Mississippi going from South to North, in all except a couple of cases. Within the States, too, the rectangle shaped a thousand counties. Does any human factor except the lazy measuring rod correspond to such boundary lines? Did the Indian nations live behind straight lines? Were not their territories more natural? Indeed they were, and it took a lot of terrible pulling and stretching and evicting and eradication to get them to where they would not cross these mad lines of the White man. And the mythically rational man of the Enlightenment, Thomas Jefferson, was responsible for the straight lines more than anybody.

Montana and Wyoming were Indian country. They might have remained so forever, so far as agriculture and industry were concerned, but they had treasures in the ground that could not be left to the diffident Indians. So the mining companies came in, financed and directed from the East, using as miners whatever poor men and new immigrant group came along when the mines opened up. The process continued until the mines, most of them, closed.

We are talking big deals politically, a few great mining companies had the largest voice in these states, seconded by the railroad magnates; and we can add Idaho and Nevada, South Dakota and North Dakota; altogether they have twelve U.S. senators, six members of the House of Representatives, and a total six-State population equivalent to one Black Congressional district of the city of Chicago, one of a number of equally populous districts in the old city and its heavily populated suburbs.

Imagine the attention to African-American problems that might ensue if this one district could have Twelve U.S. Senators representing it in Congress in addition to its modest influence on the two Illinois Senators. There might seem to be a need for a second Civil War in this situation, which is, of course, national, and not confined to the example here.

It must be recalled, or rather, said in advance - that the U.S. Senate, with its over-representation of the slave states, allowed the slave controversy to persist and exhaust exorbitant amounts of civic energy in America from the beginning, up to, and beyond the Civil War, and even today.

But dutifully, the statesmen of America went ahead constructing one state after another each with two senators and almost without people while certain areas in a few states were assembling huge populations. This grotesque over-representation of thinly populated states has had uncounted effects, apart from making the Civil War inevitable.

In the period of which we speak here, the decades
nearing mid-century when the territories and
their later shadows the states were being put
together, the infinitude of crimes against the Indian
nations evolved partly from the attitudes and policies of the
territorial-state governments toward their Indian populations.
A few half-educated and half-civilized Caucasian
males were given the vast powers of the American State,
originally intended for highly experienced historical units,
to govern their internal populations, and in addition,
as if to ensure that their internal policies would prevail,
they were given representation in the Senate equal to that of
Virginia or New York or Massachusetts.

Here is one more occasion to point to
the direct democratic ideology - Jacksonian democracy -
as a damaging feature of American history:
who would be so bold in the American democracy to assert
that "those courageous men who have conquered the wilderness and
prepared it for statehood" should be deemed incompetent
to write a constitution, gauge its problems,
set its course, and operate it from day to day.
Rarely had so ill-prepared and temperamentally ill-suited lot
of men been shouldered with such enormous capital resources
and the operating responsibilities of government.

It is highly ironic that the Utah people,
probably the best prepared of all territorial cadres
since those of the original thirteen states,
should have been kept waiting at the door almost half a century,
while a score of buffooneries passed through,
on the supposition that simultaneous polygyny
was a fatal evil, serial polygyny not.

The same incident gave the laugh to the theory that
states rights and states autonomy were especially creditable,
because they provided a means of conducting social experiments,
which, proven beneficial, might then be emulated by other states.

Indeed, the reason why populous States' representatives in Congress did not do their best to block the admission of some of these territories was that a number of them had their agents in these territories wheeling and dealing on their behalf for land, mining stocks, and other favors which the mining companies and railroads might dispense. The long term interest of their own constituencies and of the nation hardly concerned them.

Furthermore, since the large interests holding these states in hand were universally Eastern, these same representatives could say that effectively the new states were acting in tandem with their own states' (read "their own corporate and speculator clients' ' ") business.

By 1850 practically every religious sect was well-represented in the Old Northwest. There must have been a hundred at least. There were more Methodist churches, 3,000, than Baptist and Presbyterian (the next most numerous) taken together. The other major denominations tailed considerably behind, the Catholics and Lutherans, for instance, with about 400 churches each. There were some 200 Friends meeting houses, 3 Jewish temples (all in Ohio). The New Northwest was not much different.

The Mormons of Utah were, unlike the Unitarians of Massachusetts, a distinctively new religious sect "made in America". Founder of Mormonism in 1830, amidst the universal excitement of the Great Revival, was Joseph Smith, a farm laborer from Vermont. Aged 14, he claimed a confrontation with God, then at 17 with an Angel named Moroni, who dictated to him from a set of golden hieroglyph tablets, later lost, and a section of the Bible, also mislaid, announcing a new way of Christian worship for the world. He composed numerous inspired

texts in his short lifetime. One need not believe him
any more than believe that his Puritan forbears had
a pipeline to God. Max Weber, dean of
Religionssoziologie, regarded him as a fraud;
this is a technical distinction that does not get one
very far in the comparative study of religions.

His calling to set up an Israel in the New World
was foreshadowed by the two-century old Puritan claim
to be the new Israel. The Pilgrims themselves were
regarded in England like the sect of Jehovah's Witnesses
of today, reason enough to abandon so unsympathetic a society.
The Mormons, soon numbering thousands,
were convinced of their moral superiority and
capacity to create a new moral order.

With their neighbors of Palmyra unconvinced,
and disturbed by the success of their new order,
they thought they should move along,
so they descended upon Kirtland, Ohio,
Independence, Missouri, then up to Nauvoo, Illinois
for five years, culminating in dissension,
betrayal, mob violence, and the mob killing
of Joseph and Hyrum Smith.
Brigham Young succeeded to the leadership and
promised the surrounding forces of evil that he would
get the sect out of their territory.

He read John Fremont's book of western exploration and
put his finger on a deserted impregnable area
with a good water supply.
It was the basin of the Great Salt Lake,
in Mexican territory.
They set up relief stations along the route,
with a major rendezvous at the junction of the Platte
and Missouri Rivers. About 15,000 pilgrims
succeeded in making the journey by 1848,
lucky ones with wagons, others with mules,
many with push-carts, and most in all or part on foot.
The land was no longer a Promised Land in Mexico;

it was part of the United States,
conceded upon the end of the Mexican War.
Had it not been, it would have become another Texas,
for the Mormons would not have served Mexico.
As it was, they did not want to serve the USA.

Brigham Young had to leave behind a wife, Emma.
She, with her sons and a few followers of Brigham,
settled in Independence, where Joseph Smith III
became Prophet, Seer, and Revelator. These
Reorganized Mormons joined Emma in denying that
Joseph I ever practiced polygyny,
taught poly-theism, baptized the dead, or
promised all would become gods.

Brigham Young did not suffer for lack of the
companionship of women. Married 27 times,
he was survived by 17 wives and 57 children.
He endorsed polygamy in 1852, which was
practiced from the first by Joseph Smith. The Mormon
establishment of Utah was more of New England than of
Middle Atlantic or Southern Culture. And from the
beginning, even while Mormons arrived ahead of
many frontiersmen at the frontier, theirs could not be
classified as a frontier culture.

It numbered many thousands of immigrants, mainly from
Great Britain, where Brigham Young had proselytized.
It remained patriarchal whereas all American cultures,
including the New England, replaced the father by the son
as the protagonist of America. Its mentality had also in it the
Yankee ability at keeping account books and merchandising.
(Joseph Smith's implication in a bank fraud in Kirtland, Ohio,
indicates a penchant for white-collar practices.)
A well-disciplined hierarchical structure
and secret proceedings out-did the Masonic order,
for there was nothing avocational about them;
Mormanism was practically totalitarian.

The Mormons got an effective irrigation system going,

a major achievement, and before long were selling
produce to the passing procession on the Oregon Trail.
Mormon culture and technology were forward-looking.
The thearchs saw to it that a proper
tithe was paid in to the treasury of the theocracy.

Bigamy was practiced, but within two fecund
biological generations was abandoned, save among extremists.
Some say that it became immoral,
some say it became needless,
others say that they had to quit as a condition
of Utah becoming a State. At any rate,
monogamy was enshrined in the Constitution.

It is doubtful that Utah could have been settled,
except as another Nevada or Montana,
were it left to the motley crowd that would have
happened in upon it in the absence of the Mormons.
Given that they were driven from New York,
and again from Missouri and Illinois by vigilantes and rioters
(the period we recall as employing the mob on
hundreds of occasions as the fourth branch of democratic
government), the hatred of Mormonism could have
aroused a holy crusade against heretics and bigamists that might
have marched upon them and exterminated them.
Perhaps the Mexican War and the Civil War
deflected the destructive energies of the paranoid and
socially atomized gun-toting population that might
otherwise have struck at them.

The Mormons, as fundamentalist people of the Book,
two Books, indeed, were paranoid to a fault,
redoubled by the persecution they suffered.
They bound themselves into a diligent tribe,
and built a civilization of true believers
in America's forbidding Great Basin,
intending to become a separate nation, not
American, but a new Israel.

A crisis occurred when President Buchanan, bowing to

media abusiveness, and hoping to divert attention from the slavery and succession crisis, appointed in 1857 a new Governor of the Territory of Utah to replace Brigham Young. At signs that the Mormons would resist the change, he despatched 2500 troops to enforce Federal rule. The Mormons feared for their lives and, worse, the destruction of their religion. So they armed more heavily, cached food supplies in the mountains, enlisted the support of Paiutes and other Indian neighbors against the Americans, sent a call to all Mormons everywhere to return to Utah to repel the invaders, declared a scorched earth policy, and figured how they might carry on a prolonged resistance from mountain redoubts.

When a large double wagon train from Arkansas and Missouri swung South to cross into California, and gave evidence of scorn and hostility, local Mormon leaders made false accusations and reports, and, not without the knowledge of topmost Mormons, organized with the Paiutes a treacherous massacre and pillaging of the train, killing some 120 men, women and children mercilessly, sparing only 18 children "too young to talk". The Mountain Meadows Massacre was hushed up for a century, except that a single man, prominently accused, was brought to trial by federal authorities after twenty years, convicted, brought to the scene of the massacre, and shot by firing squad. He was widely pronounced the scapegoat. He was later forgiven by the Church.

To the North and East, Mormon militia burned their own new villages and farms on the frontier, marched out to meet the Federal troops, captured more than half of the supplies and animals of their foes, and left them to suffer grievously from hunger and cold over the winter. A ballet of politicking ensued, which ended with President Buchanan pardoning the whole Church leadership, in a parade of Federal troops (through deserted streets past blinded windows), and in the admission of the designated Governor's

right to undertake the duties of his office.
Brigham Young and his Councillors now
ran the Territory from the wings of the stage.

The Mormons edged out beyond Utah into all five of their
neighboring states. They also established congregations in a
number of cities of the Americas. Its theocracy was
missionary as well, and began the practice of sending out the
young to proselytize around America and
in all world cultures that would admit them.
Many Europeans were converted in Europe and emigrated
directly to Utah. The Mormons were hardly more Christian than
Muslim, who adored Jesus but lived by the Prophet Mahomet,
counterpart to Joseph Smith. Yet, except to theologians,
they seemed later to be assuredly American,
cultural heroes in some ways.

Mormonism represented historically the
most successful agrarianism in the United States,
the most elegant transition to an age of science and technology.
Founded by poor men, they seemed instinctively to grasp
what was needed to prosper in a new age.
Universal education was foremost in their minds.

They combined the contradictory qualities of religious
fundamentalism and pragmatism in an
American schizotype. In a country of
extreme individualism, they displayed a complete
corporatism or communitarianism.
Religious, social, political and vocational participation was
asked of everyone, and almost universally loyally
granted to this successful utopia.
The Church of Jesus Christ of Latter-Day Saints.

Mormon Trek West

Part Seven

THE VOLUNTARY CULTURE

It is my contention that civil disobediences are but the latest form of voluntary association, and that they are thus quite in tune with the oldest traditions of the country.
HANNAH ARENDT

The first voluntary act of Americanism was mental.
Even when driven here by the direst of circumstances,
most first-generation Americans from earliest times
had to think at some point, *"I'm going to become an American"* -
half a wish, half an expectation.
To think of joining a nation is a staggering idea,
so extraordinary that it is accepted without reflection,

like the air one breathes. It is different, say,
from the English going into Ireland proclaiming
"Well, you are now English",
or the French going to Corsica saying "You are now French",
or the Germans doing the same in Alsace,
or the Soviets in Estonia.
Beginning with only a voluntary tie to the state,
the individualistic ego expands greatly.

Yes, the critic says, and that's where all the trouble begins.

Self-help is part of the voluntaristic ethic.
Specifically, it probably began with the problem of Protestants,
newly detached from the Catholic Universal Church,
who had now to save themselves in order to get to heaven.
Much of the history of Protestantism became then a
dialectic of self-help. One had to get all the way from original sin to
possible, while uncertain, salvation by one's personal efforts.

Catholicism can be seen in the same perspective, of course. But
Catholics had long lost the Augustinian sense of urgency that now
beset the Protestants. The "better kind" of people who came to
America had been reading Lewis Bayly's *The Practice of Piety*
(1612). John Bunyan's allegory of worldliness, temptation, and
successful struggle to achieve salvation, *A Pilgrim's Progress,* had
appeared in 1678. The Americans began to cook up their own share
of self-help recipes in Cotton Mather's *The Christian at His Calling*,
1701. In America, however, the Catholic Church itself became more
Augustinian, that is, intent upon self-help and self-salvation.

Self-help at its best was and is an
ordering and care for the self and the interests of the self -
family affection, work, feeding, learning - in a decent fashion,
without intruding upon the self-helping activities of others or
impinging upon the welfare of the whole group.

At its worst, self-help was aggressive selfishness, even criminality,
and the attitude usually associated with it toward others:
"Root, hog, or die!" or
"It's every man for himself, and the

Devil take the hindmost".

Social and personal training in America always praised self-help,
found much for it to do, and paid it well in respect, money,
new experience, and power. Few doubted that
"God helps those who help themselves".

One problem of self-help persists:
it was forever touted as necessary on the way to salvation;
salvation obviously is the most important achievement
any person could hope for; but, self-help as a way to solve
the mess of social problems and personal problems,
which depended upon the response of others,
failed on countless occasions.
Yet, instead of turning to mutual help as an
ethically equally good path to mundane goals, it was often belittled,
not only in neighborhood affairs,
but as an admissible major means in politics.
Mutual support in politics was highly opportunistic and personal.

If one could get to heaven only through self-help,
surely he could solve mere social problems the same way.
But what of mutual help: was it not as wonderful as self-help?
Why not, *"God helps those who help each other"?*
Or, for that matter, *"Love thy neighbor!"*

Americans during the period from 1810 to 1860 were
world famous for doing practically everything without government
except obtaining land and taking care of a few other matters
that I mentioned earlier in connection with Hamilton's
Federalist administration, and in taking charge of records and roads,
and preserving the slave system.
Both governments and people were taking on new jobs now, too.
The governments were Democrat-Republican, Jeffersonian,
and they did less than before under the so-called Federalists,
while the nation had quadrupled in size and population.

Writers, who have been so kind to the Democrats of that age,
ought be reminded that most common men and minorities
got a better deal under the conservatives

than under the party of the common man.

Truly Americans could not think of what government should do that they could not better do themselves (or so they believed). A government so close to the people and so dominated by majoritarian and crowd psychology might be imagined as immediately setting to work doing everything imaginable for the good of the people. The doctrine of individualism and self-help operated precisely as expectable of an ideology: it kept people from thinking of alternatives.

What of the immigrants, then?
Immigrants, as immigrants to America were expected to behave, and came expecting to behave, readily practiced the rules of initiative and self-help. A number of German immigrants were socialists of the new secular type (the *Communist Manifesto* issued in 1848), but they were soon assimilated. Only a few remained to keep the spark alive until the late nineteenth century, when socialist agitation broke out again.

This is not to say, however, that any generation of natives and immigrants was wholly preoccupied with self-help.

On the contrary, mutual help or voluntary associationism was exercised and practiced. And it is practically certain that the most guarded study would show little difference in this respect between the earliest and the latest Americans. That self-selection and a powerful set of environmental forces have been producing these twin behaviors is indubitable.

To avoid confounding oneself, it may be best to regard the American character as having two typical branches, the one of intensive self-help, the other of equally intensive mutual help. Experience within almost any voluntary or compulsory group in America will testify to the presence and tug-o-war between these

two tendencies, even in an involuntary order,
such as an army company or government or corporate office.

Suppose that in a historiographical *tour de force*,
after putting aside all the things that adult Americans
had to do to earn a living and were required by their
state, local, and federal governments or masters to do,
we could weigh upon the scales all the
voluntary bad and good activities of the citizens of the
American Republic during the period from 1810 to 1860.
Would the good outweigh the bad?
If it did not, would one have to retreat quickly
in a state of shock, declaring, yes,
but the bad would even have been more
if what was voluntary became compulsory.

For example, your putting aside money for a rainy day
(as people used to say long ago)
is better than the government making you do so, or
paying you anyhow. Not only are you better as a person for
doing what you should do without being told, but
the government is better for being less onerous.

But suppose you have all sorts of needs for the money now
and in the coming years, never mind the rainy day that
may put people under umbrellas at your graveside.
Are you to be deprived of all of those joys
that you cannot have when you are old?
And what has your government been doing with your money
in the meantime; lending and spending it like you would?
Or doing just what you don't want it to do?

What you pay to the government or a master
in money and services is compulsory, and
what you must do to support your household is involuntary also;
such is assumed to be true even if all gives you pleasure.
What you do with all your resources of
time, energy, and property that is not involuntary is voluntary.

Voluntarism as the word is used here means
what you and others do jointly and voluntarily.

Unfortunately a good deal of what one does voluntarily
is not even as pleasurable as what one does at work,
let as say as a wine taster, or in fulfilling, let us say,
an obligation to be a juror or a soldier.
Think in this connection of the church-goer
who goes because she feels that she must. Or the
person who exercises reluctantly in
order to keep healthy.

Americans have been famous at least since the early
1800's for their cooperative activities.
For the first century of the Nation's two-hundred-year history,
voluntary activities accounted for more time and
resources and projects than did the state, local and federal
governments put together. Insofar as the
settlement of a new area,
organizing it into a territorial government, and
bringing it into the union, were tasks undertaken
voluntarily by people without compulsion,
often lacking direction or even encouragement from the
other states or federal government, the very process of
expansionism may be regarded as an enormous
constructive voluntary effort.
Still, it was an essentially simple process, and
we should hardly be surprised if, thereafter,
the governments that they did set up were models of
inactivity such as would warm the
cockles of Adam Smith's heart..

We hasten to assert, however, that
some highly important activities were not performed at all
and the question is why:
was it because the people did not want them to be done,
that they did not recognize their need or there was no need,
or that the nature of the activities was such that

they could only be done by the government,
either because they were never known before,
or because their peculiar qualities let there be only one solution,
a governmental way, of doing them.
How can one praise a legislature ,
where voluntarism borders upon anarchy,
with wheeling-and-dealing the order of every legislative day,
and corruption embedded cheerfully in ordinary party politics?

Is there something distinctively virtuous about voluntarism?
To answer this, we have to assume that
what is compulsory is evil, all things being equal.
Things are often not equal.
It was better to force the whiskey rebels to pay a tax
than to let them destroy the system of law and order, or so we say.
While this may be true, we have to go back to the question
whether all that is voluntary is good.

No, because the whiskey distillers were not good,
and doubly naughty when they refused to be taxed.

Still, it is possible, and probably well, to believe that
a voluntary good act is superior morally to a compelled good act.
And what of the person who voluntarily submits to compulsion,
as opposed to the person who hates and tries to
reject all forms of compulsion or a particular form?

Are not discipline and order, and the ability to
organize such and submit to it, good types of conduct?

But is this true of a voluntary bad act?
Surprisingly not. On the contrary.
We say that a person who willfully commits evil is behaving worse
than if he had been compelled to commit the same evil.
But can we not say that a person who voluntarily is good is
superior to both a voluntarily bad person and
a person compelled to be bad or to be good.
We have here the reason why

a person who of his own free will commits a good act
is regarded highly.

Still, how sure can we be?
Perhaps the voluntarist is aesthetically more pleasing
than the obedient person who is someone else's servant.
Perhaps it was the exotic attractiveness of American associationism
that so bemused young aristocratic Alexis de Tocqueville,
when he was traveling about the country.

And, although they may not be called evil in intent,
but just the opposite,
how should one judge all of those voluntary groups and movements
aimed at getting government to make more behaviors compulsory?
Alcoholic temperance movements, for instance, and
evangelistic movements of the nineteenth century
imposing prayers in the factories, schools, and halls of government?

And, furthermore, the same person is thought to be
especially superior, if he does not obtain pleasure from his action,
or may even suffer in the act of doing good.
The parent who spanks his child saying sincerely,
"This hurts me more than it does you", is thus better than the parent
who feels nothing or even a pleasure in spanking his child. We
abandon the discussion now, because it appears to be
getting more complicated: is spanking
itself good; is the parent ignorant or mean; is the
punishment proportionate to the crime?
And so it goes.

Although we must race through the abundant materials on the
American as an associative animal, we can now at least avoid the
supposition insinuated by so many historians and publicists,
that all such conduct is blessed and helped make the nation great.

We may rather even entertain the notion that
at least half of the voluntary and cooperative activity was
dedicated to causes one might not wish to support.

Homesteaders in the 1880s

Chapter Thirty-four

Individualism and Affection

Not everyone in America has felt the surprise of the hero of *Moby Dick*, who found himself bedded down at a lodging house and squeezed by a massive stranger named Queequeg, a completely tattooed harpooner of Australoid race. Still, there must have been countless anxious incidents. A custom shared by all races and cultures, and to be found in America over a long period of time, was sleeping together:

men and women, men and women and children, women and children, men and children, men and men, women and women, and children of one or both sexes. Their relationship was usually of the nuclear family, plus grandparents, but often included other relatives, friends, and visitors. This, one would think, should settle the problem of intimate relations in America.

Body contact was ordinary unless a person sought to avoid it. We may wonder at the incidence of perversion, too much of a good thing, perhaps, but there should have been no general problem with physical love and affection.

Perhaps the Indians had as many versions of love as they had cultures and sub-cultures, and since they were healthy individualists, so far as we can tell, the squaws and braves of any given tribe may have varied greatly in their conception and practice of love. When a census of Cherokees was made in 1832, it appeared that about 150 Caucasian husbands and about sixty Caucasian wives were present among the 15,000 or so people. Multiply this proportion by the number of tribes and the considerable number ensuing would seem to guarantee that we would have a certain volume of erotic literature. Unfortunately such is not the case. One cannot make a Colette out of a Puritan woman, randomly fallen victim to strangers.

Much earlier, I alluded to the findings that colonial men and women with Indian partners seem to have been sexually and socially compatible. There is no reason to believe that conditions changed so long as we speak of an intact social system; once the couple were thrown into the outer world, prejudice, alcohol, loneliness, and economic insecurity made interracial couples as incompatible or more so than Caucasian couples. A lone Fox Indian in Des Moines, Iowa, was not likely to stay fixed with his New England squaw, much as she might wish to appease her guilty conscience with his help.

Caucasian couples had from the beginning a high rate of divorce

and a much higher rate of abandonment than
were to be found in Catholic or Protestant Europe.
In the third biological generation, the second political generation,
we note the beginnings of disintegration of patriarchal family and
a heightened self-reliance in affairs of the heart
among young men and women, as reported by the
first memorial generation. Independent and individualistic behavior
increased in all four cultures of America, the fourth, the frontier,
acting as a tempting devil to the others.

The English idea was paternal:
treat the colonials and Indians as children,
whether it was the King trying to make his voice heard like
the Wizard of Oz from far off, or his officials seeking to sell the
Indians a bill of goods. The Indians were quick to appreciate the
phony quality of this appeal. Yet American officials
followed the English formula of authority for lack of better.

Perhaps, with all their experience of brotherhood,
they realized that they could not be brothers or big brother,
for that would give the Indians rights that only a father
could take away. They also felt that Indians were too uncivilized
to talk in terms of constitutions, natural rights, legality, or, again,
feared that the use of such concepts would backfire.
Notwithstanding the Iroquois confederation and a few others.

The Cherokees did adopt the symbolic equipment of republican
Enlightenment - alphabet, printing presses, constitution, etc. - they
even could say, *"Look, we are like you, we have slaves too"*.
To no avail: they went out in a trail of blood and tears.

Every President from the beginning believed the country must be rid
of independent Indian nations. Andrew Jackson was especially
two-faced and treacherous, but Martin Van Buren, his hand-picked
President, will do here; he said, *"No State can achieve proper culture,
civilization, and progress... as long as Indians are
permitted to remain"*.
Besides: Indians made bad company:
disorders of the frontier were owing to Indians, whereas the
misbehavior of Whites came from emulating Indians.

They talked of Indians becoming civilized and even assimilated, foreseeing every brave owning and cultivating a modest piece of land like any poor White. Yet they had few illusions that the Indians would put up with this solution. Nor did they. The White "fathers" resorted to ridiculous language and rationalizations, as frustrated fathers have a way of doing: one favorite image reduced Indians to the status of infants.

As infants they could not be held responsible. They should be taken into the custody of the father and relieved of all propensities for harm. The final end of the idea and process of infantilization was the Indian reservation, the small stipend, the strict controls and the staff of the Indian administrations of State and Nation, minding the children.

At the other end of the world was Australia. The Black aborigines there were treated worse than the American Indian. The policy decided upon was cultural genocide. It was felt that the greatest favor that could be done to the natives was to stop slaughtering and starving them, and change them into civilized beings like oneself.

So, without notice or due process of law of any kind, squads appeared before the native camps and seized thousands of children. These were to be raised like White Australians, so that when released at the age of fifteen they could get a job and settle down. The results were a traumatized people, general hostility, hopeless resistance, universal drunkenness, and few dutiful young workers.

In Hispanic America, the policy was to baptize everyone within reach, by hook or crook, and then to regard them all as backsliding sinners for non-observance, with death-bed repentance to save them from Hell. The Mestizo population continued to grow rapidly, and cushioned the Indians against Caucasians emotionally and to a degree materially.

What, then - to proceed with the American experience - would be the state of affections among African-American slaves and freemen? And among Blacks and Whites of both sexes? Despite all fear, hate, and prejudice, the innumerable rapes of African-Americans by Caucasians that patterned White-Black relations over a three-century period, despite all the excuses offered by the offending male, to the effect that "nothing was meant by it", was proof positive, a thousand times over, that miscegenation is a normal behavior between races and groups of the human species.
One estimate has the average American with 5% black genes. Another points out that the average American is an octoroon. So much for averages.

But restrictive or permissive laws are also normal behavior. (By "normal" we mean normally schizoid. In Louisiana, that paradise of racial and ethnic mixing, the law defined as black anyone who was one thirty-second of black ancestry and refused to re-classify a woman of three thirty-seconds in 1982.)
The whole system was set against lending permanence to interracial liaisons. One result was the diminution of the meaning of love and affection among both Whites and Blacks, and as a corollary, the restriction of sex very often to non-loving relationships.

In the slave-free South, North and West, as well as in the slave culture, the separation of sex from affection was occurring by the preaching of a Puritanical morality: bodily lust was sinful and should be suppressed. Of course it did not work much of the time bodily; but it did work in the mind, where affectional ties are arranged.

Further, the great mobility of Americans, boys and men especially, and the lack of better occupation for women, led to a proliferation of prostitution around the country, in cities and back of villages certainly, but off in a cabin or on a barge. The railroad gangs that sweated out a hundred thousand miles of track in a century's time were in all cases followed faithfully, but at a reasonable distance for propriety, by a caravan of prostitutes, their fancy-men, and the gamblers; somewhere around, more of a loner, would be the wagon and tent of a priest or minister with the paraphernalia needed to save men's souls. And to hitch them to women. For so few women were on the scene, that a pimp could do double duty as a proxenete. As Chicago became the world's greatest rail center, it also became the world's greatest center of prostitution.

No country in the world imposed abstinence upon men like the developing United States effected. The large population of single immigrant men, the innumerable gangs at work upon the infrastructure of the country distant from homes and families, the troops of Indians and Indian-fighters chasing each other about, the scarcity of lodging facilities everywhere for women and children, the large percentage of jobs that required prolonged absences from home - at sea, in the forests, wagoneering and barging long distances: all this meant that sexual and other female companionship had to be hasty, strange, risky, frustrating, and mis-educative.

That a pleasant courtship technique - French literature of the 1700's and 1800's provided many volumes of this, untranslated - would be practically absent, and that sexual harassment would be a typical American male's idea of courtship was to be expected. Dreams and illusions of affectionate heterosexual relationships were difficult to put to the test.

The minister and the priest performed usefully as match-makers. American girls went more than half way to help out, too, by contrast with their counterparts in Europe; they were chaperoned less and more was forgiven them. Nowhere was "petting" so widely practiced, to the point of being a substitute for sexual intercourse. Joining a church group was always the more productive way to meet the opposite sex; often the problem thereafter was how to escape the church group with your prey. Contraception was well-known, and may have been in some small part responsible for a diminution of the birth rate in the nineteenth century.

❖❖❖

There was a widely read literature on sex, containing such works as *Chastity*, by a food freak named Graham, the same as invented the graham cracker that lucky American children ate with warm milk before retiring. He foresaw the most destructive consequences emerging from masturbation and frequent marital intercourse. They were affronts to God as well as the human body, or so he would admonish in his quasi-revivalist lectures.

A reading of the American classics on sex and affection is disturbing. Nathaniel Hawthorne, whose "Scarlet Letter" gave millions of young scholars a definition of adultery, gave them little else, since the act took place well before the action of the book. Hawthorne seems more concerned to make a Protestant Virgin Mary out of Hester Prynne, nursing her illegitimate baby with the finely embroidered "A" for adulteress on her dress. The male characters are hardly dreamboats, mainly a stand-in for a severe father and a milquetoast preacher as lover.

His evasion of genitality is fully common. Of the group that grew up and therefore learned its mores between 1820 and 1850 - Bret Harte, Mark Twain, William Howells, Henry James, James Russell Lowell, Walt Whitman, Emily Dickinson - life is portrayed very well but without "normal" sexuality. (I do not deny - indeed, it should be stressed –that Mark Twain had a hand in writing and publishing pornography and scatology.)

Nor is one impressed in this regard by the earlier and first generation of productive literati. The beginning of the century, the end of the Federalist Period, witnessed Washington Irving, James Fenimore Cooper, Hawthorne, Edgar Allen Poe, William Cullens Bryant, James Whitleaf Whittier, Ralph Waldo Emerson, Oliver Wendell Holmes, Henry Thoreau, and Harriet Beecher Stowe. Eros bows out of this group as well.

Edgar Allen Poe, the unique American writer who influenced high literary circles in Europe, and who invented the detective story, was sexually supine. He overtly subjected men to women in his stories. His women are commanding, masculine, beautiful like hard jewels, witchlike, tyrant mothers, approachable only when dead. No guide to love and affection he.

Killed by alcoholism, he lay in an unmarked grave for many years until the city of Baltimore scraped together the price of a tombstone, at the unveiling of which the only literary personage present was an all-loving homosexual, Walt Whitman.

Others speak of love, of course, Whitman and Melville, for instance. Whitman makes a philosophy of love and democracy, beginning by loving them both with an embarrassing sensuality (considering that they are abstractions) and extending into a grandiose lush love for everything in the world, culminating in what experts in poetry read as masturbatory celebrations.

"The main purport of these States is to found a superb
friendship, exalted, previously unknown,
Because I perceive it waits, and has been
always waiting, latent in all men".

Whitman, a volunteer nurse in the Civil War, got a job in Washington in 1865 as a clerk in the Office of Indian Affairs of the Department of the Interior. Secretary of the Department James Harlan peered *en passant* into a copy of "Leaves of Grass" on Whitman's desk, and fired him as a "free lover".

But then, everyone knows that Whitman's drive was homoerotic: does that mean that only homosexuals can love everything, be panerotic? Critic Harold Bloom wondered

"that our national poet should be an egotistical onanist,
who proclaimed his own divinity in a series of
untitled, unrhymed, apparently prosy verses"..

Whitman became unquestionably America's national poet. At Camden, New Jersey, where he lived last and died, a conclave in 1998 celebrated his "Many Cultures".

On Whitman as teacher and how to teach Whitman,
on Whitman as influence on poets of the world,
on religion, on photography, on journalism, on pragmatism,
on sexuality, on the city, on song, on publishing, on music,
on politics, on war, and on gender. One could concentrate upon
him because he had no family except all men,
which he nobly projected to all mankind.
He would have embraced the Internet, for its vastness and
its permissiveness, and the word-processor for he continually
altered his poems as time went by. Too,
he was an unabashed self-promoter and inscribed himself on
the roster of world-class authors publishing themselves, and
this would have made him a booster of desk-top publishing.

Herman Melville approaches the panerotic also,
with the Great (dreaded) Mother, "Moby Dick",
his enthusiasm for the male figures of his book and
revulsion against the bad father, Captain Ahab,
"castrated" by the loss of a leg,
who lives only to kill Moby Dick.
His loving descriptions of the harpooners culminate in a
final book of his old age, Billy Budd, portrait of the beautiful young Christ-figure
finally sacrificed for doing a good deed, killing a wicked mate.

Theirs are great achievements, wonderful to watch,
and bear in mind as we seek love and affection
in ordinary Americans of this age.

A clue is to be found in the concept of brotherly love - the French
revolutionaries put it hopefully in their motto of
"Liberté, Egalité, Fraternité" - That goes back
to early Christianity and is incorporated into the
friars, fraternities, monasteries of the intervening ages and then
enters the radical Protestant sects, like the Quakers. All belong and all
are capable of being saved, including for the man moving along the
highways and byways of America, *"Brother, are you going my way?"*
and *"Brother, can you spare a dime?"*

The concept of brotherly love fits well into egalitarian republicanism as well, and especially among groups of truculent men the notion of brotherhood is soothing, whereas that of superiority or strangeness or patronage is offensive.

Two large expressions of American ideas of fraternal love were the outbursts of fraternal orders and humanitarian movements. The Masonic Order was most formidable, but before the Civil War every major occupational and social segment of society had its brotherhood, containing a little of religion, a little life insurance, many social gatherings, and ego-aggrandizing symbol-laden rituals.

Free Africans, and after emancipation, African-Americans generally, founded similar groups. The fraternal lodge reached into the remote rural recesses of the land. Founded in the 1790's, Charleston's Brown Fellowship Society limited membership to free mulattoes, whereupon an exclusive Society of Free Dark Men of Color was also organized. Some say that such fraternal societies reached back to African roots, but every region of the world had its fraternal society, from the Masons to the Chinese Tong and German Bund, and generally the societies sought international affiliations. As American society specialized into more and more components, each of these gave rise to associated fraternities. Collegiate fraternities were no more than a superficial variant of the sociological tintype.

We may wonder whether the changing character of immigration from Europe and Asia over the generations has altered much the kinds of affectionate relations discoverable in the population. Did the increase in Catholic immigration weaken the position of women in families, change the way children were treated, stress authority over persuasion in the family and schools? Yes, on all counts. Did sexuality become more exploitative even as it was more restricted in expression? Yes. Did not Catholics of different national origins have rather differing systems of affection? Yes.

But, besides Roman Catholics, there were Greek and Armenian Orthodox, and besides these were Jews and Asians, non-Christian. Perhaps ignorance rather than insight rules this area, but it might be correct to say that Mediterranean origins were likely to signify more passionate family and sexual relations than the average, Asian systems of intimacy more on family, less on sex. And the whole society of systems - Protestant and regional and occupational, and ethno-racial all together - was moving the other way, even while protesting to pursue the oldest values, the other way being toward a loving partnership as the norm at best, and an indifference and promiscuity of affection otherwise.

The best way for Protestant sects to go in accommodating sex relations was the fraternal idea of partners. Over several generations they made great progress away from the unusable or at least difficult patriarchal relationship, toward the notion of man and woman, and men or women together, for that matter, finding in one another an affectionate partnership, with a de-emphasis of brute power and maleness worship. Even the Catholic Church to whom such an idea was foreign - but which had gone surprisingly far in getting their men and women in America back into the traditional household mold - was heavily impressed by the partnership notion.

Partnership also was a most helpful concept, indeed a necessary tool, for portraying the situation of an increasing number of families toward the end of the nineteenth century, when both husband and wife went to work outside of the home.

The conception had, however, two major problems. Sex in natural biology seems to have been so universally a exercise in which the male plays a dominating and aggressive role with respect to the female - cases like the praying mantis aside - that a "normal" majority, or ecstatic minority of people may feel progressively deprived by the concept of partnership.

In such cases, the concept of individualism may intervene, pushing aside the partnership: the man and the women, the husband and wife, are independent persons who are together because they match well, and as long as they do, and each finds satisfaction and fulfillment in her or his chosen spheres, then the relationship is one of love and affection, sexually more exciting.

This type of relationship is a minor third to the masterful and the partnership, but has been making headway in recent years, and with a history that goes back to the heavy individualist ideology, with the need that it presents, to find one's way in life by oneself, in so lonely and mobile a society.

Masonic Certificate, 1876

Chapter Thirty-five

Movements

A second Great Awakening broke out around 1795 and lingered into 1837, always countering reason with faith. It drew a million people into its momentary embrace, then released them into about the same individual condition as before. (Probably, while seized emotionally, many were kinder and gentler.) It was millennialist: the Kingdom of God was about to take over, if not tomorrow, then surely within the next generation (the millennialists were not very patient).

The optimism of salvation permeated the soul of many Americans, for the nonce, but possibly rendered them all the more anxious and uncertain and prone to other movements, fads, hatreds, and paranoia. In the end, the Awakening sent off unintentionally hundreds of thousands of people into a hundred reform movements that promised changes obviously needed right here and now on earth. Faith, like logic, slips readily from one function to another.

The Awakening crossed denominational lines, excepting Catholics, Unitarians, Universalists and a few other groups; these were often preached against. Free-will Methodists and predestinarian Presbyterians could be found in the same throngs. Occupational lines, too, were crossed. Some breeding grounds for revivalists also became breeders of reformers, like Oberlin College.

The United States was patriotically well-treated in the proceedings, granted a special place in God's plans, even if its people were more wicked than most. Revivalists often disagreed on small points, but when it came to recognizing the degeneracy and vice of the American West, they were all one, and in 1829 launched a great revivalist campaign there, thus, to their mind, saving the nation.

Direct communication with God, a conversion of the heart rather than the mind, brought a feeling of perfectionism to the leaders, and they wished to make everyone perfect. They did not quite succeed but managed to make a lot of people optimistic for a time about their chances. It may be that this impossible idealism was a body blow to the pragmatic temper that characterized so many Americans. The two could not be compatible. Neither gave way, and a common ambivalence in Americans came to be a mixture of both of these attitudes in the personality.

Large doses of moral preachments could hardly live with the functionalist notion that what works well creates the good rather than the other way around. The propaganda of fundamentalism beat incessantly upon the heads of the people. The American Bible Society was formed to paste the nation with copies of the Bible, and the American Tract Society pinned to these Bibles innumerable pamphlets, directing which avenues to take in order to abide with the Lord. For another 100 years these groups were fully active.

The wealth as well as the piety of America could be witnessed at a later day when the Gideon movement managed to place a finely produced Bible in most hotel rooms of the United States, and could express a certain wry gratification at the large number of these that were appropriated by the guests.

If there were no evangelical propaganda in hand, there would be certainly approaching a minister with a packet of it. As every proper priesthood should behave, the Protestant sects whose potential parishioners were mobile went with them or after them. The Methodists and Baptists were especially famous for their circuit riders. They organized assemblages, arranged to cooperate in revival meetings, searched out the last cabin to save a soul. Not being celibate, these roving preachers bred, and their progeny were not quite ordinary.

We have to assign a significant portion of the ideas and energies pervading America then to its army of itinerant pastors. To them are owed some American typicalities and contradictions, the simultaneous presence in the character of materialism and generosity, of accumulativeness and carelessness of property, of hypocrisy (for, after all, most people can be morally persuaded no more than half-way: that's all they can manage, and, besides, one has to be back on the road again). Camp meetings were continuous, revival meetings supplemental.

The Baptists and Methodists moved far into the lead in the competition for souls. They could function well in city or country, particularly the Methodists. The Congregationalists functioned only in "civilized" areas. A Plan of Union of 1801 between Presbyterians and Congregationalists failed to revive their joint membership. They were unable to cope with free competition in the marketplace, so to speak. For the masses, the camp meetings provided a desperately needed sociability and fraternal and sisterly love - often an occasion for finding romantic and marital love, also. A veritable applied science of rustic religion was contained in the Camp Meeting Manual of B.W. Goram of 1854.

The older Puritan groups were priced out of the market literally: their ministers earned between $300 and $400 annually and their church property had a range of values from $3000 to $13,000, whereas the Baptist and Methodist pastors were receiving only $60 to $100 in settled areas and the property of their pastorate averaged only $1200 in value. By 1850, the statistical shape of the membership distribution in 1776 had drastically altered:

Total Church Adherents, 1776 and 1850,
Per cent of total held by six denominations

Denomination	1776	*1850*
Congregational	20.4	4.0
Episcopalian	15.7	3.5
Presbyterian	19.0	11.6
Baptist	16.9	20.5
Methodist	2.5	34.2
Catholic	1.8	13.9
Total	77.3	87.7

Drinking was a sport for many, too, thinly disguised then as it is now, sociability, or a ball game on television. "Joe Six-Pack" of the 1990's was then "John Barleycorn". The number of licensed distilleries came to 2,579 in 1792. The population doubled by 1810 but the number of distilleries jumped to 14,191, a sixfold increase. And the number of illegal distilleries, concentrated in the rural areas, was legion. White adult males would have been consuming on the average a pint of hard liquor per day. America was in the same state that the Soviet Union came to be respecting vodka, when Gorbachev blew the whistle and declared the Cold War over: a third of his comrades were drowning in the sauce.

Agitation for laws governing the sale and consumption of alcohol was minimal before the War of 1812-15. Then, Methodists (hastened by the abominable experience of Britain), took up the cause. Soon Quakers entered upon the scene. Then New England congregations. The motives were not so simple as a desire to save people from going to the devil. Or even to preserve the mass of people from ruin. It became a mark of social status to be engaged in the temperance movement. (The same motive was to be found among anti-slavery agitators, beginning soon.)

For the older respectable classes that had lost power and respect in the Jacksonian movement, here was a chance to espouse the public weal and to lead once more the masses. Later the reform movements would be called contemptuously the "blue stockings", because of the preponderance of proper ladies in the pressure groups for temperance and feminist causes. The poorer congregations such as the Methodists tried to avoid domination by the upper classes, reasonably, but as so often happened with good causes in America, thus split the movement, and made united action directed at a special objective impossible.

The Connecticut Society for the Reformation of Morals (organized 1813), and the Massachusetts Society for the Suppression of Intemperance (1813) were founded and led by clergymen and wealthy laymen of Federalist persuasion. So was the American Temperance Society (1826). It was not only the egalitarian direct democrats that had pushed them from power. It was also the commercial classes, who were entering local politics and buying places and men in national politics.

However, we must not forget the Methodists and then, too, the Baptists and other sects. They were to be continually in agitation against alcohol use for the rest of American history. Only the Catholic Church did not see fit to engage in the movement to any large degree, partly because its priests often liked to drink and had a measure of authority and control over their drunken parishioners. Or perhaps they knew how to get money out of drunks. No church or movement took out after the tobacco system; people consumed the plant in unlimited quantities in its strongest forms. (At least Turks employed the civilized and leisurely water pipe, and did not spit all over the place.)

By paying no attention to what was going on in Europe, one tends to allow America its slower pace in some regards. By 1850, the basis for most modern solutions of social problems had been offered in Europe. Socialism in different forms had been presented in theory. The social sciences were already developing with such giants as Auguste Comte and St. Simon. It probably would be fair to say that America in the first half of the nineteenth century was a political generation behind Europe intellectually, scientifically, and culturally. Exceptionally, had the country been composed only of the region from Concord to Baltimore, it would have stood modestly in the second rank, comparable to Portugal or Switzerland.

Still, look at the matter of pacifism. The two chemicals of reform and pacifism could and did combine. A man named Joseph Sturge worked at the marrying of American and British cities, - Boston to Boston, Manchester to New York. (Note the striking precursor of "sister cities" under the auspices of the United Nations in the late twentieth century.)

His mentor was Elihu Burritt, "the learned blacksmith" of Worcester, Mass., who crossed the ocean to England, and there walked the country with a knapsack and staff to call upon Worcester, England, but en route conceived the great idea of a League of Universal Brotherhood dedicated to peace. He stopped at a village called Pershore and there promptly signed up twenty country folk in a pledge for peace. Within a year he had 30,000 associates.

The League promoted pacific intercourse between France and England. It sought a penny stamp that would encourage international understanding among common people. It then moved into a boycott of American cotton as a blow against slavery. A Congress of Nations was advocated, too. An American judge, son of John Jay, William Jay, President of the American Peace Society, proposed the inclusion of arbitration clauses into treaties.

With the backing of Sturge in England, a prolonged and persistent campaign was conducted, until Richard Cobden, the English reformer, introduced legislation into the House of Commons calling for compulsory arbitration. The Senate Foreign Relations Committee also reported favorably on the idea. A signal victory was won with the inclusion of an arbitration clause in the Treaty of Paris that concluded the bloody Crimean War.

Young and old convicts were cast into prisons. Jail for debt was common, an estimated 75,000 unfortunates per year in the thirties, many for debts of under $50. Punishments for crime were still what would be considered by the courts of today as cruel and unusual punishment: branding, ear-cropping, whipping and jails as foul as hell. The teachings of William Penn and of the American followers of Beccaria like John Adams, who argued the idiocy of the punitive system, were universally ignored.

From the Auburn Penitentiary of New York came the first remarkable study of the causes of delinquency and crime, an intensive interrogation of and report on 173 prisoners in 1829-30; fully two-thirds appeared from the record to have gone wrong because of family circumstances; childhood made the man. The thesis was to become the leading doctrine of the next century for explaining and suggesting remedies for criminality. Notable in the history of social science was the systematic interviewing and analysis.

The moral leaders and many more plain citizens of the American republic - not to mention the millions of millennialists - really believed that the society, which had hardly ever seemed to be together, was in imminent danger of falling apart. It seemed to be the first case in history where anarchy would prevail without anarchists. (The perverse workings of the direct democratic ideology were simply not sensed.)

Americans over the age of eight years who were not in school or at work twelve hours a day except Sunday on largely displeasing tasks,

necessitated by some condition or some authority, were presumably slackers or in desperate straits for lack of work. Under such circumstances, there would be little time for activities other than personal care.

Actually shirking, slacking, and soldiering were most common. The eccentric mass movements, like molecules in a gas, may have had the unconscious purpose of avoiding work, as well as responsibility, not to mention getting away from the demands of governments. It takes time to walk alone or *en famille* from Cincinnati to nearby Akron, Ohio. Allowing a week to go look for a job there gives hardly enough walking time. Think how many people got many months of vacation going from Maine to Oregon by foot or wagon or horse or sailing ship - or would you prefer to be standing at a loom twelve hours a day six days a week?

Unemployment itself has a good side: not working. There was plenty of this. And farming in America was hardly what it might be, if the average American farmer were as diligent as he might be; I am not accusing him of lying on a haystack half the time, but simply warning ourselves to take seriously the expert depreciation of the qualities of the farmer. Elsewhere, even in efficient factories, machines broke down continually and could not be set up to outspeed the machine tender ordinarily, both of which features were taken care of in the course of three political generations, by the time the 1920's came along.

No one except a new band of socialists looked to the workers as the saviors of society, although there would soon be as many workers as there were farmers (who were supposed to be the backbone of the nation). It is a wonder that the workers were not more criminal. There was very little chance for workers to save their money. They received 75 cents a day for most of the year, if they were more fortunate than most. In the depression of 1837, which began in England, a bank panic followed by business failures disemployed fully one-third of the total urban work force;
farmers, of course, lost their markets.

When unemployed, they were taken care of by others, as they would do in turn, when roles were reversed. The effect was hardly adequate and family relations suffered. Sporadic union efforts accomplished practically nothing in the few places where they were tried. Nowhere was the helplessness of the brave American individualist so manifest as in the life conditions of the wage worker. Here we include not only the ever larger work gangs and factory workers, but also the ever-increasing number of slave and tenant farmers and share-croppers.

Perhaps it is just as well that the free workers did not succeed in organizing powerful unions and parties. For the nativists, anti-Catholics, anti-foreigners, anti-Africans, and mad schemers would certainly have been in charge. Later, feminists, pacifists, intellectuals, communists, etc. would enrage the unionists. Most of the hundreds of riots that raged through American cities in the decades before the Civil War were inspired by such elements; and a riot mob, like the lynch mob, is a rather pure expression of voluntary action.

The mob has the basic self-confidence of the majoritarian direct democrat, too. Just as the King's decree ordering a head chopped off read: *"It is my pleasure"*, so the semi-spontaneous crowd was prefacing its behavior by the sentiment, often expressed loudly, *"We the people do ordain this shooting, burning, beating, and hanging"*.

The anti-Masonic Party, founded upon the suspicious death of an ex-Mason planning an exposé, found myriads of adherents, mostly workingmen and farmers, and ran successfully for many offices for a few years. The Know-Nothings, already mentioned, depended heavily upon the workingman's vote. They finally dissolved into the party of Abraham Lincoln, the Republican Party, on the eve of the Civil War.

During all this time, Karl Marx worked steadily at his economic research in London, but never seemed to position the facts properly vis-a-vis the character of many, if not most, workers, and did an enormous harm, in Europe but also to a small extent in America, by positing the worker as congenitally a hero of society.

The Bible Tract Society knew who were pulling the puppet strings in American society and published a pamphlet telling merchants and employers how they ought to behave. They were to revere honesty, spend sparingly, keep accurate accounts, observe their religious faith, and tend to the moral and religious supervision of their employees. Nothing said about profits, or workers' rights, or ethics of competition. They were to pledge their purse for the good order and morality of the community.

As for employees and laborers and slaves,
the morality, like the wealth, trickling down
from their betters, should suffice; no special virtue
save obedience need be cultured.

Youth tore itself away from age at the beginning of the 1800's and never returned. One sees it in the terms for old age that changed from affectionate to contemptuous: old gaffer, fogy, codger, fuddy-duddy, oldster, geezer, etc. Most writers changed in attitude from favorable to unfavorable to the elderly. Politicians averaged younger. Forced retirement was entering in the few establishments where it applied. It was still the custom for the youngest daughter to remain at home until the parents died. Provided that parents possessed a home. Inasmuch as only 2% to 3% of the population lived to the age of sixty-five, this would ordinarily mean fifteen years of drudgery, but hopefully associated with love.

Men worked or tried to work until they died. The normal tragedy of old age, the interim between an occupation and death, was apparent in the urban centers. What was concealed were the million hovels of rural areas where old people lay unattended and waiting for death. Over all hung the "work ethic", that *"you ain't no good unless you got a job"*.

Little was done for the mentally ill, save for the first studies of the problem and the provision of asylums where persons obnoxious to the public were consigned to live in the most degraded and disgusting conditions. (Conditions in Europe were not much better.) The insane began to be thought of as a social problem in a few minds as early as the mid-1700's. They were usually dumped into prisons along with criminals, cruel and unusual punishment for both.

Dorothea Dix, a Massachusetts schoolteacher, was shocked at finding a group of the insane abandoned in a freezing corner of a prison, and took to the road researching the problem and reporting, uninvited, the disgusting results to the state legislature. Her insistent pleas won results, not alone in Massachusetts but in a score of states before the Civil War. Asylums were provided specially, but we shall not go into the administration and financing of these and others; woe betide the person of slipping mind, then, thereafter, as now. When Dix led to victory the lobby for federally assisted care for the mentally ill in Congress, President Pierce, sitting on top of a balanced budget, vetoed the bill.

Exclamations of distress and horror can be found from time to time in newspapers of the age, but otherwise gangs of children were left alone to live and die on the streets or individually on country by-ways. The philanthropically organized and governmentally assumed asylums for various disabled groups - paupers, cripples, the insane - began in the early 1820's, and included orphans. The number of states and counties providing orphan asylums gradually increased, at about one-tenth the rate of the problem, so that, by the time that the problem embraced millions of children, thousands could be taken care of, badly it must be said, in grim institutions.

Charles Loring Brace is a man to be remembered: in 1853 he founded the New York Children's Aid Society. He had a singular respect for the children of the streets, even admired the cunning and grace with which they could make off with a pile of wood from a dock, and believed that the best that could be done for them was to place them with a family out west, send them there, and hope for the best. (Horatio Alger in the next generation lived in a CAS lodging and got the background for many of his popular "rags to riches" stories from the experience.)

Brace assailed the insistence upon drill, discipline, uniformity, and cowering obedience exacted by the institutions. This, he argued, was no way to prepare a child for practical life. He brought about the building of numerous lodging houses and vocational schools, all of them wholly voluntary.

Sending children West was an old idea, called "placing out" in New England; some were speaking of a mass removal of the indigent, sweeping the cities clean of them. But Brace confined his recommendations to the young and regarded being despatched West as an opportunity for them, and a free act; he even had little regard for the blessings of the countryside. He had little faith in the family; he did not want to put the pieces of broken families together; he felt such families only bred more crime, poverty and disorder. He was interested in avoiding revolutionary gatherings and rioting, however, which was his main excuse for the hard-hearted and uncomprehending to go along with his scheme.

Some 90,000 boys were sent West over a forty-year period. By 1929, 150,000 children had been despatched. Follow-up studies were regarded by Brace as superfluous: whatever happened had to be for the better, he thought.

The Young Men's Christian Association originated in England in 1841 with George Williams, a dry-goods clerk, stuck among a crowd of clerks with little to do with their little free time except make mischief. He started up a library and out of this grew the YMCA, which came to America ten years later with George Van Derlip, a divinity student, and George Petrie, a young merchant, who had visited together a YMCA premise in England.

Within a decade, 200 local associations had been founded with 25,000 members. The "Y" provided meeting places, libraries, eating places, and rooms for young men. From their many modest offices, the Secretaries of the YMCA's moved into pressure group tactics to get the law on the tails of saloon-keepers, prostitutes, and pornographers. The notorious Anthony Comstock got his start with the YMCA-created New York Committee for the

Suppression of Vice.

Although the hand of religious men may be seen in the beginnings, the movement was taken up by businessmen. It was especially dear to self-made rich men from the country, and the institution applied with poignant relevance to the problems of the young aspirant to the commercial world coming in from small town or farm to the city. They were the clerical wave of the future. There would be millions of these migrants.

The abundance of land encouraged Americans from the beginning to set up settlements conforming to an ideal plan that they had in mind. The most successful, if least exciting utopias for philosophers and idealists, would be the aforementioned new territories and states. From the primitive Protestants emulating ancient Israel, up to the scientific Enlightenment and later socialists, utopian communities were a large part of reform thinking. We recall that the Pilgrims were such utopians and so were the hedonists of nearby Merry Mount. Most of the utopias were attempted by Anglo-Americans, a sizeable minority by Germanics.

Many successes were registered by religious cults, which, surviving the community stage, expanded into numbers of congregations in many places. They fed of course into the maw of the national society, whereas the aim of utopias has always been uncompromising and, if anything, to set a model that the state or some group of institutions, like schools or factories, would follow. Most early utopias were religious, but perforce had to adopt a posture with respect to all the values - production, wealth, affection, hierarchy, education and power. And, if they were not religious, they were by definition moral schemes anyhow.

Some produced communistically, and divided the wealth; some produced for the market using community sanctioned methods. In some all wealth belonged to the community and small sums were retained by the members. In others capitalism was encouraged provided a tithe was paid in to the community. Some wrote elaborate constitutions and rule books; others called upon love and a benign human nature to settle all conflict. Some were dictatorships, some oligarchies, some male-dominated, others quite egalitarian.

Nor should one ignore a common utopian phenomenon
going back at least two centuries: communities of
hoboes, tramps, bums, unemployed, homeless.
Aloofly hospitable to their kind, , knowledgeable about the wide world,
usually peaceful though anarchist,
enduring a high turnover of occupants over many years.

Some utopias denied offices, others created many.
Some put education into the family sphere,
some segregated education
from the family at an early point.
Some were sexually abstinent, others permissive.
Some were intellectual and artistic,
others manacled themselves to their plows.
Some were ritualistic from morning to night,
others atheistic. Some derived from international
or national movements, others were one-shot
affairs with no evangelistic impulses.

German Mennonites created Ephrata and nourished an unparalleled school of hymn singers. New Harmony was a communistic settlement of German celibates; it lasted a century and had imitators. The Shakers were founded by an Englishwoman, Ann Lee, on the basis of a French group specializing in a convulsive dance. She became the mother in Christ, standing alongside God, to her followers; settled soon in America, she spread her doctrines especially among the frontier folk, who were astonished by the acoustical effects and bodily contortions of the entranced devotees.
Sexual intercourse was banned (she had left her husband);
men and women were largely equal for once;
private property was abolished.
A number of such utopian settlements resulted.

Hopedale and Brook Farm are famous for the intellectual discussions that went into their planning and execution, and demise; the literati of New England knew about them, wrote about them, even at times visited them; each lasted for some years; one sold out as a business in the end; the other collapsed delicately into a private school.

Although most utopias did not last as long as the Pony Express, they deserve the greater attention they receive in American historiography. Utopias sparked a thousand localities in America and enlivened the minds of generation after generation. Every American, commented Emerson of these times, had a plan for a utopia in his pocket. Utopias have changed, but the pockets are still stuffed.

The Hudson River School - Samuel Colman: Storm King on the Hudson (1866)

Chapter Thirty-six

Arts and Sciences

George Bancroft, a superb historian of the age, who had spent a long time lapping up culture in places like Germany, Italy, and England, nevertheless believed America to have a greater future in store than any other nation because of its reliance upon the people. "The measure of the progress of civilization is the progress of the people", (1854) and he considered that the people of the United States had gone far. He was typically the American scholar as optimist.

True, much of America, about one-fourth, could be deemed civilized at the time - meaning places where people possessed recognizable arts and sciences - but most of the Americans of the time seemed to be trying to occupy as much space as they could and trying to carve out some humble life-style. Civilization to them meant rather what Indians were not.

But then the moment has come to speak of the fun and games of Americans (and here once more, alas, the slaves remained simply slaves, worsening or bettering in small increments with the economic state of the masters, and the women remained in bondage –as we shall shortly confirm - and also the workers young and old except on Sundays).

Did American have a full array of civil games and sports, thus qualifying in one way to be civilized? ("Savages" didn't play many games; all of life was a game, including torturing prisoners, drinking whiskey, and watching the White man make a fool of himself.) Somehow there was time for the European types to enjoy games. Games had once been condemned, in early New England. New York and Virginia had strict seventeenth century laws against many games, especially where gambling or sex was involved, and never on Sunday.

But now there were so many games, that we are unhappily confined to a mere listing. There were : cockfighting, bear-baiting, pit-bull fights, rough and tumble fighting, turkey shoots, round-up animal shooting, fishing for sport rather than food - to name a few less humane sports that were popular. Should the "necktie party" be named; lynching was a crowd sport, setting the tone for a hot summer in many a dull town; there is no accurate count; I would suggest a figure of 20,000 victims for the 1800's and 1900's; many more such "parties" were aborted, by local heroes and heroines. The "game" began in America in the early 1800's, apparently authentically American.

Horse-racing, dog-racing, mule-racing, sled-racing, wagon-racing, sailboat and steamboat racing, even locomotive racing in a later day. (Tragic boiler explosions were not unexpected.) Gambling at dice and cards and betting on everything that might happen two ways or more. (A classic homicide case in American law turned around a bet that the town drunk could not consume a quart of whiskey in one sitting; he was happy to oblige, but died, and the bettors were convicted of murder by the court, despite their defense that, though obviously drunk at some point, he had consented to begin with.)

But let us mention more gentle pastimes: visiting (usually involving long walks or rides), hiking, dancing, music, conversation, draughts, chess, dramas, vaudeville, painting, poetry clubs.
Girls would nurse and dress dolls, skip rope (so, too, later, boxers in training), play hop-scotch and tag (also boys), and jacks.
The athletic engaged in foot racing, football, cricket, tennis, quoits, sledding, ninepins, skittles and bowls, shooting at targets with guns and bows and arrows.
Billiards were fashionable.

Baseball would soon take over the fields, imported from England, where it was called rounders and had stabilized a set of rules as early as 1827. (Abner Doubleday copied the rule book and popularized the game in America twelve years later.)
Practically all of these games and sports were from England, and beyond England in time and space Europe, Rome, Egypt, India.
American football derived from Anglo-French rugby.
We need await basketball as the only American invention, this by James Naismith in 1891.

The Mexican rodeo came decades later, and was transformed for amusement and sent from the West to the East culminating as part of the great Barnum & Bailey Circus, and Buffalo Bill's Wild West Show. The circus was European in origin but grew, of course, Bigger and Better in America. Revolutions in the media of communication and the means of transportation, that began at about the same time as the Civil War, pushed a number of sports into the realms of regional and national attention and competition, and spurred their professionalization and development into major business enterprises.

We are already into the performing arts, for that's what the circuses, side-shows, and carnivals amounted to. Would the Dime Museum belong to the performing arts? It went back to before the Revolution, when various mountebanks, entertainers, and strollers went about exhibiting animals, freaks, mechanical and scientific oddities, peep shows and wax figures. Some were collected. The greatest was Phineas T. Barnum's American Museum in New York beginning in 1841.

Small boys and the poor, native and immigrant, could find in a proliferation of expositions that began to add live performers to museum material an understandable entertainment. The medicine show paralleled the museum, sometimes combining with or traveling together with it, and the assembled folk might purchase patent medicines, elixirs of various types, cures for all ailments.
Show business in America started with the Minstrel Show. About 1828 Thomas D. Rice of Cincinnati created a "Jim Crow" show with a song and dance routine performed in blackface by White men. The first full-length show called themselves the Virginia Minstrels and was organized by Dan Emmett. The characters could be clever or foolish; the blackface came to be more a mask, as was done in early drama in Europe, than an anti-African caricature.

The genre caught on and by 1846 its structure was in place, consisting of a repartee with an interlocutor and endmen, followed by a variety set or "olio" and culminating in a farcical skit. It became rapid-fire, highly skilled, and witty at its best. Descended from the Italian *commedia dell'arte* and the English music hall, the minstrel show, before it expired at the turn of the century, handed over some of its characterizations, skills and ideas to vaudeville, along with several types of jokes and humor. The immigrant was a favorite butt and fool: so this variety show of the 70's jested Germanics:

He: "A man he stole away my trunk,
In dot was my new pants.
She: Unt ven we asked him how dot vas,
He called us emigrants".

Such low humor risked the penalty of having to go on stage after a dog act.

The dramatic stage in America was now professionalized and commercial. Theater was active in the cities, playing a steady stream of London hits. American plays were moving in, none of consequence - nor were the British for that matter, except for the classics, of course. The audiences were lively and likely to become rowdy, if too animated by the action on the stage. The plays were long, usually with a main offering followed by a farce.

The Drunkard opened in Boston in 1844 and became the most popular play ever to grace the Boston boards. In it, a wicked lawyer conspires to ruin a feckless but good young man, and almost succeeds, mostly by making a drunk and wastrel out of him, much to the dismay of his pure wife and child, but ultimately gets his come-uppance and all ends happily (*sic*).

German drama received some play. Schiller's *The Robbers* came to New York in 1795 in translation, and returned over the years. Several years later Kotzebue's succession of sentimental heroic dramas, translated from the German, aroused sizeable audiences. Between 1830 and 1864 among some forty-five German poets to be translated and published in American collections, Schiller led with 123, followed in order by Goethe, Uhland, Ruckert, Heine and Geibel. A considerable literature appeared directly in German in Pennsylvania, Cincinnati, and St. Louis. This American literature written in German has never been properly assessed, nor made generally available. There mains still to be uncovered original music, essays, and theatre, written in various languages by immigrants or conoscenti; Yiddish, a Jewish dialect of German, appeared later and provided an American literature. More is to be expected from the variations of Spanish that have begun to clothe the work of Hispanic-Americans.

The lower you were on the social scale or the more subtle your vices, the more likely you were to listen in on the most original development of American music in this period, occurring in the African-American forms of the blues, the syncopated march and gospel hymns, the oratorios, the ditties, the mumbo-jumbo chants, and the downright better-performed White music. Ludwig von Beethoven made close friends with an American violinist, a half-African slave who had become a classical musician; Beethoven regarded him as world-class. (Since Beethoven himself was grandson of a Black, he may have been prejudiced.) The locales were the plantation slums, and the ghettos of Southern cities. The Blacks also interacted with the poor Whites who had their own country music.

White country music was not mountain music alone. It carried on wherever the Anglo-Celtic and otherwise mixed, poor population existed - on the tidewater flats, in all the hills that stretched from Maine to Texas, and in the towns and cities wherever Southern culture spread. The bearers of Southern culture were not the plantation aristocrats, but the poor folk, ignorant, Bible-ridden, rickety, oscillating between drunkenness and teetotalism, and amply aggressive and hostile when they were not being called to the love of Christ.

Their country music was not much when it arrived with them in America, a handful of tunes in the mournful bagpipe intonation (without the bagpipe) of five, not seven tones, to work with, and no instrument except occasionally a feeble-sounding dulcimer. Occasionally a background set of local voices chimed in. Over time, Old Country songs were given an American setting and plot and a few musical variations. The Americans selected out the sad themes from Anglo-Celtic sources, especially parting and death, a sentimentalism founded upon the harsh realities of poverty, poor health, social disdain.

The fiddle arrived, and life changed. It may have been toted over the caste line by Black violinists, more privy to slave master possessions and habits. With the fiddle, things perked up, feet began to smoke, the scale grew to a full octave, though the lamenting minor key was usually preferred. An accommodation was made with the men of God, so that music could be admitted without embarrassment. Hymns of evangelic content came in; evangelism was successful in the poor South in part because it brought in hymns and encouraged people to sing them.

New secular songs began to be sung: sad, nostalgic, worrying about lost loves, love unrequited, and the death of loved ones. (Again the death theme of American literature and song of the first half of the nineteenth century: could there have been a death drive, a Freudian *thanatos* that brought on the Civil War?) Behind the secular songs there played the theology of evangelism and the revival. No songs were against religion.
No superior songs originated, nothing so beautiful as "Loch Lomon" or "Danny Boy" of the Celtic homelands.

Patriotic recitals were sung,
like "The Battle of New Orleans".
Hardly the typical American go-getter kind of song.
Yet it came to be the favorite, almost only music,
of most of the people of half the states in the Union.
How come? Because of another typical trait of Americans,
the loneliness and anxiety beneath the hearty sociability
and boastful self-confidence.

After the fiddle came harmony in the nineteenth century, of voices and instruments, for other instruments were added - the banjo (out of Africa) and the guitar (from Spain and Italy via Mexico). Country music was developing and the butterfly would soon leave the cocoon to become a billion-dollar business, a stupendous extravaganza. The poor Southerners would be still back there somewhere, but a person could not help but listen to their songs once one bought an automobile with a radio.

There was no music of protest, no music appealing for social action. Some of these came much later. Rock music had much of country music in it, and, as it bounced to and fro between Elvis Presley and the Liverpool Beatles, carried many a fetching complaint.
Bob Dylan (*née* Zimmerman in Minnesota) composed
the words and music and sang and twanged
many a ballad of love and social protest
in the sixties, in the war against the war in Vietnam.

Many songs of country music deplored the cities and extolled rural values. Rural Southerners, but also the rural person everywhere, had to reject the city that had grown up without them. The roots of anti-urbanism in America go very deep. The people of the British isles who came early to America were mostly rural. The same held true of Irish Catholics and the Germans. Scandinavians when they came were rural. So there was already a built-in hostility to the city. The Southern plantation Jeffersonian hated the city. Jefferson was more anxious about the cities than about the sources of American destruction underfoot.

There was sheer hypocrisy in urbs-phobia or bucolism; by every indication Americans have always hated and feared the wilderness and the vast spaces, so much so, that they were helped to tolerate it by insistent songs and stories of the wickedness of the city.

The immensely popular "Home on the Range", that cowboy Teddy Roosevelt so cherished, was composed by two Eastern tenderfeet stuck on a homestead in Kansas.

The coming of immigrant groups of different lineage built up urbs-phobia too. It came about that the country boy from the hills of Tennessee journeyed to Chicago expecting only the worst to happen to him, with only his country songs to comfort him.

Too, of course, Hollywood promoted bucolism, the image of rural sweetness and light. The Jesse James gang, a despicable collection of desperados, was cleansed in the blood of Hollywood cameras. Wyatt Earp was another, cut out of whole cloth by Director John Ford. The real Earp was a horse thief, a villainous gangster, murderer, buddy of gamblers, killers, and prostitutes - elected sheriff once in a not uncommon turn - consorted to the end of his life with Josephine Marcus, a "Jewish princess" from San Francisco. In the film, "My Darling Clementine", (1946) he was resurrected in heroic, benign, handsome flesh.

Given their bad public image of violence and stagnation, it could not be the poor Southerners solely, and had to be the New England and North European Northerners that made America give rural life its blessing and brought a curse down upon the city - with all the rurally caused political malapportionment, financial stringencies, tax disproportions, crazy-quilt governmental units and districting that fleshed out the stream of abuse.

Surprisingly, the very media that would be expected to come to the aid of their own - the city newspapers, magazines and publishers - went to all lengths to make the cities ashamed of themselves and the rural people thrill with virtues that they could hardly have dreamed of possessing. Only a hundred and fifty years later did we begin to receive an urban setting for country music themes.

Between 1837 and 1857 a longish period of prosperity for the well-to-do and rising urban middle classes brought a flood of heavy furnishings into the homes of the well-to-do, including the piano. In 1829 there was a new pianoforte for every 4,800 persons, two decades later, a new piano for every 2,777 people, and in 1860 a new piano for every 1500 persons.

The piano was more an index of rich consumption than of musical talent. Jonas Pickering in Boston made 1000 pianos annually by 1860, at which time there was already a piano factory in California. In 1850 the Steinwegs, who had been making pianos in Germany, emigrated to New York, and in a few years established themselves as Steinway and Sons. The family was at first preoccupied with improvements in quality, but gradually public relations and advertising took most of their attention. Eminent musicians were promoted playing on Steinway instruments - Rubenstein and Paderewski among them - and their name became the hallmark of gentility in homes around the country and abroad. The Steinways repeatedly bribed juries at international competitions; they ran their factories paternalistically but intelligently, and kept unions out. Ultimately they would succumb to fresh foreign competition, the decline in the prestige of a piano in the parlor, and electronic recording and electronic instruments of several kinds.

Evangelism called for more and better singing of religious music, and
industry responded with many church organs,
a great many home reed
organs or melodeons,
and a vigorous business of hymnal composition,
led by a prolific composer and promoter of hymns, Lowell Mason of
Boston. He also produced "glee books",
collections of secular songs for singing,
from which grew "glee clubs"
that invested most towns and neighborhoods with
tides of loud song.
This was the time of Stephen Foster, erstwhile Cincinnati
bookkeeper turned composer, whose songs like "Old Kentucky Home"
and "Way Down upon the Sewanee River" were to be
crooned endlessly in America and forever. His folklike melodies
merged Anglo-Irish ditties, Afro-chants and Italian arias.
He himself did not fare too well, owing to
John Barleycorn and a disheveled life,
"losing his grip on things".
His songs were of a subdued melancholy, escapes
into old time and Southern space, or old age, or childhood.
He sings of the Mother sentimentally, and of Maidens who
are dead (one notes his consistency with other American authors
who dwelled upon dead women or symbols thereof).

German-Americans founded the earliest music societies in the
1700's. In non-Germanic America, except for Louisiana,
music was a weak art.
Lorenzo da Ponte, who wrote the Italian librettos of Wolfgang
Amadeus Mozart, emigrated to New York and opened a
food produce market, which he ran for twenty years.
In the later democratic age, classical music was imported
in large quantities via the concert stage. At first,
with a shortage of proficient musicians -
despite two centuries and 100,000 pianos -
solos, duos, trios and quartets sufficed.

There came Ole Bull, a giant from Norway with a marvelously

evocative violin. He composed a number of pieces that he played He came and came again repeatedly, giving in the end 200 concerts after 100,000 miles of travel. So, too, Jenny Lind, the "Swedish nightingale", presented by the notorious promoter Barnum, who paid her $1000 per concert plus half of the net profits, which were large.

In 1848 the Germania Society philharmonic orchestra came to play. Then other symphony orchestras, and finally America started up its own - remarkably the pattern followed with every art form. Anthony Heinrich came over from Bohemia to compose symphonies in classical form and many songs.

It was a vastly enthusiastic and imitative nation. All the while shouting, *"We are the best!"* When a man could not think of what else to say to an Englishman, he might offer, *"Here you know, the sun shines"*.

Two notable art associations operated before the Civil War, the American Art Union and the Cosmopolitan Art Association. They hired reproductions, they bought contemporary art, they published pictorial magazines. The Union, for example, bought works of the German-American Emanuel Leutze, whose wholly fictitious painting of "Washington Crossing the Delaware" he painted while in Dusseldorf. Probably it was to be the best known of all American paintings.

George Caleb Bingham, a "realist" of typical American scenes, polished up his paintings so that even a mongrel stray seems washed and brushed for the occasion - a true predecessor of the peculiarly American Hollywood gift of patining reality. The managers of the Art-Union premeditated practically all of the purchasing, packaging and distribution devices of the art clubs and book clubs of the twentieth century. They were to the American art audience as the Sears Roebuck Catalogue would one day be to the American peasantry.

One might go on with the several painters, sculptors and "schools" such as the Hudson Valley landscape school, but one learns little about art from them. It seems, too, the Americans were more influenced by novelists than by artists. Charles Dickens was of course in the possession of every literate person, he and Sir Walter Scott. Their American publishers made large sums of money.

Some of the better American writers published themselves, perhaps most of them. Walt Whitman is one instance. Longfellow is another. Longfellow learned to reformat his poems, put out variant editions in different setups and collections, and, with occasional co-publishers,
sold 179,000 volumes
between 1839 and 1861.
Books of exploration and travel were especially well-received, as if people had not enough exploring to do near home. Charles Dana's *Two Years before the Mast*, an autobiography of a brief period on a sailing ship voyaging around the Horn, was one. Herman Melville's *Typee* was another, an idyll of the South Seas. Bayard Taylor's *Lands of the Saracens* was a bestseller in 1854.

Books of self-help grew rapidly in this period. History books were popular, and famous names like George Bancroft on the United States, William H. Prescott on the Spanish Empire in the New World, John Lothrop Motley on the Dutch Republic, and Francis Parkman, occur.

All forms of publication expanded in print runs and titles during the ante-bellum years. In 1840 there were 138 dailies, in 1860, 372. Improving technology (better papermaking machines, the rotary printing press, 1846, for example) and faster communications (post-roads, telegraph, railroads, faster steamers, trans-Atlantic cable) gave an illusion that newspapers were improving in content; standards of journalism were base.
In 1840 there were 1,266 weeklies,
in 1860 2,971.
The magazine of choice was, however, the *Edinburgh Review*. *Harper's* first issued at mid-century.

Farm income doubled with the population over a thirty year period, book sales trebled, to $9.5 million in 1860 - but so did all receipts from manufacturing, to $495 millions, already 40% of all farm income.

Public education in its modern sense began in this period in America. It was emerging rapidly in Europe at the same time, under government and Catholic Church auspices, so that there is no reason for believing that the element of volunteerism was all-important. The Catholic bishops of America had as first priority to find priests who could handle the vastly increased parish populations. The not so faithful, who had quit the Church upon arriving in America, before priests and churches were present to serve them, according to a greatly exaggerated estimate, might have produced up to three millions when, in the eighteen twenties, Catholics were counted as a few thousands.

No doubt many of the so-called Scots-Irish were Irish Catholics, forbidden or unable to practice Catholicism; they would rest in some cases with Protestant churches, but it would have been they also, whom the revivalists of the second Great Awakening trumpeted about as given over to atheism and vice on the frontiers.

The next priority was to build churches, and these had to be pretentious; that was the Catholic mentality. A number of the first priests were French refugees from the great Revolution, and, put in charge of parishes composed of Irish clod-hoppers, they proved to be over-qualified: give us a priest who can orate in Irish-English, demanded the people, and of course they were right. They wanted fine churches, aggressive priests and parochial schools: stubborn parishioners they supplied themselves, and had enough of already.

They got all three. Schools were begun by the 1830's and progressed rapidly thereafter. Their curriculum handled the normal three R's well: reading, writing, and 'rithmetic. Their strong catechismic discipline split the child's character neatly into the rational secular and the metaphysical religious: the law of gravitation was one thing, Christ's ascension quite another. Parochial schools kept up in numbers with the public schools until the 1940's, then declined steeply, as did the number of nuns, friars and priests.

Schools espousing reformed theories of education were Protestant and secular and private at first. In 1837 the Massachusetts legislature created a Board of Education with Horace Mann as its first Secretary. There had been already some community public schools, and one state-supported high school. Now a new teacher's training college or normal school was set up (whose capabilities became uniformly drab in pace with its general adoption and imitation around the United States). In 1852 school attendance for the State's children became compulsory. Private schools and Catholic schools, by dint of diligent lobbying, were able to continue their separate existence.

The agitation of Horace Mann and his colleagues at home and elsewhere could attract numerous elements in the population, even granted that the well-to-do often wished that only a select few be provided with schooling at public expense. Protestants needed children who would read along and be captivated at their Sunday School Bible classes. The ambitious and skilled workers felt that schooling was the proper goal of a democracy and of the respectable workman. Women wanted their children to get ahead through literacy. The White collar class was growing by leaps and bounds.

The democratic ideology and rhetoric were crucial to universal public education in the last analysis. Mann believed that an educated population would be a tame population, if only because it would be prosperous. Virtuous activity, morals, were to be an integral part of every child's program. He asserted that an educated people cannot remain poor for long - an important observation that must be part of a democratic ideology. That is, education is a determining variable with regard to wealth. It might also be considered the most important - the most independently operative - of the other values conceived of as variables: power and respect, notably. Education could and can bring increased shares of these. Yet it could subsist profitably without them.

For a time a Protestant version of Christianity was taught,

without interference from law or courts. Ultimately, Catholic, Jewish, liberal Protestants, atheists and agnostics got the Bible out of the schools in most areas. But it was a long struggle that never ended. Millions of Americans never ceased to believe that governments should preach their particular brand of religion. Most likely this would be an anti-papal Protestantism of the most general kind, considering the lack of accord among Protestant denominations. In America the conglomerate of interests surrounding the schools finally settled almost everywhere into a stable truce - no Bible.

The U.S. Census for the year 1880 is cited sometimes for the figure that by then 78% of the total population and 91% of the White population could read and write. That might mean 65% and 75% of the total people. But even so, the figures are incredible. I doubt that so many people could make a sign other than "x" for anything besides their own name. Possibly half of the numbers would be acceptable. That is, less than half the White population could read advertisements and hymn books, and almost none of the Black and Red and Hispanic population, which would give us an overall figure of perhaps 30% literacy. That was not bad, but neither was it good.

Here as elsewhere along the spectrum of social concerns, the dominant groups of Americans knew what ought to be done, but were too individualistic, busy with other things, and racially, religiously, and ethnically too prejudiced to do it.

In those times Harvard was a hospice for Unitarians. There was not much to be said otherwise about its educational mission. For want of competition it perforce turned out a large fraction of the literati and cultural leaders of the country. The student body was socially benighted. Students gave considerable attention to forming exclusive cliques, discriminating against the poorer classes, displaying family distinctions, putting down women, and discovering the latest fashions from London.

They could on occasion provide a mob to harass abolitionists and Democrats. They hissed down Senator Charles Sumner, the quintessential Harvard man, and Ralph Waldo Emerson, when they appeared to lecture against slavery. (Stephen Foster was similarly treated at Dartmouth, one of many instances everywhere.) In 1864, no man of the Harvard or Yale boat crews entered the Army after graduation. Harvard men could also riot on account of bad food, antagonistic professors, rote learning, fellow students undergoing "unjust" punishment, and the usual unconscionable rules of institutions. A revolt of 1823 was especially grave, but had small effect save for some expulsions.

Colleges nourished few social reformers on campus, although some of the great reformers had schooled there. At Lane Presbyterian Theological Seminary in Cincinnati, there appeared the first student political leader, Theodore Weld. He was a charismatic man who, before they could stop him, had conducted soul-searching meetings at the college and had brought a number of sons of slave-holders to denounce the institution. The group was strong, older on average than other college students elsewhere, and readied for action.

When the Lane trustees and faculty asked them to hold off political action until they had graduated, they refused, set up separately, and declared the issue one of free speech as well:

"Proscription of free discussion is sacrilege!
It is boring out the eyes of the soul...",

and went to join the Oberlin College student body. Oberlin, already nearly radicalized, now moved strongly to the center of anti-slavery agitation among the colleges of the nation. Like-minded students came from other schools, Phillips Andover Academy and Marietta College, but not the fancy schools of the country.

In what might well be famed as America's greatest marriage, comparable, say, to the marriage of the British writers, Leonard and Virginia Woolf, a century later, Theodore Weld became the husband of Angelina Grimke.

Princeton students were agitated by the same issues that aroused the Harvard men. They were more destructive, burning down their main building and library on one occasion, other buildings at other times. Bringing a slave along to school was a Princeton practice (it had a strong Southern contingent); liberating him upon graduation was another, certainly superior infinitely to the usual high-jinks.

Not until 1910, in a politically turbulent period nationally, did Harvard students set up a socialist club to consider and take positions on large national and world issues.

Harvard intellectuals were subjected *ante-Bellum* to a large Germanic influence in philosophy and science, which jacked up the intellectual and creative level considerably. Transcendentalism, philosophical idealism and even pragmatism (a reaction) might not have come about, were it not for the influence of Goethe, Hegel, and Fichte.

They were a relief from English philosophy, so dry and empirical. They also relieved the earlier Germans, Kant and the Enlightenment rationalists, whose work had landed in America earlier. Notably these two waves of German philosophy took each a political generation to get to America and exert their full impact. Also noteworthy is the snubbing of Karl Marx and Friedrich Engels, as their work began to appear.

The prototypical proponent of a pragmatic point of view, Charles Sanders Pierce, was the son of a Harvard Professor. William James went to school in this period, where, under Pierce, he began the process of creating pragmatism, using his new-found, German-based experimental psychology as a control over his ventures into the sociology of religion. He it was who gave the most vivid definitions of democracy: democracy, the process of giving one group what it is hollering for, then responding to the reactive hollering from another group, and so on indefinitely. (One notes here the essentially pragmatic method of not asking for absolute truth and ideals, but determining what should be done by observing the consequences of what has just been done.)

❖❖❖

The year 1836 saw the beginnings of what became the Transcendental Club, an intellectual circle meeting here and there in the Boston area to discuss the most important universal problems. The term transcendental implies a world spirit tying in everything, a denial of the material and rational as ultimately productive of the best and most lasting effects.
At least a dozen top-flight American writers and reformers had a hand in the proceedings.
They published a magazine, *The Dial*, which brought them fame and attention in distant parts.
Chief transcendentalist was Ralph Waldo Emerson, who edited the *Little Review.*

He said that *"whoso would be a man, must be a nonconformist"*, and

"It is easy in the world to live after the world's opinion;
it is easy in solitude to live after one's own;
but the great man is he who in the midst of a crowd
keeps with perfect sweetness the independence of solitude".

He wished to down-play all the statistics of production and wealth, and called nations but collections of mobs. He demanded a stop to *"boyish egotism, hoarse with cheering for one side, for one state".*
He asked that America become a nation of world-servants.
He called the Native American Party (the Know-Nothings) a dog in the manger. He believed in a new race of Americans, compounded of many peoples.

He wrote polemical essays; he drew a large income from lectures.
He was America's best epigramist, an inspiration to Friedrich Nietzsche;
he could strike an attitude better than anyone else;
he could go the heart of a matter.
He was a sounder of reform, not its engine.
Detailing precisely the steps he proposed taking, and betaking them himself were not his forte;
he left popular agitation, organization, governing, to others.

Nonetheless, Emerson may unto this day have been the most
eloquent and correct definer of "the American Dream",
of the ideal American person,
of the need for total respect for humanity and brotherly love,
of the contributions of the lowliest in society,
when compared with the most elevated,
of world peace and union.

Parker, Ripley, Thoreau, Brownson, Hawthorne, Margaret Fuller,
Sophia Peabody and her sister Elizabeth were of the group. A related
School struck up in St. Louis, more Germanic, and sent its signals
back East. So nationwide was their media coverage at the
time and in thousands of classrooms and millions of class-years to
come in America, that the transcendentalists have to be regarded as
one of the several top influences acting upon
American minds of high intensity.
(To say an intellectual influence exists is one thing,
to prove it another, *viz* the attempts to show effects of the much
heavier television immersion of young American minds.)

The total number of intellectuals was then minute,
if only because higher education was so rare;
only one or two out of a hundred of the Boston population
attended college in the 1830's and 1840's.
New England women did catch up with the men in
literacy at this time, although they had no chance at a
college education.

The period saw a fruitful re-connection of England with America.
The history of Anglo-American influences may need revision:
for now we had both a heavy English immigration resuming,
about 600,000 of a new sort of
non-American, revised Englishmen of the working classes,
and a new set of cultural bridges among the cultural elite.
The flow of ideas and personages had never been
so large and consequential.

The Unitarian sect was a nuclear factor

with its atoms revolving wildly between the two countries,
engaged in trading goods and ideas.
Intermarriage became more common.
Joseph Priestley, 1733-1804,
was discoverer of oxygen, an experimenter with electricity,
a clergyman, and a political radical - also a
founder of Unitarianism, who organized
a utopian colony on the Susquehanna River.

Harriet Martineau was not just any writing traveler;
she was of a highly engaged English Unitarian
political-religious-business network and family
that went back to the Dissenters of old. Now a
new New England connection was made that was
heavily influential in the intellectual development of the
United States, and, one must add, England as well;
most of the English Unitarians were colored
by republicanism.

Interest in natural sciences was happily more widespread in
America than interest in the World-Soul.
Once more, as with idealism, German influence was strong,
especially in chemistry, biology, psychology, and geology.
The French were active in geology, astronomy, social psychology.
The British were strong in statistics, astronomy.
These are mere indications; what should be remembered
is that this was a fecund period for science.

Practically every science had a "Father of".. in this half century,
Cuvier, "Father of the Science of Paleontology", Auguste Comte,
"Father of Sociology". Alas, there were no fathers in America, only
sons and daughters, practically only sons. Beaumont might have made
the grade of "Father of American Physiology"
when in 1833 he seized the opportunity of
gazing through a glass into the stomach of an injured
Canadien lumberjack, and meticulously detailed the
digestive processes.

Americans did somewhat better in inventing things, although the notion of the Yankee inventor is more mythical than real. There was a host of tinkerers, improvers, clever improvisors, connectors, appliers, handymen, jacks-of-all-trades, all summing up to an advancing tide of technology and industry, but of fundamental inventions and discoveries, what do we have: the eternal Eli Whitney with his cotton gin; Alonzo Phillips and the friction match, 1836; Samuel Colt and the revolver, 1836; Samuel F.B. Morse and, independently, Charles Wheatstone and William Cooke of England, the telegraph, 1837; Charles Goodyear and the vulcanization of rubber (with some counter-claims); Walter Hunt and the safety pin, 1849; Cyrus McCormick and the mechanical reaper (he had some justified patent problems); Jacob Perkins and the mechanical refrigerator, 1834; Elias Howe and the sewing machine, 1845.

The French Revolution and Napoleon developed the sciences of large-scale organization and logistics in military and civil administration. In America, corresponding moves took place: the Du Pont de Nemours explosives company was set up by French refugees; John Hall and Simeon North mass-produced firearms; Alexander T. Stewart opened the first department store, a French invention, in 1846. In the USA, however, the federal and state governments were non-functional compared with the now highly centralized France and Prussia.

Overall and in the Northeast especially, an age of technology loomed up. The *American Journal of Science* issued forth in 1819; Yale and Harvard set up science schools; the Massachusetts Institute of Technology was founded; the United States patent office was systematized and became fully operative. The great Mesabi iron range at the western tip of Lake Superior in Minnesota was discovered. Ether began to be used in surgery. Bigger and better bridges and railroad locomotives were built. The industrial iron age was well along.

In all such affairs the United States was on the trailing edge of Western Europe. The USA was tied to Europe and to a lesser degree to the rest of the world. It was a great thief of ideas and methods. It could figure out how to use them; it was productive. It let other people steal from itself - a wonderful virtue - unless you were to regard it as sheer carelessness; still, if you spend too much time on guard, you get little done.

The myth of equality conjures a myth of inventiveness. A perennial favorite plot has been "the superb creation of a reputed blockhead". Most Americans believed that genius crouches everywhere. They also believed training and education not to be essential. From a hovel or a flat would emerge the genial talent. Inventions would flow therefrom.

Given the capacity of Americans, particularly of the Northeast and the Midwest, for frenzied pursuit of mechanical goals, it would not take long to come abreast of Europe. In Latin America, material resources and cheap manpower were available but little else, and the Iberian Peninsula, their chief European inspirator, had long been in a technological drowse. To the North, where attention to Europe was keen, ideology, material resources, interest in and flexible use of capital investment, and both skilled and cheap manpower were coalescing to the same end, an industrial democracy.

Elizabeth Cady Stanton in 1848, the year she organized the first women's rights convention in Seneca Falls.

Chapter Thirty-seven

Women as Feminists

Whether from a guilty conscience, or in condescension,
or for lack of better to say, historians and orators
speak kindly of the role of women in American history -
pioneering, strong, caring, religiously devout,
willing to brave the dangers of...,
sharing the hardships of menfolk....
Actually, women were characterized by many of
the same vices and virtues as men and children;
women supplied as many opponents to raising the
status of women as did men.

A large proportion of women was incapacitated by
chiliastic religious ideology, waiting for
God to carry forward social reforms.

Another large proportion, not entirely overlapped by these others,
cowered under a domineering master,
who brooked no complaint of woman's role in life.

Against these facts one sets the large fact that
highly commendable deeds - besides keeping house,
bearing the young, sharing education, and amusing
the world around with sex, affection, and social intercourse -
were performed by women.

In the often ignominious struggle for equal rights, too, the
Constitution, the nation's heroes, and the democratic system of
government are excused, as if they were faultless, and the issue of
women's rights dangles out in the social atmosphere by itself, as an
anomaly in an otherwise just and righteous land. In fact, almost
none of the nation's touted leaders were out in front for the
rights of women before these were practically obtained. Name any
ten top heroes of American history before 1915:
you will be lucky if one of them had a record of advocacy
of women's rights before these rights were
in some cases adopted.

It could happen naturally that a woman who was a feminist and
educator might still write a book that proudly found "no examples of
profligate females" or "of bold and criminal ambition".
Compared with England and France,
*"..old and wily nations, the character of America
is that of youthful simplicity, of maiden purity;
and her future statesman will say, as he reads the story,
my country was the most virtuous among the nations".*
Thus Mrs. Emma Willard, whose histories of the United States
sold 400,000 copies
between 1828 and 1860.

A political system that does not provide the possibilities of change is
imperfect; if it does not encompass change that is needed to make it

consistent with itself, it is disabled. Such could be said about the American system of government and the leadership it provided for a century and a half, for it could not manage to cope with the glaring inconsistencies of women's subjection, in a system full of self-glorifying praise of equal rights.

A full philosophical equipage for winning women's rights, that American women could use, was even then available. The Enlightenment philosophers had cleaned out human nature to provide room for nurture to equalize all persons regardless of sex. Human rights were equally inherited. The Declaration of Independence and many Bills of Rights created all "men" equal but women knew that here "men" stood for all humans, all of mankind. That's what Locke and Rousseau meant.

At the same time women might look to romanticism and transcendentalism as showing the ultimate unity and harmony of all creation, women and men included indiscriminately. Many of the utopias were communitarian and socialist, as such providing the full bag of equal rights for women and men. Tasks were often apportioned according to logical, efficient and/or philosophically tenable rules that redefined workplaces.

The American radical sects established areas of sex equality, beginning with the Levellers of the seventeenth century in England, but now two centuries later strongly notable in Quakerism, especially the Hicksite Quakerism of Elias Hicks. Radical Protestant sects got rid of much of the clerical opposition to women's rights that had been ensconced in the ministries of the larger and more disciplined groups. Unitarians were prominent in the movement, too, they and their less intellectual brethren of the Universalist Church. The number of women leaders was perhaps a hundred in ten million women, yet one study of fifty-one feminist-abolitionist leaders revealed that 21 grew up in Quaker, Unitarian or Universalist households, and that another 9 of them changed from their early religion to one of these three sects in the course of their lives. Most apparent here is the tiny proportion of top elite among a great mass of people.

Intensity of the reform movement for women's rights rose sharply in the decades before the Civil War, and indeed brought forward most of the arguments and reactions to be experienced until the renewed agitation of the late 1900's. Like every other reform movement called in under the new umbrella of direct democracy, it was largely a failure. It raised consciousness and opened all cards on the table.

Women of the age were asked to possess the virtues of piety, purity, submissiveness, and domesticity. The terms were and are clear enough. They bespeak religious conformity within one's family sect, the wearing of modest dress, abstinence from tobacco, and sexual confinement to the spouse or celibacy, obedience to the husband's wishes or to one's father, and contented devotion to household maintenance and child-rearing. The prudent woman pretended to all of the virtues. If none of this brought the male into a corresponding virtuous state, there was prayer.

By then an increasing band of women sought not only more personal freedom but legal equality with men. They pointed out with indignant perplexity that the whole democratic movement, taking such pains to apportion votes among the mass of White men, was unconcerned with giving a vote to even a few women. Nor did the vastly extended new White electorate turn to a resolution of any other of the oppressions weighing down upon women. For women had many more grievances than men.

But anyone, male or female, who dared to challenge the

fundamental virtues, was widely condemned as an enemy of God and of the Republic. Religion, of course, was deemed to be the proper sphere of women if they must leave the home for any reason, and the reform movements that subtended from their church sects were only sometimes tolerated. Margaret Fuller, a prominent editor and literary critic, ran seminars for upper class ladies on the subject-matter of feminism. Her book, *Woman in the Nineteenth Century* (1845), argued for erasing all intellectual and economic disabilities of women. She asked for the fulfillment of women's powers in every sphere. She was hardly permitted to proceed with her activity.

The pecksniff was legion in American life. You needed not to rub a magic lamp to evoke the crowd, the so-called public, Thomas Jefferson, who was not always right, deemed women to be too sensitive for politics, that they should be preserved from its rigors. But he recognized the enemy:

> *"This country, which has given to the world the example of physical liberty, owes to it that of moral emancipation, also; for as yet it is but nominal with us. The inquisition of public opinion overwhelms, in practice, the freedom asserted by the laws in theory".*

With women, as with slaves, children, foreigners, and just about every other category of the population, the Bill of Rights of the Federal Constitution did not provide ample protection for most reform activities, nor even for cases at law; neither did the states' bills of rights cover a full range and, what was worse, were not believed to apply to a great many circumstances where today people would be shouting for a lawyer. Freedoms of speech, press, assembly, religion, movement, occupation, education, dress, and association were often available, but only when the shadow of a presumed public opinion did not fall upon them.

Liberty could be nothing, ever and now, but the
freedom to act as one wished. Without moral guidance,
be it Jefferson's directives or the Gospels, or the
very devil, it was a lust, libinal and genetic,
stronger in some people than in others.
Like sexual lust or avarice or craving for dominance,
lust for liberty has no morals to begin with,
no restrictions in nature save impotence and impossibility,
but must be culturally defined, formulated, constrained, and
released according to cultural norms -
the metes and bounds of society working upon
the "yen to do whatever I want".

The biography of any one of a dozen well-known agitators
would tell us much the same story of the feminist movement.
Sarah and Angelina Grimke, Elizabeth Cady Stanton, Lucretia Mott,
Lydia Marie Child, and the aforesaid Margaret Fuller were
perhaps the most prominent and effective workers.

Englishwoman Harriet Martineau nearly belongs.
An economist, journalist, and feminist,
her visit to America in the thirties and the
publication of her three volumes on American civilization
brought the problems of women in themselves, and in the reform
movements, before the British and American publics.
It is a commentary both upon her conscientiousness
and the isolation of American centers of learning,
that not a single visitor from Britain had come
to the University of Virginia until 1835 when,
to the delight of professors and their families, she showed up there.
(One feels that she must be mistaken, that she believed those
indulgent Southern voices, hospitably exclaiming.)
Martineau was exceedingly kind to Americans.
She thought that the women were basically pretty,
if the prettiness were not spoiled by generally poor health
and a nasal twangy way of speaking.
She also sensed that they did not bathe frequently,
and wondered at the lack of sanitary facilities

aboard large steamboats. (Perhaps her acquaintances were hoity-toity: common Methodists would have been cleaner.)

She found the hotel floors, boat decks, and walks slimy with tobacco spit, but tried to overlook it and exclaimed instead over the beauties of the empty countryside. She was appalled at the mob spirit that would appear so quickly and do such extensive damage.

She particularly liked Cincinnati, a healthy city, she thought, with many nice dwellings surrounded by fine gardens. The large number of public school children impressed her here. (This would be even before Massachusetts, and ahead of England and France.)

A rich and respected citizen, she says, told how he had come less than fifty years ago when buffalo browsed among the cane brakes and Indians outnumbered the one hundred Whites, but now over 30,000 people dwelled in the city, coming from several nations, prospering in diverse industries, directing the teeming traffic of the Ohio River. Land that was bought for a dollar an acre brought now $40.

She described a later famous incident of anti-slavery crusading that occurred during her visit. A committee of women had called a meeting at the Hall of Liberty (Faneuil) in Boston, there hopefully to meet William Lloyd Garrison, editor and prominent leader of the anti-slavery agitation. But posters had been plastered around the town calling citizens to assemble and block the proposed meeting. Hundreds of men came. Many women were kept from passing through to the meeting. Abuse and filth were hurled at them. The mob threatened to break in. The mayor said he could do nothing.

The women nevertheless persisted in conducting a full meeting. Meanwhile Garrison with his wife had been caught. A rope was hung around his neck, and he was dragged through the streets. Finally he was released when a burly stranger intervened with a show of authority and escaped with him.

An especially appealing character was Sarah Grimke. She wrote books, carried on a heavy public correspondence, organized meetings, lectured, pressured politicians, and co-directed an advanced kind of elementary school in New Jersey - coed, with a broad curriculum, and pragmatic. In the late nineteen hundreds all of these activities would be gladly tolerated, but in the early and middle 1800's such feminists were hassled by individuals, newspapers, and mobs; abuse both personal and general fell from every quarter.

Hardly had women begun their protests against slavery, and by inference - because they were publicly assertive - against the suppression of women, when the Council of Congregational Ministers of Massachusetts issued a pastoral letter denouncing their conduct as unwomanly and un-Christian. Prayer for religious causes in religious settings is acceptable for women, read the letter,

"but when she assumes the place and tone of man as a public reformer... she yields the power which God has given her for her protection, and her character becomes unnatural".
In other words, she deserves whatever happens to her - along with other fallen women.

Grimke came from a leading family in Charleston, South Carolina. She had every opportunity that one might then hope to have; of course, she was not let to practice law, as she would wish. Her younger sister Angelina was thoroughly sympathetic and, while Sarah stressed feminism, Angelina pressed against slavery before all else - never mind that her family owned slaves. The sisters were the first female "professional" agitators against slavery.

They were the only women in Theodore Weld's gang of seventy that toured New England in the late thirties declaiming against slavery. Born in 1792 and 1805, the sisters lived long, moved about in the field less as they grew older. Over the years, Sarah was especially concerned with the dreadful circumstances of working women. At the ages of seventy-eight and sixty-five, in 1870, the Grimke girls led forty-two women through a snowstorm to cast ballots in an election. They were not let to vote, but deposited their ballots and marched home.

In her *Letters on the Equality of the Sexes*, addressed to Mary S. Parker, President of the Boston Female Anti-Slavery Society, and printed in William Lloyd Garrison's *Liberator* before being published in book form, and in other essays, Sarah struck at the deprivation of women with regard to the full range of life's values. The total dispossession of power was paramount in importance, for with power, other values are more easily won. The laws that practically seized a woman's property and earnings on behalf of the husband were reviewed. The unavailability of proper and sufficient educational opportunities for women, the restrictions on their mobility and occupations, and the suppression of their freedom of expression were exposed. Today most of this is an old story, yet many of the vital facts stay unchanged.

Of the goods of life, affection, love, is most independent of the agglutinative effect observable, of the tendency of all values to be enjoyed at a high or low level together: if you possess one, especially if it is power, you are likely to gain the others. Except that affection is semi-autonomous.

Giving and accepting love does not explicate one's situation in regard to the other values. Into exchanges of affection go various currencies. Grimke's attitude to sex in marriage is an objection to the brute in the husband (the American male was not then, at least, the world's greatest lover), and to the male's purely exploitative use of his wife.

Sarah Grimke's position changed from minimalist to maximalist in the course of her life, to use terms that were unknown then, but

bring her into current relevance. From a vision that is
male-centered, touting minimal sex-differences,
to a maximalist women-are-different gynocentric vision,
means that her earlier concerns were colored by
justifiable jealousy of male attributes
(Freud's concept of "penis-envy") and the
injustice of not being permitted to compete for and aspire to them,
whereas her later interests came to reside in the strength,
beauties, and bonds possessed by women.
Obviously, given one or the other of these dispositions,
the character of love and affection will be different

But, also, these two visions of women logically
present more dichotomous dispositions toward the other values.
If the inherent position of woman is determined
at least in part by her identification with the Earth Mother
and a uniquely feminine model of fulfillment,
then her philosophy of life must be substantially
different from men's.

Statistically she can be measured as to her power, wealth, respect,
knowledge, and experience on any items that are proposed, but the
measures will be less reliable; the human meaning of the measures
will vary between the sexes. Properly construed, this would bring
about a much expanded and richer gamut of life's values, not so
male-defined and male-centered, but human-centered,
meaning universally variable in people .
Power, wealth, respect, knowledge would acquire
vastly broader horizons. And so affection.
For this situation a pluralist, yet truly individualist,
society would be convoked.

Thus one may pursue the logic of Sarah Grimke's ideas,
while admitting that the practical achievements of her movement were
disappointing. One may well ask:
What did the women's movement do wrong,
that prevented it from obtaining at least the vote for
generations to come?

True, as was said in rebuttal, they had not the vote in Europe.
Still, the suffrage reforms of America were generally
ahead of those of Europe, and were not Americans forever crowing
about the progressive nature of their society? Is it one more indication
of the fraudulence of Jacksonian democracy?

In 1848 at Seneca Falls, New York,
a conclave of women was called.
Lucretia Mott and Elizabeth Cady Stanton were among its primary
sponsors. They prepared a "Declaration of Sentiments"
that followed the pattern and style of the
Declaration of Independence, detailing all
the wrongs of women and asking equality.

The document was more valid than the Declaration of Independence.
The signers were mostly of rural roots, with experience of
working on equal and reciprocal terms with men,
who typically engendered large households and extended families.
They might be distinguished from urban feminists who came to demand
equality in the course of their benevolent social work.

Soon the movement would take a back place to the abolition
movement. More should have been accomplished.
Did the failure originate in what was perceived as
the snobbery of the bluestockings,
that alienated Western and working class women?
Did the Catholic priests throw their weight
on the side of most Protestant ministers
against women's suffrage because they were
trained and disciplined to do so;
did they serve women faithfully only in order to make
the lot of the downtrodden male more bearable?
Was it the reluctance of the Southern belle to speak out
against discrimination, for fear that after women's rights would
come the rights of slaves?
Should not the movement have concentrated its
resources upon one state and
only the vote to begin with?

Did American males all this while nurse an unconscious grudge against domineering Moms?

Reform movements in most cases began
in religious settings, the peculiar American Protestant scene, later
Catholic as well, where the congregation was the most important
bonding agent of half the population for community welfare
extending beyond rites and doctrine: did churchmen fear that women
would soon thereafter dominate church elections and
control church funds?

Was it the Civil War, that would ruin so many good things
or put them off for a long time?

These nine questions find their place
in the total explanation, with the answer always, "Yes!"

And what of the long-term effects upon women
of discrimination and their frustrated attempts to overcome it?
One would expect to discover the same psychic
phenomena as would be enhanced among all groups
suffering from invidious discrimination. Certainly there would
be bred in many women more than a modicum of resentment, an
undercurrent of aggression (including the use of children as
unconscious champions against men),
an unwillingness to respond to the prompts of men and society,
a higher than average paranoid quotient, and
some nasty internecine controversy among women
(frequently stirred up by men),
all of which would tend to compound the problem of
establishing a fair and affectionate relationship
among *(sic)* the sexes. So here is a tenth "Yes".

That only multiple causes suffice to explain
does not excuse the stubborn, sluggish, negative response.
Their consequences added up to a shameful social
condition and continuous failure of the American political system
that was to endure at least into the year 2000.
But while the system failed, it elicited instances of
civil courage of the highest order.

Comparing the records of the foremost fifty women with those of the most prominent fifty males of American history in the nineteenth century, and assigning scores for that precious quality of a republic, *civil courage*, there can be little doubt that the women would emerge with a higher average score.

Elections polling place scene.

Chapter Thirty-eight

Political Parties and Legislatures

Partisan spirit has always been high in America,
although often denounced. In the hubbub it generates,
one can rarely distinguish between emotion and enthusiasm
on the one hand and an actual confrontation
over meaningful issues on the other hand.
Politics, though vociferous, have been
vaguely focused and opportunistic.

What happened all along, as today, was that the significance of an issue came to be measured by the turbulence surrounding it. Jacksonian democratic and populist politics frequently have used acoustical waves to make a hash of issues. A few men who want to succeed with an issue, for whatever reasons, try first for secrecy, but, if that will not work, will deal in decibels.

In 1850 the only country in the world with a political party in the modern sense of the term was the United States. Elsewhere in constitutional regimes, factions, clubs, and political circles could be found. The British had not gotten around to organizing at the lowest levels, complete with intra-party elections and conventions; the suffrage was still quite limited. By this time, the American party consisted of its present forms in large part; it was a sprawling, unmanageable network of committees at all levels of government, clustered like phagocytes around the aspirant to office.

There were as many different versions of the political party as there were local, county, state, and federal governments. Fortunately, the varieties were homologs: know one, know all. A useful definition of the American Party in those times would be: a hopefully national network of persons who believed that they had enough in common to warrant their cooperating in electing selected candidates for public office.

There was a great deal of talk in the early years of the republic about the evils of factionalism in a country, as if any government in the world ever lived without factions, or with factions all good. The Framers have to be docked points for not appreciating the significance of this fact for their baby. They knew all about the Tories and Whigs of England; could they not have drawn the conclusion about themselves: there would be parties. All the more so, since there was no monarch to confuse the issue. How to organize them was the question. The problem solved itself, non-constitutionally.

The political elite could hardly wait for George Washington to bow out of the scene before dividing into two factions overtly to dominate the succession. John Adams managed a difficult term denying the need for a formal opposition. Then came the horrendous election of 1800. The party system arose from the mire of politics full-blown. No better proof of its existence (many doubters and wishful thinkers were still about) could be had than in the results of the electoral college.

Every elector who voted for Jefferson voted for Aaron Burr as well. The Federalists, more sophisticated, arranged so that Adams would have one more electoral vote than his acknowledged vice-Presidential candidate, Pinckney. However, Jefferson had a clear majority and so Burr. But each had 100 and it took 36 ballots in the House of Representatives before Jefferson could out-tally Burr. (I pointed out earlier that this episode so frightened everybody that the Twelfth Amendment to the Constitution passed quickly, so as clearly to distinguish who was running for what office.)

Although it is true that the first parties to form were recognizably divided according to those who thought the well-to-do should rule and those who thought all adult White males should have a crack at ruling, there were other reasons for parties to establish themselves and reasons why, once established, they could only go so far in running the country.

The main reason for parties to occur was not that there would always be two or more sides to every question, nor that the government needs to have a concerted set of policies to act upon, nor that people should know who is responsible for the mess they are in, nor etc., but basically it is twofold:
politics is so confused and nonsensical
that some simple explanation of it all has to be given,
enabling people who elect the people to run affairs
to group themselves in some semblance of order
for the purpose of choosing.

Second, and tightly tied into this, is the need
universally felt on occasion for
some kind of change, meaningless though it be, and the
superior sense of power it gives people to know that
they can effect such a change.
As for what happens once the change occurs, that is anybody's guess. If one took all the pledges, prescriptions, programs, agendas, plans, policies, manifestoes, declarations of principles,

platforms, etc of all the parties and then associated them,
after cleaning them like fish,
alternately with the blade of one party then of the others,
and afterwards compared these results with the historical record,
the correlation of claimed goals with subsequent real
happenings would be low and
equally low for both parties in a two-party system.

For three or more parties the result would be the same.
They raise a sharper set of issues, but they are therefore
shunted aside with their faithful small fraction of votes.
That is, party programs were practically nonsense
in the golden period of party formation in America;
voters for one party might as well have belonged to the other party,
from the viewpoint of the legislation and the
administration of the laws that followed.

Profoundly, the very act of voting begs its own proof: that the total nominating campaign, electoral campaign, results and effects in the processes of legislation are and were and would be rational. The meaning of the party, as of the vote, is that the voter is facilitated in a triumphant exercise of self-deception. He can, in casting his vote, unite himself with the mass of people in a universal rite. He is at the same time assured, just as surely as by a priest at a sacral ritual, that the political party has framed his views into a universal demand and presented them for enactment by the Godlike State, and that all that happens subsequently is therefore his work, too.

The party is the priest that helps the voting acolyte get to heaven. That the voting participation may range from 20% to 90% of those eligible means little, here, only that people are often backsliders. But they will be back in church perhaps at the next election, if only the party religionists would invent more persuasive promises and assurances and explanations as to why his dreams died the first time around.

Hardly had Andrew Jackson come and gone when several first-rate theorists were rationalizing the American political party. Francis Lieber immigrated to South Carolina from Germany and wrote the first systematic book of political science since that of John Adams. He defined the political party, which by now was witnessed all about him, as a group of men organized in lawful pursuit of a common interest that they thought sincerely would help the country. He believed citizens should join a party, or be considered weak or self-interested. Importantly, he believed that *"it is impossible for civil liberties to exist without parties".*

John Hammond wrote a history of New York (1842), affirming throughout lengthy volumes, that parties must and should exist. They clarify public issues, argue policy, check corruption, and are a peaceful substitute for political violence. He supported the use of the spoils (that is, a free replacements) system as a way of getting things done expeditiously. He also stressed and advocated stronger party discipline, a common demand and plaint ever thereafter.

Frederick Grimke, remarkable brother of the great sisters, like them, moved North, where, in seclusion, he wrote *The Nature and Tendency of Free Institutions* (1848), under the inspiration of Auguste Compte and Alexis de Tocqueville. He offers the singular theory that the system of checks and balances is inadequate. It must be socially holistic.

*"Parties take the place of the old system of checks and balances.
The latter balance the government only,
the former balance society itself".*

The composition of the party being so diverse, the accommodations that parties make become social compromises of large scope and effect. The clash of opinions is healthy, vital; the encounter of rival opinions imposes a discipline of thought upon the society. There is no place for unanimity, a false notion.

The structures of political parties of America have burgeoned since the beginnings, often of their own accord and often by dint of reform movements which sought to improve them. Essentially, then, as now, the party system came to display the traits that I already indicated in the first paragraph above, the plethora of committees. And the whole was extremely decentralized.

Generally nominations began with state laws prescribing an application or filing and a number of supporting signatures. The parties, however, "owned" a valuable label and sought to pin this label only upon approved candidates. Therefore, before long, party leaders in a legislature, often in touch with influential outsiders, would designate the party's candidates for the various offices to be contested.

Then, since a hue and cry was raised against caucuses for being undemocratic, the parties began to set up conventions in the county, the city, the state, and the nation. In this regard state parties were innovative: a new and weak but obstreperous party, the Anti-Masonic Party, was the first to hold a national nominating convention. This pushed the great parties also to hold Presidential nominating conventions, with varying ways of bringing together a number of elected and specially chosen party stalwarts.

The Anti-Masonic Party was a grouping of religious fundamentalists, liberals, and Catholics who sympathized against a common enemy, against what they believed to be - helped in this by a sizeable paranoia - a secret conspiracy by non-believers to take over the country. All this excitement was occasioned by the alleged murder by Masons of an ex-member, who threatened to tell all. It expired after several years of influence in local and state elections and was a flat failure with a Presidential candidate in 1832. But it denigrated the Masonic order in America for decades.)

Another minor party later on was the Know-Nothing or Native American Party, officially termed (and not Amer-Indian), a native workingman's party mostly, for agitating and legislating against the foreign-born, Catholics, and African-Americans. It, too, waged several campaigns in the states with

limited success and raised a large vote,
which fell into the lap of the oncoming Republican Party.
(Samuel F.B.Morse was an excellent painter and
an inventor of the telegraph,
but also a bigoted author who accused American Catholics of
conspiring to destroy liberty, and who
ran for office with the "Know-Nothings" in 1836.)

The two-party system was multiple, not only in these cases of novel competing parties, but also from the split factions of the larger parties, the Whigs and Democrats (Jefferson's Democratic-Republicans). These splits were fatal and exhibited the ineptitude of the American party system.

The Constitution did not preclude anyone who was a natural-born citizen of the United States from running for the Presidency.
So how could the possibility be eliminated?
There were now parties, but no one laid down a law preventing anyone else in the party from running for President.

In 1824 the question became critical. The Congressional caucus that had taken on the nominating function was discredited by democratic sentiment. First the Tennessee Legislature nominated Jackson. Then the Georgia legislature, which favored William Crawford, resolved that only the Congressional caucus of the Democratic Party could legitimately nominate the candidate. So a minority of Congressmen made up a caucus and nominated Crawford. Three other candidates were nominated by caucus or convention:
Clay, Calhoun and Adams.

For the second and last time, the House of Representatives received the job of selecting among candidates no one of whom had a majority of the electoral vote. Adams was elected then by the House (with the states' delegations casting each a single vote). The thought that there would be several candidates often, and that the House would be soon electing the President, was too much for the country to take, and the

national convention of the party for the nomination of
Presidential and vice Presidential candidates
took over the task forever after.

The effects of the decentralization of the American party were great. Its beneficiaries defied numerous attempts at centralizing, and succeeded, because decentralization was locked into the system. The Framers, without quite realizing it, accomplished their chief aim of keeping any party from developing and representing a majority that would be fixed upon a sentiment opposed to their interests.

But what they wanted instead - a nice nest with eggs of their own kind perennially hatching at the time of election in the name of the whole undivided nation - did not come about either. They did not get what they wanted, but they denied what would have been the heart's delight among the party organizers and the great mass of the public, an unconscionable majoritarian centralized government enacting one set of foolish laws after another.

The parties became rickety electoral machines.
They could never manage to get complete control
over their party operations in all states.
They could not select nearly all of the candidates that the
top elite would have preferred. They could not get their
candidates to work in unison, or to sacrifice anything substantial for
the common cause. They could not guarantee any
program of legislation or administration.
They could not guarantee that the President and a majority of
one or both houses of Congress would be of the same party.
They could not make either the President or the party
Congressional leaders the actual leaders of the party
over the whole country; the same-named parties
in state legislatures and local governments would rarely
feel compelled by them.

Thus we had a complete decentralization of
parties, making impossible of realization
the concept, idealized in many liberal minds, of a

responsible party government in the United States. The remote possibilities, looked at from the perspective of that day, were that the executive branch of government in Washington could control so many jobs that a party of patronage would tie in all of the party offices around the country - which happened only once, during the New Deal, as we shall see - and a second possibility, more remote than it sometimes appeared to be - the possibility of a national leader with such charismatic powers that he might obtain a centralized party working for his program and under his will, regardless of the formal limits to his power. In such a case, there would be the danger of a government of a single-minded party, as was feared by some in the time of Jackson, Lincoln, and Franklin Delano Roosevelt.

Given the effective federal system and state control over elections central control was practically impossible. (Congress, strongly tied to local interests within its districts, always delegated the conduct of federal elections to the states, although the Constitution would have readily permitted Congress to set up a separate federal system.)

Given sectionalism, too, there would be no central party program except at the risk of offending North or South or west, or subdivisions thereof.

Inasmuch as political parties were not mentioned in the Constitution and were at least in their beginnings fully extra-legal voluntary associations, there could have been little support in Congress for granting to the parties nationwide authority to control and discipline their membership; furthermore, any attempt to dictate party organization and membership to all state and local candidates would have correctly aroused a clamor of "unconstitutional"!

Hampered by the Constitution and by it own dependence upon local politicians, and by its resulting modest estimates of itself, Congress did not give the impression that it would a century later, of being the most powerful legislative body in the world. The individual state legislatures had many more powers over their constituents. But they, too, were kept by the doctrine of limited government and by their own modesty from undertaking grand projects.

The Erie Canal and other such works, and the railroad land and bond arrangements were indeed large and important. State legislatures were almost forced to act in these cases; it was the Governor of New York, Clinton, it will be recalled, who backed the Erie Canal vigorously for some years to get it finally inaugurated. Ordinarily the legislatures were content with budgets and fiscal flows the size of a supermarket's on today's typical mall. Their vast police powers went unused. They worried over many matters of election administration, land titles, and the naming of people to the still few offices. They worried over their own election, and over the elections of their friends and enemies down to the most local of elective offices.

The idea of justifying federalism by the innovative designing of laws to fit the geo-social-economic conditions and human welfare of the state was nowhere perceptible; possibly one could detect it in Massachusetts on occasion. State legislatures, whether 13 or even more so when 30, were like a collection of vases whose slight variations in style and lip would pass quite unnoticed by most observers, although the slight differences might arouse furious debate among connoisseurs.

Congress adopted most of the very rules of the Congress of the Articles of Confederation. It took no pleasure in innovation. Its members were not usually intimate with the President and Cabinet, no more than today. It relied upon *ad hoc* committees for many issues coming before it. It began then to appoint standing committees, to whom bills of special types might be referred by the Speaker.

Presiding over the House and determining often the introduction and passage, or the death, of all legislation, the Speaker, elected by its members, became for a time the most powerful officer of the

Federal government, a kind of Prime Minister. Henry Clay of Kentucky played this role for many years. He had his troubles with the sometimes unruly and disorderly House members. He dueled with one of them, a nasty chap named John Randolph, whose conduct was regularly so obnoxious that, if he had been anywhere except upon the floor of the House, he would have been booted out as crazy. If he had been anybody but a Randolph of Virginia, he would have been incarcerated in one of the foul lunatic asylums of the time. Neither man was hurt in the exchange of gunfire.

In the Senate, standing committees also developed. So long as the House had a membership not too greatly in excess of the Senate, and because it controlled the purse strings without challenge, the House was the more powerful and respected of the two bodies.

Other factors favored senatorial power and prestige. For one, like it or not, only the Senate, affording a disproportionate representation of the Southern population was upholding the crisis of sectionalism in the country.

And Senators had long terms of six years.

Too, in a later development, the allowance of unlimited debating time and the resulting right to filibuster *ad infinitum ad nauseam* to block disfavored legislation fell to the Senators.

When, two political generations later, direct election by the voters of the state was prescribed for Senate seats, instead of selection by the legislatures, the Senate gained new authority in the public and political mind.

Soon now, one could say that Congress was ruled by a system of standing committees, whose chairmen gained their exalted position of command over the bills relative to their committee by the customary rule of seniority. Like the malapportionment already apparent, that was giving rural areas preference in all legislatures and in Congress over urban areas, the seniority system in the Congress and legislatures gave the "safe districts" of the legislature - seats whose incumbents (and political party) were invariably reelected -

much greater than average influence and power. Since such safe districts came disproportionately from the more unchanging country than from the cities, the system was once more predisposed to the rural point of view.

The great issues of the first memorial generation, 1790-1860 - meaning by issues specific economic-social preferences that politicians and people believed to be the subjects of their disputes - were only six: whether the tariff schedule generally should be high or low; whether the federal government should actively manage the banking and currency of the country; whether the government should actively promote public works construction; how the public land should be granted and sold; whether and how slavery should be contained; and how far a state might go in rejecting the application of federal law within its borders (states rights).
To these would be added the questions of war and peace: how did the parties differ on the War of 1812 and the Mexican War, and in the Indian Wars and in the boundary disputes with England in Oregon, and Spain in Florida.

The resolution of these questions has already been revealed or will soon be. The tariff was continuously raised and lowered as elections seemed to demand. Often what was at issue was not a general tariff schedule, but a tariff on specific items to which one region or even one district of the country was sensitive. The tariff issue continued forever, and a scholar would be rash to denote high or low tariffs, and any particular tariff, as generally beneficial or harmful.

The South wanted low tariffs, the North high, the agrarian West low. The idea (Hamilton's), we recall, was that high tariffs encouraged American industry and allow higher workers' wages. The former is true in that the extra charge on a foreigner's goods profited entrepreneurs, letting them not only stay in business with higher costs, but also giving them extra money to invest in expansion or new enterprise. Planters and farmers would have to pay higher prices for domestically produced machines and stuff, and also for foreign-produced material.

The worker's wage was kept level by low-wage immigrants, slavery and the political system.

But there are several intervening variables: both foreign and domestic producers might become more efficient in the situation, one because he must, the other because he has the larger production and advantages of scale. Too, the country should welcome a charge on its goods occasioned by tariffs, if as a result its life and industry become more varied and its population more skilled.

However, against this goes the pollution resulting from industrial production. The trading partner may now slap a duty on incoming cotton or wheat or tobacco either in simple retaliation or to use the money in some way to support its own injured people. Smuggling goes up and down with the tariff, too.

These are mere beginnings of the complex causal interactions that occur with (or without) tariffs. It might be useless here to go to great lengths in the analysis of even a single tariff struggle.

People of direct democratic persuasion were likely to be agrarian (most of the country) and favor easy money, meaning by this the easy availability of ordinarily inflated currency that can be used to pay back debts, because farmers were usually in debt. Furthermore, with easy money, one could borrow to buy more land with which to speculate, and to plant additional land once the present land collapses from exhaustion; to buy slaves; to buy the machines newly coming upon the market; and to buy consumer goods, also becoming available in large quantities from the industrializing countries and the East.

Most bankers were not frauds and therefore would wish to have a stable currency. If they were frauds they would play several kinds of games to extract wealth from others. They would issue bank notes without gold or silver backing, or the backing of one of the world's stable banks (although none were available except in the several large American centers of commerce).
They would obtain assets in cash, titles, and possessions,

hide them and declare bankruptcy.

(Foreign observers were struck by the readiness of the better class of citizens to declare bankruptcy whenever convenient, maintaining one's social position, and then returning to banking or another risky enterprise with newly obtained or retrieved capital. The early experiences were not forgotten: rather than diminishing over time, the number of bankruptcies reached an all-time high in 1997-8.)

The United States National Bank came and went twice and would soon come again. The Treasury of the United States would also be used as a central banking agent for the mixed-up internal fiscal affairs of the government, and it would issue bonds or convert bonds. State legislatures engaged in highly risky practices (showing that the reluctance to innovate does not arise out of a fear of taking risks so much as from a void of principled motives).

They brought on a steady stream of bankruptcies by letting bankers issue paper money, and by selling land to people without the ability to pay for it. (No matter how "ridiculously cheap", the mass of people was too poor to buy.) Corruption in land and banknotes were a normal part of legislative proceedings in all parts of the nation.

Both federal and state legislatures occupied themselves regularly with debate and legislation over the disposal of public lands. Ultimately the issue became tied up with the slavery issue and the secession-states rights issue. For, do you give land only to men without slaves, or to anybody otherwise qualifying. And the great stretches of land bred one Congressional struggle after another. In a chapter to come, we shall return to this complex of issues over the creation of territories and the admission of states.

While apparently doing little in the way of constructive legislation for improving the welfare and culture of the people of the country, the state legislatures and particularly Congress began to position the Union for disaster over apparently unresolvable issues.

They failed, the party system failed, the Constitution failed,

in providing the chief and most beneficial operation of government,:
to block access to power of those who would
paralyze it, bring it down, or rule it absolutely.

The next most beneficial operation - that of creating a climate of
free opportunity and creativity - failed, too.
As for civil rights,
some could be had, by some people, here and there.

Battle of Mobile Bay, 1864

Part Eight

CIVIL STRIFE

The real war will never get in the books.
WALT WHITMAN

By the end of the period of egalitarian illusion,
when wealth and deference and power
were as concentrated, at least in the original states,
as they ever were and would be,
a class of accomplished, dedicated agitators had grown up
in the Northeast, that went from target to target of the
many evils of the country, until, finally,
the largest, most consecrated group of all settled down
upon the issue of slavery.

When this occurred, a fatal commitment overcame them -
politicians, educated men and women, publicists,
fanatic undistinguished citizens, and ministers -
to engage in struggle by all means necessary against
an equally adamant resistant group of Southern
editors, lawyers, politicians and planters,
until the slaves should be freed.

Political agitators were never suffered gladly in America,
whatever their variety and number. They had to be tolerated
in many places. Then, with the flow of communications speeded up,
and enhanced, and the facilities of travel greatly expanded,
barbed arrows from Massachusetts drew blood in South Carolina.
Soaring statistics of the rapidly populating,
industrializing, foreign North sandpapered
the always tender sensibilities of the Southerners.

It is about time to talk of the Civil War, we sense,
but I would approach the subject by denying it
the neat encapsulation usually provided:
from the firing upon Fort Sumter in early 1861
to the surrenders at Appomattox Courthouse and elsewhere
in the Spring of 1865, conceded it has given a handy
frame for the myriad buffs and military men
who have made it the
world's most popular war game.

Speak as they will, with all the media in amplification,
of "brilliant tactics" and "heroic generals" who march
their soldiers up the hill and down again (with severe losses),
they only persuade me that the
Civil War's meaning has been swinging in too narrow a compass.

"God forbid", orated Senator Robert Y. Haynes to a
Congregational Church of Charleston in 1831,
"that the Union be now dissolved", but tyranny in the
new form it had assumed in Washington must be
resisted to the death.

Back of this pietist rhetoric was typical
paranoiac overreaction to high tariffs,
a paranoia that would assume plague proportions
with the human issue of slavery,
which insulted all basic values:
well-being, freedom, and justice, in their several parts.

Hence, I urge that we consider the Period from about
1830 to 1965 as three wars:
The first evolved and fought the slavery issue
by all intellectual, moral, political, propagandistic,
agitational, and terrorist means,
until the struggle escalated into
full-scale organized violence;

The second bloodier war dealt with the supply, management, and
conduct of combat operations until the formal surrenders.

Whereupon the third war took shape as
a prolonged period of sporadic violence,
disposition of surrendered resources,
the regaining of the resources by the rebels,
the struggle to provide and to block and erase
the liberties and opportunities of the African-Americans
and their Allies, continuing uninterrupted
for a full one hundred years ,
until there finally arrived, with the Civil Rights Act of 1965,
a point in time when the liberties and opportunities of
African-Americans, after seeming to have been hopelessly lost
became operational and ordinarily assured,
though with still a sick-making need for
constant vigilance and patrolling.
Countless millions of personal injuries had yet to be suffered,
to the endless disgrace of the United States.

The period began with one kind of federal law and ended with another, so I am beginning and ending the 135-year "war" with a discussion of the old and new federalism.

A concluding word begs to be spoken even before we begin: the treatment of African-Americans - and to a lesser degree because they were mobile, the Indian-Americans - reduced the quality of life for many millions of considerate White Americans for over three hundred years. A temporary relief was given by a supposedly victorious war and legislation on behalf of the victims, but then the shame resumed its gnawing upon the intelligent conscience. Civically, religiously, politically, philosophically, materially, Americans were living a lie, a big lie.

Only in the last third of the twentieth century could an American feel reasonably confident that the processes of extending equal opportunities and liberties to ordinary Blacks and Whites were significantly operative. If a new happiness was not generally felt, it may be because of the excessive ravages of history, and because of the aforesaid myriad daily blows against blacks and their (unequal) retaliations against whites.

As if the motley multi-hued population were white and black..

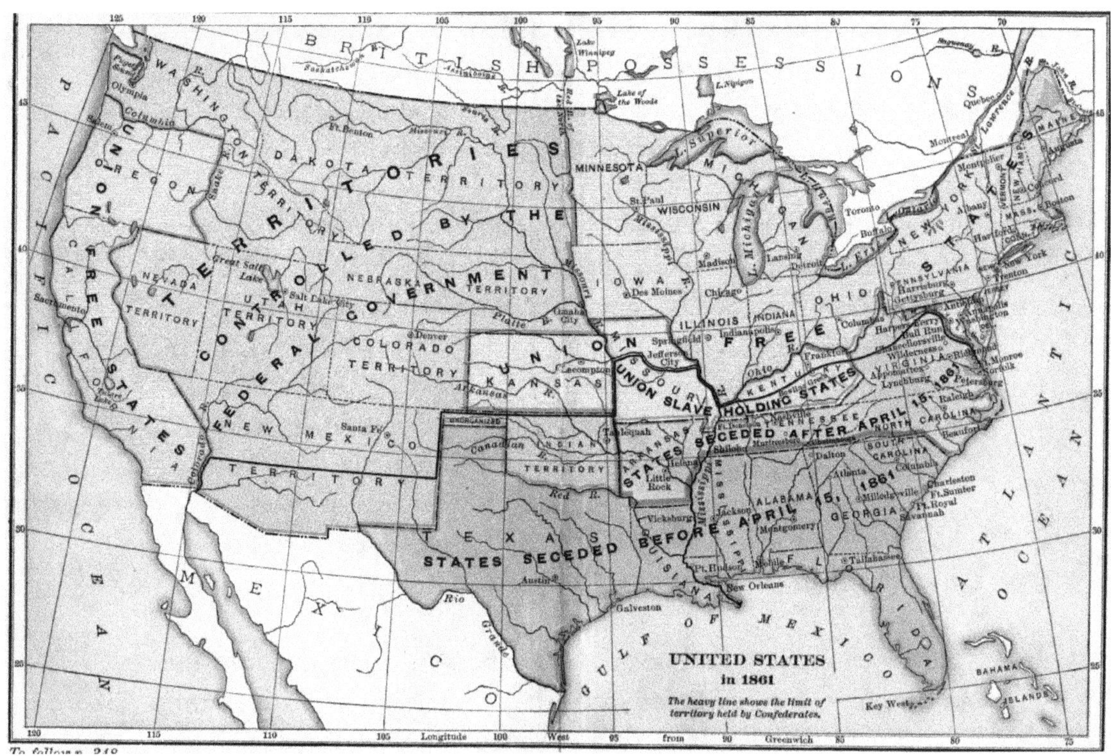

How Civil War divided the Nation

Chapter Thirty-nine

Constitutional Law and States Rights

How stood the federal courts, especially the Supreme Court of the United States, in the long-drawn-out struggles for reform and the containment and abolition of slavery? Given its growing prestige, could not the Supreme Court have found a solution in some cases coming before it, perhaps declaring outright that Blacks were naturally among all men who were created equal and therefore could not be held as slaves, citing the Declaration of Independence, and other documents and cases in support of the ruling? (We recall that there is "law" to be found somewhere, with which to decide every conceivable case, once a court assumes jurisdiction.)

The Court might have seen in the guarantee of a republican form of government grounds for questioning the manacling of a fifth of all persons in slavery. Suppose a favorable court and a plea of individuals (slaves or persons willing to free slaves) based their rationale on the Constitution's stipulation of a republican form of government: given universal male suffrage everywhere else, a condition of being a republic is that no person be deprived of the right to vote. Once again, we are fantasying history; but it may be more useful to do so than tell the story of one more bloody battle.

As for counting three-fifths of other persons (slaves, that is) in apportioning representation in the House of Representatives, this, like about one-third of the Constitution, could be ignored, which the South would like, and Congress could proceed to counting slaves as full persons.

There were other ways of skinning the cat: the Preamble of the Constitution, claiming life, liberty and happiness to be its objectives as well as its goals, could be declared law, and its words and implications applied to ridding the country of slavery; after all, English common law was also being applied in cases before the American courts, and there was something called "natural law" and something else called "international law". These were often cited in legal cases.

The Court could have declared at the same time that inasmuch as claimants to such property (slave-owners) had entered in good faith into transactions involving their purchase, the federal government would be liable for their reasonable compensation. By entertaining suits against the government, and allowing overly-generous compensation, the courts would ease the shock of manumission so slave-owners could cuss all the way to the bank. And, as for the "new" non-slaves, they might be compensated by their holders

from one-half of their holders' compensation,
paid out annually according to the number of years
from age 7 to x that the non-slave had been held as a slave.

I allude to such dreamlike solutions to mark the stark contrast between conceivable reform and possible reform. Also to show that the "Great Debate" over States Rights was largely puerile and inexcusably narrow. My dream was impossible for the judicial system to handle, even though there have been several occasions in history when the federal courts have taken it upon themselves to mastermind enormously complicated schemes in order to bring reality in conformity with the Constitution.

Examples would be the break-up of the American Tobacco Company monopoly into numerous components a century ago, the disassembly and reassembly of the components of the American Telephone and Telegraph Company monopoly, the determination that capital punishment and other forms of punition can be construed nowadays - never mind the past three hundred years - as forms of cruel and unusual punishment and therefore unconstitutional, and the repossession of Indian lands from the States and Federal Government, and their redistribution among the Indian tribes.

After all, when the evils of slavery and the struggles over it had gone on for a century and more, bringing interminable violence and property destruction, the dreamy way might have been the practical way.
There remains, however, a large gap between technical competence and heart and will.

We bear in mind the way Gorbachev handled the dissolution of the Cold War and averted possible worldwide destruction. But that is not the way history ordinarily goes; it is neither the way of the courts nor the way of politics. When he ran for President of Russia in 1996, Gorbachev received a pitiful 0.5% of the vote cast from the communist serfs that he freed.

Courts have always been creatures of tradition and

rationalizations of the new in terms of the old.
Legal procedures and language are as puzzling as politics, when it comes to discovering why the judicial process (or the political process) goes one way rather than another. Well into the 1820's, for instance, American judges and lawyers considered that the common law was still the basis for American law, unless it were to be specifically overruled by constitution, code or statute, and could even accept the thesis of Chancellor Kent of New York and others that America was a Christian nation and Christianity a principle of common law and enforceable. The States were getting around to codification one by one, the Federal government, with less law and jurisdiction, yet moved more slowly.

American lawyers and judges were from the earliest times poorly trained and non-theoretical. Only within living memory has there been any systematic efforts to come to grips with the chaos of laws and legal practice.

Writers of law textbooks, much more than political scientists and historians, have from the very beginning described and prescribed for a non-existent world.

And passed apprentices and students of the law into the courts unprepared for reality of the judicial process.
But, too, there was no legal reality to be clearly defined.

Even if judges and lawyers leaped at the presentation of a statute of the state legislature, they would be at odds in interpreting it, for legislative drafting in the United States did not become systematic until the mid-twentieth century.

If one were to try to mentally survey the total court record, itself a jammed massive collection from many jurisdictions, local, state and national, one would find that it exhibits little attention in practice to the famed due process of law in procedural and substantive matters, and whether in criminal or civil law.

What has become the history of the law is an

Empress Catherine facade, built of a handful of cases on most topics, which are lined up along the avenue of legal studies.

For example, the injunction against passing any law respecting the establishment of a religion has had a tortuous history. It was never absolutely observed (and philosophically it probably could never be, except upon taking a narrow view of what religion consisted).

Oaths in court cases, and everywhere else they were required, were sworn in the name of the Bible and the Lord. Legislatures, military forces, *et al* appointed chaplains. Tax exemptions were always given to religious groups. And so on. Was male circumcision a religious practice and therefore neither to be encouraged nor forbidden by any agency of government? Would female circumcision be subjected to the same rules? The principles of religious freedom have never been able to carry beyond blocking and attacking special religious and anti-religious groups; a perfectly acceptable theory cannot be devised.

So it goes with the principle of free speech, which seems absolute enough: free is free. But to read the foreign travelers' accounts written in the first half of the nineteenth century, you would have to say during this hot season of direct democracy that one of America's salient problems was free speech. De Tocqueville was astounded at the censorship of free speech by the opinion of the crowd. And, although we are anticipating our story again by many chapters, one would have to say that the only period of free speech in America worthy of unique praise would be the last third of the twentieth century.

During the first half of the 1800's, whatever the changing fortunes of those who called for growth of national powers, the Supreme Court could be counted upon to lean toward the nationalists. Having established without much resistance the doctrine of judicial review in the case of *Marbury vs Madison*, the court could expect ample opportunity to overrule state laws in cases where obstreperous legislatures thought that they might invade the powers of the Constitution.

The case of *McCullough vs. Maryland* (1819) is here most notable, because the Court took a dim view of any transgressions of state law or activity upon an area of concern that by implication had been consigned to Congress under an expressed power: With the approval of the Bank of the United States under the general authority to coin money and regulate the currency, the Bank of the United States itself was deemed to be constitutionally established; and therefore a Maryland attempt to tax the Bank of the United States was ruled unconstitutional. The federal power was considered to extend into large areas of "implied powers" thereafter.

But before then, cases had come up wherein the Court had prevented state laws from interfering with United States treaties with foreign powers.

The Judiciary Act, by creating a set of national courts instead of relying upon the state courts to do the job for the federal government under the supervision of the Supreme Court, guaranteed uniformity and discipline in federal law, and prevented state courts from forever chipping away federal powers.

Also, Congress, by opting to give the Supreme Court an extensive appellate jurisdiction, tied the federal and state lower courts into a unitary organization, and the Supreme Court, in extending its power, began to make distinctions between the kinds of cases it would and would not hear. With an eye to its power and prestige, it would accept for review only those cases that promised to establish important principles of law, cases of wide application to important interests. The appointment as Chief Justice of John Marshall, a man with a full-blown theory of federalism to carry into practice, began a 35 -year period of consistent centralization of constitutional power.

After *McCullough* came cases that prevented state legislatures or officers from breaking a contract with a private corporation. In the leading instance it pitted Dartmouth College against the State of

New Hampshire. *Cohens vs Virginia* (1821) houses in its opinion a superlative expression by Marshall on the supremacy of the federal government in many spheres and the unitary character of the American nation. *Gibbons vs. Ogden* (1821) further tightened Congressional power over the States.

However the Court, while it would not permit the State governments themselves to get into the printing of currency, did allow the States to permit private banks (so-called state banks, because state-chartered) to issue bank notes - with inflationary, speculative, bankruptive consequences all around.

(Indeed, and perhaps this should not be said in parentheses, the only explanation for the great economic expansion of the age may be the logically disastrous financial policies of the country's banking and financial system; for it doesn't matter that a great many individuals go broke or rich or both, if, in doing so, the overall result is an expanded population in an expanded territory doing expanded tasks - this is sheer pragmatism, of course.

To counter such an argument pragmatically, one would have to assert that the country should not have developed so crazily and destructively, and that the enormous human costs of the booming and crashing economic cycles should be reckoned. A steady, more humane development was possible, but only if there were a different elite and popular mix.)

The Court tried to intervene to keep Georgia from defrauding and bullying the Indians within its grasp, but Georgia, with the help of President Jackson, tossed the judgement into the wastebasket. Still, the court was moving steadily toward a stronger federal union, even under the successor of Marshall, Chief Justice Roger Taney, a friend of the slave states.

And when the decision came that shocked the North into stronger abolitionism, it was Taney's opinion that mattered, but his opinion was along national lines. I speak of the Dred Scott case. After all, to declare that a slave, property under the law, remained property, and certainly did not gain freedom, by being transported into another state or territory, even where the local law prohibited slavery, was merely repeating what the Constitution enjoined the states to do: refrain from any action taking the property of the citizen of another state.

Taney did not say this in so many words. He pronounced that Dred Scott was not a person or citizen who had the standing to appear before the court. (If so, why did the Court then bother to make a decision, a vastly disturbing one at that?).

Taney also made scurrilous remarks about Negroes, and said in effect that Congress had no right under the Constitution to prohibit slavery anywhere.

He became a hero of the South and a villain of the North. The Supreme Court would now lose much of its prestige, until, in the latter part of the century, it would begin to uphold and gain the favor of the great economic and financial interests and mass media of the country against both state and federal governments, the favor of the South anti-African forces, too.W What liberals came to think of the Court was another matter.

Even though Taney and the Court could hand down so troublesome a judgement, the Court never accepted a case that would have enabled or required it to determine whether nullification of a federal action by a state or a state secession would be a constitutional act. Of course, if ever there were cases of pure political power - eyeball to eyeball - here they were!

And the Court - not that its precedents were ever so compelling as rolling the phrase *stare decisis* off the tongue made it seem - had clearly announced in 1842 in the Dorr Case that it would have no truck with a political decision, this when two groups appeared before it, each announcing itself to be the legitimate government of the State of Rhode Island, and asking the Court's favor.

This, pronounced the Court, was a political decision from which it was excluded, as distinct from a judicial decision. The case involved an uprising led by citizen Dorr to select a legislature by manhood suffrage after futile attempts to get the State legislature to extend the voting privilege. The upstart assembly confronted the existing one. In the end, the direct democrats won, without further violence.

Such cases, whatever else they do, and they go along with many another, tell us that the Supreme Court was assuming powers and building nationalism up to the time of the Civil War, and therefore doing the slaveholders a disservice. For it made any Constitutional claim to the right to nullification or secession implausible.

When, one may ask, would the nationalizing trend go so far as to allow the federal government to begin imposing all kinds of welfare requirements upon slaveholders. If Congress had once been instructed by the Constitution to eliminate the slave trade and count the slaves according to a three-fifths rule, and regulate interstate and foreign commerce exclusively and as it pleased, etc., a nationalistic court might have found an implied power to legislate so extensively regarding the welfare of slaves that the slave-holders might have given up the task of compliance in disgust and laid their burden down. But then the idea of welfare was in the earliest stages of consciousness and agitation in America, so could all of the people's welfare and happiness been rolled into an omnibus bill? Impossible.

"Worse than slavery", most people would say of life-long imprisonment. Worse than life imprisonment, most would say, would be death by public execution. When America was invaded by Europe in the fifteenth century, England was punishing eight crimes by death: treason, malicious murder, larceny, robbery, burglary, rape, arson, and androcide.

Two centuries later (1688), the "Glorious Revolution" could boast of fifty capital crimes. Even though the "Bill of Rights" of 1689 proscribed "cruel and unusual punishments", several practices such as burning at the stake, strangling, and even worse continued. The penalty for an attempt on the life of the King was unspeakably gruesome.

About 100 capital crimes were added to the list under George II and George III. In 1819, by which time the Americans had been luckily cut off from this fount of justice, the number was estimated at 223. Attainder, forfeiture of property, and "corruption of blood" (denial of inheritance) accompanied the death penalty.

Annually between 2000 and 3000 Britons were sentenced to die, but often the sentence was commuted and the convict transported to a colony elsewhere than America, now that America was free, and, there, usefully consigned to servitude.

Early Massachusetts (1636) added idolatry, witchcraft, blasphemy, and kidnaping to the English capital list. These were referred back not only to the Authority of the Crown and Colony, but also to the Old Testament of the Bible. A century later, the code of the new state brought the number down: treason, piracy, murder, rape, robbery, arson, burglary, and - evincing a concern more American than European - buggery and sodomy. South Jersey and Pennsylvania, thanks to William Penn, let only treason and murder be capital, but pressures from England brought all the colonies up to London's lofty standards.

The states then diverged. Since the police power was conspicuously lacking in the early Federal government and would take two hundred years to find by reading between the lines under the direction of a liberal Supreme Court, some states became imaginative and vindictive. North Carolina, pointing out weakly that it had no penitentiary, posted a long list of capital crimes, including bigamy and having anything to do with freeing a slave.

A breath of wisdom entered with the Enlightenment when Cesare Beccaria's book on *Crimes and Punishment* moved English and American reformers not only with its historic formula of the object of legislation, "the greatest happiness of the greatest number", but also with an elegantly reasoned defense of humane punition. Dr. Benjamin Rush, Dr. Benjamin Franklin, and Attorney-General William Bradford of Pennsylvania (who first divided homicides into first and second degree), gave that State a solitary excuse for taking a life, murder in the first degree. Beccaria also influenced Jefferson's agitation to limit the death penalty in Virginia to crimes of murder and treason.

The Louisiana legislature commissioned lawyer Edward Livingston to draw up a penal code, and in 1824, moved by the above precedents and a continuing if belated influence of the French Enlightenment, he proposed the abolition of capital punishment. The legislature said no.

Agitation elsewhere continued with "anti-gallows" societies, who joined the rest of the pressure groups in this, the first age of the lobbies. Lobbies were already called "the Third House of Congress" in 1857. Senator Benton of Missouri claimed that they could get any bill passed if they were prepared to bribe Congressmen liberally.

On March 1, 1847 Michigan became the first Anglophone jurisdiction in the world to abolish the death penalty (save for treason, which practically was a federal offense). Rhode Island went all the way in 1852, and Wisconsin followed in 1853. Thus could the states be innovative in criminal law.

Then came a weakening of voluntary associations, with a growth in public paranoia and aggression. There were several moves back and forth, a large revival under Clarence Darrow, a famous attorney, and Warden Lewis Lawes of Sing Sing Prison in New York, who aided in the foundation in 1927 of the American League to Abolish Capital Punishment.

In a bold legal step, the Supreme Court, half a century later, found capital punishment itself to be a cruel and unusual punishment, but later cut back on its promises, so that a pent-up variety of death sentences around the country were carried out.

Perhaps the main reason why the death penalty persisted

was the ease with which a part of the population could be enraged or panicked by a crime; and especially since less painful means of administering death were being found, people generally did not feel the issue so acutely. Public opinion polls kept turning up opinions on the penalty near the 50% mark.

The profound antinomy goes to the principle that the government should never kill its people. For, when the state is restrained, the police, criminals, impassioned individuals and crowds become more hesitant to kill.

Other movements accessory to that against capital punishment progressed in fair order. Allowing the jury discretion in capital cases was instituted in Massachusetts in 1636 for rape - and may have been anti-female; in 1809 in Maryland for rape and arson; until half the states finally allowed juries to determine whether the death penalty should be imposed.

New Plymouth Colony (1646) ordained the first income tax, on the "returns and gains" of craftsmen and tradesmen. Six states adopted income taxes in the years 1840 to 1860, and in 1862 the Federal government levied its first income tax, to help pay for the war. (It was declared unconstitutional not long afterwards).

In the rush to write new constitutions at the beginning of the Revolutionary War, innovations occurred. New York established a seven-year census of the population and electors according to place of residence. Pennsylvania had a single-chambered legislature and for a while an executive committee instead of a governor. In the early 1800's the states had been occasionally innovative. Penal and corrections systems, general education systems, institutions for paupers, orphans and the mentally disabled were being built here and there. Laws trying to ease the lot of children doing factory work were starting to appear.

With all the powers they possessed,

and the possibility of learning from one another's experiments, it is a wonder that no state could devise a formula tending to end slavery. During the colonial period and Revolutionary era, social inventions were not rare: the earliest period was, of course, the most inventive. The Massachusetts Puritan theocracy, for instance, was novel, as such. There were even experiments in the beginning in defining the status of slaves, involving, for example, ultimate release, or non-inheritance of slave status. Anumber of states with few slaves came to abolish the institution, but their methods were scarcely more that sovereign fiat. Still, by 1804 slavery was doomed in all of the urban industrializing regions, all Northern states, that is - evidencing the rural agrarian character of the institution.

The slave states were more innovative in devising means for controlling, governing, punishing, and trafficking in humans. And, as we shall see, following their military surrender, the Southern state governments were especially inventive when it came to finding means, whether through state or voluntary action, to lash back at and circumvent the United States Constitution, federal law, the army and agencies of the federal government, and Congress and the presidency.

A typical place for buying and selling humans

Chapter Forty

Slavery and State Sovereignty

We speak now of the agitation and propaganda against and for slavery, and of the right of States to secede from the Union: hence we speak of the numerous causes of the Civil War, argued at the time and ever since. Two points dominate our own explanation of the war. First, the poor White Southerners were the principal block

to solutions of the slavery crisis other than by civil war.
These had their own representatives in local governments,
in Congress and especially in the State legislatures,
and the plantation class was trapped by the class
logic of racism and pride, a perverted *noblesse oblige*.

Second, paranoia, masked in piety and legalese,
motivated both principal groupings who brought on the struggle:
the Southern racists - planters as well as poor Whites -
and the Northern abolitionists.
The "other" side was out to get them!
Inasmuch as one must choose between slavers and abolitionists
and both are heavily paranoid,
one chooses the paranoids who are in the right.
This would be the abolitionists.
It doesn't matter whether one would rather be sipping bourbon
on a veranda after being out with the good
ol' boys hunting wild pigs, or, on the other hand,
be sitting stiffly in a lecture hall listening to a harangue
on good causes by a presbyterian minister.
Right is right. History must be judged.
For eight years, the House of Representatives debated whether to
table automatically all petitions proposing the abolition of slavery on
grounds that these were obviously unconstitutional.
Such a gag rule was steadfastly opposed by
former President, now Member of the House, John Quincy Adams,
as an abridgement of the freedoms of speech and petition
guaranteed by the Constitution.
(It was generally accepted that the slaves enjoyed no such rights,
but here white men were to be deprived of them.)
In the end (1844) the proposed rule was voted down.

Politician-lawyers were in charge of the problem
in the State capitals and Washington. They argued,
compromised, from time to time engaged in debates
that generations of schoolteachers since have called great -
the Haynes-Webster Debate, the Lincoln-Douglas Debate, and
so on. No other subject so occupied Congress as slavery and
secession. The idea at first was to resolve the problem of slavery
through giving some of the unlimited national domain

over to slavery and the rest to freeholding.
The last State to be admitted without a furor over slavery
was Alabama, onto whose fertile cotton-growing soil
slave speculators and slave-owners had avidly pounced.

But by the following year, alarm bells had rung in the North:
admission of Maine and Missouri became controversial. The
Missouri compromises of 1820 admitted Maine as free
and Missouri as slave, but fixed "forever" the great balance
of the Louisiana purchase territory to the North of Missouri
(lat.36 degrees, 30 minutes) as free.
We recall that the Texas and Mexican wars raised strong protests
over the advances which slave-owners were making.

In 1846, in a debate on a bill to fund possible purchases of land
from Mexico, Congressman Wilmot tacked on an amendment to the
effect that any territories received from Mexico be barred to slavery.
This stirred up sentiments, but was turned down. Again and again
the "Proviso" came forward; always a bridesmaid, but never a bride.

In 1850 another "Omnibus" compromise bill took care of various
matters and kept the peace for the nonce: California was to be
admitted free; a line at the 37th parallel would separate the
territories of Utah and New Mexico, and their constitutions
(effectively then Congress) would decide whether to permit slavery
or not; $10 millions went to Texas as compensation
for giving up claims it had in New Mexico.

Slave trade in the District of Columbia was to be abolished;
a new fugitive slave act would be passed making it easier to
recapture slaves escaped into free territory.
All orators turned out upon the occasion.
Daniel Webster culminated grandiloquently two decades
of hard selling of the Union. Calhoun asked for equality of South
and North in the territories, approved steps to return fugitive slaves,
and spoke of guarantees of an equilibrium between South and North
so that either section could refuse the demand of the other section,
an equilibrium that came to be known as the theory of the
concurrent majority - an idea of two separate nations on
whatever issue was deemed by either side to be of greatest

importance, like slavery (a century later, political philosophers were
saying, what a clever idea, which it certainly was not -
a clever dialectical quibble, yes).
The Compromise of 1850 was duly enacted.

The Compromise of 1850 lasted until 1854
when Senator Stephen Douglas of Illinois
sought to facilitate, not without pocketing the change,
a railroad line between Chicago and the Pacific Coast.
The result of his efforts was the Kansas-Nebraska Act that repealed the
Missouri Compromise, organized the territories of Kansas and
Nebraska and promised to let the principle of popular sovereignty or
"squatter sovereignty" in the territories decide whether to admit
slavery or not. This administered the *coup de grace* to the
Whig Party that had been struggling along as the
ghost of the old Federalists for many years.

Sam Houston complained from the Senate that the Act would
deprive the Indians of territory promised them for eternity;
no one could deny this or be surprised: if one were
at this time to calculate the number of broken promises
and agreements in Indian and foreign affairs
relative to bargains kept, the ratio might be 50/50.

The Know-Nothing Party and the Republican Party appeared
in the same year of 1856.
The Free Soilers and the Independent Democratic Party
also picked up some of the Whig adherents.
Fear in the North grew that free country might become
surrounded by slavery. Settlers, paid to migrate, poured into
Kansas. The New England Emigrant Aid Society was formed to
outfit abolition enthusiasts, and they came in with "Beecher Bibles",
that is, gun-toting, named after the New England preacher,
Henry Ward Beecher, who championed abolition.
Pro-slavery settlers, mostly border ruffians from Missouri,
arrived, too, and hundreds of killings and burnings occurred.
Fanatical John Brown appeared with his several sons,
striking at Pottawatomie after slavists had burned Lawrence.

In the middle of this, two governments sprang up,
the first, slavists, tried to get a Constitution written and accepted
by Congress so as to control the territory.
They drew up the Constitution at the town of Lecompton.
Students of referenda voting, who would one day marvel
at how dictators managed such favorable results with referenda,
might begin their studies here. A first referendum,
slavists in charge, voted 6,226 for the slavery constitution,
569 for the constitution without slavery.
The territorial legislature, not at all impressed,
responded to the new acting Governor's wishes and
called another referendum to vote
up or down the Lecompton constitution.
It went down 10,226 against,
138 for the slavery constitution.
Now a third referendum was held, supervised by a
Congressionally designated group of managers, and the Lecompton
Constitution went down for the full count, 11,300 to 1,788.
The date was August 2, 1858.

As if he had not enough troubles, the Democratic Party
administration of President James Buchanan ran into
a financial storm followed by a depression,
a typical affair whereby the common people suffered
in many countries and no one could pinpoint responsibility.
Speculative bubbles bursting,
a reduction in demand abroad for American cereals,
and the chaotic State bank note system
were chief culprits,
at least in the press and halls of Congress.
Southerners trumpeted that agriculture was more stable -
the cotton market happened to be spared -
proving that slavery was the preferable system.

The Presidential elections of 1856 had shown up
the Republicans as the second largest party in the nation;
their candidate had been John Fremont. The American Party
"Know-Nothings" had run Millard Fillmore and came in
far behind Buchanan and Fremont.
Buchanan was a Southerner, a compromiser, who hoped to sit tight

and weather the storm; he barely managed to get out
before the roof blew away.

Consonant with the Kansas-Nebraska Act, Congress had enacted a
Fugitive Slave Law that ordered slaves found anywhere to be
returned to their masters. Northerners foresaw horrors of federal
agents entering their closets looking for fugitives.
The Dred Scott decision had added fuel to the flames.
Few slaves escaped the tight system in the South,
notwithstanding heroic efforts on the part of Black and White citizens
to facilitate their escape. But of these some hundreds
per year, ever fewer were caught.

Several riots over attempts to enforce the law persuaded the
authorities that other forms of delinquency
deserved closer attention.
(It is of note that Douglas, consoling Northerners
about his legislation, opined that the local police would
have to cooperate with the federal authorities to
return a slave and they could be counted
upon –heh, heh! - not to cooperate;
but, in the century that followed the Civil War,
a continual protest issued from the North that the
local police in the South were preventing the
Constitution from being enforced.)

Other incidents occurred.
One that shocked the Northern public was
the brutal cane beating and disablement of a helpless Senator,
Charles Sumner of Massachusetts, by a nephew
and member of the House, whose uncle had been berated
by Sumner in a speech. The assailant
was praised for the atrocity, not tried or removed,
and was later re-elected.

Even worse was John Brown's raid of
October 16, 1859, on Harper's Ferry,
where stood a federal arsenal, then in Virginia.
He crossed from Maryland with his gang, including sons
that survived the Kansas killings and several African-Americans,

and seized the arsenal and hostages.
He had probably been wanting to incite a riot
of slaves and sympathizers, to spread rebellion.
He was besieged, supporters killed when they came to
dicker under a white flag, and
the next morning a marine detachment came up,
attacked and killed or captured most. Still, several escaped.

Trapped, they were quickly tried by Virginia authorities
for treason against the State and hanged,
including the wounded John Brown. Later,
Union soldiers would sing to the tune of Hallelujah,
a *"Battle Hymn of the Republic"*,

"John Brown's body lies a-mold'ring in the grave,
but his soul goes marching on..."

Abraham Lincoln was born in Kentucky in a log cabin,
of a mother for whom he always claimed a tender affection
and a father of typical backwoods irresponsibility.
She died when he was small, and his
father married a firmer and more demanding type.
She taught Abe and imbued him with ambition.
Lincoln's ancestry was sufficiently clouded so that he has
been claimed to have English and German origins,
and was probably of New England ancestors
who crossed the Ohio River border into Southernity
a couple of generations earlier. His swarthy color of
eye and skin might even have signified Indian or
Black genes along the line. He ended up in
Southern Illinois, then and still a country of heavy
Southern cultural influence.

Lest one crow about freedom to rise high from
low circumstances, his antecedents were no more
ignoble than those of Adolph Hitler.
Neither man could now qualify for a credit card.
Hitler was of uncertain Austrian parentage,

hardly schooled, failed as often as Lincoln,
was shell-shocked, suffered from a variety of lifelong
ailments and phobias (among them hypospadia and
spino bifida occulta - whence he had obsessions of
syphilis that he called a "Jewish disease" -,
recurrent war wound and gas traumas,
explosive rages, sexual inhibitions, and paranoia
replete with delusions), painted and sold postcards,
and then, instead of becoming a "mouthpiece" became a
loudmouth agitator and adored monster of the Germans.

As troubled as he was, Lincoln was angelic by comparison.
Lincoln's store went bankrupt. Haled into court, his
few possessions were seized. Several insolvent
years passed. He failed time after time in politics.

He bucked against marriage, leaving his girl standing at
the church door. His relations with women,
beginning with profound sentimentalizing of his true mother,
were stressful. Gore Vidal and Douglas L. Wilson,
mainly by way of Lincoln's law partner, Herndon,
conclude that Lincoln had a problem with syphilis,
and may have been infected in an episode with a
Sangamon whore whom he himself blamed.
He worried over resorting to prostitutes from time to time.
When he did marry, after years of agonizing and
on-again, off-again determinations, his wife,
Mary Todd, brooked no nonsense from him.

Possessed of an earthy sense of humor,
such as backwoods folk enjoyed, he displayed
also a sharp wit, such that, with his melancholy -
sometimes fully neurotic - and his oedipus complex and
his sensitivity to personal obligations (guilt feelings),
he became a most interesting man -
physically, too, with deep brown eyes,
whose pathological (say some) height
and angularity lent him both distinction and absurdity.

He was driven to succeed, worked several jobs as a young man,

and ran and was elected to the Illinois legislature while preparing for a law practice. He fashioned a decent practice and could probably have become quite wealthy at it had he not been bitten by the bug of politics. He had no compunctions about fighting Indians, and volunteered in the war to put down the Sac and Fox tribes.
He stayed in the state legislature several years,
ran for Congress, served one term. He opposed the
Mexican War, antagonizing his constituents.
He campaigned for U.S. Senator (then chosen by the state legislature), lost to Stephen Douglas on a respectable showing, and developed a viewpoint on the slavery issue that did not lose him too many votes, except in the South, and did not arouse much hostility in the North.
Generally he was for confining slavery to the South,
but intended no large harm to slaveholders.

This Douglas could not boast of. And with Buchanan happily quitting, Douglas "the Little Giant" did become the Democratic choice, but only after a large chunk of the party was bitten off at a first convention in Charleston, South Carolina - of all places - because he was not slavish enough, while John C. Breckinridge, a full Southern sympathizer, came on with an independent Democratic party. John Bell was the candidate of a new Constitutional Union party with the merest of "hold-the-fort" slogans for a platform: " the Constitution of the Country, the Union of the States, and the Enforcement of the Laws". This still brought him the electoral votes of Virginia, Tennessee, and Kentucky. Breckinridge got all the rest of the South including Maryland.
Douglas won Missouri and Delaware.

Lincoln, who had been a Whig, became a Republican, following upon that new Party's remarkable successes in 1856 and 1858.
Lincoln hardly budged and merely repeated his prior ideas, which called for reserving the territories for free men and for holding the Union together, while reassuring the South that he had no intention of interfering with its peculiar institution.
(By no means a radical reformer, he inclined to racism in regard to African-Americans, and nativism

in respect to Irish and German Catholics.)

In the elections of November 1960,
Lincoln captured all the North and West. He received a plurality,
not a majority, of the ballots cast: 1,866,000,
while Douglas won 1,183,000,
Breckinridge 848,000, and Bell 593,000.
But the Electoral College, counting the vote by States,
rather than districts within States, gave the official count
as a majority for Lincoln, 180,
as against only 12 for Douglas, 72 for Breckinridge, and
39 for Bell; so he was elected President.

What would happen now? Lincoln would not
take office until March. Buchanan did as little as possible,
hoping that the problem would go away.
Lincoln passed the buck to Buchanan, justifying himself weakly.
Virginia called a meeting but the delegates could not agree upon
anything but "hold tight". The American constitutional system, the
American party system, the American theory of democracy, the
American leadership, the American people - all failed in the final
analysis. The Union turned out to be a house of cards; the great
spread of symbols of unity and patriotism meant little in the
face of a single grave issue.

One would be quite critical, if the same had not happened to
many countries in the course of history - Athens, Rome,
Florence, England, Ireland, the Netherlands, France, Spain, Brazil,
Mexico, and more to come.

America extricated itself no better than
than any other revolt-wracked country. (It would soon
forget itself, hypocritically, and go after those
weak South American countries who couldn't
hold together internally without revolution,
exhibiting, said the American jingoists, an unfortunate,
severe cultural, probably racial, weakness.)

South Carolina, deeply offended, as always, called a special convention to consider succession, which met on December 20 and voted to secede, declaring that threats to slavery were rife, that Lincoln had promised its forthcoming extinction, and that therefore and henceforth South Carolina was resigned from the Union. (It is fairly certain that South Carolina secessionists believed Lincoln to be an abolitionist, which he was not - and a century of contrary propaganda since then should convince no one otherwise.)

By February six States added their own secessionist declarations. These were the Deep South and Texas. Texas was last because the secessionists took up time in arranging the *coup d'état* forcing out loyalist Governor Sam Houston.

The popular votes for secession were fairly close where they were held (in Georgia and Louisiana, for example). Votes for delegates to conventions on the issue also evidenced some strong Union feelings. Secession was opposed in Northern Florida, Southern Louisiana, Central and Far North Texas, in the back counties of every State from Virginia to Alabama, also in Northern Arkansas and much of Missouri. The South was not united: war and defeat unified it.

The secessionists thereupon convened in Montgomery, Alabama, and in several days - with a bewildering speed that should have put down all myth about Southerners moving slowly - organized the Confederate States of America, adopted a Constitution, elected Jefferson Davis President, and set up the offices of government. By this time the American political elite, South or North, could organize new governments blindfolded.

Now then, the federal government - what had Lincoln been brooding over all this while? - should have had some sort of plan in the event of the promised secessions. One would have been a plan for governments-in-exile. That is, a joint resolution of Congress could have been readied, and even publicized, labeling any declaration or act

of secession unconstitutional and illegitimate, stating, too, that a
State which claimed to secede, by that token was un-republican,
and was in violation of its commitments, as
voted by its members in Congress over the years,
and was in contradiction of its ever-continuing consent
to the Federal nation.
The President and Congress must then designate
loyal citizens who should elect Members of Congress
and officers of every such State
(from the abundant citizens of those States opposing secession)
who would constitute the government of the State,
residing as always within the Union and conducting the
business of the State at an appropriate location within the State or in
Washington or another designated location across the State's border
until such time as the State was liberated
and republican government restored.

Under these circumstances, the whole secession movement
would have found it difficult to proceed and
might have collapsed within a year.
Warfare would have been minimal.
No such plan was generated.
Most of the politicians, national and State, were
committed to a derring-do contest.
Bluff and bullets, bullets and bluff.

Fort Sumter in Charleston Harbor became famous.
In January, a ship sent with reinforcements and provisions
was driven off by South Carolinian fire.
Both houses of Congress debated compromise schemes
for the containment of slavery, consuming two months, to no avail.
Both houses approved by two-thirds vote
a Constitutional amendment permitting slavery wherever it existed!
President-elect Lincoln was prepared to accept this first
usage of the word "slavery" in the Constitution,
although a terrible setback for the ideals of the republic.

After several misunderstandings and conflicting moves,

eager General Beauregard, with the approval of the Confederate government, began to cannonade Fort Sumter.
Some 3,000 shots failed to kill anyone, but,
since ammunition was running law, and food, too,
Commander Anderson, after some 30 hours, struck his colors.
In a ceremonial explosion to mark the surrender,
two soldiers were killed - "friendly fire" began
the death toll of the Civil War.

A second wave of secessions followed the violence at Fort Sumter.
Virginia, Arkansas, Tennessee, and North Carolina quit
the United States and joined the Confederate States.
On the other hand, several slave States remained in the Union,
held by a combination of belief and force.
These were Delaware, Maryland, Kentucky, and Missouri.
Western Virginia seceded from the State of Virginia, was
formed into a regular State, and admitted to the Union promptly.
It possessed a non-slaveholding population, more of mountain than
of tidelands Southern sub-culture, and had coal mines. All along the
borderlands, from Delaware to California,
Union sentiment ran strong, even in very poor areas.

The results would be hardly felt. If no further shots would be fired, the *status quo ante* would have survived indefinitely, two nations instead of one. The Federal presence was not noticeable around the vast Southlands. The Federal government gave little to the South - land to individuals by sale or grant, but the States would now have done the same. The South was practically self-sufficient in foodstuffs and could be quite so with little extra effort. Customs service and coast guard could easily be provided by the independent States or confederacy.
The North could continue to sell its goods to the South,
but only when the prices beat out European competition.
The Federal record in handling the common currency was unworthy
of a boast, so that could also be handled or mishandled.
The South would have had to build railroads,
which it had been doing already; but a single balky State
would create problems.

The Southern States were and would be much in the situation and condition of the sovereign States of Europe that formed the European Community after World War II. Interstate compacts would have had to become a common way of governance. For those who wanted to keep slavery at any price, a confederacy guaranteeing Southern culture was a negligible concession of desirable arrangements. Moreover, as the Confederates and Unionists of perspicacity already knew, another two decades of rapid industrial and communications development in the North would have bound the South into the Union with a crushing embrace.

We might better ask whether it was not the North that needed the South. In 1842, William Lloyd Garrison called for dis-joining the Union, letting the South go its own way. The American Anti-Slavery Society officially adopted the idea of disunionism two years later. The idea was shocking and it made people see how absolute was the chasm between slavery and anti-slavery. The solution would be immediate; an interminable and costly struggle could be avoided.

But most elements of the rapidly burgeoning abolition movement disapproved. It would put them in a position of fighting against slavery as external enemies, instead of citizens and therefore responsible for the institution. It would deprive many of a cause, for they would no longer feel responsible for slavery in another nation. Northern industry would lose an army of customers, for, whatever the weaknesses of the economic determinists, it has to be granted that Northern financial, trading, transportation, and industrial interests were exploiting Southern markets. If Northern pressures against slavery in its neighboring nation became strong, they might set off a boycott of their manufactured goods.

The abolitionists numbered half a million activists as the showdown neared. Led by geniuses of the media, like Garrison, agitators like Weld, preachers like Beecher, and writers like Harriet Stowe, with stern driving politicians like Charles Sumner, they made up a tremendous force, second to none, exceeding even the temperance activists, in their capabilities for applying political pressure.

Never before - not even the pre-Revolution Patriots - nor after -

not even the later Progressive movement, the agitation against Nazism, the anti-Soviet movement of the fifties and sixties, never again, was such a large proportion of the American people so agitated and demanding of change.

A sizeable portion of the energies that had been mobilized by religious revivals and other reform movements of the time were drained from them and flowing into abolition. The human devils - the slaveholders and their protectors - the human victims, the slaves - presented a human problem of sin, crusade, liberation of the soul, penance, and redemption, resounding over the vast country.

Harriet Beecher Stowe's book, *Uncle Tom's Cabin*, quickly sold over a million copies and was translated into the major languages soon after its publication in 1852; it was a soul-wrenching story of an African-American family endeavoring to survive as decent folk in the throes of a brutal slave system.

And abolition was a civic problem, which the federal government could do something about, even though the problem was fundamentally religious or could be looked upon as such. One could feel superior to the government for doing nothing, worse than nothing, for thinking of one way then another of containing, not abolishing, slavery.

Now if the government were so wicked, naturally, as to tolerate the slave system in the bosom of the god-given republic of the free and equal, then the government had better be brought down too. It is extraordinary and indicative of the lack of faith in democratic politics as developed in America that abolitionists for many years declined to intervene directly in politics.

The Liberty Party, an abolitionist party, put up candidates in Presidential elections and won few votes. A single-issue party, abolitionists recognized, would go nowhere, and if it became a multi-issue party, it would sell out like the others to diversionary issues and situations. The movement would have to also become in a contradictory sense, more responsible. It would have to recognize that the Southern slavists, for all their faults, were on firm Constitutional ground. They could declaim until everyone was blue of face over issues of constitutionality. There appeared to be nowhere to go to get rid of the hated institution by constitutional and legal means. Direct, increasing pressure was the only recourse, and, eventually, if necessary, force.

As the evangelists wanted promptly to reconciliate God, abolitionists wanted abolition now. Immediacy was Garrison's main contribution to the ideology of abolition: freedom now. This suited the chiliastic predispositions of Americans, the same who had gone into the revivals and camp meetings hoping to be spiritually transformed here and now.

The elite of the abolitionists were descended from the theocracy and ideocracy of New England. This class was no longer the richest and most powerful group; the rising class of manufacturers paid ever less attention to its pretensions. Foremen, managers, artisans, the workers - they did not look to the old upper class. These were attending to the new upper class, so imperfectly amalgamated with the old.
Abolition could restore the leadership of the older theocrat and utopian groups. Many of the clergy could find new life. The Congregational Church had gone down steeply in its number of adherents and churches.
So too, Presbyterians and Episcopalians.

The mass churches now were of the Baptists, the Methodists, and the Catholics (pass over these last for the moment, for they were busily organizing and anyhow could not appeal to their poor Irish immigrant constituents to take up the cause of the Africans, a principal competitor for jobs even now - and imagine how things would be if they were freed!).

The Baptist and the Methodists began to fight over the issue of slavery, and by 1845 had split into North and South branches, a terrible blow to national unity, everyone agreed, just when the nation so needed agreement and unity. But, you see, it was slavery that caused them to split, not States rights.

The doctrine of States rights and the right to secede were gigantic camouflages of the basic issue of slavery. People fooled themselves, a great many people, and yet the issue had to be used; few would go to war and risk their lives to free a people of different race who were universally deemed inferior, presently if not by nature.

Strange it was, therefore, that the true issue was denied, except by the abolitionists and by those in the North who tried to avoid the issue and appease the South. But the issue had an enormous subconscious appeal in the North. And in the South the same was true: slavery, not States rights and secession, was the moving force. In the end, over half a million men would die in war believing that the issue, if any, was the Union, for the Northerners, and was the right to be free for the Southerners, whereas the undertow that dragged them along defying its force was the issue of slavery or emancipation.

Abraham Lincoln himself is a splendid example of the introjection of the true issue and its denial, with the adamant exclamation of the false issue, States rights and secession. He was fully determined to tolerate slavery everywhere it stood but to fight its extension; he disliked the institution, but had no love for Africans; he had little personal contact with them.

He was in many ways a typical Kentuckian. (When Kentucky stuck by the Union, after many difficulties, he was greatly relieved because of the problems in controlling the Ohio River Valley otherwise; but he probably also was emotionally gratified.)

The South, we recall, had a poor White population of large dimensions. It is doubtful that this people shrank in numbers with the growth and development of the nation. Rather the obverse. Southern culture throughout its length and breadth probably would number no less than 80% poor of the White population, 95% poor of the Blacks.

By poor is meant a household or individual who can put all his household's possessions into a single trunk or cart, but half the time had no mule to draw the cart or carry the trunk, may have had a horse to draw a hand plow if the mule could not, who was a tenant, a sharecropper, or the owner of under 100 acres of improperly cultivated and deteriorating land, and whose cash income in the course of the year would not exceed $70.00. His tools would be no better than his ancestors' from wherever, six centuries earlier.

His household diet would be inadequate, but supplemented by a wild bird or wild pig or rodent now and then. there was a jug of whiskey on hand (or hidden if the wife were a teetotaler). There might be one rifle in the family. The family would dwell in a two-room cabin with a plank or dirt floor, and heating and cooking would depend upon a stone fireplace. Clothing would be homemade with occasional purchases of footwear. The condition of slaves would be considerably worse.

Expectedly, according to the agglomerative principle, material conditions would be matched by low levels of education, manners, medical care and health, and power over other persons. Their education was meager, hardly better than their ancestors' of five or ten biological generations earlier. They were isolated from the news-bearing, object-bearing immigrants who were everywhere in the North.

The household's social position was low, higher in the eyes of his society and his ilk than the respect tendered any Indians who might be still nearby, or foreigners far away, especially the immigrant workers of the cities up North, but most emphatically higher than the Africans near or far away, the slaves (He did not like to think of the free Blacks, who composed a noticeable and progressive group in the towns and cities South and North of the Mason-Dixon line). The greatest certainty in the life of the poor White Southern household was that it was socially superior to the slaves and other Blacks.

Upon breaking with their Northern brethren, their preachers had preached of this superiority, finding its justification in the Bible where the descendants of Ham were cursed and supposedly were Black. The omnipresent preachers gave the poor White Southerners no trouble on this score. If they had, they would be threatening to take away from them their most precious social and psychological possession; the preachers would get short shrift.

In fact, and this may be the key to the lock that could not be found at the time, the poor White Southerners asked of their rich White governors, who thought very poorly of them in general, only two things: that they be let alone and that the Africans be kept in their place, as deep and broad a servitude as possible. And since there was absolutely no conception yet, and wouldn't be for a century, of a central government that could assist the poor of all types, anything whatsoever that benefitted the Blacks was an insult to the Whites.

The poor White Southerners, respecting the top position of the planters, fighting for the system of the masters, resented any signs of kindliness toward the Blacks, any improvements in their standards of living, any freedoms granted them, and they hated the abolitionists of the North fervently for threatening to place next to them a full equivalent class of free people. The people of the poor White Southern class were disproportionately of Scots-Irish and North Border English stock and their attitudes, and the way they tried to cope with these attitudes, trailed back to their origins. John Calhoun, for instance, was of the border stock, and he was a nationalist as well as a slavist to begin with, but when he saw that he would not be let to become President by one of his kindred folk, Andrew Jackson, he became the principal rationalizer of the slave system in constitutional and legal terms. The Calhoun and related families had grown to power in America, but had not lost their chieftain-and-clan ideas of political and social organization. When the Army of the Confederate West was organized it fought under the Cross of St. Andrew, the Scottish saint, and used other clan symbols of the Anglo-Scottish border and Scots-Irish.

When war broke out, the poor Whites were quick to volunteer for the confederacy. Hundreds of thousands enlisted. They fought well and for years against odds. It is impossible to understand the voluntarism and enthusiasm of the poor Whites for the Southern cause except on grounds of the devil's bargain they had unconsciously struck with the ruling class. The ruling class must not concede to any degree an extension of liberties or of better conditions to the slaves.

Realizing this, albeit often unconsciously, the planters and their professional and service auxiliaries were not free in dealing with the Northern politicians and abolitionists. They could not begin to free the slaves. Their whole system would start to fall apart, not only because of the freed slaves but because of the demeaned poor Whites. The planters would lose the respect of their mass following; to whom could they turn, then, to recognize their claim to "honor?"

It was a classic case of the French Jacobin's cry: *"There goes the crowd; I am their leader; I must follow them!"* The planters were prisoners of their population and had to lead, that is to follow, them to their own doom.

By this time, the 1840's and onwards, the Southern ruling class knew full well that the nations whom they had to respect abroad had banned the slave trade, abolished slavery, and were chasing American slave-traders on the high seas. (One-sixth of British naval expenditures were going to hunting for slave-traders, many of them Americans operating in Latin America and smuggling illegally to the United States.) The Southern elite knew that the British upper-middle classes condemned slavery.

The European nations and even the South American nations were closing shop on slavery. The Mexican government, as poor and needy as it was after independence, had abolished slavery and, we recall, after first inviting Americans in to help populate Texas, tried to bar further immigration because it would re-introduce the slave system to Mexico; whereupon the Texans revolted.

The Southern upper classes realized that the world was turning against them and that they would be more and more isolated if they persisted; they sometimes concealed the truth from themselves and/or believed that their client nation had to have their cotton. Still the pull of their own people, even those they held most in contempt, was undeniable.

A parallel is suggested by the experience of Poland in the eighteenth

century: there the poor farmers had been continuously exploited and
driven mercilessly by the Polish aristocracy,
their daughters taken away,
whippings commonly employed, but it wasn't until the
aristocracy had become Frenchified and in the process more
humane, that the peasantry rioted
and insurrections became common.
The Southern planter class had to stick by the
poor Whites who laid claim to it.

Death deals no distinction between North and South.

Chapter Forty-one

War among the States

The civil war that broke out was often referred to, pathetically, as a war of brother against brother. Although many families counted relatives on opposite sides of a shifting three-thousand miles of hostile confrontation, few families were cross-cultured, North and South.

The war in general was between free and slave cultures, that had been separated to begin with by different sorts of immigrants, by persons coming from different regions of the British Isles and the European Continent, and by two centuries of contrasting forms of development.

The armies of the South, especially of the upper west, were more representative of rural Anglo-Celtic elements;

they behaved or tried to behave as warriors out of a
romantic historical novel of Sir Walter Scott,
an immensely popular author of the time. The Northern
armies groped for a contrasting ideal, the new army of Prussia,
as a model, bureaucratic in structure, of interchangeable humans,
with God marching along in His proper order.
There were two ways of looking at Prussia;
from the planters' perspective, they were the junkers who
provided the high officers corps; and, while some
of these American junkers failed, and many died,
their overall performance was excellent, such that the
calamitous end of the war did not dislodge them
as the ruling class.

Furthermore, one may ask, if the two sides were brothers,
why had the two denominations whose aim
had been to make much of the fraternity
of all humans, the Baptists and the Methodists, split
unfraternally fifteen years earlier into
Northern and Southern denominations? For that matter,
why was not the question of fratricide raised when
three million German-American and Italian-American
soldiers, not to mention the Japanese-Americans of the
Army's most decorated unit, fought against their
fully civilized counterparts in World War II?
A matter of their having voluntarily separated themselves
from the Old Country many years before, one might say:
except that the Southerners were doing precisely that,
separating themselves from the Old Country, in the only way
anybody knew how, forcefully if needs be.

Anyhow, civil or fraternal conflicts have been long infamous as
exceedingly bloody - if not the Revolutionary War where the
Loyalists fled or were miserably imprisoned or joined the British
ranks, then the English Civil War of the mid-1600's,
the War of the Roses, the French Revolution, and
all the ancient and modern cases, of ancient Rome,
the Russian Civil War between Reds and Whites,
1918 to 1923, the Spanish Civil War
of the 1930's, the Chinese Civil War of the 1940's,

the Cambodian Civil War of the 1970's, and so on, down to the Bosnian fraternal carnage of the 1990's, where the largest visible difference between the three peoples was that some of the Croatians were dedicated Catholics, some of the Serbs dedicated Orthodox, and some of the dedicated Bosnians Islamic; this was enough for Serbian political gangsters to begin their massacres.

A prime case of fraternal conflict would be the Lincoln household itself, where Mary Todd Lincoln, the President's wife, had a brother and several other close relatives in Confederate ranks. There were those who suspected that she may have influenced the President to be accommodating and lenient with the Southern cause. She was so often nagging the President, however, that one would hardly have been able to tell the ideological quarrel from a household one.

In the broadest sense, a cultural overlap existed in the border regions: here men were brought into conflict who looked, acted, and talked like they might be related. In a civil war, borders are always important for this reason, and there were valid economic reasons for the border to cut both ways here. The border states happened not to be suitable for plantation agriculture, hence had fewer slaves, and the people of the border states had that free-flowing Celtic element in disproportion and these, whether they believed in slavery or not, were psychologically unequipped to develop a slave culture.

There were, we recall, Kentucky, Missouri, Maryland and Delaware (with West Virginia to become a state in 1863). They tended toward neutrality, but in the end, after it was obvious who would win, they abolished slavery, or accepted the Thirteenth Amendment that towards the end of the War abolished slavery everywhere in the United States. They did not become the centers of conflict, such as border areas often do in civil wars, but at least Kentucky and Missouri saw a great many skirmishes.

Centers of the struggle were a limited area South and West of Washington, D.C., and the Tennessee and Lower Mississippi River valleys. Much is made of Sherman's March from Tennessee down through Atlanta and thence to the Sea. It was, however, a *contretemps*. The war had already been won in effect, and while he was cutting a swath of destruction, dragging the enfeebled armies of Hood and Johnston behind him, the decisive action South of Washington had turned into a chess game in which the King (read the Northern Army of Virginia of General Lee) was trying to avoid entrapment and checkmate by the powerful ever-enhancing pieces of General Ulysses S. Grant. In addition to these theaters, there was the sea blockade and the early cleanup of the far Southwest. Strangely there, not even Texas caused grave problems. There were already many Northerners on location, and nationalist German-Americans in the crucial Southeast, who remained loyal. Within the year, Federal troops were in charge in Texas, in New Mexico Territory and in California. Utah was never in doubt, nor any other territory except Oklahoma, still the center of the civilized tribes removed from the Southeast.
Here the Cherokees, instead of turning now against the people who had persecuted them, robbed them of their land and almost exterminated them, they actually joined the Confederacy as an ally. And held on to their few slaves. Indeed the last active command of the Confederacy in the Civil War was a Cherokee troop. The Cherokees suffered in the end: they were cheated, and their lands dismembered once more, with rather less sympathy from the North than they might otherwise have enjoyed.

The war itself took four years, in a formal sense. In a real sense, it took 145 years, or even only two years, depending on other points of view. For two years of the formal war (beginning with the declaration of the blockade of Confederate ports according to international law in April 1961 and ending with the battle of Gettysburg in July of 1863) the outcome was less certainly a Union victory, and therefore could be called the determining warfare. The second two years of the war were "unnecessary", but typical: a period of destruction, heavy casualties, often slaughters, of mass

desertions and collapsing opposition, all of which
takes much time to come about.

Resources - usually one need not bother with the campaigns, as thrilling as they may be to inveterate veterans - were the critical measure of the future of the bellicose.
The North contained two-and-a-half times the population of the South, 22 millions to nine,
and 3.5 million Southerners were slaves.
It would be wrong to deduct the slaves from the active belligerent population. They were an enormous resource for the South, probably more so than if they had been free Whites. They could be worked without relief and pay, fed the minimum for survival - men, women and children. They had no rights. They could not quit. They could not go West or back to the Old Country. They took up many of the tasks that uniformed troops performed in the Union Army. They could do everything but possess and use weapons; yet they could make and repair them. It was feared that, given weapons, they would turn them against the Caucasian Confederates.

As the war ended, the Confederate government was about to draft African-Africans into the Confederate Army, assuring them of emancipation when and if the war were won. It was a bad bargain, but a shrieking irony. In the North, after considerable delay, units of Afro-Americans were formed, more and more then, until they composed about ten percent of the huge Union forces. In battle or when captured, they suffered more from ill-treatment, murder and massacre than ordinary White troops.

The Confederacy produced less than a tenth of the goods put out by Northern manufactures. This included firearms and all of the equipment of war. The only large heavy industry was the Tredegar Iron Works, located at Richmond, Virginia, one more reason for fighting desperately to hold onto the Capital. Leather goods were almost exclusively Northern manufactures. The advantage in coal mining was 38 to 1.

The transportation system of the North was much superior. Its railroads held over twice the track and were more standardized. The one trans-Confederacy route that existed carried various lines to Chattanooga, Tennessee, from where the line arrived finally at Memphis. The North had two cross-national railroad lines; it could do without the Mississippi to get its goods overseas; it also had the canal system for the same, of course.

Used to the absolute necessity of industrial comparability in twentieth century wars, we are inclined to overestimate the value of heavier production to warfare in 1860. Aside from the railroad, we were still in the age of the horse and wagon, and inestimable mule. Ten thousand slaves knew how to cut leather into shoes. The plantation in some ways was a perfect decentralized factory for men and materiel useful in the warfare of the age.

The average Northern soldier was more handy than the average of the South, more used to machines, gears, variegated work procedures. The Southerner was more likely to pride himself on his mastery of the rifle, and it may be supposed that many a poor man volunteered so as to have a rifle that he could call his own, with plenty of free ammunition. The will to fight and attack is probably associated with the strong individualist and a rough breeding; it would be the Southern rank and file who would be more likely, in most types of engagements, to have this quality.

On the sea the Northerners had a numerical superiority of seafarers; the navy went Federal, officers and men, and throughout the war had a ten-to-one superiority in gunboats. The Confederates took over and transformed the ship Merrimac into the Virginia, plated it heavily, and proceeded to destroy numbers of Federal ships. A conveniently invented, smaller but heavily armed, iron Federal ship, called the Monitor, arrived propitiously from New York and took on the Virginia off Newport News, Virginia. More balls bounced off the Monitor than the Merrimac, and the latter withdrew from action permanently.

Confederate raiders did great damage, the average kill per boat before capture or the end of the war being a score and more of Union vessels. Worse was promised; like the Germans with their V-1 and V-2 rockets in World War II, the Confederates had a secret weapon, ironclad warships reinforced to ram enemy ships. But the British government, sensing the end, perfidiously delayed deliveries from the shipyards where they were being built, and the ships never saw action.

The Federal Navy performed notable feats, an amphibious landing at Roanoke, for instance, involving close coordination of bombardment and ferrying assault troops to the beaches. Navy barges and gunboats were put to good use, ferrying troops down the Potomac and up the James River, back and forth on the Ohio and Mississippi, blasting Confederate shore positions and troop concentrations on various occasions. Admiral Farragut's invasion of the Mississippi delta, his capture of New Orleans, and his juncture with the Army to the North, with minimal casualties, was a model naval operation. Indeed the Navy had all of its missions in hand, if not completed, before a year was out!

Neither side could maintain a fully effective blockade. By one ruse or another much cotton found its way to Latin-American and European processors. In the final analysis, the South was short of everything, but not to the point of surrender on that account. On the other hand, the blockade also kept large Southern forces tied up at its major seaports, for if they were withdrawn, an attack from the sea might take and hold the ports.

Technology of warfare was changing, but not so much that either side could find a definitive advantage in it. Before the War and during it, cannon barrels came to be rifled for accuracy in spinning the ball to its target, and were loaded at the breech instead of the muzzle. Rifles replaced muskets. The Winchester repeating carbine of 1861 and an improved French-designed bullet added to the deadliness of the firearm. Trenches - a cowardly invention by Waterloo standards of courage - had been used by Americans to good effect in the Revolution and

1812. They were employed regularly in the Civil War, and
where not employed - as General Grant failed to do at Shiloh -
more severe losses occurred. The Gatling gun,
a very slow machine-gun, came into use.
Wire entanglements proved serviceable.
Mining behind enemy positions was sometimes
attempted; the most notable effort in the last days of
the war was a large Union tunnel, blasting out
into a large crater; but, without a properly prepared
follow-through, the operation ended in heavy Union casualties.
Observation balloons, rising by letting the hot air
from a transported fire fill a cloth envelope,
proved useful for scouting and targeting.
Of horses, mules, and wagons there was aplenty.
And now there were available everywhere the telegraph wire and
the telegraph transmitter; the Civil War, fought upon one
of the largest of historical terrains, had the best communication
facilities for coordinating elements of any army
until that time.

The South was more combat-ready. Its population was
closer to the ordinary instruments of violence
in its very "backwardness". And it pulled out of the
Federal ranks the largest number of competent
Army officers. Even in sheer numbers of officers,
the South came first: it had a number of military
academies, more than the North.
General Robert E. Lee comes readily to mind,
West Point graduate like many others,
the Lieutenant Colonel who led the capture of the John Brown
conspirators, affectionate son of Virginia who turned
her way when the decision had to be made,
violating his oath to the Constitution incidentally.

Isn't one officer as good as another?
One is tempted to guess so, at least on the average.
And, as I shall be mentioning shortly, the best
officers, by reputation, made terrible blunders.

However, the greatness of command lies largely in the organization,
training, logistics, and morale functions of leadership.
Generalship in the field is the tool of the preparatory phases.
The use of the word "brilliant" is almost always excessive.
There are only several basic precepts of military strategy.
All kinds of folk wisdom of statesmen and military men
may be alluded to and have value -

"Git ther fustest with the mustest", is one,
attributable to a Confederate general.
There is the choice of an offensive strategy or a defensive one.
There are the overall assignments and divisions of troops.
There is the choice of fighting in depth or at a line of battle.
There is the choice of introducing one or more points of confrontation.
There is the choice of placing greater or lesser reliance upon
artillery as opposed to infantry,
of cavalry as opposed to these other two arms.

Lincoln was no warrior, nor even a proven officer.
His experience as a Captain of Illinois militia in the Blackhawk
Indian War was negligible, if not downright harmful.
He was not aggressive, atypically, while many of his associates,
appointees, and generals were typically so. He was not
a rabble-rouser. He was not an accountant of funds,
and let much corruption pass.
He appeared to be giving many commands, but hardly did so.
It is to his credit that most of his commands were versions of
O.K., or, "Git goin'!" He rarely needed to say "Go slower".
He appointed and removed generals - McClelland, Burnside,
Pope, *et al.* - usually without success.
He finally appointed Grant, say the books, but Grant
was already sticking out like a sore thumb, and perhaps Grant the
General was not so great as historiography
has made him out to be.

Lincoln did not panic, given many occasions to do so.
He was a morose man, given to mourning rather
than rage when disappointed. He did not fire
people right and left, when he had ample excuse to do so -
fortunately, for this would have enhanced the already dizzying

confusion. He was responsible in his speech, not a fire-eater, not a bombaster, but measured, sensible, and full of political cunning. His principal fault was his misinterpretation of the will of the Southern, elite and Whites generally. He misinterpreted it before the War began, during the War itself, and in his plans for the Reconstruction following the war. His character, more Southern than Northern, led him to sympathize with typical Southern ideas. He demanded much of himself, yet did not ask for too much for himself, and he did not expect or ask too much of other people, which was on occasion a mistake. He sympathized with the slaves, but did not expect much of them, whether as slaves or as free men.

Emancipation of the slaves possessed the double-edged quality of several basic war issues. The abolitionists pressed to free all slaves within Federal jurisdiction in the border states or conquered areas immediately, and the rest upon liberating the South. Practical arguments for abolition were strong too. If liberation came now, it would not be a problem for post-war governments - not that so many people thought ahead. If liberated, the free Blacks and the Blacks still in slavery would aid the Union cause in every possible way. Recruitment of Negro soldiers would increase greatly. Handling the increasing numbers of slaves entering Union lines would be eased: they would be inducted into the armed forces. Abroad, sympathy and aid to the Union cause would be forthcoming, whereas the South would be put ever more on the moral defensive.

On the other hand, Lincoln and the Republicans had promised that this would not be a war against slavery, where it already existed. They felt even now in the middle of the war that emancipation would alienate supporters in the existing slave states of the Union, would anger the South to fight ever harder, and would meet with resistance among the millions of racists in the Northern population and Union army. It was widely believed, and was probably true, that most Northerners and soldiers were racist, who were projecting blame upon Afro-Americans for causing them moral and mental confusion.

Nevertheless Lincoln felt that there could be no ultimate resolution of the problem of unity without emancipation and that the end of the war would be hastened by it: so, after a trial balloon announcing the intention of the government, he issued on January 1, 1863 the "Emancipation Proclamation", as people came to call it.

Despite votes by Congress in 1862, abolishing territorial and District of Columbia slavery and declaring free the slaves of all Confederates, Lincoln had sought a long-term liberating arrangement, with compensation. His Proclamation freed, on grounds of military necessity, all slaves in rebel areas. This was a clear seizure of power as military commander, such that the Constitution, already buffeted by non-constitutional Reality, could barely endure. Not until December of 1865 were slavery and involuntary servitude abolished throughout the whole of the United States, and then by virtue of the Thirteenth Amendment to the Constitution. Once more here, the Confederate States, who were fictionally determined never to have left the Union, were deprived of a voice.

It was enthusiastically welcomed abroad, where even intellectuals and officials assumed it meant all slaves were henceforth to be free. Abolitionists approved it, but felt it did not go far enough. Southerners surprisingly were rather apathetic to the report; it was not worse than they had expected all along and they were numb with the costs of the war.

Yankee soldiers were divided among practical enthusiasts, approving abolitionists, the great number who were apathetic, and those who disliked having brought liberty to the slaves while they themselves faced nothing soon but more suffering. The troops would discover that freeing the slaves as they went along would be a pleasure, both for the exhilarating power of releasing people and from the discomfiture of enemy soldiers and civilians. They could also put the former slaves to work, as compulsory volunteers for the Union.

Lincoln's perpetual stress was on Union, but why he, who had been a congressman opposed to the Mexican War (and was subsequently defeated for this reason) should have such strong feelings is not easy to understand (and a later strongly nationalist scholarhood took the strength of his feeling for granted). It may have arisen out of his border state origins: in history, sociologically marginal border regions have produced a disproportionate share of intense nationalists and nationalist leaders. (Napoleon a Corsican, Hitler an Austrian, Stalin a Georgian, for example.)

When the fighting began, both sides asked for volunteers, and the response on both sides was excellent. The new men and the militias called to arms promptly gave the conflict the proportions of a large war by historical standards, comparable to the armies who fought the wars of Napoleon. Photography was just maturing into an art form, and we have thousands of photographs of the soldiers in camps on both sides, at the road *en marche*, at the line of combat, and especially on the ground dead, an effect occasioned so often because the subjects of the camera had to take a long deep breath and remain still.

The strategy of the North and South might have pleased Leo Tolstoi, who had served in the Crimean War a few years earlier and was writing his novel, *War and Peace*. He found that generals had very little to say about the course of large historical events, but capered pretentiously atop a mass of hard facts; these small facts it was that composed destiny by solidifying into some collective form.

Where could the South have chosen to fight? If it marched West, it would promptly lose its most symbolic, progressive and rich area, the Virginia complex. It would give up half of its traditions, practically the same as losing the war then and there. If it put too much into the Eastern theater, it would lose the great cotton kingdoms and combative populations of the West. So it had to fight both East and west.

Its sea strategy I have already referred to: it was foreordained also.

Its border strategy had to be simply to cause as much destruction of property and communications as possible, to try also by terrorism or harassment generally to get the border populations to demand peace. Many ambushes and much raiding went on in divided Kentucky and Missouri. William Quantrell's guerillas, with Jesse and Frank James and the Younger boys, committed hundreds, if not thousands, of murders in Missouri, and ravaged and looted large areas. The Kansas Territory was brutalized. The level of suspicion was at the paranoiac stage everywhere. Countless slaves were tortured and killed on any evidence that they were considering action against the Confederacy or for freedom.

General Ulysses S. Grant, commanding the Northern border areas, decided that Jews were a threat and issued an order to expel them. This incredible action, soon rescinded by Lincoln, was to be repeated against the Japanese-Americans in World War II, and was not to be rescinded by President Roosevelt, or even officially regretted until long after that war.

Grant, emerging from a history of alcoholism, was also prone to paranoia. His case was not as bad as General William Tecumseh Sherman's. Sherman went into profound depressions and was convinced that the Washington crowd was out to get him, although he had a faithful brother high in the administration there, and a wife who was a skillful saleswoman of his abilities.
When assigned a command in Kentucky, he was seized by a totally illusory notion of the huge size of the opposing forces. He was

plagued by as many self-doubts as Lincoln. He dwelt continually upon the idea of resigning.

What seems ultimately to have happened psychologically is that Sherman was seized with a hatred for the enemy and focused his more than ample punishing instincts upon the Confederates; later on in life, he would be hunting Indians and buffalo herds with the same venom.

The North had the same border policies as the South. Moreover, it had little choice but to engage the enemy in the area of the Potomac and Northern Virginia. Washington may have been only a detail of the national industrial, transportation, communications, and manpower network, but London, Paris, Madrid, and Mexico City would regard its loss as most damaging and might even recognize and lend aid to the Southern Confederacy as a result.

(As it was, the Confederacy appeared imposing enough to elicit the status of a belligerent from France and Britain, enabling its vessels, material possessions, and personnel to be treated as the belongings of a respectable nation; not enough is made of this fact by historians, who consider it non-American and therefore not part of the war, whereas it was just about the only thing the Confederacy could hang onto in the external world.)

So Washington had to be held and Richmond assaulted. Early voices were prophesying a quick Union victory, but the Battle of Bull Run in July of 1861 ended in a disgraceful rout of the Federal forces. A succession of bitter battles grew in bloodiness and indecisiveness: the Peninsular Campaign; another second Bull Run; Antietam Creek (in Maryland), Fredericksburg (Virginia), and Chancellorsville (Virginia), this last fought in May of 1863. The stage was set for Gettysburg.

Meanwhile, to the North and West, control of the rivers had to be denied the South, and its only major railroad line cut. So it was thought, and two years were occupied in doing so. It is permissible to challenge this notion. Suppose the North had decided to hold fast on the North side of the Ohio River and the West side of the Mississippi. Small armies would have been detailed to defend critical points and even to behave aggressively wherever men and resources permitted. The powerful and loyal Navy would help. The Confederate armies could not have proceeded across the Rivers, at least not where they would have liked to cross, at the industrial ports of Ohio, for example. Then the North could have assembled overwhelming force at the decisive point where the Confederacy would have to make or break, the Northern Virginia sector. The South would have had to march most of their forces from the West to the smaller region of the East where their provisioning would have been difficult.

Meanwhile out of Southern Pennsylvania and Maryland, the Union could have launched an enormous flanking attack, sufficient to turn the whole South around into the Northern Virginia area, at the same time as the Northern armies out of Chesapeake Bay and Baltimore would have descended upon the main body of Confederate troops, the Army of Northern Virginia.

Actually something like this happened in the end. Larger Union armies than necessary were deployed into the Tennessee River and Mississippi Valleys, moved down and up, converging upon Vicksburg on the Mississippi, Memphis farther upstream, and Chattanooga. All this done, at considerable cost to both sides in a dozen major engagements, General Tecumseh Sherman was unleashed to march obliquely Southeast from Chattanooga following the railroad trunk line to Atlanta, Georgia, and from there to Savannah by the sea.
John Bell Hood, the Confederate choice to block all of this, stormed into several battles, each time being repulsed, while the Federals marched on, and on, toward the sea, destroying everything in their path.

General Ulysses S. Grant and his generals of the Western Theater had been circling about and conducting the costly but eventually successful battles that left the Confederates with a force inadequate to cope with Sherman's army. Grant's bulldog disposition attracted Lincoln who brought him to lead the Army of the Potomac.

Here the Union might earlier have won the war on several occasions, but had failed owing to the inflexible, slow, and bungling tactics of its generals and the resourceful and rapid responses of the Confederate generals. At one point, Lincoln had wondered whether he should not bring in somebody like Giuseppe Garibaldi, who was terrifically popular at the time in London and New England liberal and abolitionist circles for his daring liberation of Sicily and Naples and his dashing republican confrontation of nobility and Papacy in Italy; but Garibaldi wanted the major command, not a simple generalship, and nothing happened.

However, Grant did inherit a severely wounded adversary. Lee's army had been severely damaged by a foolish expedition into the North. It was part of the impossible options of the Confederates. The Union could hold out and build up as long as the Confederates stayed on the defensive. It was highly questionable whether they could command the thrust to go on the offensive in the North.

But go they did and the result was shameful. I speak of Gettysburg. The Confederates attacked in an area where the attack was brought on frivolously, by mistake, by a group of marauding soldiers who needed shoes. They attacked a larger army, under the command of Meade. At a critical juncture, their best troops, a division led by General Pickett, were ordered by Lee into an impossible attack against entrenched Federal troops on a hill. The kind of reserves that Lee needed to follow up Pickett's charge were not available, supposing the charge to have succeeded. It did not. And Lee retreated from Pennsylvania into Virginia.

One has to surmise that, facing the general election of the Confederate legislature, dreading the thought of retreating after so short a sojourn on Northern soil, he took an inexcusable gamble. His foolhardy venture provided a convenient "turning point of the War", such as historians are prone to seek. It might have been nearer the end if General Meade had followed in hot pursuit.

But he was like the rest of them; he was afflicted,
in Lincoln's phrase, with "the slows".
Common soldiers of the Union Army of the Potomac
knew well the string of slow-paced loggy generals
and even sang appropriate songs,
viz.,

General Meade, a slow old plug,
for he let them away at Gettysburg,
and we'll all drink stone-blind,
Johnny, fill the bowl.

It was at Gettysburg, to commemorate the prodigious sacrifice there,
that Lincoln delivered the address which half a billion American schoolchildren had to
memorize later on, a mercifully brief, elegantly styled, and simple moving
statement culminating in the prayer that there should not
perish from the Earth this "government of the people,
by the people, and for the people"
(an expression heard for the first time from the lips of the radical
French Revolutionary leader, Georges Danton,
guillotined in 1794:
"gouvernement du peuple, par le peuple, pour le peuple",
and picked up by New England radicals.)

Now Grant enters upon the scene in the East. He had done well usually; he had escaped near disaster from his own incompetence at Shiloh, where by acting aggressively after having been unnecessarily surprised, he avoided having his heavy losses counted as a defeat. He had seemed to perform brilliantly at the relief of Chattanooga; there his troops, sitting at the foot of Missionary Ridge, were exposed to cannon fire from above; instinctively they climbed to get below the angle of fire of the cannon and kept on going; when the Confederates saw the advancing lines, they panicked.
The battle was won.

Lincoln believed that Grant's genius was confirmed and brought him East to put an end to Lee. Probably (his Secretary is the source) Lincoln noticed Grant's willingness to accept disproportionately high casualties to come to grips with the outnumbered enemy. After Meade failed to take the losses of close pursuit on top of the heavy casualties of Gettysburg, Lincoln calculated that the losses through disease over a lengthy period without engagement were heavier than the losses in even the heaviest battle. Grant did slog on, in his imitable fashion, employing the greater weight of his armies to push incessantly, never too fast, never too slow.

Subjecting his soldiers to great losses, over 60,000 in a month at the Wilderness Battle, at Spotsylvania Court House, at Cold Harbor, he nevertheless ordered his army on - he had begun with a two-to-one advantage in numbers - so he could not be said to have lost a battle. In this manner he rounded Richmond and came before the railroad junction of Petersburg.

A small Confederate army moved in to defend the site, led by Beauregard. Instead of using his overwhelming force to break the siege, or cut around it to Richmond directly, Grant, the indomitable irresistible mover of armies, lay there encamped from June to April. Why would he have ground up his men in such a slaughtering in the weeks beforehand, if it were only in order to sit before a railroad junction?

One must conclude that Lincoln, the poor judge of men, had made another misjudgement; but the North simply had too many things going for it to lose.

The siege was conducted along extended lines of many miles above and below the junction. Knowing that Lee could not match his manpower, Grant pushed the tentacle of his left flank westward, farther and farther. Encirclement of the whole Southern army was threatened. Far to the West and through the Shenandoah Valley and then out upon the Eastern plain went Union General Philip Sheridan, capturing one after another town, forbidding supplies to the main Confederate army.

To the far South, Sherman had taken Charleston, and defeated an attempt by the depleted army of Joseph E. Johnston to stop him at Bentonville in central North Carolina.
It was time for Lee to abandon the Confederate capital to its fate.

He escaped from the Petersburg siege, and headed South thinking possibly to join up with Johnston's remaining forces. However, Sheridan had cut East and barred his escape.

The Confederate leadership gave consideration to carrying on a guerrilla war, but, imagining the characters who would turn up to lead the bands around the country, men like the notoriously evil Quantrell, they decided to surrender like gentlemen. Lee, dressed in his best dress uniform, met slovenly Grant at a private home in Appomattox, and on April 9, 1865 yielded his Army of Northern Virginia to Grant. His principal request, and he was lucky to have it granted, was that his men be allowed to keep their private horses and mules, and the officers their sidearms. Remaining Confederate forces soon followed suit South and West. The formal Civil War was over. The freed African-Americans didn't do as well as the surrendering enemy; they had not horse nor mule, neither sidearms.

The attention to casualties in the Civil War is excessive and comes because of their naturally gruesome quality, exhibited in many striking photographs, and because people have too few explanations otherwise for victory and defeat. It is known that the Confederates lost about 100,000 soldiers in combat (including amicide or "friendly fire" such as caught their second greatest general "Stonewall Jackson"), a rate of 25,000 a year, quite bearable for a nation of nine millions; they lost another 150,000 men owing to the diseases that plagued an army.

The typical hospital killed the wounded and sick more than cured them; there was one private hospital owned and superintended by a woman, Confederate Sally Tomkins of Richmond, where the death rate was several times lower than in the typical military hospital. The same miserable hospitalling was true of the North; personnel tried to discourage poet Walt Whitman's volunteer nursing because he might go public with revelations of the care they were providing.

Confederate military strength was officially 326,768 men in

December 1861; the peak number was 473,058 in June 1863 (a month before Gettysburg). It still counted 358,692 in December of 1864. But these were men listed as enrolled. Many were absent without leave, actually deserters. The desertion rate in the first instance was 20%, on the latter two occasions between 40% and 53%.

The picture is clear: the Confederates had a large-enough military manpower potential. But the actual size of the army was determined by hundreds of thousands of individual soldiers; they voted with their feet. It was they, not General Lee or General Grant, who determined that the war was over.

The Union troops suffered much heavier casualties. They lost 200,000 in combat, and the same proportion through disease. Combat losses tend to be greater with an attacking army, and the Union Army was dedicated to an offensive strategy. As I indicated earlier, about half of these losses, not nearly so many among the Confederates, came in the course of rash charges.

Nine out of ten frontal assaults brought defeat, a break and retreat - on whichever side charged. The same schoolboys and poolroom habitués who had hooted and howled at General Pekingham's disastrous charge at New Orleans now found themselves marching across killing fields just as bad. The bayonet was rarely used except to cut bread and scrape mud off boots. We were already in an age of massed firepower. All that was needed to murder a great many more men was the machine gun.

The home fronts were often troubled. Riots, particularly in connection with the forced conscription of soldiers, occurred in many cities. Richmond also saw food riots. During the four years of organized and border warfare, there had of course existed two nations to lead and administer, insofar as either was possible. Southerners found themselves with a government whose devotion to slavery and states rights could not be gainsaid. It was a one-party government, whereas the North operated with a coalition government of Republicans and Democrats.

The Confederate Government found itself with pressing needs to behave out of form: it impressed labor, conscripted soldiers, suspended the writ of habeas corpus, and would have liked to compel the states to pay their badly needed assessments but could not. It issued vast quantities of currencies that came to be worthless. It borrowed all the money and obtained all the credits it could, but these were hardly sufficient and of course in the end it could neither back its paper currency or pay its debts.

Inasmuch as the South fought the war as a congeries of state "clans", the independent states, the source of morale lay in states individually rather than in the total vision of a central union. There was no great abstraction like the United States of America that claimed the allegiance of men from Vermont and Iowa alike. Southern soldiers therefore referred morale questions to their buddies or to their own personal State. They judged fairly well the situation. Whenever there was a defeat, the desertion rate, always high, went up even more. During the last year of the War, over half the soldiers had decided to call it quits on their own part and deserted (telling themselves that they were on leave, of course). The Federals suffered, not so severely, from their own desertions.

Both sides contained numerous disloyal citizens. In booming Chicago, early in the War, there was a fear that the city would be taken over by Confederate sympathizers. Several associations of friends of the Union carried on secret activities to end the war, or even to slow the war effort. Almost no measure was taken on either side but that excited strong opposition.

The draft riots of New York City in 1863 turned out to be a racist riot against the free Blacks of the city, more than being a riot against conscription. Hundreds of civilians were killed by the rioters and by the militia and Federal troops sent specially into the city to quell the disturbances. Irish Catholic elements, now prominent in New York, and still laboring under the cruelest economic disadvantages, rampaged against the African-Americans, poorest of workers, yet competitive with the Irish.

No deaths are recorded among the rich of the city, some of the most distinguished names of Wall Street and monopoly industry, who could pay the pittance for substitute soldiers. They played it safe, and their names adorn some of the most distinguished university buildings, corporation headquarters, and foundations of the land.

The Union soldiers had much to complain about in the conduct of the civilians back home. As many new farms were planted during the war as there were casualties. The military suppliers all too often sold shoddy goods and rotten food to the Army, and the corrupt on the outside found their counterparts in uniform or as civilian officials. In one famous case, J. P. Morgan, an English immigrant of a rich English father who was backing his banking company in the United States, was party to a deal whereby the Army had sold a batch of defective guns at $17, 486 to the same persons to whom it had promised to buy the same guns the day before for $109,912.

The Secretary of War, a kindly Scot named Simon Cameron, proved to be the ringleader of the largest corrupt gang of the war. He had been a prime operator in Pennsylvania politics and had bought a Senate seat before joining the Lincoln Administration. Lincoln could not like him but tolerated him, while the man was dispensing incredible bargains to his railroading friends and giving agents funds to buy supplies for the Army as they pleased. He had cost the government millions and killed a few soldiers indirectly by the time Lincoln had him resign and accept nomination as Minister to Russia in January 1862.

Politics during the War were as dirty as beforehand. The Union coalition of Lincoln did not drive the Democrats out of business; there would be soon another party, essentially of Democrats. Peace Democrats were especially active in Indiana, Illinois and Ohio, most of them of Southern lineage from the Ohio River area. They called him "King Abraham" and he and his friends called them "Copperheads". The peace party had an imposing candidate, none other than General McClelland, the quality of whose generalship was not indisputable. He was a good organizer, and had in fact, after his early military career, become a successful businessman before he was recalled to serve the Union.

The political campaign was hardly ennobling. For instance, two McClelland journalists published a campaign book called "Miscegenation", that purported to be a Republican document encouraging racial mixing as a Republican policy. Presumably the "Peace Party" would be readier to grant the South easy terms upon receipt of a pledge to return to the Union. But Lincoln was not speaking of harsh terms either. It is remarkable that McClelland did so well in the popular vote, gaining 45% to Lincoln's 55%. The electoral vote was more disparate, as usual. Obviously "Honest Abe" was not the idol of the people of the North, never mind that he was the most hated man in the South.

If little positive were gained aside from Lincoln's re-election, there was a loss in Lincoln's choice of Vice-President, Andrew Johnson, a Unionist from Tennessee, a poor boy grown to hate Southern planters as a class, but conservative in his social opinions and bereft of education and culture.

A history of the Presidents could be written with reference to what their choice of Vice-President shows about their inner character. Lincoln gave out that he had picked him because he was pleasing to the border interest, or so he thought. Johnson was also committed, like Lincoln, to reconciliation between North and South, in this respect being target of well-founded suspicions on the part of the hard-nosed Republicans of the Joint Congressional Committees on the Conduct of the War, who were getting ready to conduct the peace.

What happened in the Congress during the War in the way of civil legislation gave proof positive that the United States had been composed of two different nations: Congress passed most of the legislation that had been controversial since the founding of the republic! It could be seen now that the North and West composed a national unity.

Congress enacted a high protective tariff schedule, twice what made

South Carolina shout secession. It established a National Bank and provided hard currency reforms despite running up a large debt to carry on the war. It passed the Morrill Land Grant Act that gave each state large acreages, all proceeds from whose sale were to be used for setting up agricultural and mechanical colleges around the nation.

It passed legislation (The Homestead Act) giving away 160-acre lots to settlers who hung on for five years. (It soon worked to the advantage of speculators, who dealt in the titles, once the farmers failed, and to banks that lent capital for the enterprises.)
A great deal of land was given over to the capitalization of a transcontinental railroad route from Omaha, Nebraska, to Sacramento, California.

With all this progress,
one might think that they should have let the
South go its own way, but of course there had remained the overriding issue of slavery.
There was great relief and happiness in the North
upon the collapse of the Confederacy.
In the last months of the War, Tennessee and
Missouri abolished slavery. In 1865,
the Thirteenth Amendment to the
Constitution was adopted,
abolishing slavery throughout the Union.
Only Kentucky and Delaware had remained to be
affected by the Amendment.

Now all the slaves were free and most people wished that they would vanish into some sultry Southern back fields. Northerners wanted to do even more business, without shame at the sacrifices others were making. But the casualties of the war stayed with people, as would the fate of the freed slaves.

The condition of the Southern veterans
was bad, generally closer than ever
to the level of the former slave.
The North was not ready to
spend any resources on their rehabilitation,
a mistake to be sure, and

did not require that the Southern States take measures to help its veterans. (Later on they would get some state help.)

The Northern veteran was another matter. Nothing was too good for him, to hear the politicians and media talk. And, indeed, a system of payments was begun that brought the equivalent of social welfare payments to a large proportion of the Northern population, enabling them, wrapped in the flag as patriots, to more comfortably oppose the welfare needs of others.

African-Americans suffered a caste system even
100 years after the War that 'freed the Negro. '(1911)

Chapter Forty-two

Civil War II: 1865-1965

A War of Reconstruction, largely conducted by
terror, mob action, and civil disobedience,
began with a terrorist act in a Washington theater,
on the evening of April 14, 1865.
Earlier on the same day, a large gathering at Fort Sumter,
offshore of Charleston, South Carolina, had marshaled
major symbols of Confederate humiliation:
Afro-American occupation troops,
William Lloyd Garrison and Henry Ward Beecher

(principal orator for the occasion), Major Anderson who had surrendered the Fort just four years earlier, and all kinds of boats festooned gaily and booming salutes. The week before had seen the surrender of the Southern Armies of the East and the dissolution of the Confederate States of America.

But here in Washington, from a band of terrorist conspirators, came a man who like Lincoln had been born in a log cabin, a man who had won fame in the difficult profession of dramatic acting: John Wilkes Booth. He walked into the Presidential box, where sat the President and Mrs. Lincoln, and shot the President fatally. The security guard was nowhere to be seen.

To bind himself to history, Booth shouted in the manner of Brutus assassinating Julius Caesar nineteen hundred years before, *"Sic semper tyrannis!"* When trapped twelve days later and about to die himself, he called out, more typically American, a message of love to his mother.

A sense of grief, remorse, and loss shook most of the Northern population. The act was called criminal, insane, vengeful, futile, and many people said that nobody could handle the problems of the country as could have "Ol' Abe". Few thought it to be - for this it also was - an opening signal to the unreconstructible South that there were other ways of winning a war than by full-dress battle.

With minimal help from the Federal government and their Northern compatriots, the freedmen of the South had to engage the Southern governments and the Southern population in a continual war of resistance, fighting to protect themselves from reduction to a condition worse than slavery and from the destruction of the most meaningful parts of the Federal Constitution and its amendments.

The Southern people and governments, most of them - let there be no doubt of it - wanted to reduce African-Americans to a point where they would regret their freedom, and reduce the Federal

Constitution to a dead letter in those parts that hinted at or denoted the loss of the War of the Rebellion.

The North was supine, and worse. For 100 years African-Americans of the South felt like the Polish people of Warsaw in 1944 when, fighting for their existence against the Nazi army, they could see their supposed allies, the Soviet Army, across the River, declining to come to their aid, watching them being annihilated.

Too, like the Poles, they had to wait a long time before even their voice could get through to proclaim what had happened. For there was nothing but censorship in the South of Whites and Blacks, and false historiography on questions of the Civil War and reconstruction and the struggles that followed. It is up to honest historians to abandon the characterization of the United States as a democracy or a republic of law and order even until the mid-twentieth century, given that, minimally, Blacks, Indians and Hispanics were outcastes to these terms.
"Reconstruction" was the term used by its proponents to stand for the civil and physical regeneration of the former Confederate states. Historians and the Northern public described prejudicially the attempted Reconstruction of the South; they set an arbitrary cut-off point to the period of troubles at 1877 when Federal troops were withdrawn; they gave only intermittent attention to the progress of the South from that time onward, until something called "the New South" was supposed to be generating around the turn of the Twentieth century.

The total and integrated significance of what was occurring in the South with reverberations in Washington especially was missed, with unconscious purpose. The technique, charitably we can call it unwitting, was to speak of the long period as full of incidents, with the eternal implication that progress was slowly being made, and that the African-American was a victim of prejudice, but he did have bad qualities, and prejudice was better than slavery, after all.

The story of the War of Reconstruction may be understood better if we declare in advance what were the terms and conditions of the final victory against slavery of 1965. In them we can see what should have or might have come with the surrender of the armed forces of the South in early 1865. Yet practically all of these victorious conditions came about near the end of the century of struggle, with most Southerners waging war against the Constitution, the Federal government, and the African-American population - man, woman, and child. For reasons to be explained later the end of the struggle has to be tentative, but may be tied temporarily to the passage of the Civil Rights Act of 1964 and the Voting Rights Act of 1965.

By 1997, one political generation later:

1

- Most of the population had ceased continually to badger and oppress African-Americans.

2

- Overt respect for the achievements of African-Americans was commonly expressed.

3

- Fear of uncommon criminality and irresponsibility of the African-American population was more common than 140 years ago, but there was a determined successful effort by authorities everywhere to stop at individual punishment for an individual crime.

4

- Fear of a large-scale Black revolt, that had worried a great many Southerners in 1865, was much diminished.

5

- The national police of the United States, particularly the Federal Bureau of Investigation, itself still blighted by racism, were now interfering with the despotic, cruel, and unlawful tactics of most Southern police.

6

- The United States armed forces were in readiness to suppress riot and rebelliousness by racist crowds, racist police forces, and racist state militias.

7

- African-Americans eligible to vote were registered and could actually vote, and rebels against this new order of affairs were sought out and prosecuted.

8

- The power of Southern Senators to engage in filibuster until their points were won was sharply curtailed.

9

- Schools and universities of the South and North were opened to African-Americans students with little regard to race and some positive inducements (these being termed "affirmative action").

10

- The armed services were de-segregated and promotional opportunities for African-Americans expanded greatly.

11

- Access to government welfare benefits and other government programs were no longer withheld from African-Americans.

12

- African-Americans were elected to many offices in Southern towns, counties, cities, state legislatures, Congress, and appointed to courts of law.

13

- Due process of law in criminal and civil cases was typically extended, both procedurally and substantively to African-Americans.

14

.- Public places such as restaurants, waiting rooms, hotels, toilets, trains and buses, were opened on a non-discriminatory basis to African-Americans.

15

- A number of government programs to give special benefits hitherto not available were provided, such as small business loans, minority business loans, etc. Again "affirmative action" was put into play.

16

- Hundreds of active, passive and obsolete state laws and local ordinances and administrative rules by which invidious discrimination was practiced against African-Americans were repealed, and a great many equal-rights ordinances and rules and laws were promulgated.

17

- Laws effecting invidious discrimination in the apportionment of seats in legislatures and other elective bodies were redrawn or repealed or nullified.

18

- The constitutions of thousands of voluntary associations, clubs, schools, scientific and professional associations, that had discriminated against African-Americans, were altered to abolish such practices.

19

- The right to assemble in public places, to march, and to demonstrate was handed over to the African-Americans and the same level of delinquent and illegal disorderly behavior and rioting was tolerated for Blacks as had always been tolerated for Whites.

20

- The right of questioning and protesting without severe retaliation, against the thousand picayune ways by which Americans of Caucasian race typically tormented African-Americans, became ordinary.

To be explicit, the foregoing constitute the peace terms of the Hundred Year War of Reconstruction. They represent a proper victory, not the happiest and most complete of victories, but a substantial one. The reforms alluded to above are felt throughout the South and ramify throughout the nation. Their positive effects are greater than those of the victory won in 1865.

But the agonizing question remains: why were not all of these terms of victory part of the complete victory of the North in 1865, with the complete capitulation of the South? The answer to this question lies in the study of the peace terms of 1865 and how the new war began and was carried on by variegated means for a century.

Furthermore, although the recent listed changes amounted to a general victory, true racial equality and harmony were still distant. A later chapter can assess the chances of there occurring another breakdown of the civil order.

All over the South, in 1865, disorder bordered upon chaos. Hysteria and panic were common, led by paranoia: outlandish rumors of freedmen conspiracies, of horrendous crimes committed, flew about. Many freedmen were beaten or lynched in consequence. Not enough federal troops were available to patrol the huge region. Although psychological surveys cannot be cited, ample personal observations and documents go to show that a profound depression afflicted many White Southerners. They could not work, they felt exhausted, they were totally apathetic.

Examining this fact exposes the importance of deference as a value.
Recall the plight of the planters, who could neither avoid the war nor end it.
For the nub remained unshaven: the Southern poor
lived off a social deference requiring the Blacks below;
they continued to require this deference, in fact, needed it
even more, after defeat. No idea of progress -
old or new - floated in the atmosphere.
They had nowhere to turn except, like the
fundamentalists waging global warfare
a hundred years later, to their historically-employed
miserable solution.

Union soldiers frequently clashed with disbanded confederate soldiers roaming over the countryside begging or stealing whatever could be eaten, drunk, or carried off. Innumerable confederate soldiers wandered westward and Southward; many of them had never had much of a home before joining up.

The freedmen, who many planters thought would stay and work the plantations as laborers, loving their locales as they did, did not love it enough, apparently, for they, too, moved out in every direction, looking very often for some agent of the Union who would show them a piece of land and start them up in farming. In some areas, the post-war disorder did not end for fifty years.

Center stage for Reconstruction in 1865 was Washington, D.C. The ascendency to the Presidency of Andrew Johnson was an ugly surprise to the Radical Republicans, the group of Congressmen who had prosecuted the war most fiercely and had the most concrete ideas of what should be done now. To them, Lincoln had been disappointing, but Johnson would be worse. (One would expect that all the while the Confederacy was staggering to an end, plans would have been properly laid for the hereafter.)

Generally the Radicals believed that seceded states should be treated as conquered provinces, to be admitted to the Union under whatever restrictive conditions the Congress might impose. Reflected in the Wade-Davis Bill, one idea was to require a loyalty oath from a majority of White male adults of a seceded state before it could be considered for admission, and to deny the suffrage to all who had fought against the Union.

Lincoln pocketed the bill and Congress adjourned without its having passed into law. Lincoln, with his presumption that the States had never left the Union because they legally could not - a position later upheld by the Supreme Court (1869) - proposed that all who accepted the Union and swore allegiance to its laws be forgiven except those who had held high office or had left the Federal service to join the revolt, and further that a State might return to Congress after one-tenth of its 1860 qualified voters would take a loyalty oath.

His death put Johnson in charge, who began to rule by decree, granting amnesty to all Confederates except top policy-makers and the richest men. (He was a populist, unsurprisingly also was self-contradictory, and of ungovernable temperament: when he first learned of the Emancipation Proclamation, he exclaimed *"Damn the Negroes, I am fighting these traitorous aristocrats, their masters".)*

He proclaimed provisional governments and authorized loyal Whites to draft new state constitutions and to elect legislatures instructed to repeal secession, and repudiate their war debts - a forced default, but they could not pay anyhow - and ratify the Thirteenth Amendment now making the rounds of the states.

However, the provisional governments began to enact so-called Black Codes that subjected the former slaves to disabilities, depriving them of most civil liberties, including the right to vote, and limiting their economic activity to farming, for instance.

This may all seem incredible, but the slave states and even some of their conquerors might well be confused with all that had been said about the war having to do with secession, not slavery, with Abraham Lincoln to be quoted and fairly as of this opinion, nor was there any law or even governing opinion to the effect that the freedmen were now equals - all states had laws making "some people more equal than others".

The Radical Republicans, now dominating the Congress, were led by Senator Charles Sumner of Massachusetts and Representative Thaddeus Stevens. When the Congressmen from the provisional governments showed up at the convening of Congress in December of 1865, Congress refused to seat them.

Then Congress created a powerful Joint Committee on Reconstruction of 15 members with jurisdiction over all questions determining the settlement of the war. Earlier Congress had created the Bureau of Refugees, Freedmen, and Abandoned Lands, which came to be called the Freedmen's Bureau. In 1866 Congress extended the life of the Bureau indefinitely in a bill that Johnson vetoed. An even stronger bill was passed, however, and overrode his veto later in the year.

The Bureau opened offices throughout the South and sought to ticket abandoned land for the use of newly freed Blacks, to feed and house the homeless, to set up schools, to peacefully and equitably settle Blacks and Whites in old and new forms of employment.

Some attempts were made to give the freedmen small parcels of land to farm. This was the dream of the former slave, as of the poor Southern White as well. And many poor Whites were incensed at being passed over for Negroes because they had not been slaves and had been Confederate soldiers.

The White planters fully expected Johnson, who had long said the most vicious things about them - including that he would like to have them all shot - to begin a systematic confiscation and parceling out of their land. It never happened. Running a chaotic and resentful population was a tough job for a crippled nation that had little experience with social welfare programs, North or South.

Congress passed also a Civil Rights Act to confer citizenship upon the Blacks and to seek equal treatment for them under the law. The

President declared that the measure invaded States Rights (*sic!*) and tended to revive the spirit of rebellion.
Understandably, the Republicans saw Johnson as playing ball for the wrong team. So the Joint Committee proposed and got passed a Fourteenth Amendment to the Constitution. This created a national citizenship for every person born or naturalized in the United States. It prohibited any state from passing laws abridging the privileges and immunities of any citizen of the United States or depriving any person of *"life, liberty, or property without due process of law"*. Moreover, any state that deprived any males of the ballot would have its representation in the Congress cut by the proportion that the deprived ones constituted of all males. Former confederates could not fill any offices similar in character to offices they held before the war. The Confederate debt was repudiated and the debt of the United States affirmed for repayment.

Johnson denounced the Amendment as unconstitutional (*sic!*) and advised the former Confederate states not to ratify it. It was, however, ratified, in July, 1868. The President and the Republicans locked horns in the 1866 Congressional elections; former "copperheads" joined with the President. His candidates were roundly defeated; the Republicans now had a clear mandate.

Now Congress passed the Reconstruction Acts. These divided up the ten unreconstructed states into five military districts. Federal generals became in effect their full governors. To be readmitted to the Union, a state had to hold a constitutional convention under full male suffrage; draft a constitution that guaranteed full male suffrage,
pass the proposed constitutions under the approval of Congress,
elect state legislatures under the new universal male suffrage
that were pledged to vote for the fourteenth amendment,
then finally apply for representation in Congress.

Seeking to tie up the President more securely, Congress passed a Tenure of Office Act in March of 1867,
forbidding him from removing the top appointive officers without the approval of the Senate (who of course would have had to consent to the appointment in the first place).

When Johnson fired Secretary of War Edwin Stanton,

a Republican stalwart who had served first and well under Lincoln,
for refusing to obey an order properly,
the Congress decided to get rid of the President entirely.
The House impeached him, and the Senate tried him
on the impeachment.

There were eleven charges, including the violation of the Tenure of Office Act, all of them said to constitute "high crimes and misdemeanors". Some were trivial or silly, the one on the Tenure Act was defending what looked like and would ultimately be termed an unconstitutional law. The charge that bore most weight was that he was *"unlawfully devising and contriving"* to evade the Reconstruction Acts in violation of his constitutional function of faithfully executing the laws.

Counsel for the defense argued for one thing that the Tenure Act was unconstitutional and he, Johnson, could not violate his oath of office and in good conscience obey it.

Nevertheless, the vote to convict and remove him from office was 35 to 19, only one vote short of the two-thirds required. Johnson's powers were in fact circumscribed; he was frightened from blocking Congressional will thereafter. His chief function, in retrospect, seems to have been to encourage Southern resistance to the spirit of Reconstruction.

The new state constitutional conventions convened.
(The occupying Army ensured full and equal suffrage.)
One-third of their total membership was African-American.
Their work was commendable. For instance,
the need was recognized for equally peopled legislative districts
to complement the right to vote by preventing gerrymandering
and other forms of deliberate malapportionment of representatives
to a favored partisan group.

"Unreconstructed" Southerners poured abuse upon their conduct and upon the legislatures elected afterwards. They popularized two epithets for the White men who took part in the new politics:

"scalawags" for the White Southerners who tried to implement the Reconstruction Acts, and "carpetbaggers" for the out-of-state-Whites who participated to the same end.

Fourteen African-Americans came to serve now in Congress, and larger numbers in the state legislatures. Almost without exception the African-American legislators were superior in mind and morality to the average of their Caucasian colleagues.

Most of the ten states under surveillance qualified soon, but Mississippi, Georgia, Texas, and Virginia took until 1870, by which time they had also to ratify the Fifteenth Amendment, which was making the rounds of ratification and which forbade any state to deny anyone the vote on grounds of race, color, or previous condition of servitude. The Amendment passed in that year.

In the same year and the next, Congress devised the "Force Acts", that decreed heavy penalties for violation of the Fourteenth and Fifteenth amendments, which allowed federal authorities to control Congressional elections, and which gave the President authority to use the military to suppress violent disruption of the exercise of civil rights.

The flow of legislation - punitive, reconstructive, beneficial - appears to have been timely, reasonable and well-directed. But Johnson's premature creation of provisional governments helped to organize immediately the forces of a new rebellion. Before Congress could react to the situation, an image of the intended rebellion was created - led by many new men of populist and strongly racist disposition, eager for personal gains, contemptuous in many cases of the half-destroyed planter class, convinced that the war need not have been lost nor need be lost now.

Unfortunately, as often will occur in occupying armies, the fraternization of soldiers and populace turns to the advantage of the interests and people that brought in the soldiers for protection of others in the first place. So that Southern anti-reconstructionists - who could be also termed racists, or anti-Yankees, or Dixiecrats (for adhering to the ideology of Southern culture, the region defined roughly by the Mason-Dixon survey line and the popularity of the song *"I wish I were in Dixie"..*) - were informally encouraged in this manner as well.

Both African-American freedmen and Anglo-Celtic poor Whites were victimized by planters and merchants. Planters marked out the Blacks as their economic servitors, the merchants signaled the poor Whites. Planters and merchants fought to preserve their stake in the victims. Planters in many places had state laws passed that would forbid selling anything at night in order to control all sales to their Black workers. They also obtained legal and actual control over the lending of money, credit, and supplies to Blacks, while the merchants did the same with regard to poor Whites.

Half the poor Whites were forever in debt. So were most Blacks. Both groups cried continually over being cheated. Redress for either Black or White was almost impossible. Both groups lost their farms over a couple of decades of time to their "patrons". Instead of becoming a vast land of small independent farmers, the South became a region of tenants, share-croppers and farm laborers. This happened by 1890, in the generation following the War.

County courthouse gangs - a sheriff, a court, a few deputies, a few landowners, several lawyers, a couple of merchants, a land surveyor, a county recorder, a council of friends of these - this was the typical Southern elite in over a thousand counties during this century of which we speak: they were the local troops of the "Second Army of the Confederacy".

Cries of corruption were raised on all sides. There is no question, but that all the reconstruction governments could be accused of inordinate corruption at all levels, and that the army brought in its share of crooks. The Dixiecrats raised the cry most successfully, and, given the prevalent racism in the North as well as the South, the stigma of waste and corruption branded the governments, in which were to be found African-Americans and White collaborators.

The propaganda victory here was complete; for a century the whole nation was given to believe that the reconstructed governments were ridiculous and corrupt failures. Such was not the case. They appear now not to have been worse than the average in these regards when compared with pre-war or post-reconstruction governments; in any event, the civil liberties and fairness and hope that they allowed to the poor population might compensate for a large amount of corruption. Too, the budgets that provided for the first time for public education in some of the reformed states were commendable, not wasteful.

Supplementing the accusations of illegitimate (that is, Northern-enforced) government, and of incompetence and corruption, was a propaganda depicting general sexual and moral promiscuity and conspiracies against the White communities and White property. Then came the propaganda of terror, promising that active Blacks and those cooperating with them could expect to be punished economically, socially, and physically by the ever-swelling Dixiecrat movement. And reality soon succeeded the threat.

In 1866 in Memphis, the Ku Klux Klan was formed, not with any grand conspiracy in mind, but as a civic and social club. The idea developed its full form and large interstate membership quickly. It became a general revolt by all means against the efforts to make of the South what losing a war, any war, would have been expected to make of it. Similar secret "reform" associations, parading in awful gear, had been long known in Europe, usually being gilds of artisans or Catholic lay groups or Mardi Gras clubs. There were similar organizations with the same goals, also: the Knights of the White Camellia, the Boys of '76, etc. They wore outlandish costumes - white robes and hoods for instance - pledged secret vows, and used guns, knives, whips, clubs, branding, nooses, torches, fires, and burning crosses to impress the world and break the will of the opposition.

Once the repertoire of Dixiecrat tactics was learned and spread, local vigilantism and the local communities knew just what they had to do to "keep the Negro in his place", and to frustrate any local or outside intervention on behalf of the African-American or - and here was the equally great tragedy of the White South - to alter any conditions that might interject wider opinions, progress, new faces, or measures for the general welfare.

The expression is sometimes used pridefully in the history of a country resisting oppression, "the whole people rose against the occupying power:" this might be applied to the whole of the South including the areas of Southern culture that escaped membership in the Confederacy.

Indeed, the Confederacy gained allies; the border States that had fought for the Union now turned against the Union and the Constitution and joined the enemy! An enormous reinforcement of political, economic, population, and propaganda power blessed the Old South in the Reconstruction War. In these States - Maryland, West Virginia, Kentucky, Tennessee, Oklahoma, and portions of Missouri, Illinois, Indiana, Ohio, and wherever else the borders of the Confederacy were touched - Confederates, overtly or in disguise, came to dominate.

But surely there were Southerners who knew what should be done to recover from the war and achieve equality in agriculture, commerce, politics, and social well-being with the North? They were a minority, a subdued and silent minority who could hardly muster a quorum of opposition to the general tenor and pace of Southern affairs.

Few could realize, not then nor now, how wretched were the souls of the gentle and kind in the old South, particularly of the Coastal region, who were citizens of the State, nation and world, but were condemned to everlasting custody by vicious prejudice around them, the contempt, too, and hatred of the cultured national public, feeling no longer at one with peace, plenty, and progress, cast into the ignominy of the whole Southern culture.

The War increased the number of poor and destitute of the South to over 85% of the White population, and in this same category had to be placed practically all - say 98% - of the Blacks. This state of degradation would not be alleviated before another three biological generations.

But it was from this poor White population that the initiative and the battles of the hundred-year Civil War sprang. Once more, the poor Southerner valued more than anything his pride; this pride had been mercilessly crushed by the Northerners; and the only way he could think of to restore it was to continue what had been his tactic of self-respect for centuries, the further degradation of the Blacks, fortified now in his determination by Union's attempts at the legal and forced emancipation of the Blacks.

The poor Whites of the South would continue to fight their kind of war violently, socially, illegally and legally, economically, too, until a great many of them (and the Blacks) had left the South and until Federal troops descended upon them once more.

One *coup d'état* succeeded another. By illegal and violent means the Dixiecrats expelled the cooperating Blacks and Whites from the state governments. Efforts to organize biracial militias could not suffice against the forces developed by the illegal elements. The national army was sent in once by General Grant to curb Klan violence under the Force Acts. Between 1865 and 1868 in Texas, an official and perhaps correct report came up with 509 White and 486 freedman killings, but almost all the White deaths came at the hands of other Whites. There were scores of lethal riots occurring throughout the period.

The Republican Party of the South, that the congressional radicals had hope would develop, weakened rapidly until it lost control of all states, and existed thereafter by tolerance, often serving its Democratic political masters, discriminating also against Blacks, and called "Lily White Republicans" by contemptuous Northern Republican associates.

In 1872, a combination of Democrats and moderate Republicans

enacted a General Amnesty Act that gave back political privileges to thousands of former Confederate leaders. The number of Black office-holders declined farther as a result.
As if to lend the Dixiecrat rebels further assistance, the Supreme Court in 1873 decided in the so-called *Slaughterhouse Cases* that the fourteenth amendment was not intended to protect civil rights in general, but only to protect the rights of U.S. national citizenship.

In 1875 Congress passed a law prohibiting racial discrimination in public places, such as restaurants and hotels. It was not enforced, but even so in 1883 the Supreme Court was pleased to find a case for declaring it unconstitutional on grounds that the Fourteenth amendment forbade acts of discrimination by States, but not by private parties. By this time, most hopes for a changed and cooperative South were lost.

Barely, one might accord a period of promise for African-Americans, one-third of the Southern states' people then, in the years 1865 to 1872. No sooner had the war ended, when Black freedom and national unity, the two main objectives of the war, which never were established anyhow, began to erode farther.

The new Southern State legislatures, whose historical record before the War was not at all positive or innovative, suddenly began to show the ideal possibilities of federalism, but in the wrong way.

They became exceedingly crafty in laws to resist Reconstruction and to discriminate against African-Americans. They learned how to evade federal jurisdiction and laws.

They wrote a new version of Southern honor, which boiled down to ways of making a Black "respect" a White man regardless of merit, and States Rights, which amounted to all the ways to circumvent, cheat and milk the federal government.

In 1876 a Presidential election was held. Grant had served two terms as a Republican, winning easily, yet doing nothing for the public welfare in any part of the country. He encouraged speculations, many of them practically swindles, and had nothing to offer when severe economic depression struck the country and millions of people suffered dismally and miserably. He tolerated a high incidence of graft and corruption in his entourage.

The war that his supporters claimed him to have won
was continuing under his nose without his
demonstrating frustration or regret.
He would have run for a third term,
but his following deserted him and
nominated a non-entity named Rutherford Hayes,
an Ohio politician. Against him the Democrats,
sensing the first victory since 1856,
ran Samuel Tilden of New York;
he was a millionaire, a lawyer,
and reform governor of New York State.
He had broken up the grafting Tweed Ring.

Tilden won more votes than Hayes
but, with 184 electoral votes, was
one short of the necessary majority.
Once again, the Electoral College
would threaten the federal system;
luckily neither Tilden nor Hayes
had a Jacksonian following.
In three Southern states, where fraud and
intimidation were extensive, rival boards of
canvassers appeared, giving different totals. The Republicans
conceded Florida, but not Louisiana and South Carolina, where,
also, two different governments came forward to claim legitimacy.

The Constitution owning no word on this subject, Congress set up an Electoral Commission of fifteen members, five each from House and Senate and five from the Supreme Court, for the particular purpose of reporting recommendations to Congress. The swing member became Justice Bradley, a Republican, there being only Republicans left in the Court, and he voted with the other Republicans in favor of recommending Hayes to Congress.

The House finally accepted Hayes by a narrow margin, and it developed that the margin had been provided by several Democrats, who voted for the Republican because he promised to withdraw the Federal troops that had been policing the reconstruction scene in South Carolina and Louisiana.

The Republican governments in those states soon collapsed and they became Democratic far into the future, along with the rest of the "Solid South".

The Democrats in on the deal had promised to observe the Reconstruction laws and Constitutional Amendments, but had never the slightest intention of doing so, as Congress might have realized. Other promises were exchanged no less irresponsibly.

The election proved to be a major victory for the Caucasian South against the North and African-American South. Like the other victories, this also helped to perpetuate the degradation of Southern culture and minimize its capacity for national leadership.

The Southern states now embarked upon a voyage of inventions designed to eliminate the African-American as a voter and respectable American citizen. These were accompanied by the continual violence and intimidation already described.

At first the South was led in good part by an element that came to be called "Bourbons,' for having connections with the pre-war elite, and not so opposed as the poor whites to giving Blacks some small role in civic affairs. They maintained stingy governments that gave little in public education or social services. They offered the nation an amusing panorama of romantic decadence.

They lost ground as time went on to harder and more populist elements - rabble-rousing "men of the people" like Ben Tillman, James Vardaman, and Jeff Davis. These wanted easier money, that is, inflation, laws against extortionate interest rates, laws against fencing their livestock from common lands, and laws restraining monopolies such as railroads, docks, and grain elevators. The populists sometimes tried joining with Blacks along social class and income lines, but in the end, despite a few victories, the populists went the way of anti-Black forces and abetted the degradation of the Blacks.

In 1896, the Supreme Court took up the case of *Plessy vs. Ferguson*, a Louisiana situation in which a Black refused to be evicted from a railroad car section reserved for "Whites". (He was one-eighth Black, but as everywhere in the South, any amount of proven Black ancestry placed a person in the discriminated category of Black) Now was announced the infamous "separate but equal" doctrine, holding that the states had every right to discriminate between Black and White provided only that they provided separate but equal facilities for each race.

To the complete segregation by private groups and facilities, often resulting in a total exclusion of African-Americans from services, there was added the whole range of possibilities for the states to make life worse for the Blacks. Every facility and service that the states provided became superior for Whites and degenerated for Blacks. Blacks had to ride to the rear of Whites in buses, they were seated separately practically everywhere, and barred from many recreation and other public areas. Their schools were maintained to be universally inferior.

Laws were passed making literacy a requirement for voting, or requiring a satisfactory rendering of the constitution of the state: laws that would discriminate against the poor and uneducated, but, as applied in fact, could let Whites pass through and make Negroes fail.

A shocking evasion of the Constitution occurred in the case of the "grandfather" clauses, measures that allowed to vote, in the failure of other qualifications for voting, anyone whose ancestors had voted before 1867.

The poll tax was widespread as a limitation on the vote. One could not vote if he could not tender to the registrar of elections a receipt for having paid last year's poll tax. The tax was low, but sufficient to discourage a man who had nothing.

In 1900, 181,000 Alabama Black citizens were registered to vote (already a severely reduced number); two years later the number had dropped to 3,000.

Texas passed a law excluding Negroes from voting in the Democratic Primary elections, rationalizing that the Party was a voluntary association and therefore could determine who might be allowed to belong or vote in to act in concert with the Party. But the Supreme Court could not swallow this, for the law governing the Party was a law of the State and therefore clearly prohibited.

Later on, the Democrats passed a Party resolution to exclude Negroes, but this too was regarded as an act that had come from an association, the party, that was effectively an organ of government. One way or another, however, Blacks had been almost entirely excluded from their constitutional suffrage rights all over the South by the turn of the century.

The perpetrators of these crimes, effectively the Southern political elite, were aware of the unconstitutionality of the laws they were passing, a bizarre collection, often nonsensical. They expected that sooner or later the laws would be demolished, but they would meanwhile and for some years be "victorious", and, upon the loss of one law, they might pass another, equally ridiculous on its face, equally pernicious in its effects. Like the mills of the gods, the legal mills were set to grind exceedingly slow when it came to the rights of Afro-Americans.

Meanwhile, it should be clear, African-Americans in the South (and much of this rubbed off on Northern practice) had no chance of enjoying a wide range of civil rights, of economic possibilities and rights, of educational rights, of social rights. As late as 1930, Birmingham, Alabama, passed a law forbidding a White and a Black person to play dominoes or checkers with each other.
Blacks were never called to serve on a jury.
Nor were they allowed to act as witnesses in a court proceeding.
They found it practically impossible to sue a White person.

They could not enter professional schools, because none existed in many places. They were excluded from most of the skilled trades, and in dealing with Whites, except on the most simple level of the selling of produce or purchase of supplies, while having to rely upon the Whites for the borrowing of money at usurious interest rates, the employment of Whites to draw up their documents, etc. Laws against mixed marriages of Whites and Blacks were universal. Churches were segregated. The Black paid more for whatever he bought. He had no professional medical care worth mentioning. He had to step aside to let a White person pass. And by he, I mean, of course, she, too, and the children.

Probably less than one in 100,000 (*sic*) violations of civil rights ever received the sympathetic attention of the police, politicians, press or courts. The world's foremost financier, whose advice the White House lapped up, J.P.Morgan, was so impressed by the Congo, then being exposed as a stable of horrors owned personally by the King of Belgium, that he recommended the region as *"an ideal dumping ground for the South's surplus Blacks".*

To conclude here, the African ethnics in America by the year 1905 were in most regards in a situation worse than under slavery. (Nine out of 10 Blacks lived in the South still.) They had practically no economic value in their community, where the Whites were measuring value. The Republican Party still raked in their faithful votes up North, yet gave nothing in return, since the Party had found that it could win the Presidency and Congress with the Northern White vote alone.

And, hoist by their own petard, the Southern Caucasians were practically as badly off, except that they could escape into the North and lose their cultural markings, or by competing successfully achieve the limited opportunities to succeed financially in the South. At great cost to themselves, greater even than the cost to the South of the Civil War, which latter costs historians duly and continually lamented, the South won the first fifty years' battles of the War of Reconstruction. The next fifty years saw a turning of the tide.

Black Americans were becoming more numerous in the North and West. In the 1870's 7,000 Afro-Americans moved from Kentucky and Tennessee into Kansas. In 1879, outdoing the Mormon westward trek, 60,000 in families moved from the lower Mississippi Valley to Kansas. Between 1891 and 1910, there was a major migration into the Oklahoma Territory. Blacks were settling everywhere, hoping for a majority. In 1907, Statehood was granted, and the first act of the legislature was to segregate public facilities and transportation. In the 1920's the Ku Klux Klan reactivated.

But then the Northern trek was on. Some 170,000 headed North in the first decade of the twentieth century, 454,000 in the next decade, 749,000 between 1920 and 1930, 349,000 in the depression years, and 1,599,000 in the nineteen forties. It must be appreciated that these were people with the same zero cash reserve as most millions of other immigrants from abroad. They brought no property with them. And, as with the European ethnics coming to America, they may have left behind their families and a parched or swampy patch of land which they owned.

New York, Philadelphia, Washington and other cities had a fairly complete social class pyramid of Blacks, with all the distinctions of White social class pretensions, plus a couple of distinctively Black ones, such as the fairness of skin, although even this was to be found among the Whites, with degree of blondness marking a socially desirable feature.

It was mostly from this elite that the first generations of Black scholars, university teachers and administrators, and professional men came. It was also from this group that, despite their pretensions to superiority and desire to separate themselves from the overwhelming majority of Blacks, that the first agitators and activists of the African-American counterrevolution to the White Southern assaults came.

Generally, educated African-Americans had recourse to two schools of thought on to proceed to complete emancipation and equality. One was represented by Booker T. Washington: it held that Negroes and Caucasians had to learn to work peaceably together in mutual respect, but that meanwhile much could be done while the two races remained segregated. Negroes, he felt, should not press for integration as a necessary part of advancement, nor should they demand immediate large changes, which were the views taken by W.E.B. du Bois, the most influential agitator of the times. Of course, White people liked Booker Washington; he was so sweetly reasonable. He founded Tuskegee Institute in Alabama to provide Blacks with a higher education. Later generations of Black agitators found du Bois much more to their liking.

In the first years of the century, the National Association for the Advancement of the Colored People was organized. Whites participated from the beginning. The old abolitionist group had not vanished. Much diminished and without a national audience any longer, it worked through the *Boston Transcript* journal under Edward Clement, who termed the South Carolina complete disfranchisement of African-Americans in 1895 a *"second nullification"*, William Lloyd Garrison, Jr., a merchant who called for the Blacks to rise up in combat against the savagery of the South and the racial contempt of the North, and Fanny Garrison and her husband Henry Villard who took over the *New York Evening Post* and the *Nation* magazine and converted them into weapons of liberation and equality.

In 1909, Mary White Ovington, William Walling, and Dr. Henry Moskowitz (a Jewish name, indicative of a new source of strength for reform causes in America, that would grow immensely influential in the course of the century), enlisted Villard's leadership in calling a National Negro Conference in 1909, from which grew the NAACP. After it was formed, major outrages against the Blacks were met by some kind of protest, lobbying, publicity, and meetings (wherever in the public halls, schools, and social gathering places the gatherings would be tolerated).

❖❖❖

With the coming of World War I, however, a considerable immigration of rural Blacks from the South - and poor Whites as well - occurred to fill jobs in Northern industry, not so much vacated by men joining the army as created by heavily increased orders for war materiel of all kinds. In Chicago in 1919 grave riots occurred. Blacks were moving into the worst neighborhoods, taking the worst jobs available: still this was not enough to ward off persecution and rioters. At that time not a single Black was to be found in any lowly managerial position in Chicago industry, then the world's most productive. Black workers moved into Detroit as well, where the automobile industry was booming.

Much worse was the riot of 1921 in Tulsa, Oklahoma, where merely a rumor of an attempted assault by a black of a white woman led to an attack by an armed mob of white men against the mostly black neighborhood of north Tulsa; blacks responded in less numbers and firepower. From 75 to 300 persons were estimated to have been killed, many more wounded, while the neighborhood was destroyed. The National Guard stopped the battle, but 79 years later new facts emerged, engendering suits against the government.

A second KKK Had been formed in Atlanta in 1915. It grew far beyond the old South and beyond even the border states into the Midwest and West, with the Blacks as a secondary target - being already completely suppressed - and Catholics, Jews, and foreigners as the primary targets - yet at the same time the Klan went out heavily to get at White Anglo-Celtic Protestants offending against "Bible Belt" morality. (The Bible Belt is the large portion of the States that entertains a high proportion of revivalists, evangelists, and literal Bible-readers; its area correlates well with Southern culture.)

The Klan dominated the government of Indiana until scandals of

sex and graft hit its own leaders.
Even states such as Oregon, Colorado, and Illinois were affected by the tactics of the Klan. Over two million White Protestants joined the Klan. The Bible Belt was churning out racial and religious prejudice and hostilities as fast as ever.

"The times they was a-changin'"

New personnel were being appointed to the Supreme Court. A new climate of opinion was supportive of a people's yearnings. The New Deal turned out to be a great victory for the African-American. First it had to be a great victory for the poor Southern White.
Then the Blacks could share modestly.
But, in the North, Black opportunities soared.
Jobs were made for the pick-and-shovel man and the artist. And a range of welfare and education benefits suddenly became available.

President Franklin D. Roosevelt approved a Fair Employment Practices Commission of 1941 that directed American industry in all of its ramifications to make jobs available to persons on an equal basis regardless of race and creed. It had mostly a symbolic effect for many years. Between 1933 and 1946 the number of Blacks employed by the Federal government rose from 50,000 to 200,000. But the rise appears to be less spectacular when viewed against the great increase in government employment as a whole .

The Supreme Court, frightened by Roosevelt into a liberal attitude, ordered a separate and equal law school to be constructed by a State that did not admit Black law students; it reordered trials where Negroes had been systematically denied selection as jurors; it directed the Railroad Brotherhoods to grant membership rights to Negroes or forfeit its right to be a bargaining agent for railroad employees; only in 1946 did it ban separate seating in interstate buses.

In 1948 the Court would rule that restrictive covenants of private groups that aimed at barring certain areas for housing to African-Americans were unconstitutional and unenforceable.

After a wide attack upon racism, after racial riots again occurred in Detroit and other places, and while Blacks were widely discriminated against all over the South and Southwest, and had fought and were still trained in segregated units under principally White officers, President Truman finally and under pressure ordered the Armed Forces to admit and incorporate African-Americans on a non-segregated basis. Truman's actions on behalf of racial justice were not impelled by civil courage; on the contrary; he had done almost nothing on his own initiative to boost African-Americans.

But once he was informed that enough Blacks were now voting in the key states of the Union to determine the election of 1948, in which a third "Progressive Party" candidate, Henry Wallace, a great Agriculture Secretary and formerly Vice-President under Franklin Delano Roosevelt and a proven life-long advocate of social justice, could capture some of the old New Deal Black vote and thus let Republican candidate Thomas Dewey win the election, Truman somersaulted before the African-American leadership and missed a pratfall on Election Day by a few votes.

Truman's new administration was also characterized by a political witch-hunt, led by the FBI under J. Edgar Hoover, Senator Joseph McCarthy, and the usual clutch of red-baiters. Their continual tactic was expressed well in the words of Cardinal Richelieu, chief of the government of Louis XIII of France, long before:
"If one gives me six lines written by the most honorable of men,
I will find in them something with which to hang him".

In all of the Congress there were only two radical voices regularly denouncing and voting against the long-drawn-out persecution. A great nuisance and infinite minor injustices were rendered incidentally, but at most only several true "burnings", not at all comparable to what Stalin, Mao, and other great men were simultaneously doing to their peoples.
So, the usual expression was in order,
"It could be worse. Look at what's

happening in Lower Slobbovia".
The two voices were the dashing dusky Adam Clayton Powell and Vito Marcantonio in the House of Representatives, both from New York City.

During much of this time, the Supreme Court was working against the national popular current. It found Alabama's allowance of wide powers to its voting registrars to discriminate against voters without due process of law to be unconstitutional; it ended segregation in railroad dining cars, and it ruled in 1954 in the case of *Brown vs. Board of Education* that segregation in public schools was inescapably invidious discrimination and ordered the educational systems of America in effect to integrate the races. Chief Justice Warren of the Supreme Court led some of these major advances.

Numerous cases were bring brought in lower courts, and increasingly the judicial system and the factory and the public sector gave racial equality its due. The favorable edicts issued with greater frequency. And so did pro-African-American agitators - college students Black and White, the Students Non-violent Coordinating Committee, the Committee on Racial Equality, both with short-term spectacular histories in this period, and the more enduring Southern Conference organization of Dr. Luther Martin King.

The national media were alive and friendly now. An informal system, a network of groups birthed, typically beginning with a state-federal patterning, with local oligarchic control and rising nationally to a pyramid peak of a few individuals with national media exposure.

"Sit-ins" at discriminatory restaurants and other public places proved to be highly effective, once the high risk of violence and bloodshed was assumed; in the end, few disastrous encounters occurred. The capacity to turn out great crowds on critical occasions had striking effect upon national elite groups. They, including many Southern politicians, made significant concessions; the elites of universities, industry, government, non-profit groups, religions, the military, the presidency and the legislatures –many of them caved in.

The techniques of stressed democracy - the grand demonstration, the threatened picketings, and the like - proved able to do the job, in part at least, that the traditional representative government devices had failed at doing.

When President Kennedy was assassinated in 1963, President Johnson "got religion" and pushed through the Civil Rights Act of 1964, which put government squarely on a day-to-day basis into the business of eliminating bias in many fields. The victory was theoretically won, as it had been won a hundred years earlier.

No matter how important, the Civil Rights Act of 1964 had to be succeeded by even larger and violent episodes. African-Americans were accumulating an an irresistible rage.

Malcolm X was born in Omaha, Nebraska, in 1925, changed his last name from "Little" to "X" because he wanted no white man's name but knew not his African surname. He led a most troubled life despite his splendid appearance and intelligence. With his father killed, his mother insane, he spent his youth in white foster homes and then in jails and finally a freed man of extreme though eloquent anti-white racism and attraction to Islam invited around the world, attractive to both rulers and crowds. He broke with his original sect "Nation of Islam," whose famous leader, Elijah Muhammad, converted him and founded his own sect. He proposed a separate black nation, preached anti-semitism on occasion, and advocated violence in defense of black rights. He may have increased his followers to 150,000 by the 1960's. In February 1965, at a rally, four gunmen charged upon Malcolm X and shot him dead. Likely, they were of the Nation of Islam. Many memorials celebrate Malcolm X in different locations.

Now then, in 1968, the Reverend Martin Luther King was assassinated, the killer captured, a typical befuddled poor Southern White. Victory in the Second Civil War ended like the first, in the assassination of the paramount leader

Rev. Martin Luther King, the most effective and prominent African-American civil rights leader, was assassinated in Memphis on April 4, 1968, aged 39. On June 10, James Earl Ray, a repeat criminal offender and active racist, was arrested for the crime at Heathrow Airport in London, as he attempted a flight to Rhodesia, where white racists ruled. On trial in America, he pleaded guilty and was sentenced to 99 years in prison, but then he tried to withdraw his plea, without success. He died in jail but not before attracting supporters to his having been framed. Even some of Rev. King's circle believed that only an organized conspiracy could have arranged the murder. Also they believed the FBI, President Johnson, and Vietnam "War Hawks"were behind his murder, because King had lately become increasingly persecuted as a presumed communist, for his increasingly strident calls for basic reforms in the economy and political system, and a wrecker of the US war effort in Vietnam.

But most Americans, reneging on promises and influenced by the deplorable Southern poor White culture, continued in a hundred forms to begrudge only second-class citizenship to African-Americans. The promise of integrated education was dispelled, despite the busing of millions of children tediously and expensively to various schools in search of a racial balance. Black colleges remained almost entirely black, whether public or independent. Housing segregation continued to obey the laws of sociology rather than the law of the land. In Chicago only 110 of 1,169 neighborhoods could be termed integrated, containing 20% to 50% black residents, in 1990. Five years later, only 27 of the 110 remained integrated.

Granting that the gains won by African-Americans by the year 1965 leveled the playing field for blacks and whites so far as much formal law was concerned, we would have to say that racial hostilities in thought and informal uncontrolled activity continued . One might also ask what were the gains and losses of the White Southerner by the degradation of a century of guerrilla warfare, of economic and social hostilities against the North and Blacks everywhere, and against the liberal Southerners who wanted to accommodate to the new age.

The South won in Congress more and more. Because of the one-party system, the Democrats always triumphant, over a long period of time, the important committees of Congress came to be dominated and chaired by Southerners. Since the committees ran much of the national government, the Dixiecrats had many ways of blocking the equal rights of Blacks throughout America society. At the same time, they lent to the legislative process and politics a cunning and negative conservatism.

They, too, brokers for their districts and states (more truly ringleaders of "good old boy" cliques), wormed disproportionately large sums of federal money out of the more prosperous sections of the country. But on the whole their influence was baleful. The South brought itself to a low moral, psychological and cultural level in order to suppress Blacks.

Personal accounts, biographies, autobiographies, histories local and regional, newspaper files - all sources of information describe a tragic apathy alternating with irascibility, of deterioration of the environment and widespread greed - often called the "new South" - of pandemic illnesses - rickets, pellagra, ringworm, trachoma, malaria - largely defeated elsewhere by preventive care and medicine.

When a Jewish businessman was lynched in Georgia in 1915 for allegedly raping and murdering a young factory worker, almost all of the Jews of the State moved out, in disgust and fear, a loss of the State's most progressive element, making it a little easier to understand why Georgia spent the twentieth century vying for bottom place on the social indicators that bespeak the welfare of the people of a state.

In a nation most of whose state and local governments have persisted in various stages and forms of corruption, the Southern states were notoriously worse than average. In education, the South was universally at a lower level than any of the Northern states, no matter how poor these were. By the turn of the century there were more distinguished professors at the state University of Wisconsin than in all Southern universities combined.

Northern businessmen were invited to establish factories and services by many local Southern elites. They found no law to impede them from a disgraceful exploitation of the White Southern population - men, women, and children. Wages and opportunities were less than those allotted to Northern immigrant arrivals.

By 1890, Northern political mouthpieces of business were working against efforts to reduce the oppression of African-Americans, warning that the tender shoots of commercial cooperation between North and South would wither in consequence. Call the roll of many sections of the Northern elite and very few would respond with an "aye" to commend the useful and nobly inspired work of the Freedman's Bureau. Yet it was the total elite, not the Bureau, that failed to give the freed Black his promised "forty acres and a mule".

Crimes of violence occurred in the South at higher rates than anywhere else even if crimes against and between Blacks were put aside. In the year of the infamous St.Valentine's Day Massacre so-called, when Al Capone's gang wiped out a gang of Dion O'Banion, killing 7 of them, there were in Mississippi, Alabama, and Georgia, all of them together having no more people than the world-shocking City of Chicago, ten times as many recorded murders, a larger number of poor people's and police-enforcement murders, unrecorded, and certainly as much wholesale intimidation and robbing of the poor, the Black, and the liberals, as the again infamous racketeers accomplished in the stores, construction industry, and speakeasies of Chicago.

It was the attitude that Southerners adopted toward the Civil War, their intent to carry it on by all means possible and *"Ah hates the Constitution"*.. (as a doggerel litany went), that brought out the floods of violence throughout the South and borderlands, even besides racial aggression. Thousands of Americans, White and Black, were murdered every year. The family blood feuds that had nearly disappeared before the Civil War broke out everywhere, especially violent episodes characterizing the Southern Appalachians, even at their western extremity in Texas. Texas saw every kind of violence through the hundred years, including vicious Indian war with the Comanche and Kiowas.

The same Southern culture that had moved from Arkansas and Missouri, and from East Texas into Central Texas and then over to New Mexico and Arizona, continued the history of violence. From 1886 to 1892, the Tewsbury sheep family and the Graham cattle family waged a deadly feud to the last man; only one person survived; numerous Black and Chicano cowboys also bit the dust in the fracas.

A few Blacks in this gory and gruesome panorama of the Southwest gained a measure of protection and dignity by serving under White officers in the Army cavalry. Nicknamed the "Buffalos", they fought, ironically, the other notoriously oppressed American minority, the Indians.

A hatred of sheep was manifested in the wide West, and many battles between sheep-herders and cowmen were noted. Wild West fiction amplified the incidence of conflict, and sided with the cattlemen, so that four generations of boys learned to hold shepherds in contempt and would prefer eating beef to eating lamb. The canard was circulated that sheep ate the grass down to its roots, killing it. Cattle were instinctively conservationist, it seemed.

Nobody dared admit, even if they realized it, that a major source of all of this nonsense was probably the appalling series of enclosures in Britain and even on the continent that, to make way for sheep, made homeless hundreds of thousands of peasants, ancestors and clansfolk of the cowmen, and started them on the road to America.

Vigilantism was everywhere in the South and west. Often the "better element" of a community was enlisted to keep order and run out of town the frequent disorderly and criminal visitors and new settlers. Vice and virtue lived cheek and jowl as everywhere in America, but the case of the Bald Knobber vigilantes of the Ozarks was outstanding: there gangs rose to wipe out theft, liquor, gambling and prostitution in Christian and Taney counties; the militia had finally to be called in.

Most vigilante groups were used to put down the Blacks and poor squatters, also gypsies and tramps on occasions ,others to combat vice; the White Caps were in different localities of differing habits. In Northern New Mexico the White Caps were a poor farmer and rancher movement of the native Hispanics against rich Hispanics and Anglo-celts, who wished to seize their land and water.

In the twentieth century, a hundred years would pass and the South would still try to solve its problems, as would the North to a lesser degree, in the shadow of the Civil War and racism. The cost to African-Americans of the history of slavery and the struggles aimed at excising its baneful influence has been enormous. One could offer in dollar terms a figure of five trillion dollars and justify it, by assigning a cost, in current dollars, of the deprivations suffered. These five trillions would be made up of the less than average portion given the African-Americans out of the total product of values.

By values, we mean of course, power, wealth, respect, knowledge, welfare, and affection. Of all these only affection, despite frequent splitting asunder of families and friends, could be said to have been possessed and enjoyed by the African-American with his fellow beings, as much or more than the Whites managed to bring it about among themselves.

In dollar figures, the White South in addition lost at least half as much because they crippled their own cultural, economic, and affectional development in order to preserve an evil institution legally and then illegally. But theirs was voluntary activity, the Black loss involuntary and therefore, if anyone should pay, it may be said, it should be the Whites to the Blacks, and then the Whites to themselves.

Then there is the ecology of the South, not counted in above, that was wrecked by three centuries of abuse, its forests, its bays, its river valleys, its soils, its fisheries, its animal life. What was the damage here in dollar terms - another two trillion dollars? Quite so.

Then the total damage amounts to nine trillion dollars, without
considering the North's fate. What is a trillion dollars?
It is what the whole American people earn in a year.
They would all starve to death a hundred times
trying to repay the sum.

In a later section, we shall enter farther these realms of heuristic accounting. Religious people like to say that ultimately we shall each and every one come to an accounting before our Lord. There is some point to fabricating a preliminary accounting at the end of a history of a people - to present it to the Sovereign People.

Homestead Rioters Assailing the Pinkerton Workers Guarding Carnegie Steel Works

Part Nine

NATIONAL INDUSTRIAL DEMOCRACY

Men have become tools to their own tools.
HENRY DAVID THOREAU

The War of Reconstruction contributed heavily
to making the federal government disjointed,
lurching every which way,
unable to lend guidance to the Nation.
No doubt the loss of the country's most skilled politicians,
the Southerners,
made something of a mockery of Washington, and

the Southerners who turned up upon the resumption
of Southern representation hardly improved the ambiance
of the Capital and the business transacted there.

Without more than a by-your-leave from the federal government,
American enterprise and a massive number of immigrant men and
women turned the nation into a world-leading producer of material
and goods. The population kept rolling over: immigrants and migrants
ensured a majority of new faces in most communities
of the country every several years.

This period of national democratic industrialization
can be stretched from the Civil War to the First World War arbitrarily,
or be contained in a smaller time capsule of 1870 to 1900, say,
a mere Jeffersonian political generation. We must employ the word
democracy because of the broadness of the suffrage,
the host of myths of democracy floating about,
an increasing unionization of workers,
protest movements against anti-democratic forces,
a heightening of many forms of crowd behavior,
a rugged extreme individualism, let pass in
every sphere of life as self-expression,
innumerable unrestrained efforts,
many successful, at building
business enterprises of all kinds,
spreading monopoly,
disgusting social and
welfare conditions.
What a democracy!
Yet no wise man ever said
that democracies act saintly.

Misbehave is
what the United States
did in this period,
and on a grand scale.
In a race for the worst
society in Christendom,
the USA would be right up
there with the winners.

All that can be said is that in this nation of
many million bodies there
were many beautiful souls.
We ought to name some of the good,
being careful not to distort history by
exaggerating their number.
If you could only locate more of them!
For they would be mostly out of sight, and out of mind.

As for the others, the elites, they were painfully apparent and crass.
Histories have glossed them with Hollywood myth.
And the behavior of many elements of the population was
deliberately, or, if not purposive, then cravenly,
malfunctioning.

I have explained the situation in the South,
a third of the nation, during these years.
In the following pages the North will bear the
brunt of the equation.

Much will be said here about immigrants,
the international migrants.
That they came to America
did not make them better sorts.
That they were abused also
does not make them better.
Like most of the abused of the world,
they could hardly wait to imitate their tyrants.
But, they were the muscles and guts of the
expanding industrial society - men, women, and children.

They were a godsend (the word is blasphemous) to the rascals
building the world's greatest agro-industrial monster.

Indeed, the basic reason why
huge numbers of immigrants
were let to enter the United States,

in this period as well as always before,
was that there were present,
lips drooling in anticipation of their arrival, a
numerous and varied class of exploiters, ranging from
the farmer wanting a helpless farmhand,
to the Schenectady *hausfrau* wanting a house-drudge,
to the railroader seeking gangs of powerless laborers,
to the tycoons demanding countless factory hands,
to the cities calling for street-sweepers and sewer-layers.

The process ended up by the turn of the century with the
creation of the world's most productive nation
(minding that "productive" has always wrongly meant
gross, not net, value, and that environmental destruction
was dismissed in the calculation, and
so, too, other human and material costs.)

The new beast was urban industrial America,
a nation composed mainly of city people,
ruled by fools and scoundrels.
One and all, ruler and ruled,
expected as their reward that a bucolic dream would materialize.
A large majority expected "Progress" -
palpable personal benefits in their own lifetimes and
therefore infinite improvements for the nation.

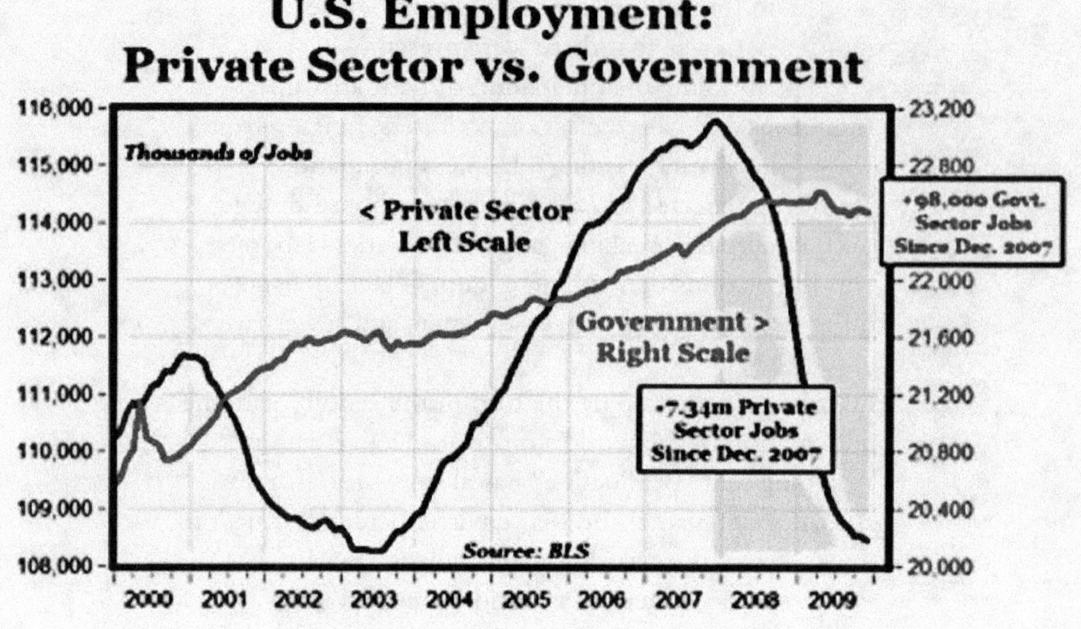

Civil Service grows relative to Private Employment

Chapter Forty-three

Entangled Federalism

The United States was more than ever a tangled invertebrate society as it moved into the latter half of the century. From the Civil War and for two political generations, the United States endured clashes of forces that were separatist and others that were unifying and centralizing. Some worked inside the formal structure of the government, others from without, and interactions between the two were many.

Some country-wide situations would be resolved by the will of several men in New York or Washington, other "national" problems could only be resolved by countless local groups in their own way.

The nation that had passed from imperial colonialism into confederation, then into federalism, then into weak federalism, then into tight unionism briefly, now moved into an entangled federalism, that would evolve into a more and more collaborative and rationalized federalism, until as the new millennium approached, the system would be on the verge of a nationalized federalism.

Between the Civil War and the end of the century, Washington was a growing city. It had grand public buildings, but was in large part also a slum where servants and underpaid employees and would-be employees lived, where saloons were frequent, prostitution was rampant, footpads commonly prowled, lobbyists were few only because government functions were few, seekers of individual favors were innumerable, and highly moral remnants of the reconstruction radicals suffered indignantly in a humid atmosphere of corruption.

Still, swamps were being drained, parks laid out, pigs and chickens were forbidden to venture upon the streets, and in the '70's the Secretary of the Navy procured a telephone into which he could shout to the Navy Yard three miles away.

Several years later plans were made to replace the gas lighting of the streets with electric lighting. Politicians' wives sought to create a social milieu capable of snobbery. Maryland and Virginia ladies were reconstructing their own society under the noses of the Radical Republicans. African-Americans supplied the logistical underpinnings, but there were always a few around with the status of confidantes and as agitators for Black causes.

The Civil War did much to centralize and nationalize the American federal system. It settled seemingly forever the issue over whether a state could constitutionally secede from the Union. More than that, the huge central army, the far-reaching national income tax, invasions of civil liberties, Presidential power extensions, Supreme Court restrictions upon State powers, wartime conscription, and other laws and practices coming out of the war gave precedent for more such laws, even if they were repealed afterwards.

Events seemed indeed to give the lie to fine political philosophy about virtues of federalism. The Federal government gave practically nothing of a positive sort to the States, save some land to be used for educational purposes, although it did end slavery in some of them. The northern and western States infrequently tried social reforms, which usually failed or were nullified by the Federal judiciary. The Southern States governments, we have witnessed *ad nauseam*, showed how viciously States rights could be used against their own people and the Union. Not until another memorial generation had passed would a few of the States, all Northern, begin to shape up a plausible political system and a functional social apparatus.

The war psychology stayed with people of the North and West; it imprinted immigrants: the myth and feeling that there was only one United Sates, indivisible, with liberty and justice for all. The civil service grew, the armed forces expanded and stayed rather large.

The habit of looking to Washington became more widespread. The Presidential office acquired new powers as commander-in-chief that it never gave up; precedents could be cited when issuing civil and military orders. The President as the sole representative of all the nation became more prominent, even though the theory that Congress represented truly the people and was responsible for legislating held on strongly for the rest of the century, after which the ideas of Theodore Roosevelt and Woodrow Wilson became popular.

Young Professor Woodrow Wilson (he was at this time) published a shrewd analysis of the functioning of the Congress, in which he showed how Congress (and therefore in major part the United States Government) was in effect an oligarchy of the Chairmen and their coteries of 47 standing committees and a few special committees created on occasion. The Speaker kept the machinery running but did not concentrate the powers of the committees any further. He was the

Party leader of the majority party of the House. He had much to do with designating the leaders of the Committees, the Chairmen, but after that they progressed more or less beyond his control. Once a Chairman took office, he would be there for a long time, usually until he left the House or died. He was coming more and more to be the most senior member of the committee, in terms of longevity in the chamber. The choice of committee posts themselves were the function of seniority.

So the thousands of bills that piled up in each session of Congress were parceled out to the committees; there certain favorite bills were dressed up properly and prepared to take a brief run of a few minutes on the floor of the "full House" in session (actually, a small fraction of the House was normally present), with no more than a few words controlled by the Committee's manager and authors of the bill - allowing a couple of opposition voices to be raised briefly, rebutted by the manager's side and then voted up or down.

If up, it had to pass through the Committee on Appropriations to determine whether the funds it called for were to be had, whereupon the bill might pass and go to the Senate, there to be voted upon, and accommodated, in a conference committee, to any discrepancies of thought between the House and Senate.

This Committee and the Ways and Means Committee were the only ones that permitted a larger participation by members of the House, especially by other committee chairmen, because to give to one might take from the other, and to raise a tax, say, might mean more money for everybody to spend.

Congressmen spent most of their time not on legislation, but upon getting favors and jobs for their constituents and supporters - two-thirds would be a close estimate of the proportion of their long workdays spent on these matters This, as well as the committee-ruler system and the relations between the two houses contradicted the expectations of the Framers of 1787. They had believed that the House would be closest to the people, not the Senate, that the House, too, would be subject to popular passions of the day, to which the Senate would counterpoise a reasoned conservative defense.

In this period, the Houses was the ruling body of the nation, the Senate still under the state legislatures for the most part, and renowned for being a body where a senator could orate at length, a privilege denied in the House; so on record are thousands of pages of guff on currency, tariffs, land policies, railroads, race differences, and the peerless virtues of the United States and its People. The most banal and trivial subjects were blown into great hot-air balloons. Bombast was ever more of a substitute for passion after Reconstruction.

The Radical Republicans lost their radicalism after two decades and turned to other less hopeless issues than the reconstruction of the South. Still, the country and the Congress as well as the Presidency remained dominated by Republicans. Only the two administrations of Grover Cleveland - with an intervening term out of office, then only Woodrow Wilson - by a fluke - for two administrations, were Democratic before 1933. Wilson was elected in 1912 as a result of a three-way race, in which Theodore Roosevelt decided to come back and try for a third term of office, rationalizing that his first term did not count, since he actually took office from the newly re-elected but assassinated McKinley. Teddy Roosevelt's Party was called the Bullmoose faction of the Republican Party. It drew enough votes from Charles Evans Hughes, the regular Republican candidate that the election went narrowly to Wilson. Hughes went to bed believing himself elected President, but the vote from California, coming in tardily, turned against him, and gave its electoral votes to Wilson.

The Presidents of the period were no better than those of the first part of the century. All except Grant and Cleveland escaped personal scandal and kept their nearest associates out of trouble. (Grant had so many scandals going on about him that one might well wonder how he could ever have controlled a huge army.) Cleveland was embarrassed by a nationwide smear campaign to defeat him because he fathered a child out of marriage - he supported mother and child. Lincoln, a special case, we have placed in the middle. Hayes we have said a word about.

Garfield came next, of long legislative experience in the Congress, an honest and thoughtful exception to the run-of-the-mill politician. He was a thoroughgoing anti-welfare specimen, however, believing, it would appear, that federal funds should go to anything but welfare. He was unfortunately assassinated and succeeded by Chester Arthur, who, like Polk, did not live up to expectations: in his case, he became honest.

Cleveland was a remarkable man who put the Democrats on the national map again. He was defeated by the vagaries of the Electoral College more than anything else, and then came back for a second try and won. Harrison was the intervenor, and there is little to be said of his tenure. In 1884, Republicans marched to the chant of *"Ma, Ma, Where's my Pa?"* in reference to the illegitimate child of Cleveland; his victorious partisans chanted

"Gone to the White House, Ha-Ha-Ha!"

Typical thoughtful campaign discussion.

McKinley liked high tariffs and led the country into an easy war, the Spanish American War, from which the country emerged with numerous problems, all of them badly handled. He was assassinated, and Theodore Roosevelt succeeded to the White House, and of him we have spoken and will say more later on.

All of the men had their very rich supporters; their ideas and outlook were most conventional, practically stupid. Mark Hanna, a rich Pennsylvania businessman and political manager, was the angel of McKinley; steel magnate Wharton Barker underwrote Harrison, Amasa Stone, industrialist, carried along James Garfield. The Presidents were one and all troglodytes on welfare matters.

When President Grant wondered incautiously whether some public works laborers' jobs ought to be created for the starving in the depression year of 1874, he was quickly subdued. Wrote future President James Garfield to a friend, *"We had somewhat of a struggle to keep him from drifting into that foolish notion ... But the Secretary of the Treasury and I united our forces in dissuading him from the scheme, insisting that the true remedy for the finances at present was economy and retrenchment, until business restored itself'.*

Political parties in these years could not do much more than stretch slogans to the point of nonsense, then crow that they appealed to everyone. They gave an indifferent and large, widespread electorate a few hints upon which to base a vote. A reading of the record of a Congressional legislative session would see no coherence, and what went for Congress went for the state legislatures and city and town councils for the most part.

Law as a general command to a large population seemed destined, in some jurisdictions some of the time, to be descending into directed messages authorizing individuals to pick up a pension, move to an office across the street, buy a wagon, build a railroad, take up a million acres of land, etc. *ad infinitum.*

Parties were independent in the smallest types of local jurisdictions - townships and towns. Loyalty was like the wind working from a personality through a windmill (then beginning to dot the larger part of the USA) onto some part of the voting public which, having sensed the breeze from a new turn of the mill would follow the wind as an authentic voice of the Democratic or Republican party.

Throughout American history, grounds for forming a party, such as the Greenback Party that split from and rejoined later on the Democratic Party, seemed to be that, if granted power, it would print more and therefore cheaper money so that debtors could evade grasping creditors or get more for their farm produce and livestock.

Greenbackers, Populists and the like could throw the nation into panic, fearing the dissolution of the bonds of society represented by the gold dollar. These were the national issues: cheap money, cheap land, big business busting, high tariffs, and, with luck, some foreign enemy to provoke excited debate. I am being generous: these composed the grist of the talk-mills; the real issues, defined as whatever activated people and politicians to behave as they did, were the aforementioned scrambling for jobs, favors, and subsidies.

Civil service reform, too, was a big issue, recognized by a few thoughtful citizens like George Curtis and Carl Schurz, who organized the National Civil Service Reform League in 1881. The issue was blown out of the cellar by Garfield's assassination and some tests of merit were prescribed for some jobs: it is remarkable how agitated the American people repeatedly became on the heels of an assassination of the President. It originates from their believing him *"washed clean in the blood of the lamb"* by popular election. It derives also from wishing, after having deprived him of many powers, he might right all evils nevertheless, from imagining him as a champion of the country against the world, and from feeling him for these reasons invincible. There has been a rush of guilt, too, because more than half the people would have been indifferent to him until the deadly moment, or scornful and opposed. It is normal public psychopathology.

The city political machines came to fruition in this period. For example, Tammany Hall, the most famous of them all, was in existence, but not in control of the Democratic Party or New York City until 1890. Boss Tweed had to treat individually - buying them, making deals - with many men in the post-Civil War period. His successor as leader of Tammany was John Kelly, during whose chiefdom factions squabbled incessantly. During the '80's half the members of the Board of Aldermen were non-Tammany Democrats.

In 1886, even the labor unions got in a crack at the mayoralty, putting up Henry George, whose famous book proposed all government finance be based upon a single tax of real property, and purporting to show that this would greatly expedite social and physical development of the society. He came in a close second to the alliance of Tammany and New York County Democrats' Alternative Tammany.

From 1890 on, Tammany monopolized the political power of New

York City (County), with exceptional victorious but short-lived intruders, until finally catastrophe struck the Hall in the person of Fiorello La Guardia.

New York's experience was common among the cities around the country, South as well as North, it should be pointed out. These cities, full-blown now, grotesquely wealthy, stinking of poverty, constituted in themselves a set of republics, indirectly federated through national and state governments. However, they had almost no relations with one another except through harboring common business, criminal, and national civic associations. They fought against the states in the name of urban rights and against the federal government in the name of local self-rule. The political parties of the nation were not able to unite either the state or local parties on matters that counted for much.

Lincoln was enabled in a single term to appoint five Supreme Court justices, a majority of the Court as it turned out, for an earlier increase to ten justices was reduced to nine before long. He appointed men who appeared to be unionist and anti-slavery, but behaved as often as not as if they did not deserve the labels. Still, like Lincoln, they were conservative in both economic and social affairs. On the whole, they did not add to Lincoln's credit as a judge of men's character and opinions.

The Court did little to help African-Americans during these years; in fact, their view of the Fourteenth Amendment was so restricted that people as individuals and groups might exercise whatever evil they fancied upon race relations and the lives of Black people. The Court assumed a role of self-restraint and often declined to interfere with the asserted rights of the legislature, the President, and the state governments.

The Court took up the interpretation of the Fourteenth Amendment, particularly the wording: *"No State shall make or enforce any law which shall abridge the privileges and immunities of citizens of the United States"*.. This was adjudged to mean that only rights which Americans possessed as national citizens would be protected, not those held as State citizens. The States could now play hob with civil and property rights, which they did for some time to come. The Court had divided 5 to 4 on this matter, and the ever stronger adherence of the Court to the doctrine of *stare decisis* meant that it would be stuck with this constitutional interpretation.

Not only did Blacks and the poor generally, that is, most of the people, suffer from this ruling, but for a time the large economic interests - railroad companies, grain storage operators –also could complain. For, under the influence of farmers and consumers generally, the states began to pass a spate of laws regulating economic activity, until one could foresee a return to the condition of interstate commerce before the Constitution, when each state managed to interfere with the commerce of every other state. Now the Court found in the Fourteenth Amendment a clause forbidding the States from depriving any person of life, liberty, and property without due process of law, and injected into the concept two features, the first that corporations should be considered as persons under the law, "persons", like you and me, and the second, that "due process of law" affected not only certain procedures like the right to obtain a lawyer and have a fair trial, but also the right to be free of onerous obligations and discrimination in connection with the ownership and management of property great and small.

The turnaround came in 1886 and for the next half century the Court served as a dike against State regulation of economic affairs, while the Court simultaneously used the Constitution to keep the federal government from involving itself in all but explicitly permitted governance of business. An extreme laissez-faire view of liberty of contract dominated the court (totally unreal when some of the unequally drawn and unfairly one-sided contracts were examined - such as between the great railroad company and the individual passenger). Thus the Court contributed, without planning to do so, to the growth of a national sentiment and centralization, by forbidding the states' entry to important socio-economic areas, while simultaneously frustrating the Federal government.

The federal government had escaped for some years

the court's clutches in regard to an income tax that it had levied during the Civil War to raise new funds. In an especially messy case, decided on a tied vote and with a switch of a justice's opinion in the middle of the proceedings, the court held in *Pollock vs. Farmer's Loan and Trust Company*, that a federal income tax could not be constitutionally levied, even if called an indirect tax, because it was really a direct tax.

A wave of opprobrium washed over the court, the heaviest since the Dred Scott case. Eighteen years passed, however, before the Sixteenth Amendment to the Constitution enabled the federal government to levy a tax directly upon incomes. The tax was then considered more useful than experience has shown it to be for equalizing the incomes of the rich and poor, whether by proportionate or progressive [exponential] rates. Power elites typically retroject new burdens upon the powerless.

The Court also knocked out the Erdman Act of 1898 that had tried to assign to the federal government the task of regulating labor relations: the Act had required employers to bargain to some extent with unions before engaging in riotous provocations and heavy police and dismissal tactics. The Court held to this ruling until 1930, for a full political generation.

In 1913 a federal law (the Mann Act) prohibited and punished the transportation of a woman across State lines for immoral purposes. It was also popularly called the "white slave" Act (as if Black and Asian women were not being transported for fun and money). The Act turned out to inconvenience a great many gentlemen who were taking their mistresses across state lines, like from Newark New Jersey, to Coney Island in New York. The Court thought this measure constitutional, but when, five years later, Congress reached into the states, saying that the products of child labor could not be shipped interstate, the court declared the act unconstitutional! Is this the place to pass judgement on the Court, with another hundred years to go? I am tempted, but... No.

In 1881, after a paranoid office-seeker killed President Garfield,
Vice-President Chester Arthur, who succeeded him,
quickly mended his evil ways as a New York spoilsman,
and signed a bill thrust upon him by an aroused public and
gung-ho Congress. It was a great step forward,
although for many years it was only partially carried to its
logical conclusion, a Civil Service system totally
recruited by considerations of merit.

Before 1883 and for some time afterward in the federal government
and for a long time in most states and localities of the country, whether
urban or rural, public administration in America was one of
the most backward in the west, back of China and Japan, ahead of
Russia only because the American civil servants were more restless
and mobile, It was a century behind the thoroughly
reformed administration of France.

The federal and the other services were expanding rapidly. The
federal service neared collapse as it extended.
It numbered 53,000 in 1871,
107,000 in 1881,
166,000 in 1891,
256,000 in 1901
(five-fold in 30 years). There were few new agencies:
Departments of Justice and Agriculture, the Civil Service Commission,
the Interstate Commerce Commission, the Bureau of Labor.
Inefficiency, politics, and rapid population growth
brought on the exponential increase in personnel.
Auditing and personnel were now services
tendered to all agencies.

Congress intervened in administration at every turn, and
controlled the President's office meticulously.
In 1871, President Grant
was permitted a private secretary, a stenographer,
a couple of executive assistants, a steward, and a messenger -
for a total allowance of $13,800.00.

The Civil Service Act and its subsequent expanded coverage by Presidential Order reduced the patronage available to national, state and local politicians around the country. This was universally lauded and still is, but one of the unforeseen results was that fewer Americans gained first-hand experience of public office, and another was that the politicians made up the deficiency of sources of financing by becoming more dependent upon business and special interests. (Practically in all jurisdictions, kickbacks of part of a new appointee's or contractor's receipts from the government went to the sponsoring politician.)

Special interest politics, which came to characterize politics in the twentieth century, was given a push in these years, the golden age of the uncontrolled lobbyists. With more civil servants, lobbyists turned their attention to influencing the executive branch more systematically.

A Civil Service Commission, to be appointed by the President, was created to form and administer the system, and to set up a classification of federal jobs, some of which were promptly placed under civil service rules. Examinations or other proof of merit had to be supplied before appointment to the federal service.
Once a person was hired for a position in the classified system, he would have permanent tenure.
He could not be forced into helping a political cause.

Presidents gained in power over time by the Act, because they could demand the undivided loyalty of the large body of permanent civil servants. Despite the fact that all the Presidents expanded the number of classified jobs (except McKinley), the number of exempt or patronage positions only increased. Whereas in 1884 federal patronage positions numbered 118,000, in 1901 they amounted to about 150,000. The service as a whole was growing, and the merit system was falling behind, but only relatively.

A considerable debate ensued over where to draw the line between the administrator and the policy-maker, who presumably should be fully responsive to the President's will. Over a century later, the debate would not be ended. The Cabinet members who were Department heads argued usually that their assistants, bureau chiefs, division chiefs and chief clerks should be exempt from the permanent Civil Service.

The Civil Service Commission believed (1890-1) there to be *"very few of the many offices in the gift of the Government which are really political in character, after we pass below the highest, such as the members of the Cabinet and the ministers to foreign countries".*

What seemed to be a technical determination has turned out to be resolvable only by a full theory of society and politics, setting forth what jobs require popularism, broadness of experience and education, and wide connections with non-governmental elites.

The Western States and territories were large factors in the centralizing of American federalism. They owed to Washington their existence. While still territories, their governors were appointed by the President with Senate approval; they and their gang of appointees looked naturally to Washington for opportunities and favors.

The largest concerns of the West for a long time to come would be Indian relations, national transportation networks, mining, and land distribution. (Most of the land remained in Federal hands even after many million acres were sold or bargained away.) Westerners were acculturated and trained in the West. Out of sheer laziness, if for no other reason, they tried to bring in the things that they knew, the law codes, the political routines. (The belief that, when politicians know nothing of the past or have no past they will innovate, is as mistaken as its contrary.)

They were content to be as uniform in their government, and social practices as were the geometric lines of their boundaries, external and intra-state. They lacked traditions and history, except Indian and Hispanic ones, which they tried to reject as substantially as possible.

The telegraph and the railroad permitted them now to be in close touch with Washington, too.

There were other institutions creating their own federalisms
in these years. State and Federal constitutions helped,
in that they granted the needed liberty of association and press.
They, the governments, also had very little on their minds.
So there was a lot of room to occupy.
More detail will be supplied upon them later, but here it is
well to remark that distinct trends toward nationalizing associations
and activities through national organizations became apparent and
strong. Practically every considerable occupation and activity -
medical, business, academic, athletic, hotel,
educational, press, and so on -
began to sprout federal organisms.
These would continue to grow exponentially as the society
became specialized in its every manifestation.
More and more their attention turned
to what was being done or might be done
through federal government activity.

We speak of what can be called "functional federalism, "
primarily of the corporations that stretched their tentacles
far and wide and of investment bankers whose
interests in many large ventures ramified,
and of voluntary non-profit organizations -
farmers' groups such as the Grange,
religious associations such as the YMCA,
labor unions such as the Industrial Workers of the World
(the IWW, also known as the "Wobblies".),
and the Knights of Labor, together with a variety
of fraternal and religious groups, whose communications were
intensified along with the expansion of railroad and telegraph, so
that even if their intent were to decentralize,
they would end up by centralizing.

The National Association of Manufacturers was now formed to agitate, propagandize and lobby for measures deemed to aid the largest firms of the country, descending into the smaller ones; it was oligarchic, with but a few leaders.

Even lawyers were part of the centralizing picture, although they were dependent usually upon local opportunities, and had a special interest in local and state legislation. They were tied into the development of constitutional and national law, and even from the beginning they tried to practice law in the state from which they came, and before that and afterwards they tried to use precedents from various jurisdictions to win local cases.

Since their most powerful clients were involved in inter-state problems, lawyers, too, had to become nationalized in their thought and in their expectations of uniform standards around the country. The larger the industrial concentration the more influence directly on Washington was needed, until many a Congressman and high official had specific business backers for whom it was understood that they would work while in Congress and office.

As for the state legislators and city and county officials, they went directly to work for business interests. Only a minority, enlarging or shrinking with the degree of popular indignation, were free of corporate control and the local elite generally. All other interests that they may have had - religious, conservation, welfare - had to realize that they must take back seats.

In the severe depression of the nineties, 40% of all American railroads went into forced or voluntary bankruptcy and had their affairs straightened out by a group of profiteers led by the bankers; it was an improvement on the old system. (They pared the bonded debt and converted it to stock shares.) J. P. Morgan sometimes played a positive role in stabilizing agglomerations of business, in the process gouging enormous profits, taking control of them, and creating monopolies damaging to the interests of smaller concerns and the public.

A great Centennial Exhibition opened in Philadelphia in 1876 of a century of progress and industry since the Declaration of Independence. In the two decades thereafter there were more strikes and more people killed or injured in labor disputes than in any other country in the world, even after taking into account that the USA had a larger population than most.

There was a paralyzing railroad strike in 1877, only nine years after the first transcontinental junction. Chicago had the Haymarket Riot, a police-killing bomb incident.

The Civil War ended with hundreds of thousands of veterans of the Grand Army of the Republic, all of whom, from unscathed drummer boy to severely disabled riflemen to widows and orphan, learned soon enough to feel that they had a claim upon the government which the Radical Republicans in the Congress were willing enough to support, especially since these would form a voting body in their favor and there was precious little else to spend money on in a nation without a large conception of welfare and with high tariffs that brought in large sums to the treasury.

The pensions went on and on, shaping a privileged aggregate among the Northern poor and middle classes, such that still in 1910 one-quarter of all men over 65 were pensioned veterans and hundreds of thousands of widows and orphans were drawing stipends. Not since the Roman Republic pensioned its veterans and sent them off to the far corners of the empire to take over seized lands and celebrate the Senate and later the Emperor, were veterans so incorporated into the political patronage system. Naturally all of their eyes were turned to Washington over the whole period of time, from the first enlistment onwards.

An unanticipated effect, possibly so uncomfortable that it has gone unrecognized, was that welfare to veterans arbitrated against welfare for others. Several psychic mechanisms were at work:

First, sheer greed made many holders of pension rights wish to keep these to themselves.

Second, pensions were rationalized as something owed them by the grateful nation for saving the Union.

Third, other people who needed help were deemed less worthy and should be kept in that position - other old people, aliens, immigrants, sick, disabled, unemployed, and so forth. A division was impressed between those who had immigrated to the US before 1845 and those who had come in later, marking more sharply ethnic, economic, respect, and power distinctions between the two categories. It was a way of being a Know-Nothing, wrapped in the flag.

Fourth, potential reform groups and crusading editors, appalled by the epidemic corruption in most other government activities, resisted starting up new activities in the welfare field, even were the Supreme Court to allow such, believing that these, too, would shortly succumb to corrupt influences. The veteran crowd did not press the point.

Civil service reformers were dismayed at the heavy preference given to veterans under the classified "merit" system, a feature that was continued to the Twenty-first century for all wars. In the Treasury Department, over 50% of all appointments between 1887-1882 were veterans, their widows, or orphans. In the Department of the Interior, one-third were, in the War Department from 1865-1882, 60% were.

Southerners might well feel resentful, because confederate veterans were barred from preference even after receiving amnesty for having worn the grey uniform. Moreover, Southerners had withdrawn from Washington during the war. So it took some time before the South could return in force. Meanwhile the North and West largely filled the ranks of the civil service, both before and after the Pendleton Civil Service Act of 1883.

When they did return, under the protecting wings of their

Congressional representatives, they reversed the flow and were over-represented proportionate to the Southern population by the time of World War I. The more depressed the South, the more the desperation there to get a job in the federal service.

The Civil War veteran and the huge aggregate of people subtending from him became a nationalistic preternaturally proud possessor of a role as well as an income that would be periodically reaffirmed by Congress, and publicized upon every Fourth of July celebration. Until the last veterans of the Civil War expired, they were trundled out and mounted upon the speakers' stands on every patriotic occasion.

It was to their interest, too, to carry on the traditions of the Civil War, so that it became an ever grander feature of the American popular and historian's memory, to which the South responded with intensified, if less compensated, recollecting in their own right. In consequence, there occurred a media bloat.

Welfare principles were scarcely tolerated anywhere. National, state, local governments - all were largely unfriendly to the needy of all kinds. No attention was given to the first paragraph (preamble it came to be called) to the Constitution which spoke of providing for the general welfare, and when a surplus would threaten the federal treasury, Congress tried to think of how to give it away otherwise, ending up with the idea of giving it to the states, or, more usually, of fashioning ever-larger pork-barrels. The surplus of 1836-7, the $37 millions surplus accumulated, was handed over to the 26 States, which usually spent the funds upon schools or general expenses and debts.

Appropriation measures were handled like Christmas gift lists, but were much lengthier. Tariff schedules had little underlying rationale; once a tariff in principle overall was accepted, which the Republicans always did, the Democrats much less, then every Congressman tried to get his own friends' business into the schedule to be subsidized by a customs duty on his foreign competitors' incoming products.

There was little of the humane in dealing with humans in their generality. Militarism came to mind immediately as the preferred method of handling labor disputes. *"A crack on the head"*, not a benefit, was the due of a complaining worker.

All over the country there was a sameness of government, which helped Americans feel comfortable as a single nation. People expected little and asked little of their governments. Administration was incompetent generally, so that what was legislated upon was rarely what was acted upon to ensure conformity.
But power was widely distributed, too, more than anywhere in the world except among "primitive" tribes. Russia, a second giant empire of the times, possessed a highly centralized czarist regime stretching over two continents, and its people were in worse shape than the Americans - with neither bread nor liberty, and corruption everywhere. Given that the number of positions in Russia subject to corrupt potential, was much smaller than in the United States, the volume of corruption in America was much greater and of course decentralized.

According to Charles Francis Adams, writing in 1876, *"All political systems, no doubt, have some tendency, greater or less, towards corruption. The peculiarity of ours is that it moves, and for fifty years has moved, in that direction with accelerating pace"*... He placed the blame, in true Federalist tradition, upon political parties.

The election system of the United States, now taken over by political parties as agents of and pressures upon the local, state and national governments, had been from the beginning usually tainted by corruption and manipulation; it may have reached its acme of corruption now. The ballot had come to replace the *viva voce* voting of pre-Civil War days, but since the ballots were privately printed by candidates and sponsors, they lent themselves to more devious corruption.

From two to thirty dollars a vote would be paid in numerous elections, depending upon the closeness of the contest and the availability of slush funds from contract peddling, favors granted, appointments obtained, and honors dispensed. Often employers drove their workers to the polls in company carriages, and then watched them as they held high the properly identifiable ballot and dropped it into the ballot box.

A great reform came with the importation from Australia of the officially printed ballot obtainable only at the time of voting, marked in secret, and therefore held aside for only a few minutes before being cast. Massachusetts initiated this reform in 1888, and within four years most States had adopted the method. Given the widespread will to cheat, the perquisites of the successful cheat, and the problems of corruption in the election process still to be solved, the reform, one may guess, carried American elections only a fourth of the way to pure elections by the beginning of World War I.

The role of business in corruption, first fouling its own nest and then spreading all over the government could not be denied. E.L.Godkin, editor of *The Nation*, wrote of the *"...immorality which pervades the commercial world, and taints nearly every branch of business,...moral anarchy..."*. The scientist, Simon Newcomb, granted not only the wide extent of corruption in politics, but decried also *"the decay in the public sense of delicacy and propriety"*.

When Benjamin Bristow was appointed Secretary of the Treasury in 1874 he was told by a private party that a large network of tax evaders was operating with the connivance of internal revenue collectors. He infiltrated secret agents and soon had evidence enabling him to seize sixteen of the largest distilleries and sixteen rectifying houses in a single day's raids, then more, implicating collectors in numerous great cities - St. Louis, Chicago, Milwaukee, Boston, and Galveston. Some 230 persons were indicted (although only 20 were convicted).

No one could be trusted in the Department, it appeared, and the trail of the Whiskey Ring led directly to the indictment of President Grant's assistant, General Babcock. This was too much for Grant, who, as soon as Babcock could be acquitted (with the help of Grant), forced Bristow's resignation, along with that of most of the honest men in the Department, who had worked with Bristow.

Congressman Hoar, who became for many years an enlightened voice in House and Senate, wrote in 1876 feelingly of the situation he found himself in: *"My own public life has been a very brief and insignificant one, extending little beyond the duration of a single term of senatorial office. But in that brief period I have seen five judges of a high court of the United States driven from office by threat of impeachment for corruption or maladministration. I have heard the taunt from friendliest lips, that when the United States presented herself in the East (at the Philadelphia Exposition) to take part with the civilized world in generous competition in the arts of life, the only product of her institutions in which she surpassed all others beyond question was her corruption... When the greatest railroad of the world, binding together the continent and uniting the two great seas which wash our shores, was finished, I have seen our national triumph and exultation turned to bitterness and shame by the unanimous reports of three committees of Congress - two of the House and one here - that every step of that mighty enterprise had been taken in fraud.... [the Credit Mobilier scandal]"* His other examples were also impressive: the court system of New York State and the government of New York City; the sale of nominations of cadets to West Point by four Congressmen.

Throughout the period was developing a class that had best be called liberals for that is what they were and would always be - developed out of old Yankee Eastern strata. They were nationalist, middle class, Republican, intellectuals, perfunctory Protestants (stamped unconsciously with the ideology), soon to be joined by large new immigrant elements and grass-roots self-selectees from here there and everywhere, having in spirit moved from anti-slavery into government reform, especially *vis a vis* corruption, and strong for the civil service merit system everywhere.

Partly because of the Civil Service act and partly because of the liberal thrust that could sometimes penetrate the system of sloth and corruption, the federal government experienced an influx of pioneers deeply involved in some subject matter.

For instance, the first steps toward the rescue and conservation of the environment –land, waters, forests - were taken in the 1870's. In 1864 George Marsh published an account of how human occupancy ravaged nature; he appealed to America's romantic nature myth and its engineering myth to combine in a restoration of a civilized natural world; he could be called America's first ecologist.

In 1889 John Wesley Powell envisioned a great network of water power works to generate electricity, just then coming into use; he also proposed that local democratic communities should properly own and develop irrigation farming in the West (the old Hispanic system). Prussian-born-and-trained Bernhard Fernow worked his way into the direction of the Forestry Service and devoted himself to raising the level of professionalism in the care of natural resources.

Sociologist Lester Ward, termed by some admirers the American Aristotle, called in 1893 for human reconstruction of nature by a corps of trained experts on the environment. Gifford Pinchot, most famous of the group here, largely because of his association with Theodore Roosevelt, stressed, in a puzzling fashion, conservation for development, which could materialize in terms warming the cockles of a timber-cutter's heart.

Scot-born John Muir was more concerned about enjoying nature as she lay, and had to fight for many years to preserve most of Yosemite Park, founding the Sierra Club on the way.

For environmentalism, the impetus for reform and honest administration was almost entirely federal; state governments and territorial governments were the stooges and dupes of western economic, banking, railroad and mining company interests. When the nation's liberals practically induced public panic over fear of loss of its domain, President Theodore Roosevelt called all the governors to Washington in 1908 to lecture them on their moral responsibility; his effect was not electric, unless he shocked some of them to go back and get their piece of the pie before conservation became serious. Conservation became part of the liberal creed forever after, expanding into general environmentalism only in the latter half of the twentieth century.

All the above, and much more,
brought on the shift from weak
federalism to the tangled, invertebrate,
but stronger federalism of the
late nineteenth and early twentieth century.
Small town and country images
still gassed the minds of Americans on all levels of society.
They lived in one world and imagined another: pastoral
(peaceful, sometimes, but usually the rugged cowboy world)
and agricultural, for the most part, destructive of realistic attentive and
calm consideration of the present and future of the nation.

Aborning was a new centralized, bureaucratic, managerial, technocratic, urban nation, but the attending doctors thought that they were helping to give birth to another bucolic type of world, nor could they be persuaded otherwise even after the baby was born.

Popular culture and some
of the sophisticated dwelled upon the myths
of the explorers and cowboys of the Wild West,
the rural heroes of the wars,
the virtues of the small town and the lost warmth
of relations between master and slave.
Not that exceptions were lacking:
Hamlin Garland and others were beginning to write
realistically about country life,
which was still nasty, brutish and
short for most country folk;
Horatio Alger was beginning to sell his
millions of novels about poor boys
making good in the business
world: at least he wrote of cities.

Along with the centralized federalism

was coming a new kind of
nationalism -
some of it progressive
and some of it racism among
elements of the would-be United States elite
that foresaw themselves
part of an Anglo-Saxon master race,
after the contemporary English
fad, connecting this with Darwin's theory
and that of Herbert Spencer
even more, the survival of the fittest.)

Perhaps it was a sign of the centralizing of great wealth and the backlash by older wealth, that much publicity attended a book that clustered the social elite into Four Hundred, shaping into a pyramid the countless small and jealous local elites seeking to add respect to their modest wealth and uncertain ancestry. Progressive nationalism had its own problems, veering crazily toward imperialism and performing other feats, more often bad than good.

But there are later chapters allocated to these developments.

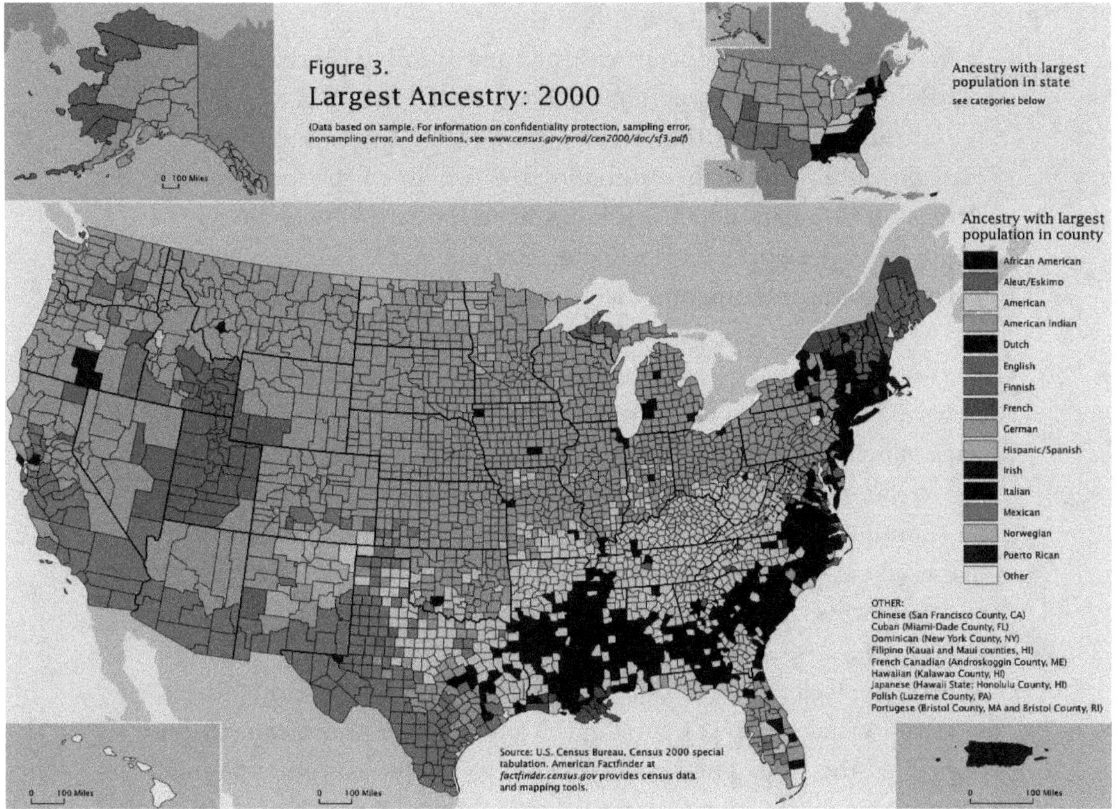

US Ancestry Map as of 2000

Chapter Forty-four

Immigration

Americans are ethnically (that is, in culture and race) the most heterogeneous of all nations. To find an unrepresented nationality may be impossible. Gypsies are well represented, coming from many countries, from Asia Minor to Ireland ("The Irish Travellers"). Icelanders are present. Australian aborigines are rare.

Inasmuch as all Americans except a few unmixed Indians have descended from immigrants arriving after 1500, and we have already guessed at the origins of the Indians, we might well introduce this chapter by estimating the origins of the total present American population. This task has been rendered easier by census inquiries of the population to determine ancestry. The results show what had been happening demographically and culturally in the course of four hundred years.

We would not wish to set forth all the problems of defining race; still, race is one factor in nationality and human relations, so that some guessing as to the ethno-racial components might be illuminating, after which we can examine the more pertinent national components. To speak of race we could begin to think in terms of about three thousand years of migrations.

Before the Celts arrived in now-called France and the British Isles, an ethno-racial group resembling the ancient Mediterranean peoples populated the land. Their ancestors are still there in some unknown minor part. The Celtic is a vague yet stubbornly meaningful label, more a cultural and linguistic grouping than a physical one. They were the earliest Central Europeans and spread from there.

Then these were overlain by new racial-cultural strata, Romanic and Teutonic. In the grand confusion that characterized the settlement of North America, it was probably the Celtic or partially Celtic that was the largest fraction.

Among the Celts of America one would include the French-Canadians (who came mostly from Bretagne, Brittany, origin of Britain), and some of the French otherwise from all over France, the Welsh, the Scottish, both lowland and highland, and the Irish, whether Catholic or Protestant. A considerable part of the immigration arriving from English ports originated years earlier, if not just before, in Scottish and Irish Celtic lands and was lumped with the English. Too, in America, it appears that the Celts had higher rates of birth than the English or Germans, and that this difference persisted down to the present time. Moreover, when the

U.S. Bureau of the Census began two decades ago to ask Americans to give the nationality of their ancestors, a third of the Southern respondents claimed only American, and this meaningless answer was not probed. In the South, it may be assumed, the longer familial residence in America caused a forgetting of ancestry, but to this true amnesia must be added an evasive amnesia, such as the common truculent assumption of being the "true" Americans, and of being less literate and worldly, these perhaps being more common among the Celt-derived constituents than from the others. Hence, assigning a figure of about 25% of the total population as Celts, or in part of Celtic derivation, as I do here, is probably an underestimate.

We should recall once more that the French component in America originates along at least five lines: Acadians of early Eastern Canada dispersed by the English for security reasons and replaced by English, Scots and Scots-Irish; the French of Louisiana and the Midwest before and after the Revolution, the Huguenots largely settled along the seaboard to begin with; individuals and groups of refugees from the French Revolution, and secular workers or utopians bent upon establishing a community according to the doctrines of Fourier or other theorists; and finally the French-Canadians, mostly of Northern New England, Rhode Island, Upper Michigan, and their scattered descendants.

Peoples largely or partly of Mediterranean stock include Jews, Greeks, Spanish and Hispanics, Lebanese, Armenians, Italians, many French, and Portuguese; their presence would probably be manifested in 20% of the population.

The very large Teutonic element would be divided by some physical anthropologists into the Alpine sub-race and Nordic sub-race, intermingling. The Alpines would carry through from Russia through Southern Germany and Switzerland into England in some large fraction, broad in stature, light brunette in coloring and eyes, brachycephalic or round-headed. They might be estimated at 10%. Nordics, the taller, less robust, more blue-eyed, would come from the Baltic, Scandinavia, Northern Germany, Northern Poland, the

Netherlands, and to a fraction of the English, coming out of Saxony and Normandy. There might be 15% of these in the American population. Germanics proper, that is, by language and culture, are to be grouped differently.

Less would be the varied African component, about 13%, described in an earlier chapter. When the large Hispanic factor is assessed for its Indian part, along with the Indians, usually mixed themselves, about 10% of the population may be distinguished as in some sense Indian. The Slavic element is scarcely distinguishable physically from the Alpine Caucasians, but originating in East-Central Europe, somewhat darker of eye and complexion, with perhaps 5% of the American people.

Tiny fractions are important, among them 1% from China, Japan and East Asia, half a percent from South Asia, especially from India, and 1% from the Malayan - Vietnam and the Philippines. But 1% of the American population amounts to nearly 2,600,000, enough, if it is well-positioned and has a special fit, to be needed in a meaningful description of the characteristics of the whole.
A more usual and useful way of dividing up the people is by their historical connections. Here, it must always be borne in mind that American history proceeded apace with other highly active histories. The USA witnessed the merging of Scots, Welsh and Irish into Great Britain, at the same time as the same people came to America during the rise and decline of the British Empire, and then by the end of the twentieth century the emergence of the same people into ethnic and political autonomy.

Not one German nationality arrived here, but a score of Germanic nationalities; only after 1870 could they be arbitrarily considered as of German nationality, serving one Kaiser. Italy was in the same situation, a geographical expression and a state of mind. In the broader sense of what happened later, we can speak of Germanic and Italic origins.

Helpfully, distinctions upon entry were made between the ethnic groups of the Austro-Hungarian Empire, such as Bohemians, Slovaks, Hungarians, and Germanophone Austrians. But there has been much slipping and sliding in labeling and recalling.

Now we find the principal elements to be as follows, in millions, rounded out to the nearest hundred thousand: Germanic 57.9; Austrian 0.9; Swiss (mostly Germanophone) 1.0; English 32.7; Scots-Irish 5.6; Scots 5.4; Welsh 2.0; Irish 38.7 (divided into about 2/3 Irish Catholic, 1/3 Scots -Irish; the question was not properly put because of official squeamishness about asking people their religion); Africans 23.8 plus 2.0 Afro-Caribbeans; Italic with 14.6; French 10.3 plus 0.7 Acadians and French Canadian 2.1; Swedes 4.7; Norwegians 3.9; Mexicans 11.6; Puerto Ricans 6.0; Poles about 6 (another 3 million Poles of origin being more usefully distinguished as Jewish); and 2.9 Russians (almost entirely Jews emigrating from Russia);

important numbers of under 2 millions are recorded for Croatian, Czech, Slovak, Finns, Greeks, Hungarians, Lithuanians, Portuguese, Ukrainians, Yugoslavs, Cubans, Haitians, Salvadoreans, Koreans, and Vietnamese. These figures changed slightly between 1990, when they were gathered, and the year 1995, principally in the larger proportions of East Asian, Caribbean and Mexican immigration, as well as with fairly large contingents of Jews from the disassembled Soviet Union.

The great ages of immigration may not be over, for in 1994 the Census estimated the foreign-born population at 22.6 millions, or 8.7% of the total, nearly half of all who had ever come to America. About 25% of California's people had immigrated from foreign countries, some 16% of New York State residents.

With all of this heterogeneity of ancestry, under the compression of the majoritarian egalitarian ideology, the whole gathered itself into a culture unmistakably American, speaking an American English.
Foreign languages and dialects have died out, except for a persistent but never threatening use of other languages in enclaves, particularly Spanish (17.3 millions), French (1.7), Chinese (1.2), Tagalog (0.8), and other oriental tongues. German (1.5) and Italian (1.3) are spoken almost entirely among present-day immigrants.

Attempts at forcing the learning and use of English often

caused ethnic conflicts. A more clever policy for promoting
the prompt use of the English language among all Americans
would be to officially and generally call it the American language.
Immigrants might resent learning English,
but never having to learn American.
Even dialect speakers would move toward the norm of an
American language, who otherwise resist the teaching of English.

Language generates largely from lower classes and demi-mondaine.
By persisting in their own language forms,
these groups render themselves incommunicado
to the elite and authorities,
provide themselves with a common bond.
They obtain a secret, often erotic pleasure,
Their peculiar language is a cheap weapon
against the respectable classes, achieving revenge,
and in the end actually creating the vernacular,
the reputable tongue of the future -
as the demotic against the sacred Egyptian,
modern versus ancient Greek,
Italian, French, Spanish in place of Latin,
Saxon transfusing French,
American superimposing and intruding upon English.
Centuries of suppression have not quite destroyed
Gaelic and Welsh.

Given the profuse sweep of American popular culture
around the world, America's global presence,
power and wealth, its head start with Anglophones elsewhere,
its word-proliferating technology,
the rapidly evoluting American language
would spread perhaps twice as fast, were it not for
the bedraggled esteem of its elite worldwide.

The major component of culture is language,
followed closely in historical times by religion,
which has in America also been partially disassembled.
(*"I am a sect of one"*, said Celtic Jefferson.)

The movement in and out of cults has been rapid, continuous and large. It has been too hectic for language to keep up. Quakers of today have lost both their original English and Welsh dialects and their ethnic identity, without having increased numerically relative to the total population. More will be said later about this phenomenon of the dissociation of culture, language and religion. It may be an unnerving thought to a people continually harping upon their identity, but in America generally a person's history does not emerge from what one seems to be or claims to be.

The settlement of America was a triumph of propaganda. From the first settlements to the present day, almost all immigrants who were not forced to come had heard or read deliberate propaganda designed to persuade one to go to America. Word of mouth was a most important confirmatory persuasion. American children have long been taught that their ancestors had heard that "the streets were paved with gold", and forthwith schemed to come over. This is not so. Most Americans were brought to emigrate by a compelling desperation. They did not usually suffer grand illusions.

Military conscription, the draft, probably sent over a million immigrants to America in the nineteenth and twentieth centuries. (The introduction of conscription into the North German Confederation of 1866 by Prussia sent a wave of immigrants to America.)

They had many qualms. Many were just free enough and autonomous enough in the old culture to be able to consider a choice and make it in favor of trying out America. Concomitantly, a myth of total resolve is circulated; the fact is that a great many immigrants traveled back and forth until they got stuck one day, by marriage, financially, by illness, etc., and many got their taste of America and found it too bitter to tolerate, so returned home. We are speaking of many millions of persons, not of odd cases. The typical European village not only had its relatives in America, but also its "Americans", persons who had been there and returned.

A summary of their motives would have to include more than one and sometimes many reasons to explain each case. The vast majority from beginning to end were:

1.
Materially very poor, and increasingly at the mercy of a cold industrial civilization.
2.
Foresaw few chances for education and advancement at home.
3.
Unskilled or semi-skilled, except for a highly important very few.
4.
Without a wife or husband, or immediate prospects of one.
5.
Aware of any work being promptly available at their level of skill and /or with better pay.
6.
Between 15 and 40 years of age.
7.
Intending to return if things turned out badly or very well.
8.
Traveling to America by the cheapest route and means possible.
9.
Hostile, if male, to local officials at home, and often nursing a grudge against the old form of government.
10.
Wanting, if male, to loosen his dependence upon his church, if not upon his religion or religious institutions in general.
11.
Healthier than the average of one's locality.
12.
More frequently in trouble with family, church, state, police, creditors, and/or personal enemies than the average person left behind.
13.
Persuaded that Americans generally welcomed one (if not one's personal credentials).
14.
Of an open (slack, some might say) and receptive character, and docile (humble), realizing that a person would receive shocks and rebuffs in the new life.
15.
Coming with or informally connected to groups as close to one's kind as possible until arrived and then choosing the best possibility available even if (and often especially if) it prolonged his identity as a

"foreigner", in a mixed or native work and settlement group.

16.

Homesick and missing the home culture sorely, despised as it might be.

17.

Beginning to live more and more in the present, and forgetting much of one's own culture, more so if and when one heard that one's closest of kin at home had died.

18.

After a short while, surprised at how many "real Americans" were as poor as oneself and just as ignorant and unskilled, and often more so.

19.

At some point feeling, if male, that they must marry and have children who would be "real Americans" and that this had to be done by marrying a woman as close to one culturally as possible, even though this meant a retreat from Americanization.

To tell how all the immigrants arrived is to relate a multiplicity of means. None of them are new to these pages - I have mentioned them all before - I mention them here again to generalize about four hundred years. They came as fishermen, traders, adventurers, vagabonds, indentured servants, slaves, kidnaped, captives (Acadians *et al*), convicts, expelled, exiles deported, land-bound buccaneers, jumped ship, military troop deserters, dischargees. They might come under arrangements with individual contractors, as pay-as-you-go refugees, as missionaries, and even now, as clergy. They might be contracted to be free servants, employees, and officials of companies. They could be ex-consular employees of any country, or entrepreneurs.

They might set out as families seeking economic betterment, or under the leadership of a minister. Clan groups were made up, where the primitive clan persisted, otherwise village groups, partying groups of young men, of Irish maidens, of sectarian groups, utopian community groups, groups of hunters, gold-digging partnerships, trapping and fishing groups, parties of the demi-mondaine evading close scrutiny while passing as theatrical and musical ensembles.

Shipping agents sent consignments of workers, one such in 1864, dispatched to Northern employers, containing British *"iron puddlers and their helpers, roughers, rollers, finishers, and blast-furnacemen; engineers, comprising iron turners, fitters, planers, brass turners and brass finishers... flax-dressers, woolen-cloth weavers, carders, scourers, dyers, bleachers, colour-makers, calico-printers, calenderers, shepherds, farmers, and domestic servants".*

They came by boat and after the 1960's by air. At the docks were relatives, employers, agents, contractors, friends, landladies, cheaters, racketeers, ethnic exploiters of international scope or of ethnic areas, of language dialects, of all kinds of pretensions. All were practically uncontrolled in scenes of chaos, with a few local police, then federal immigration police after millions of horses had escaped the immigration barns. It made hardly any difference that convicts, prostitutes, diseased persons, mental defectives and some other categories were barred by successive Congressional laws beginning in the seventies; they had already come in or still came in by various means and furthermore they changed upon arrival or others took their place from among the mass of arrivals or they were there from among the native population anyhow.

In deference to ideals but perhaps as much to employers and housewives, Presidents vetoed bills by Congress to admit only literates (a fine and difficult distinction to ask of barely literate inspectors of immigration, and one could not face the embarrassment of immigrants who were too conspicuously superior to the American population itself, especially the largely illiterate South that protested indignantly against foreigners on principle) but finally illiterates were barred so that 2% of the flow was turned back for this and all other reasons at the ever more grandiose halls of reception, such as Ellis Island, with its insulting and largely incorrect inscription by a poet, Emma Lazarus, greeting immigrants from everywhere.

(First and second class immigrant passengers did not have to stop at

Ellis Island, but were inspected on board ship and passed on through the penurious steerage majorities. It was well worth a costlier ticket, if you could find the money, to avoid the bossy immigrant officers at the main halls. Implicitly, the message on the Statue of Liberty did not apply.)

Indeed, so considerably unfriendly were many Americans who had landed before to those incoming later, and from the beginning of time in the New World, and regardless of race, religion or condition of servitude, that we have to wonder why immigrants were so liberally allowed in the first place. And the answer to this question is less than flattering to the image the nation purveyed of itself and that its people prided themselves in. It stresses the absurdity of the inscription on the Statue of Liberty .

The practical absence of government was a principal permissive cause for the vast immigration to America. Realistically nobody was in charge. When feelings against immigrants became too high, mobs or the local police would keep boats carrying immigrants from landing, and they would have to sail up and down to find a place to anchor or dock. Or to get to Canada or Mexico where they could be landed and proceed on foot to cross the frontiers. This of course still goes on today, to the tune of half a million or more illegal immigrants per year.

Apart from the immigrants themselves, and those who brought them in for pay or with some special social or economic motive, hardly anyone else cared who came in so long as they did not get in one's way and could be exploited to one's selfish ends individually.

Expectedly, one discovers noble passages in American political and poetic literature extending a welcome to many kinds of people (usually with a few that the particular politician or poet disliked). This genre of expression does not wish to believe that people would have come or be coming to America just to be irresponsible or put more meat and whiskey on the table.

It is felt, too, by such sweet-thinking people that it is best if schoolchildren be taught that the ancestors of some of them, at least, came to set up a new society out of the noblest of religious and political motives - and all had better harken to those who have taken command of these ancestors and who speak in their name.

More to be respected are the considerable numbers of Americans who, having once established a decent way of life for themselves, were generous enough to let others come who thought they might be able to do the same for themselves. Sympathy and generosity for the less lucky and privileged, then, will persist as reasons why immigrants were let to come in.

Once landed, many an immigrant has pondered who in the Old Country could he possibly persuade or pay to come over to help him endure his loneliness and miseries. So, in millions of cases, the reason for immigrating was to join somebody already here - clan folk, cousins, siblings, husbands, pals, home-town, acquaintances, *paesani.* This is an exponential phenomenon, please note: once the bush is planted, it sprouts leaves ever more voluminously. In a decade, a fecund seed can bring in thousands of its kind, almost the whole of a clan or village or sect in many cases.

Employing classes, including housewives, could always get cheaper help by hiring immigrants off the boat, up to the present time and beginning right away. The western movements could thus be tolerated. Otherwise such restrictions would have made sense much of the time: to keep the fully adapted working class in place; to ensure Indian rights; to develop natural resources less wastefully; to educate and train fully the working classes; to develop exporting, capital-earning industries more rapidly; and to be more selective about immigrant applications.

The native population scattered to the winds and immigrants came in to take their places. Aside from considerations of character, religion, and cultural unfamiliarity, the immigrants coming in from nearly every country were better workers and cost less than the native equivalents. One to three decades in America usually reduced the docility, assiduity, morale, and permanence of workers.

Language compatibility excepted, the continental immigrants in most cases carried a richer bundle of cultural traditions and art forms with them. This was especially true of the Mediterranean peoples and the Jews, no matter from where they came. It may have been true also of the Irish and German Catholics, who did not have to try to wipe out or caricature a thousand years of religious history as did the Protestants.

In the final analysis, however, the main reason why the flow of immigrants to America was not cut off upon the birth of the nation was that the immigrants were infinitely exploitable by employers. To all the normal disabilities of the working class in all occupations on the land, on the sea, in the cities, when treating with the boss over conditions of work, skills offered, wages, hours, promises of promotion, etc., are added the special traits of the immigrants, nearly absolute financial, linguistic, cultural, legal and support-group fraternal helplessness.

Few employers in their right minds and a fixation upon the bottom line have ever in American history from 1600 onwards complained about the number of immigrants landing in their neighborhood.

One must greatly revise views about the usually scorned, depreciated and lampooned Irish maid who, beginning in the 30's somehow worked her way into American civilization, usually without a man. She was the key factor in assembling a populous and durable Catholic Church in America, bringing over or enticing her family and the men, marrying and bearing children, supporting the priests in a kind of professional social service worker group, assimilating to the ways of her "betters" from the superior learning standpoint of the household, and pitching in pennies that ended in towering stone churches with their ornate symbolism and colored giant pictures storying the gospels and the saints. Orders of nuns came from the first and fulfilled "total care" facilities - a pretentious concept that we seek to establish today but which came from the first as the holistic belief system of the Church - meaning that no problem was irrelevant and untreatable (even if unwisely).

Between 1821 and 1850 about a million Irish emigrated to America; between 1851 and 1901, another three million came. The Irish home population diminished from starvation, plague and emigration from nine millions to three millions. Still its people remained practically the poorest in Europe. The oppressive English government was so ideologically committed to free enterprise, free trade, and self-help that it stood by and let Ireland shrivel. A small Anglo-Irish landholding class ruled the society.

The temper of the times was such that a million Irish could cross the channel to live and work in England without raising insurrections and even without bringing the English citizenry into a responsible realization of their situation. Ireland was not the only victim of Victorian imperialism, then at its height; India, Pakistan, China, Africa were being economically exploited and humiliated at the same time.

Catholic Irishmen were a great set of troublemakers, to listen to their priests; they drank excessively, shirked work, fought continuously among themselves and with others, whether the occasion be politics, jobs, or simple rancor. The phenomenon faded over time; it is not strange; driven from their homeland after long defeat and oppression, held in contempt by the English and their Protestant cohorts, failing where their women had a certain success - a success that was itself despised because it served the descendants of the oppressors - they frequently exhibited this syndrome of bellicosity, alcoholism, machoism, inferiority-feelings, hopelessness, and low working morale - a syndrome which was so frequently discoverable among Black males of the American Northern cities a hundred years later.

The Irish Catholic experience of adjustment to America was the most painful of all European groups. The Chicago Evening Post in 1868, a bio-generation after the first famine flood of immigrants, editorialized, "Scratch a convict or a pauper, and the chances are that you tickle the skin of an Irish Catholic". In 1901 the Irish, meaning Catholic Irish, had the highest ratio of inmates of any ethnic group in the penal and charitable institutions of the country, this despite the hard labor of the priesthood and the women to keep the men in order. They sometimes held well over half the jail cells and half of the insane asylums. They were as often the victims of rioting as the provokers, but the latter increased over time. Indeed in the cities of the century from 1840 to 1940, the Irish Catholic Celts acted a disorderly role that the Irish Protestant Celts acted in rural America and on the frontier for two centuries.

I have spoken enough of Scots-Irish (the unsuccessfully implanted Celtic residents of North Ireland, commemorated there even in recent decades by the most heart-wringing forms of terrorism) emigrating to America, and may be spared further detail here save to comment that they continued to come along with their hostile Celtic cousins continuously, for never were conditions settled there, there never occurred a long period of prosperity, never a rootedness beyond challenge. As domestic workers, Irish women dropped out over time to be replaced by Swiss, Scandinavians, Bohemians and few others, until there ventured North the African-American woman and the Caribbean woman in the twentieth century to replace them.

Immigrants poured in as docile rate-busters. They were ideal therefore for householders and employers, who felt only rarely any responsibility for conditions of work, old age poverty, health, future earnings, education, etc. Some critics talked about the ignorance of the immigrants, but in fact they were no more ignorant on the whole than the indigenous Caucasian population.

When the time came to talk of educating the young, the taxpayers did not have to worry about the cost of educating the adult immigrants (many millions of people for whom schools did not have to be built). Even so, the U.S. record did not compare favorably with the progress in building European school systems that was going on in the same period. Nor of course were the Blacks educated at all until late. So an enormous educational reverse subsidy was given to the U.S. in the form of non-education of immigrants and Blacks, even while newspaper editors, politicians, and even and especially educators were boasting of the American public school system. When it did get established, it suffered by comparison with its European counterparts.

The English who came early to America were more distinguishable among themselves by cult, dialect, and location in the Old Country than those who came in the nineteenth and twentieth centuries. The reasons are clear. England was not the same country. In the interim, England had grown to be a world power, it had become heavily industrialized, it had lost most of its rural population, its religions had been watered down, its occupations had become more specialized, it had generated a great labor movement of socialist inclination.

German immigrants of the later nineteenth century, were, like the English, far removed from the types who came to America in earlier times. The new immigration Germans were inclined to be industrialized, militarily disciplined, nationalistic, unreligious, socialist, labor unionists, and citified - much different from the "old immigration" Germanics.

However, they, like the late English, were pleased to be identified with mythical ancestral American types, instead of the massive new immigration coming from Eastern and Southern Europe, revealing their true colors, of course, when it came to rivalries across the sea between the German and British Empires.

Still, although the industrial English centers were a home for the Celts from all over the islands and for the ruralites, the Scots were still coming as Scots (and as lowlanders and highlanders: a rich lady of Skye in 1884 sent three hundred poor crofters to join settlements in North Carolina still tinged as Scottish after a century and a half in America), the Irish as Catholic Irish, Ulsterites as Scots-Irish (or Catholics). The Cornishmen came as such, devilishly clever tunnelers after three thousand years of practice. The Welsh arrived as Welshmen speaking Gaelic until well toward the end of the nineteenth century, their musical voices resounding through the deepening galleries of West Virginia and Pennsylvania as they probed for coal.

Britain's wealth had become even more unequally distributed since the

American Revolution; the United States following the Civil War was slightly less unequal and in line with Western European wealth distribution generally. Britain had seen a remarkable development of a sizeable uniform urban middle class claiming respectability, and a laboring class that, too, laid claim to self-respect and manners. It had gotten used to the awkward giant of a nation across the Atlantic. It had also developed, along with other European nations, coal-powered ships that churned back and forth regularly, carrying thousands of passengers.

Its emigrants to America reflected all of these conditions. And they were by no means few in number. In the nineteen hundreds several millions entered the United States, half of them to stay, even when they thought they might not, until it was too late. They were a different breed from the earlier ones, modern rather than medieval folk. Those who bought a steerage return ticket and took a season off to make and save some money in America, or those who stayed longer but did the journey often, were called "sparrows". In a few cases they were men who had criminal records or had made enemies of their employers or of their fellow workers and took the American way out. A federal act of 1882 excluded immigrants likely to become public charges, so a group of unemployed men and women who were shipped over by the Duke of Buckingham were deported. In this one decade alone, 1881-1890, 645,000 arrivals from England,
13,000 from Wales,
150,000 from Scotland,
and 656,000 from Northern and Southern Ireland were recorded.

Most immigrants were men under contract or of trades, where the ever more rapid communications of the times let it be known that a surplus of jobs was occurring in the States. Englishmen who were skilled in the silk-making processes preceded the factories, when English employers, bankrupting from English free trade laws, moved to the States with its tariff walls.

Often the "sparrows" were known to particular employers. Earning more and saving a half-dollar a day would help a man bring home a bit for his old age and presents for his children. Surprisingly when times were good in England, workers would all the more emigrate to America to get the higher wages there. And when times were bad, they heard about hard times in America and stayed home. Thus the growth of a world that operated in parallel also operated to hold people in place when they might better have been moving.

Speaking English and mostly literate, they could angle for the better jobs in competition with other foreigners. They had their troubles; sometimes their class consciousness as workers put them into the unionizing movements; more often they could be on the employers' side as strike-breakers. They were prone to compare America unfavorably with England in every respect except wages; they felt that their working-class solidarity gave them more liberty of conduct and speech in England than in America.

They found themselves often unsteady socially;
especially did they conflict with the Irish Catholics,
who were anti-English to begin with.
But then it was a kind of war of all against all among the ethnic groups. The Welsh and the Scots, and so, too, the Cornishmen all had their quarrels with the English, and with the Germans, Irish, Scots-Irish, and various continental nationalities now making their way into American society in large numbers.
Even in the past social generation,
from 1960 to 1990,
half a million British
(including, that is, Scots, Welsh, and Ulstermen)
emigrated to America.

The floods of emigrants of the times ran not only upon the USA. Large numbers of British were emigrating to Australia, Canada and South and East Africa. The Americas were the focus of most nations. Italians, while seeming to prefer the United States, emigrated in great numbers to Argentina, Uruguay, Chile and elsewhere in the Americas.

The Age of the Steamboat made it all more possible. Ships became larger and safer; methods of despatching, loading, packaging and handling personnel on boats improved, and costs per ton-mile were greatly reduced. Never before or since has crossing the Atlantic been so cheap and easy. Too, profitable to the ship companies. Steerage class passengers engendered more net income than did First Class on the *Titanic* - admitted, the accounts were not kept for long.

Between 1850 and 1914 (when World War I began), some forty million emigrants left Europe out of a population totaling 400 millions on average. Thus one out of ten Europeans moved abroad, and probably about one-fourth of the labor force, considering that most of the emigrants were adult males. That the European population continued to grow is merely another indication of the superfluity of males when it comes to birthing. What America was experiencing was only what all the European world was experiencing, and this may have had something to do with the lack of mass panic at the influx of newcomers.

Between 1846 and 1932 12.5 million British and Scots emigrated from the Isles at the peak of imperial glory. At the same time, about five million Germans left the towering continental power and its unsurpassed scientific and educational systems. Some 5.5 million Irishmen left home. Eleven million Italians departed from the elegant and famous peninsula and islands. The Austro-Hungarian Empire was at the height of its power and glory (until 1918), but 5.2 millions left, mostly for America, comprising Austrians, Hungarians, Bohemians, Slovaks, and other peoples. From Sweden exited 1.2 millions; times had been terribly hard there over many years. The Norwegians practically emptied their country, giving off 850,000 of their people. Canadians emigrated to the States at a rate of ten per cent per annum.

The happiest country in the world (tremendous migrations were going on in South and East Asia) would seem to have been France: only 519,000 French left, mostly to go to African colonies and various spots that favored them.

The ratio of immigrants to population coming in over the years was actually fairly steady in America. The immigration rate (in relation to total population excluding Indians but including Africans) had always been high. In gross numbers, beginning with the decade of the 1840's, the number neared and passed 2 millions. It exceeded five in the 1880's, reached almost nine in the 1900 decade, and topped ten in the 1980's.

For a hundred and fifty years at least, the percentage of foreign-born to be found in the United States ranged between eleven and fifteen per cent, less than one in seven. However, the foreign-born workers constituted on the average from about 15 to 23 per cent of the total labor force. That is, for probably all of United States history, the ratio of foreign workers to all workers was better than one in five. The difference was owed to the fact that a majority of foreign immigrants were adult workers and more of them worked than did native Americans.

Here was an enormous capital contribution of the Old World to the New. In 1871, David A. Wells, who founded the U.S. Bureau of Statistics, estimated that the 350,000 immigrants coming in a year had a value in labor of $300 millions. (At the same time, a billion acres of arable land was still unoccupied.) Human beings, male for the most part, brought in a value not only far in excess of all money being invested in the United States, but also a value per capita much larger than the average native American worker was contributing.

An estimate of material value added to the nation by the immigrant generation in American history can be conceived. Add up estimates of the Gross Domestic Product over the full history of the country, and multiply the total by 10%, that is one/tenth, which represents the ratio of foreigners to the United States population over the whole period. The resulting total should exceed one thousand billion dollars. A better mode of calculating will be revealed later.

For the whole history of America from the beginning, Europe, Asia, the Americas, and Africa have then contributed in the nature of three to four thousand billion current dollars in real human effort. If Benjamin Franklin had been alive and hired as bargaining representative for this great aggregate, he would have been demanding something like these sums, plus retirement pay in lieu of interest, plus inheritance of the property produced in the appropriate shares, plus, you may be sure, a generous commission for himself for results achieved. Great nations don't come cheap.

To conclude the fantasy, practically all of the American population of today would be on a regular stipend representing one's inheritance from his immigrant forbears, as well as whatever might have been saved up by his largely improvident Indian ancestors. In this event, the nation would be over half-way to solving its largest welfare entitlement and distribution problems. An intelligent reform movement of the future might well develop the fantasy to good end.

Fourth largest element of the American population today and more or less so for the duration of the States' history, was the African. Just as Whites of inexperience and prejudice complain that they cannot tell one Chinese from another or one Black from another, there is a world of ignorance of other features of African Americans. They came from a hundred different subcultures and several giant cultures. They varied physically in color, stature, hairiness, eye shape, etc., as much as the Caucasian Europeans, but were rapidly miscegenated once in America and forced to blend and forget their cultures. They lost their groupness, and therefore today have to be sorted out individually if one is looking for a typical Bantu or Guinean or another type.

The belief that somehow they arrived at the same early time is also incorrect. Africans arrived continually from 1619 to 1865, and then afterwards from the Caribbean islands in large numbers. Just in the past generation nearly a million new Black residents have come to America, from the Dominican Republic, Haiti, Jamaica, the United States Virgin Islands (which of course are American citizens anyhow), some from Puerto Rico and from Cuba or Panama, then many from the Cape Verde Islands and even from other places, so that the African immigration has truly continued throughout the century and a half since the Civil War. The languages of the African-Americans were basic and numerous to begin with, and then transformed into the British, Spanish and French varieties found until this day.

Nor ought we forget the pure Hawaiians, of whom there are only a few thousands left after rapid and continuous inter-racial miscegenation, and who are typically as dark-skinned as the typical pure sub-Saharan African, but are classified as Polynesian in race. The haoles (*cf.* Creoles) or continental Americans who settled in Hawaii mixed frequently with the Hawaiians, whom they at the same time ambivalently rejected and grew closer to, so that they (and the Hawaiians) were both unfriendly to African-Americans, resisting any stress upon resemblances, whether physical, social, or historical.

Fifth most numerous of American elements is the mixed racial and linguistic stock based upon Spanish and Indian. Here the main element is the Mexican, several millions by origin and increasing rapidly. Usually the Caribbean population is regarded as either Spanish or mixed Spanish-African, but the Indian element in the Puerto Rican and other Caribbean peoples is not to be overlooked. Although the Hispanic populations represent the oldest European stock on United States territory, the large numbers to be found on the continental mass today are the results of recent immigration, proceeding still at a rate of perhaps a million or more a year. The increase in Hispanic-Americans in the single decade 1980-1990 exceeded the total population of Sweden today.

Puerto Ricans have for a century come and gone as they pleased, and it is a commentary on mainland American culture that most Puerto Ricans preferred to stay on the Island rather than move North to the land of higher wages and seemingly richer material consumption. Mexicans began to return to the lands they had formerly settled in large numbers in the middle of the twentieth century, as migrant workers, as small farmers, as factory workers, as poly-occupational citizens in the second and third generation especially in places such as San Antonio, Texas.

Largest of all immigrant stocks is Teutonic, Germanophone, Germanic. More Americans have enjoyed and suffered Germanic ancestry than any other kind. Their national origins are manifold:

Palatinians, Hessians, Bavarians, Prussians, Saxons, Swabians, Pomeranians, Austrians, and Alsatians, et al. Some 350,000 emigrants left Alsace following the German seizure of the French-governed but generally Germanophone borderland in the Franco-Prussian War of 1870. Perhaps two-thirds of these refugees entered the United States and were classified as German, although they were obviously not happy with the new fatherland. Austrians were and remained a nation apart, older as such than Germany.

These variegated origins may help explain why the Germanic elements in America did not unite into a single great German voice or culture, and why Germanic identifications did not cause much trouble in the two great wars in which Germany was the enemy of the United States.

But there was also the large fact, true of all immigration to America, that the coming was basically an individual or small-group perception, even when forcibly caused as in slavery or convict-shipments. Ethnicity in its nationalistic aspect was mortally wounded on arrival. In a score of ways - cordially, spitefully, suspiciously, arrogantly, amusedly, worriedly - the newcomers were asked

"How long is it going to take you to become a real American?"

And the answer in word and deed, also multiform, was usually

"Just as soon as I can".

There were occasional worries. Benjamin Franklin, an old liberal, worked well with the groups of incoming Germans, as he did with everyone, yet was afflicted with concern, and even asked for laws to prevent the crystallization of Germanophone centers in the country. He felt that his English heritage was the superior and ought to be the standard for newcomers.

Precisely this sentiment demonstrates the point, that when an ethnic group came in a large concerted body and settled in a single area, its ethnocentrism would be fortified. On a large scale it could become a problem. Except for the French of New Orleans, and the Hispanics of the Southwest, the Pennsylvania "Dutch" did become the largest most long-lasting ethnic body with linguistic homogeneity in the United States. New Mexico's Constitution, when the Territory achieved Statehood in 1912, guaranteed the legitimacy of the Spanish language. By contrast, Nebraska, during World War I, sought to annul the teaching of German, but happily it was rebuffed by the Supreme Court.

Language is all-pervasive of life, not a collection of words. The American central dialect or standard American has much of the German in it, despite its freedom of expression. Phrases, word frequencies, syntax and breath control, along with gestures, eye movements, and facial twitches have to be researched to complete an inventory of linguistic influences. The phrase "*hochzeit* " means literally "high time" in German, while the nuances are the same in both German and English. It is a big feast, a sacral affair like a marriage, a ripe time to get something done - this last being the familiar usage in American.

From time to time afterwards state and local movements sought to discourage the use of languages other than English. They gave unnecessary trouble. American English or the American language developed a capability for absorbing foreign terms and coining new terms (with the participation of the immigrants) that did not insult, degrade or force the disuse of foreign tongues. The lowliest person might feel that one was helping to shape the language. There was to be no "Queen's English", such as the British never spoke.

Aside from the contribution of many words to the American language, what was the effect of the huge Germanic immigration and settlement upon American civilization? One might argue that the effort to assimilate to American civilization, to recover from culture shock, to gather in the new experiences, was so great that the Germanics could not begin to contribute in due proportion to American institutions, habits of thought, sophisticated or popular culture. Partly true, this is also true of the settlers from everywhere - Sussex and Essex included.

The larger truth is that the Germanics needed only to modify tangentially American institutions in order to feel at home with them. When the time came to revolt against them, they were in the lead, as in the socialist movements in the nineteenth century. Moreover, their influence in American education, philosophy, science, and culture, both popular and sophisticated, was great, and continuous for two centuries until now.

The Germanic effects were not as flamboyant as the English and Irish, because they largely did not compete in the political circuses, they were not so restless, they stayed longer with their farms and did a better job of maintaining the country: one almost dare say that by comparison with general farming practices among Anglo-Celts of the country, the Germanic farmers kept America's farmlands viable for over a century; they then were joined by other immigrant types who were diligent cultivators.

The Germanics moved into the heart of the new industrial world with less commotion than other immigrant or native groups of the same times. They filled music halls as performers and audiences; they peopled laboratories of the new science and the new universities; they moved from labor into clerical jobs and management. Not so colorful, troublesome, or reckless as the Celtics, or the Italians, Jews, Greeks, ~~Welsh~~ and a dozen other types for that matter, they were the prime movers of the country, and a balance against any number of disasters coming from other sources.

Then two distinct arguments are to be added: they were often discriminated against, especially during two world wars, at which time their very presence and achievements were put down and concealed. (Frederick Stock, to whom Chicago owed its first symphony orchestra, and its conductor for many years, resigned under pressure during the first World War; he came back later.) Second, there has always been a large German culture in America (just as there has been an Italian opera distinct from the large opera houses and a Yiddish theater ignored until recently for its achievements). A bibliography of the Pennsylvania Dutch and other Germanic cultural influences contains over 9000 items.

The contributions of Germanism to functionalism and pragmatism is large (the German in a favorite stereotype being the character whose greatest joy is to exult, "I know how to solve your problem!"). The transmission of the great German scholars, poets, and philosophers occurred in part directly, but more through their actual vibrancy within Germanic America, unknown to the Anglophone media and population. Kant, Goethe, Schiller, Hegel, Marx and many another world figure were part of Germanic America before spreading to other parts of America, not excepting the top-ranking intellectual centers.

It was not possible for the largest minority of the heterogeneous population, and the best educated upon arrival and thereafter, to have submerged its leadership, culture, and language to a preponderantly British-affected American culture without a rankling effect.
Yet this tension has usually not been obvious.
Perhaps it has not been obvious because it has been suppressed and not studied.

Often, the Germanic, like the Italic, or the Hispanic, or the Hungarian, or for that matter one of the several British types, has had to descend into cultural proletarianism before coming to the surface in the new American culture, but, too, all too frequently, this cultural ascent never happened and we had a less cultivated type coming from the transformation of Dr. Jeckyll into Mr. Hyde.

This difficult problem of socio-psychological adaptation was not unknown to English immigrants until today, who were continually asking themselves,
"How much must I give up to be an American; how consciously and deliberately should I be trying to make America itself distinct? Or should I be asking myself, how little need I give up of my English heritage and behavior and speech to be an American?"

In this brief book, neither the Germanic nor the English question can be answered. What has happened in recent years is that many an American, no matter how far removed her or his foreign roots, has been impelled into self-consciousness by the ever-variegating demography of the country and by the proliferation in the elites of professional, academic, industrial, political, and other circles of representatives, of groupings that had been temporarily unqualified, submerged, and disregarded.

Culture shock, or something akin to that, will occur to a third generation American, grandchild of the immigrant, a Greek-American, say, who from a lower-class environment suddenly discovers not only a sophisticated Greek-American set, but also finds this group to be closely associated with the general American network at a high level.

Even more common has been the awakening of Irish Catholics, whose Catholicism had been of the blue-collar or police milieu, to the existence of a fully Americanized cosmopolitan Catholicism with, for them, a startling new philosophical, historical perspective, a veritable new culture.

One may take another example from Swedish experience. The original Swedes of Delaware are practically lost to sight. The million Swedes who came to America beginning in the middle of the nineteenth century headed West by Northwest. One small group led by a minister ended up at Bishop Hill (actually originally Biskopskulla), in Western Illinois, in 1846, and sent encouraging messages back to would-be emigrants, who then came in larger numbers. Erik Jansson, the founder and leader, was killed several years later by an irate parishioner.

The colony endured, with a population of over a thousand and now of over a hundred thousand, but with a newly revived sense of the Swedish heritage, reported to consist of about 65% of the population roundabout in some part at least. It has joined the national pastime of roots-recovery: remodeling, refurnishing, refurbishing, emulating material culture and cuisine of ages gone by, a purposive and meaningful antique collecting, but effectively more - as an attempt to broaden American culture, to equalize in a sense the weights given to the past from different sources.

The chintzy and the cutesy are there, to be sure, but the citizenry of little Bishop Hill can also point North to larger Scandinavian-American achievements, creation in part of the great University of Minnesota, for example, but, too, in part, of the whole Northwest.

As for where the Swedish leaves off and the rest begins, or vice versa, it is well to remember that people are very much alike wherever they come from, and most of what they do in the course of their lives is alike to begin with. A little push here, a shove there, a slight innovation here, another there, a new manner, a new word, a blending is on its way, until the naked eye cannot detect ethnicity by attitude and behavior.

The earliest Jews of America were refugees from Iberian persecution, and became individual and small-group traders with families and with extensive international and interstate contacts. The German Jews who formed part of the German early nineteenth century migrations made the first large impression upon the country. The German-Jewish association remained fairly close - despite many disgraceful anti-semitic episodes in Germanic history and despite the arrival of over a million Russian-Polish Jews of markedly different ways - until Hitler ruthlessly cut the connection when he came to power in 1933. Jews were prominent in the Germanic community of Cincinnati, as I've said, producing clothing and shoes, by advanced forms of manufacturing and distribution, in meat-packing, and in trading generally.

In fact, associated with every immigrant ethnic group from Europe and the Near East except the Italian, Irish and Scots have been Jews, separated from their co-travelers by two thousand years of uneasy relations, punctuated by massacre and discrimination. By this very fact, they could adapt to a new culture more quickly, casting off old associations in favor of the new. Jews differed from one country to another, but shared long memories, and a religion that Christians, born from it, refused to let wither on the vine of the Enlightenment and modernity.

As is said on occasion, "Had the Jews never existed, they would have had to be invented". (And they were often just that, invented. Interestingly - and disgustingly - the Japanese who lacked totally any direct experience with Jews, have a considerable anti-semitic and anti-anti-semitic literature, as if they could not bear to witness the European world alone treasuring such nonsense.)

The most deeply prejudiced Americans, settled or incoming, were Central and Eastern Europeans, including Germans. Often, however, revivalist sects thought to add an anti-semitic verse to their clamor for a new heaven on earth. Often, too, as the Jews descended en masse from Baltic Sea ships, in the last third of the century and the first decades of the twentieth century, anti-semitic cries would be taken up, some of them, *incredibile dictu*, from the mouths of well-fixed Jews of the old immigration, even in editorials of the *New York Times*, owned and edited by a Jewish family from Cincinnati named Ochs, which became after a while probably the world's greatest newspaper, certainly the fattest.

The stupid and incorrect inscription on the Statue of Liberty was written by Emma Lazarus, herself part of a rich family of establishment Jews, who must have viewed her co-religionists and the others of Ellis Island with disgust, their resembling the look of prisoners of war and refugees, after the trauma of departure, steerage, and processing like animals upon arrival.

Snobs discovered that, by making a distinction between Sephardic Jews (those hailing ultimately from the Iberian Peninsula) and Ashkenazi Jews (those descending from Russia), they could admit the former to polite society and the Germanicized Ashkenazi as well. With all immigrant groups, *ex illo tempore,* as I frequently suggest, from the original time, there was a component that no one would wish to be identified with.

The Eastern Jews had some of the habits of their neighbors, the Russian and Polish serfs - "Quiet, Cattle!" cried the great Polish pianist Paderewski one time, addressing an unruly crowd of Poles gathered to demand independence from Russia, and peace reigned –liberated now in law but still..., and some of the habits that come from treating with serfs for centuries, uncouthness, roughness, untidiness, grasping for a deal, wariness of being the target of cheating and beatings - by all classes of the population.

If Jews had been content to pass a generation or so in America sticking pigs or cleaning streets, their passage into American Nirvana would have been less noticeable, but their unquenchable thirst for learning and clever enterprise led to their appearance on many a scene without having transposed the proper decorum - as portrayed in the wonderful (to viewers not up-tight) Marx Brothers cinema phenomenon. (The Marx family came from Alsace.)

Objections were raised and are raised by eminent authorities and by Jews themselves, because these were on each and every side of every question, that Jews were a religious group, while others said that they were of many nations and should be treated as ethnics of that nation, and still others, that they should be regarded indifferently, *"just like other Americans"*. Of all American ethnic groups, the Jews were the most varied, carrying, as they did, genetic and cultural elements from every land. Despite all such arguments, contemplation of the comings and goings of Jews in history leads one to term them a nation everywhere else, and only in America, and not without some hesitation, in terming them an ethnic grouping along with all the others, characterized by various distinctions and separateness, and probably destined to remain more distinct and ethnic for a longer period of time than most other groups except for the Chinese and African, but for different reasons.

Earlier Jewish strata added up to 250,000 at Civil War's end. They seemed to be overwhelmed by the Polish-Russian Jewish immigration after 1870 and continuing until the present time. The new immigrants startled the old, first by appearing in such seemingly catastrophic numbers as to threaten the social peace, then by assimilating so rapidly, that they became more "American" than the older group. They were, however, troublesome and troublemaking from various points of view, addicted to over-performance and success, and to new ideas that were super-American and supra-American.

Already in 1908, though 2% of the population, Jews figured as 13% of the law students, 18% of pharmacy, and 6% of dental students. Discrimination in medical schools was heavy but finally gave way after fifty years to admit the flood.

Jewish Americans produced in two memorial generations (130 years to 2000) more than any other American component - relative to numbers, probably 15 times more than the English, Celtic, Italic and Germanic, the largest four from Europe - in the fields of poetry, literature, the performing arts, the fine arts, social and natural science, medicine, law, financial and business practices, banking, philanthropy, social reform, the mass media, including publishing, music (except for African-Americans), and education.

This did not end the Jewish effect, which had probably not yet climaxed as the twentieth century ended. The most educated and culturally productive immigration in history came with the Jews who managed to escape the Nazi mass murderers in the years between 1935 and 1945.They came from Germany, Austria, Hungary, indeed from all Europe. Together with those who got out of the Stalinist communist countries after 1945, they numbered over a quarter of a million persons.

Largely owing to its Jewish elements and influences, America was transformed on its more sophisticated levels into the leading cosmopolitan culture by the end of the twentieth century, a culture all of whose leading parts were integrated - science, arts, literature, learning, social attitudes, global interests, and even religion - which at the same time was more nationally centered in scope and derivation than the so-called nationalism of the end of the nineteenth century.

Rather like East European Jews in some respects - Mediterranean traditions and traits, volatility and emotionality, more brunette than the Northern Europeans, cold minds beneath, frequent slight stature, close familial ties, and unfamiliarity with the booming industrial world - Italians came with twice the numbers, but about a decade later on the average. They were largely of agricultural occupations, unlike Jews, who pursued mercantile and crafts occupations. The Slavs and Hungarians, with whom Jews were associated when immigrating and in language, were generally of agricultural background and used to dealing with Jewish merchants and craftsmen.

The Italians came as Catholics or anti-Catholics, less devoted than the German Catholics, Irish, Bohemians, Slovaks, Croats, and Poles as such, and often distrusted by some of these because they were backsliders, and yet suspected of being favored by the Italian papacy. They were almost entirely from the Southern provinces of Italy, once world-class in culture and life-style, but now beset by poverty and social strife - Campania (Neapolitans), Calabria, Abruzzi, Puglia, with numbers from here and there in the North, but especially from Sicily.

Some brought guitars, mandolins, violins, cornets, piccolos, and accordions. They came mostly with hands inured to picks and shovels. They came from sulphur mining, from fishing, from arid-land agriculture and horticulture. They had all the trades of the traditional village, little sophistication of the modern mine and factory (although it was the bitter miners' strikes and the insurrectionary and anarchic troubles of Sicily that sent hundreds of thousands of Sicilians to America late in the nineteenth century).

They brought on the one hand their *campanilismo*, a dedication to only what was within hearing of the village churchbell. They brought on the other hand up-to-date ideologies of anarchism and socialism, and the perspectives of the Italian-led universal Catholic Church. From their ancient Mediterranean cities they brought also an urban gangsterism to be inspired by and compete with the rural and city gangs flourishing already in America.

When one Sicilian gang assembled in New Orleans to control the harbor rackets there, several of its members were savagely killed by a lynch mob along with other jailbirds who were innocent, in the belief that they had murdered the Chief of Police, himself no sweet-pea, who had been probably done in by local gang foes with high connections. This was in 1893, and along with several less spectacular incidents, helped to earn a questionable reputation for Italians, with their Sicilian-led gangs, later called *Mafiosi* and "the mafia" and "mobsters" and "the mob". Louisiana authorities who had solicited the laborious and competent Sicilians for the sugar industry desisted thereafter, but not before a large immigration had taken place; within a political generation an Italo-American, head of the political machine, was elected Mayor of New Orleans. The main setting for Italic activities was elsewhere and will be referred to in due course.

Italians reinforced the Germanic thrust in music, the Jewish juggernaut in film-making. They built an expansive following for the "Mediterranean diet", low on cholesterol, high on salads and pastas. For every Italian who quit spaghetti for steak and potatoes, ten other Americans swooped it up. Imports of Italian pasta doubled between 1990 and 1994; per capita consumption reached 20 pounds a year. Zucchini, eggplant, broccoli, fennel, salami, and pizza pies were several of half a hundred foods that zoomed in popularity. In California, embraced by a Mediterranean climate, the immigrants hit their stride in agriculture. Had they been directed Southwest to the New Mexico and Arizona territories - or even to Georgia, as President Theodore Roosevelt suggested, to regenerate agriculture - they might have had more fun in the first and second generations and worked wonders with the region.

But the industrial and transportation giants and the East Coast sweatshops had first call on them. And after that business: restaurants, construction, trucking, produce marketing, wastes disposal, the docks, fishing, liquor and entertainment, and then Catholic institutions, school-teaching, medicine, the protective services, law and politics, a broad occupational spreading patterned after the Irish and Jewish models, less than either and on a smaller scale, but some of both.

Despite the agonizing conditions of early modern cities of America, the brutal and exploitative industrial system, and the nearly complete absence of social facilities to help the population, the Irish, Poles, Italians and others like them did not suffer the ordeal of the Chinese in settling America. The Chinese were one of the saddest cases, yet ultimately triumphed. Brought over under contract as work gangs for railroad construction, mining and other labor-intensive jobs, they were isolated, underpaid, mistreated, overworked, given no rights - practically total victims. Many were murdered. They responded early in atypical American ways. They were thrifty. They remained sober. They were non-violent. But then typically, they smuggled, gambled, and opened houses of ill fame. They paid bribes to have their families brought in and to get other Chinese in. (Very often a Chinese American would have two parents: his natural parent and the one in America who brought him in as a son under changed name.)

Some 75,000 Chinese were to be counted in California at mid-nineteenth century, mostly of Cantonese origin, one-tenth of the people of the state, when a self-proclaimed liberator of the White race, himself an Irish immigrant named Kearney, aroused the public with a White man's party so-called, and the Congress was stirred to pass an act explicitly excluding Chinese from debarking upon American soil. (Later it was extended to bar Japanese.)

These indignities on top of all others did not impede the progression of the contract laborers from China and Japan in California and Hawaii from moving out into society and establishing businesses and farms that were models for the population at large. Finally after World War II, oriental exclusion was repealed and immigration resumed on a legal basis (it had never ceased illegally). A cultural outburst from the East Asian groups then occurred, rendering them extraordinarily creative in American arts, media, science and the universities.

Religious persecution - although basically a cultural,

anthropological, ethnic hostility on the part of the Turks with some response, too, from the Armenians - brought the Armenians to the brink of genocide in the early years of the twentieth century. Luckily, America's gates were still wide open and a million crossed the ocean from the Caucasus and Anatolia. Strongly Christian, in their own orthodoxy, the Armenians introduced a profoundly varied near-oriental culture to America that affected food preferences and artistic styles here and there - like everything else brought to America ingested, adapted, but still a small fraction indeed of the giant culture complex. Lebanese in large numbers came to the States, too. They had been mostly Catholic Christian in a land mostly Muslim, but dominated by Christians with French as well as Arabic their language.

The Austro-Hungarian Empire was splendidly productive in the arts and industry in the nineteenth century, but wracked by ethnic quarreling and warfare. The Empire should have given itself an acronym, perhaps, to which all might belong, such as HAPSJIBBS, indicating a partnership of Hungarians, Austrians, Poles, Slovaks, Jews, Italians, Bohemians, Bosnians, and Slovenians, while indicating the dynasty as the Hapsburgs. All of them professed strong dissatisfaction with the ruling elite and had on more than one occasion arisen in rebellion.

The Empire finally deceased in 1919, but had lost millions of its subjects to the United States - to Chicago, Cleveland, Pittsburgh, a hundred cities of the North, the mines everywhere - coal, copper, iron, stone, the large construction projects under way in the cities such as sewer systems, subways and roads. As with the Italians and most others, they were farmers and manual workers, and the shopkeepers and artisans who migrated with these often found themselves behind the times, in America, therefore unemployed, therefore consigned to harder, dirtier work. They made up a large part of the Iron Age industry work force. They labored in the slaughterhouses and packinghouses. Artisanal skills became well developed –in printing and metal-working, for example. They supported heavily the Catholic Church and the Democratic Party organization, and were surprisingly conservative, given their tough lot in the economic system.

One marvels at this distance of a century and more how this multitude made its way. And there were also the Greeks to account for, a million legally and illegally entering, in shipping, as seamen (who, like their predecessors since before the Mayflower, could jump ship and disappear until surfacing as Americans), as shopkeepers and restaurant-keepers, as laborers, too - modern, not recent, America was built up from the pick and shovel. Thence they moved into store management, government and politics - "We were the world's first democrats!" forgetting the social structure of Athens - and a broad range of occupations and professions; like the Jews, and to a certain extent like typical Italics, they refused to be denied any role that others were playing.

Filipinos came, another half-million, many pausing or staying in the Hawaiian Islands as plantation workers, then into the service occupations in the continental States, forming communities in many western and Northern cities, and developing shortly the usual social group pyramid of wealth, skill, welfare and respect. A noticeable change occurred with the immigration of East Indians; so many of these were professionals that the first questions were raised about the "brain-drain", the taking away from a foreign country of its highly trained and badly needed personnel by better working conditions and higher (though not equal to native) pay. Then, too, came the Koreans and Vietnamese and the Caribbean peoples - Jamaicans, Dominicans, Cubans - many others.

Cubans always had a foothold in Southern Florida, but, with the exodus from Castro's socialist dictatorship, they came within a political generation (two biological generations) to constitute most of a million Floridians and the same number elsewhere in the USA. In Dade County, containing Miami, they held the top elective offices, headed the police and prosecuting arms, and were prominent in banking, real estate, law, and politics - where they elected half the county and one-third of the federal legislators. They energized Anglo-Hispanic art and literature.

Almost everyone who came to America was compelled to come by circumstances or authorities. Exceptions were romantics, including utopians, and persons of high skills targeted to particular places or jobs. Once settled and adapted they would increasingly resist the idea of returning or emigrating elsewhere. Typically an ethnic arrival-aggregate would split within the same generation into "go-native" who sought to dissociate themselves from all but a token ethnic identity such as everyone else might be said to possess, and a fundamentalist "nostalgic" core that, for reasons both obvious and subtle, donned the mantle of the Old Country and solicited attention, favors, respect, and even allegiance from the "go-native" and general population, claiming to speak for the foreigners from "the Old Country" on issues of public policy and respect.

The offspring of both would generally feel the grip of America more tightly, to such an extent that the difference in the "patriotic grip" on Americans of any two generations of ancestry was from the earliest times practically negligible. There are many proofs of this statement: personal and group protestations; intense ritual observances; military records; cases of treason; literature; letters; biographies and autobiographies; testimonials; attitude tests; and public opinion surveys.

The phenomenon, though associated with similar behavior in Canada, South America, and Australia, is uniquely grand in its scale and complexity. The obliteration of ethnic ties is difficult even over centuries, and to have it occur on a massive scale in all important respects within a generation or two is perhaps the largest unique achievement of the United States of America. (Comparative studies need be made on this question: France assimilated large numbers of Poles after World War I; furthermore, its Southern provinces are heavily populated by well-assimilated recently arrived Italians. The Italians who went to Argentina, Chile, Uruguay and Brazil in great numbers took no more than two generations to become indistinguishable from the citizenry, or the citizenry to become indistinguishable from them.)

Although "Kearneyism" like "McCarthyism" was endemic in America, the rhetoric of accommodation and assimilation always prevailed. Even in the Southern states the infrequency of immigrants through the years was more a product of the racial conflict overhanging Southern life and of poor economic opportunities than of direct and general persecution of foreigners. Strangely, the individual foreigner has usually been more welcome in Southern circles of his or her type than one would be in the North. It was a Virginian, Congressman John Page, who called attention to the appeal for *"asylum for the oppressed of all nations"*, and said in the agitation over the Alien and Sedition Acts, *"It is nothing to us, whether Jews or Roman Catholics settle amongst us; whether subjects of Kings, or citizens of free states wish to reside in the United States, they will find it their interest to be good citizens, and neither their religious nor political opinions can injure us, if we have good laws, well executed"*.

In after-chapters, as in the foregoing, the antecedents of achievers of the American story may be identified. Two points may be added to the treatment that they have received thus far. One concerns the effects of the various waves of immigration insofar as they altered the course of American culture and politics. The second bears again upon accommodation and assimilation.

The average American and the various parameters of the physical appearance of the American, have changed. They have never been properly conceived anyhow. The average American today (and one must insist upon including women and children in the average) has achieved a grand stature of about 5 foot, 4 inches. The average natural coloring is brunette, with brown eyes; the average voice is a high tenor.

The per capita income per year in 1995 dollars was $7000.00. The average adult American has had 10 years of education, and is occupied in a service job, reads half a book a year, has 1.2 siblings. Most American young live in households without two parents present. Few Americans know their four grandparents or even their four family names.

The average American eats an old-fashioned heavy diet with lots of eggs, milk, beef, white bread, Coca-Cola and ice cream, and watches several hours of television daily. Most adult Americans do not vote in most elections. Nor do they know the name of their senators and Congressman.

(My reader is sophisticated in the game of playing with averages, so will appreciate that the above averages, although true, are adduced in order to crack socially damaging mythical averages.)

It is highly unlikely, given our survey of American history thus far, and knowing what is to come, that this average American has been made or remade by any of the waves of immigration (including the first boatload to row ashore), or is likely to be, by any large coming, except the descent of a flock of angels from heaven. Yet the American is different. One's habits and appearance have changed and will continue to do so. But the principle of social inertia operates strongly. The total culture keeps treading along heavily, and practically nothing socially imaginable can turn it one way or another or stop its progression.

The principle of gravity also gives us a metaphor. When an individual or a group - a large wave of immigrants, say - descends upon the American culture, it is like an airplane and Earth; the theory of gravity holds that the plane attracts Earth just as Earth does the plane, but so vast is Earth that the plane will have no appreciable effect upon its movement; it seems to be all one way.

Much more can be learned about such matters than is now known. How much more quickly did America take up classical music and science owing to the impact of the heavy German migrations. How much more quickly did it alter some dietary habits owing to the appetizing examples of incoming Italians, and the Japanese now for that matter? How much has the American novel - now contending for world supremacy - gained from the Jewish immigration?

What have English, not to mention Jewish, German, Canadian, Chinese, Indian and other immigrants, done to advance the study of nuclear forces and their applications? (One recalls the coded disguise telling Washington by telegram during World War II that at the University of Chicago, the first successful nuclear chain reaction had occurred: *"The Italian navigator has landed in the New World"*, referring to Enrico Fermi and Cristoforo Colombo.)

A vast systematic research can be visualized that would be at least as interesting as most large historical projects. Very likely, the immigrant generation will be shown to have been unusually productive, while suffering the most and often robbed of credit for its accomplishments. I think of the hundreds of tricks that miners, masons, builders, gadgeteers, publicists, writers, teachers, and others have brought over and introduced into the mainstream or tributaries of American culture. And subsumed under the rubric: "Yankee ingenuity", that conjures up Henry Ford and Robert Frost.

Now the question is accommodation and assimilation. The immigrant accommodates. He or she somehow gets by in daily life and from year to year (but recall the high rates of mental illness among the Irish and other immigrants). Accommodation is an impermanent state, and no body of American opinion has wished for an immigrant group simply to accommodate; accommodation is taken for granted. What most Americans ask for has always been assimilation. Assimilation means merging into the behavior and attitudes of the culture in a thousand ways, permanently.

By the theory of gravity mentioned above, it also means that the assimilating party, behavior, attitude, trait, if it is forceful enough, will impact and change the larger culture. But most of the time, assimilation evidences movement by the newcomer rather than the culture group into which one assimilates.

American history has shown
(we might as well admit the future here)
that no group and no personality type is non-assimilable. The American culture is an omnivorous octopus: it catches, swallows, and digests everything that comes within reach of its multitude of tentacles, and it has a large brain. A problem with assimilation though is that many immigrant habits and ideas are good, originally better than the American ones and they are lost upon assimilation: what is to be done about this? Perhaps all that can be done is by way of education and publicity in the media:

de-emphasize assimilation as a hodge-podge of trivialities, and give force to the particular preferable conduct and attitudes being brought into the country by foreigners.

The process of assimilation, the ancient Romans said, goes from *commercium* to *commensalium* to *connubium*: from commerce, to sharing the dining table, to intermarriage. Taking into account the hundreds of ethnic groups in America, the factors that most influence whether any two persons, female and male, in the population, taken at random, deal, eat together and share intimacies are chance factors: who lives next to whom; the occupational factor: who works next to whom? the educational factor: who goes to school with whom? the family factor: who has been marrying whom in the past? the fame factor, the prestige factor, the power factor, the wealth factor: who shares the same amounts and kinds of these values? the religious factor: who worship and pray together? the compatibility factor: who gets along with whom, who are congenial? the lust factor: who turns whom on?

When all of these are multiply correlated, they will show many relationships of one to the other. Ethnicity is one of these; a person's ethnic background will always have been related to all of these, and therefore there will have been a correlation within ethnicity, such that persons whose ancestors came from Bath or Kilarney or Naples or Frankfurt or Naxos or Omsk or Sierra Leone or Juarez will find themselves more commonly connected in all ways than if one's folks had come from another place.

The mix is stirred by social mobility of all kinds, and as the number of enclaves in American life diminished and continues to do so, the full measure of assimilation increases. While, after 1960, many more people have spoken against the melting pot and favorably about ethnic values, the processes of amalgamation and assimilation have gone forward. For example, the resistances and incompatibilities of Jew and Gentile, Hebrew and Christian, might be expected to reduce intermarriage and consorting to a low figure. On the contrary, the rate of intermarriage alone, clocked at 15% in 1950, reached 60% in 1990.

For the whole of 260,000,000 Americans (reaching perhaps 300 million in the next century), even if immigration moves at an annual rate of a million, probably 95% of all third-generation or earlier Americans will be of mixed ancestry, before the granddaughter of one's granddaughter gets to telling her little grandchild the whole story. The remainder will be unmistakably American in culture.

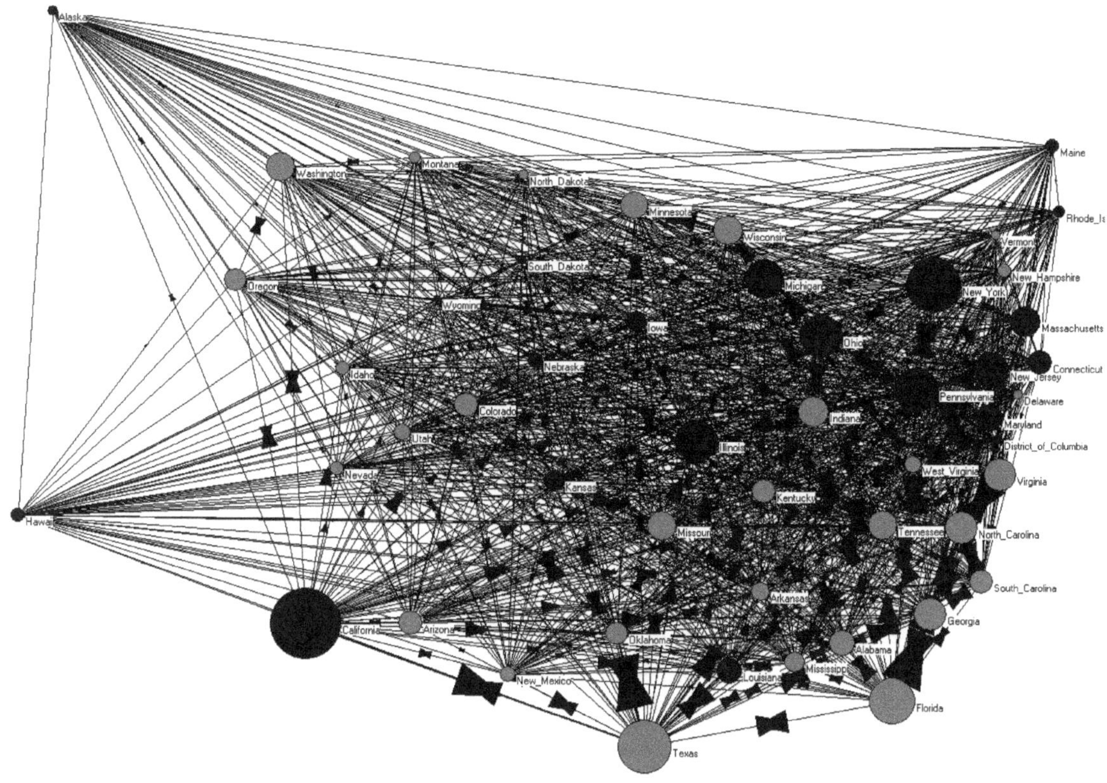

Sophisticated network display exposing recent internal USA migration, showing how people have been moving from one place to another inside the USA.

Chapter Forty-five

Internal Migration

Culture Shock was intrinsic to American experience, not only upon arrival, but time after time after migrating hither and yon. A person whose ancestor rowed ashore from a seventeenth century barque was as likely to suffer culture shock in his own lifetime as an immigrant from anywhere. Southerners moving North, Easterners moving West, and

more so Westerners moving East, all of these and
more took their turn as migrants, to be traumatized by sudden
encounters with strange character-types, ways of work,
technology, even climate and diet.

The stories of migration and immigration have been separated
unreasonably. Flight from religious and political persecution
has been taught generally to be the superior motive
for immigrating, and those who taught saw to it that
their own ancestors were of such ilk.
Actually, elementary computations readily
demonstrate that more people have migrated from
one part of the country to another
for freedom of worship or non-worship,
for liberty, equality and fraternity, for human dignity,
than have immigrated from abroad.
(In all cases, of course, there must be implicated
an economic factor.)

For every honest-to-God Puritan, Anabaptist,
Frenchman, Jew, and Irishman who could be said
to have landed in America because of persecution abroad,
ten or perhaps a hundred Americans have changed
their home within the United States because of
oppression of some kind. Many dissenting Puritans
had to leave their homes and settle elsewhere
as individuals or communes. The innumerable and
widespread Indian migrations were products largely of the
hatred and aggression of the Europeans.
Blacks fled the South at every opportunity;
it was not the Southern countryside or culture that they hated,
but their complete lack of liberty, including economic suppression.

Catholics have been forced out of towns and neighborhoods.
Mexican-Americans of the Southwest were forced into moving.
Early Mormons moved Westwards in peril of their lives.
West coast Japanese-Americans found themselves
consigned to camps in World War II, whence, released,
some refused to return to their old neighborhoods, while others
found their property had been confiscated or was occupied.

An indicator of the movements of the population was devised by the
Bureau of Census and applied retrospectively and
up to the present, the "Mean Center of Population",
a scientific fiction, a hypothetical point,
such that if a map of the U.S. surface were flattened out,
was made rigid, and everyone stood in place on it,
the map would balance perfectly on a spindle
fastened at the point. Thus, each decade, it
could be remarked that the Center of Population
was shifting westward. In 1790 it was located
East of the Appalachian Mountains, a few miles Southeast of
Baltimore, Maryland. A Southern as well as Western movement of the
Center could be noticed after World War I, because
so many people migrated to Southern California,
Florida and Arizona. The fulcrum moved markedly and
similarly after World War II, so that by
1990 the Center was calculated to be
9.7 miles Southeast of Steelville, Missouri.
We might conjecture a similar "Center of Emigration" for the world to
chart the incoming American population from abroad. The Center
would perhaps be first in Siberia, then in the United States, probably
around Tennessee, then it would move Northeastward, crossing the
ocean to Southern England, but then (artificially, of course, or
statistically) to perhaps Gibraltar because of the large incoming of
Africans, then would move North decade by decade as the larger
British and Germanic emigration came about, then in the 1880's
the Center would be moving toward Southern Europe, indicating the
emigration of Mediterranean and East European stocks, until finally by
the year 2000, hesitating whether to move East or West to denote the
large East Asian immigration, it would be somewhere
around Genoa, the city of Columbus.

Counting the hundreds of African nations, Indian nations, and
distinct sub-ethnicities of the European countries,
when their peoples moved into the American maw,
and then the Asian and North and South American nations,
we arrive at a thousand kinds of people --

whose inter-relations, beyond the shadow of a doubt,
were quite capable of peaceability,
when proper conditions were enforced.

Internal migration is to be considered in connection with foreign immigration. A fascinating pattern evolves as immigrants become migrants, for it was as migrants that some of the traits of the many nationalities that came to America were expressed: the Jewish peddler of Vitebsk starting up with a pushcart in New York and selling it to a later Jew from Lvov as he himself goes West to Arizona to peddle from a horse and wagon, then to set up a dry goods store, and finally to establish a department store;

the English machine crew from Manchester agreeing to accompany a machine system from Pittsburgh to Milwaukee to get it going;
an Italian railroad gang slurping up handfuls of spaghetti and meat balls from the great table of their boarding house in Kansas City;
the Swede languishing of loneliness and malnutrition on a desolate farm near Rapid City, South Dakota,
awaiting the arrival of his aunt and uncle from Chicago;
and so on through a million and more stories -
Armenians and Lebanese spreading around the cities of the Northeast and the farms and cities of California, exchanging places with friends and relatives from the old country,
leapfrogging each other to spread all over the place.

Between 1830 and 1860,
about 60% of the Boston population moved out
in each decade, in Philadelphia 70%.
Of the Irish traced through parish records in New York City,
in the period 1850 to 1869,
55% left the city, 17% remained and 28% died.
Similar German records reveal 58% who left,
40% who remained and 2% who died.
(The difference in death rates is real: Irish suffered
worse living conditions, a withering incidence of
contagious tuberculosis, a higher birth rate
with its consequent high mortality, and

more alcoholism and accidents.)

The immigration-migration process was often impulsive - but just as often exceedingly planned, carefully executed, an amazing story of individual and family accomplishment. It is generally not studied or taught because the social sciences that treat of these matters were unknown or undeveloped in relation to so-called history - mainly constitutional and political history - until the most recent political generation.

It seemed not part of the real America, whereas it was most of America beginning at the beginning, when the fascinating chains of communications stretched back from the first of those who left the new village and plantation to those left behind, from even the escaped slaves, convicts, indentured servants, runaway and kicked-out boys and girls, back to those who remembered them and wanted to know what they were doing and what the new world was like.

Migration consists of demographic changes within the locality; people moving in and out of a town from around the area; movement within a state; regional movements; and inter-regional movements, that is, national patterns. The rates of all of these have been rapid. A fifth of the people changed local domicile annually (about one-third of all tenants); another fifth moved somewhere within the same state; another fifth moved in the region; again a fifth moved between regions or nationally. These estimates leave a fifth of the people staying in place for at least a year. They would qualify as old-timers, except that soon they would move.

Actually there were probably more people who were substantially homeless in America over a period of three centuries than there were in the fifth who stayed at the same abode for a year or more. Once more, American history is unique. Never in the archives of history can so extreme an example of a restless (and presumably unhappy or at least anxious) population be found: and, we recall, these were all individuals or small voluntary groups, unless one were to count the armies that marched their men up and down the country during the Civil War. The statistics make of America a sort of perpetual frontier.

The Civil War veteran, North and South, was a driver of the internal migration wagon. The frontier got much of its railroad, mining, agricultural impetus and its ideology from him. The legions of pensioned war veterans acted as a kind of Republican Party task force to spread the gospel of industrialism and free enterprise. They buffered the even more insistent but impoverished Confederate veterans who would have taken over more territory in their absence. By their attitudes, they helped, too, to suppress welfare activities by governments around the country.

The USA is probably the only nation in the world where for four hundred years, when you met a farmer and asked him what he had in mind for the future, a typical reply would be, "I don't know, maybe sell out and move on.". Or you might hear "Maybe try my luck in.". The expression "It's time to pull up stakes" froze many a poor woman's heart. Land was something to be gotten at a bargain, used up, sold at a profit - I speak here of a large minority, perhaps a large majority of American farmers. Perhaps 95% of all those who attempted to farm in America.

As time went on, the immigrants from abroad and their descendants spread around. A study of the origins of the people of the States of Ohio, Indiana, Illinois, Michigan, and Wisconsin of 1850 evidences that 2.33 millions or half of the population were natives of their State, 0.28 millions came from elsewhere in the Old Northwest, 0.17 came from New England, 0.718 came from the Middle Atlantic States, 0.462 from the South, and 0.527 from Europe. If migration within these large states, each the size of England, were figured in - moves from one village or county to another, only a small percentage would have been born and lived within the circumference of a few miles.

Despite concentrations in states such as Wisconsin, Germanics came to form today the leading source of ancestry in thirty states. English ancestry is leading in five states, second in only nine, but found well represented in all states. Irish (2/3 Catholic) hold a plurality of ancestry in five states, second place in 20, African-Americans hold first place in ancestry in seven states, second place in only one. Italic ancestry holds a plurality in two states, second place also in two states. In Hawaii, the Japanese are the largest ancestral strain, in California, the Mexican, who also hold one second place. Norwegians of the near Northwest hold second place in three states. The French of New England and Louisiana are second most common therein.

Jews reside everywhere and have so since the beginning of the country (except where for a time they were excluded). Whereas for most immigrants and migrants, locating by a sizeable number of one's own ethnic or religious identity determined their movement, with the Jews a pioneering merchant spirit led them to every out-of-the-way place to establish a merchant and trading business, confident that they would make a go of it, and ultimately be in touch with co-religionists or ordinary non-practicing Jews; indeed, the process began with their setting up lines of credit and sources of merchandise with Jews established in the cities settled earlier or overseas.

This is the bolder version of the way many nationalities spread their people and customs and influence around the United States: Japanese orchardists, Italian masons and sculptors, Hungarian musicians, English metal-workers, Scottish engineers, Welsh miners, Greek café ("ice cream parlors") and restaurant owners. When immigration was severely limited, to the occupational chain was added the illegal entry chain. The Mexican was (and is) coming through knowledge of a job chain and an alien smuggling chain. Not a Greek Orthodox priest who ever served in America but had not arranged for the accommodation in parish homes and a dishwashing job for Greek sailors jumping ship and presenting themselves before him as guide to heaven on earth as well as above.

Religious cults found footholds and migrated in complex patterns. Generally the original American sub-cultures carried their religious labels westward, accumulating new legions of Baptists and Methodists as they went along. The Catholics migrated through America by several routes: their early grasp of the missions of the Southwest and Northern and Central California persisted and expanded with a new migrant population from the East; from the cities of entry and down from Canada, they spread throughout New England and the Northeast, composing an all-around plurality; their early presence around New Orleans was contained by largely Baptist elements migrating from the border states and Deep South; from Chicago, a belt of Catholicism stretched up to Lake Superior; clusters were to gather elsewhere, in Missouri, for instance, and Northcentral Kentucky.

The tendency has been toward religious diversity in the smaller centers of the country; the Sunbelt, to which Northern migration was heavy in more recent times, did not exist as a frontier concept for people and industry.

The process of westward movement from the earliest times finds itself called often "The Winning of the West". The Indians would call it "The westward plague of two-legged locusts". This was unhappily true.

The 1874 invention of barbed wire by an Illinois farmer named Joe Gladden transformed much of the Midwestern and Western landscape.

From 1872 to 1874, a buffalo-killing frenzy came upon people, abetted by the U.S. Army that used it to starve the Indians. Parties came from as far as Britain to shoot the helpless great beasts. Twelve million buffalo were slaughtered, plus countless elk, deer, and any other animals to be sighted along a gun barrel.

These were strange destructive years: the Chicago Fire of 1871, the Pestigo statewide forest fire, the Boston fire of 1872, and an 1872 plague of locusts devouring the Western plains, and then this killing mania. (One is tempted to reflect upon Ignatius Donnelly's theory that gases from Donati's comet were touching down upon the United States.)

One of the many myths about the immigrant is that in the beginning he preferred the wide-open spaces whereas, later on, he clung to the cities. Considering the myth of bucolic blessings, that made the earlier immigrant superior to the later. Some commentators, seeking to justify the latter, expostulated that the land had given out, the frontier was gone, they had nowhere to go.

Actually most humans have preferred the city to the country, when offered the choice. But in the first two centuries there were only several small cities, and few coming from Europe would have had urban experience. Cities averaged 1,000 to 50,000 in the earlier period and rose to contain from 50,000 to one million when Naples and London led the pack. It was often the case that the potential immigrant to America went first from his rural neighborhood to his nearest city, such as London, failed to locate there, and managed somehow, willy-nilly, to find himself aboard a boat to America.

There, if lucky, he would be indentured to a townsman or find town employment; else he was condemned to work upon the land or enter upon the search for land, obviously not difficult to obtain in exchange for labor, a little cash down, an application, or seize-squat-survive. Making a success from the land was another question; usually the farmer failed. Free Blacks headed for towns, and so did the emancipated African-American whenever he found a way to survive there, no matter how hard the conditions; meanwhile, however, before the turn of the century, Blacks transported themselves in considerable numbers to the far Middle West farmland.

Immigrants regardless of nationality, tended to edge westward behind somewhat earlier immigrants, for lack of town jobs, until in the end the land gave out and pioneering became obviously more foolhardy than hardy. Close examination of the records might disclose that the jobs in the cities stopped the pressure for open lands rather than the reverse, or mythical bucolism, whose scenario has the latecomers as low-grade peasants who suckered for the city, whereas the early-comers were high-grade robust farmers. Those who were kinder to the late settlers declared that these people really wanted land, but not finding it, had to stay in the city.

The opposite thesis might be more true, that the latecomers made better farmers than the earlier ones, who hardly understood the land and exploited it to the point of ruination, then moved on to wreck more of the virgin land and forests. And it is true that wherever the late-comers - I speak mainly of the Southern and Eastern Europeans - found the chance, they farmed well, or took up patches near their city jobs and turned to truck farming.

So little of the idyllic farmer has composed the Americans that it is rare to find a land title and active farm whose overseeing family goes back a century. This hardly indicates a love for the land or skill at farming. (We shall inquire whether it reflects gross mismanagement over a period of three centuries, hardly deserving the praise heaped upon the American farmer, "the most productive in the world". To be considered, too, are the immense subsidies given to farmers by the federal government beginning in the 1930's and continuing annually to today. Else the farmers would have expelled themselves much more rapidly from the land.)

The initial and persisting distinction between good and not so good farmers was ethnic. The Germanics, no matter from where, created the better farms and were followed and accompanied by Slavic and Scandinavian farmers as they traversed the continent, beginning in Pennsylvania, fostering a wide belt North into New York, and moving as such through the middle of the country to the Mississippi, into the near Northwest and later across the country from Missouri mainly.

The English, and especially the Scottish, Welsh, Scots-Irish, and Irish Catholics were not usually well adapted to farming. Although the Agricultural Revolution got a sharp impetus from English landowners, these were not the same people as those who landed in America. America's primitive conditions could not leap into agricultural revolution (the word "virgin farmland" really meant land that took far too much energy with primitive tools and barest of social support systems, without a road and market infrastructure).

As the Germanic settlers fanned out, they were preceded and accompanied and followed by a large number of other groups, mainly at first of New Englanders, who were the first to strike out for Oregon, though by this time the whole was becoming a mixed group, not moving and settling ethnically, but more likely religiously, as Lutherans, Congregationalists, or Methodists, or Baptist church groups. Both the Germanic and New England Anglo westward movement provided the cadres for numerous towns and some cities en route.

The Oregon Trail was a path very early marked out. Many Indians and traders had taken the route. In the 1840's began a large-scale migration by pushcart, wagon, horseback and foot over the two thousand miles that separated Oregon settlements from assembly points like Independence, Freeport Landing, and St. Joseph in westernmost Missouri. They had come by the same means from points South and East but most had used also the flotilla of Mississippi-Missouri Rivers steamboats. From a quarter to half a million people started out on the trail. A major fraction of these split off to go to California, attracted by the gold mines and the opportunities available there. About ten per cent died in the several months en route, not more than in the ocean crossings of the century and not so many more than those who would have back home, if there was a home. .

Hostile Indians were not commonly encountered. In fact the emigrants traded with the Indians and the Mormons who had preceded them and had come up from Utah for the purpose. (We recollect that the Mormons, after being persecuted in New York, Ohio, Missouri, and Illinois, had made their great trek several years earlier, and prospered in dealings with wagon trains pausing at Salt Lake City.)

The Oregon Trail passed through Kansas, Nebraska, Wyoming and Idaho, none of these especially tempting, then in Oregon territory, Baker City, North to Pendleton, passing through the Cascades Mountains North of Mount Hood, and over to Oregon City, Portland and Astoria by the Pacific. The attractions of the Willamette Valley caught most of the migrants. The region prospered and its people hardly felt the Civil War so far away.

Where the cities developed industry, as in Cincinnati, Cleveland, Chicago, Milwaukee, Kansas City and St. Louis, succeeding waves of Germans, British and other ethnic groups newly arrived in America joined in building industry. The great westward movement from the

Southern culture, Celtic and English by origin, was less commendable for its farming. On its Northern edges it mingled with the Northern elements and on the Southern it was *sui generis* except that it deviated around the French of New Orleans and infiltrated and took over the Mexican lands of the Southwest.

They ultimately moved in large numbers to Southern California and the great central valley, where, externally at least they began to become more like Northerners in speech and manners. But they were now among equally large Mexican and African Americans. New York and Illinois, abetted by Iowa and other Midwestern states sent large contingents into Southern California as well. They were blocked from the Northwest by the Mormons and by the new Eastern and foreign immigration settling around the mines and Northern ranges.

Numerous studies have finally come about of particular towns West of the Alleghenies and of what happened exactly in their settlement. It appears that they were composed in the first place of persons who were overly optimistic about their chances of success. Problems beset them immediately. They spent much time and energy in disputes and were unstable for a long time.

The myth of unity, community decision-making, democratic participation was rarely true. It was a shock for most people coming into a place, even there together by some chance or plan, to discover that they, Americans, had little of those wonderful talents that historians accorded them. Early Kansas towns for example did not only have to endure struggles over slavery, but conflicts between cattlemen and farmers, representing different ways of life.

Just as Europe seemed to be emptying itself of people, the East seemed to be breaking up in the westward movement. Along the trunk lines of the nation, beginning early in the nineteenth century and continuing to this day, a person never lost sight of some vehicle before and behind, carrying other migrants and their property west. It was a highly individualistic and yet highly social migration.

In the town of Jacksonville, Illinois, for instance, the outward appearances were of a voluntaristic community, with a mixed group of Yankee and Southern founders, who set up a number of voluntary associations where everybody could belong to something and do something for the community; large houses were built in plantation and Victorian style that seemed to prove a stable social order and prosperity. Peace, stability, prosperity.

Actually the town had none of these except partially and from time to time. The people fought over the Union. The ordinary run of people, whether in the beginning or in the end, entered and lived in cheap housing, that became dilapidated and was finally torn down. Depressions struck the town hard. Only a core remained, telling one another of their superiority over the "movers", as the bulk of the population was called, and publishing self-praise in a local press.
Between 1850 and 1860, only one-quarter of the residents stayed on; between 1860 and 1870 only 21 survivors could be traced in the town. Yet the town was growing in absolute numbers. When a list of "old settlers" from among the town and settlements and country people around was published in the seventies (as of 1831 or about 40 years) only 400 names showed up among many thousands. The thousands of school children with ancestors from various countries and regions who went through the town system were of course taught that these few hang-ins were the world's best people and responsible for all the good pointed out around.

The institutions, formal structures, constitutions, numerous types of voluntary associations, laws of all kinds, signposts, newspapers, infrastructures of bridges, roads, tunnels, railroads, and collections of houses, even though they hardly gave the impression of long duration and permanence of Europe, did make the scene, over let us say 80% of America throughout the three hundred years of its existence, appear durable, at least, and familiar to visitors and residents.

Whereas, in fact, these were a scenery that served constantly different troupes of players. A boarding house and a set of jerrybuilt houses would from one month to another be occupied by entirely different faces and families. Cemeteries would go unattended and were dug up after a few years. When people met as citizens of the town, they would ask one another where they had come from in the first several minutes of conversation.

Of those Americans who were not immigrants but had been born in America, the vast majority were themselves strangers in their own land, voluntarily. They could not stand where they came from, and for precisely the same reasons the immigrants had for coming to America. Where they had been, they would tell you, the land was overworked, the town jobs were diminishing or dull, one could not make a decent living, a gang of crooks ran politics, their church group couldn't support a church house any more, their loved ones had died or moved elsewhere, there was no decent schooling for the kids, and so on.

Those who remained in a town were "boosters" to the end, but the movers were the far-blown echo of the real town. There came to be thousands of local histories written in America; a half century was deemed enough to warrant a history. But with a dozen exceptions the thousands of works were unreal, untrue, flattering to the community and its presently leading citizens, and foreseeing a busy happy future. And when these thousands of communities set up monuments to their historical heroes, local or national, or to events deemed important in local or national history, historical unreliability vied with aesthetic offensiveness.

Local museums were equally trivial, but improved with time; churches were usually too plain and young to carry interesting treasures - nothing so astonishing, for instance, as was honored at the cathedral of Céziers in France: the hair of the tail of the she-ass that bore Christ on his entrance into Jerusalem.

In keeping with the "instant iconography" for which Americans were becoming world-famous, thousands of public historical sites came to be established around the country, aesthetically and historically more repulsive than Hollywoodry. A crummy site at Homestead, Nebraska, represented the first man to obtain a tract of land under the Homestead Act. He did not long remain on the land, in fact.

Did all the settlement bring an end to the frontier? The declaration by the Bureau of Census in 1890 that the Frontier had ended with the taking up of all free or non-governmental land was premature and anyhow based on false premises. There was a great deal of homesteading in the twentieth century, and one could still obtain some rather poor land under homesteading conditions just as in the century and a half before. But, as so many of the "farmers" or land-grabbers discovered when they hastened into newly opened territories for land, the land there was usually worse than the land back where they came from.

For the same reasons, the frontier did not end with the rush to take up the land of the Cherokee Strip, the last deprivation of the Cherokees in Oklahoma. It did not end with the extermination of the buffalo, brought about by soldiers and civilians with their repeating rifles urged on by Indian-haters and sporting clubs and railroad agents. The frontier had not ended with the completion of one, two, or three transcontinental railroads. Late into the nineteenth century large immigrations to America took place whose members - mostly German and Scandinavian so far as the Northwest was concerned - journeyed directly from Europe to the staging areas for farming, usually the houses of relatives or professional land dealers and farm-equipment dealers.

Good land was rare once a person left the Mississippi valley. After it became notorious that a family could not survive on even 150 acres of land in the "real West", Congress passed a Desert Land Act in 1887 that allowed a man to put down only a quarter of a dollar an acre for 640 acres and three years to attempt some kind of irrigation and then finally another dollar an acre and the title was his. The results were pathetic. An estimated 95% of the land disbursed under the Act was implicated in fraudulent sales. Practically all of it ended in the hands of large cattle ranchers.

Most of the newcomers did not last for long on the land. (In one four-year period of the seventies half the population of West Kansas fled their farms.) Destitute, the unsuccessful majority retired to the cities behind them or went to the cities of the West to find work. Some remained on the land, moving around locally, buying and selling among themselves and with the dealers of the nearest town, and beginning to organize, besides the voluntary associations, always there and with new ones on the way, political movements to facilitate cheap credit and high prices for crops and animals and their by-products, dairy and otherwise.

All too often the frontier and the West have been described as a safety valve for the nation, and there has been envisioned some large population centers of uniform traits in the East, that, upon any untoward happening - depression, overcrowding - would open and send some people spinning westwards. From the standpoint of politics, the West was more of a time bomb; instead of economic pressures and political pressures having to be taken care of in the East, their settlement was postponed by Western elements of some of the adventurous, the cantankerous, the disturbed, the poor, the immigrant, and property-owners who had failed to keep their standing - that is, those who would have constituted a turbulent social and political element.

But the same people brought many troubles to the West and the nation - private wars, public wars, violence, demands for state and national legislation of many kinds, and soon had the requisite number of U.S. Senators to shape national debates, issues and policies. The safety valve, that is, did not afford better opportunities to a great many people; they became shortly as poor as their Eastern brethren, though better off than their Southern compatriots. It lessened the pressures of law and order and radical politics on the East and moved them westward. The radicals of East and West were contemporaries and mostly took on the same ideas at the same time.

By the end of the nineteenth century, the United States could still be divided into cultural regions of some behavioral importance. There was the South, already described, with its many States, and strongly influential cultural margins along the Northern border, and the western border much extended, but with some losses in Maryland, Pennsylvania, Delaware and Southern Florida due to immigrant and migrant influences. Generally the South's basic sub-cultures were still the lowland, the uplands and the mountains. Moderating influences occurred in Louisiana French culture and Texas German settlement as well.

New England culture was now along with New York-Pennsylvania culture and their extensions all the way to the Pacific Coast a pluralist Yankee culture. The great immigrant cities stood by themselves already: New York, Philadelphia, Cleveland, Chicago, San Francisco, Milwaukee, St. Louis, Boston - they were much more alike, a mixture of immigrants and old propertied controls; they stood apart. California was becoming unique as a sub-culture of the Mid-west with strong infusions of poor Southern White and Northern big city attributes, hardly at all mixed or fully manifested at this moment in time.

In the great cities were sub-cultures, too.
It was not only incorrect but indecent to deny the authenticity of these compact neighborhoods, often composing a fifth of a great city, from the standpoint of culture. The Milwaukee Germans might be compared with the rural Pennsylvania or Texas Germans, or rural Pennsylvanians and Texans generally with respect to cultural creativity and activity. Likewise, the New York Italian neighborhoods and indeed practically all of the immigrant city ethnic microcosms were no doubt less typically American, but not less culturally active than the typical rural cultural regions of the country.

The post-Civil War Virginia inland, Chesapeake Bay, Tidewater, Eastern Bank cultures and several others of the larger Virginia complex fell into a "slough of despond" that was not alleviated by their considerable cities of Norfolk, Richmond, and even Washington (D.C.), because foreign immigration to these cities and to all Southern cities (except New Orleans) was minimal.

Nor did immigrants or their children migrate to Southern cities. The Minnesota Scandinavian culture was quite lively by contrast, but its ruralness handicapped it and not until it was securely urbanized in considerable cities did it attain a high level in the sciences and arts. Jewish city culture, both ethnic and full American, came to exceed in these regards all the others, ethnic and native, rural or urban, and remains to be treated here in later chapters. The several African-American cultures that characterized the great cities of the North and South need be compared not only among themselves but also with the Black culture of the mountains and deltas of the South.

That is, the city had its cultures, that are as important to analyze (but have not been) as the various rural and semi-rural sub-culture complexes that have arisen and in many cases died out throughout the United States. Wherever Americans went, and whether from abroad or from inside the country somewhere, they tended to group together. These affinity groups built morale and provided mutual support. They revealed in myriad instances the limits of American individualism. They were voluntary: movement in and out was relatively free.

However, wherever people were forced to live in urban colonies - whether they were mountain folk of Anglo-Kentucky or Hindustan, Jews or African-American - social problems became sharper. Trying to ghettoize them, realtors and racists (leading surrounding dwellers by the nose) figured as prime villains in the process of Americanization.

From the 1860's through the 1880's the final Indian wars and skirmishes occurred. In Minnesota during the Civil War, a forceful Sioux attack in retaliation against forced land concessions brought on a conflict in which many hundreds died. A slaughter of Cheyenne and Arapahos came at the hands of the Colorado militia in 1864, whose commander, at one time a Methodist preacher, gathered a large collection of Indian scalps for exhibition purposes. Congress began what turned out to be a hundred-year campaign in 1867, that sought to confine Indians to remote reservations. In the Southern tall grass high plains, several tribes resisted an agreement to confine them, and the Red River War of 1874-5 ensued.

In 1871, Congress decided that they were no longer treating with nations, therefore needed no treaties, but could govern the Indians by simple statute.

In the 1880's, Congress broke up tribal land systems,
assigning allotments to individual Indians,
but administering the lands in trust.
The trust made much money, it turned out, leasing the
lands for exploitation by miners and oilmen.
Badly administered, not to say corrupt,
only a century later was the trust brought to court
by the Indians for an accounting of the billions of dollars involved.

The seventies were also notable for the annihilation of
General George Custer's isolated detachment of cavalry at the
Battle of the Little Big Horn River. The
dashing, vainglorious, foolish man let his troops be
trapped despite all warning. The victorious Sioux
then retired, but were pursued everywhere.
Chief Sitting Bull, their leader, escaped to Canada.
The Far West found the Blackfoot, the Crow, the Utes,
the Modocs, and the Nez Perces harassed and increasingly confined
by the Army and irregulars. They settled finally in
miserable reservations.

Chief Cochise led the Apache nation in war and peace -
interminable frustrating encounters: it was impossible to keep Whites
from squatting, impossible, also, to keep young braves from
marauding. Wounded in a skirmish in Mexico, dying, he asked his men to
carry him up the mountain to watch the sun rise.

The Chiricahua Apaches produced a great chieftain in Geronimo, who
led them for two decades in clashes with successive punitive
expeditions of the U.S. Army. He gave up finally, though officially he
was said to have been captured..

In the late eighties, a Paiute Indian had visions of a Messiah and
predicted that he would lead all Indians to victory over the Whites.
Sitting Bull, who had returned from Canada, was killed while resisting
arrest, and a massacre of defenseless Indians - men,
women, children –occurred at Wounded Knee, South Dakota.
Practically the last incident of the Indian Wars occurred here now,
in 1890, on December 29.

Soon Theodore Roosevelt, ardent nationalist, loud-mouthed trust-buster, big game hunter, author, doughty warrior, and manic President, would be writing the epitaph of the Indian, prematurely: *"The settler and pioneer have at bottom had justice on their side; this great continent could not have been kept as nothing but a game preserve for squalid savages".* Only the total context of my book lets me dare print this seductive dogma, so accepted and so well taught to each other by so many Americans, so replete in falsehood, deception, and harmful myth.

The time had come for "benevolent" policy that would treat the Indians as Americans of unfortunate heritage. All tribal Indians were provided with reservations where they might be directly ruled by the Whites when considered necessary and where schools were provided for teaching a strictly Euro-American version of culture and history.

Between 1896 and 1990, federal government policy forbade the use of any Indian language in schools, though to suppress their language is a mortal blow to a people's culture. (During much of this period, millions of American children were reading the sad story of the last day of class for little "French" children, for now (1870) the "bad Germans" had taken over Alsace-Lorraine and banned the teaching of French (where German was the family language).

When reservations seemed not to make "good Americans" out of the Indians, a Dawes Severalty Act of 1924 authorized the President to cut up any reservation and give to each family up to 160 acres of its land, which was held in trust for the household and given over in free title only after 25 years. Soon, much of the reservations was falling into the hands of speculators. The Indians ended up with a few million acres of land under these programs. On occasion, valuable mineral and metal deposits happened to be discovered there, and individual Indians profited.

In 1924, United States citizenship was extended to all Indians. Contrary to popular belief, Indians gained little in consequence; the right to vote mattered mainly where they lived in some numbers.

A political generation later, in the Eisenhower administrations, over 100 reservations were abolished, redistributing the land to individual Indians, hoping that they would assimilate to the larger society. A decade later, this policy had disintegrated and tribal governance was restored here and there. In the couple of hundred reservations that persisted, little conventional paid work was available, and unemployment rates of 50% were common, an absurd statistic, of course, since there were rarely any jobs to be disemployed from to begin with.

Surprisingly, but in accord with the liberalizing trend of the Supreme Court, lately the Indians have been presenting old treaties and claims against the United States in state and federal courts and have been receiving (would that it were just in the nick of time) heavy compensation in certain cases.

Indians with valid racial and tribal credentials found, too, that they might legally set up gambling casinos, a highly profitable kind of operation, under their treaties and agreements of the past. The Pequots of Connecticut, who had been practically annihilated in 1637 by land-grabbing English Puritans, using other Indians as allies, still held on to a reservation in their name. The score who had remained thereabouts were able to muster three hundred, practically all of mixed ancestry - red, black and white – who qualified as tribal nationals;

they built a community economy on the basis of gambling that brought in hundreds of thousands of visitors annually in the 1990's and grossed hundreds of millions of dollars. Administering their patrimony democratically, they came shortly to resemble an upper-class suburb, giving more money, however, to support museums, education, health, and other philanthropies. As the twentieth century drew to a close, it appeared that the Indians would begin to turn the tables, debauching Whites by the same techniques as were used to ruin Indians in generations gone by.

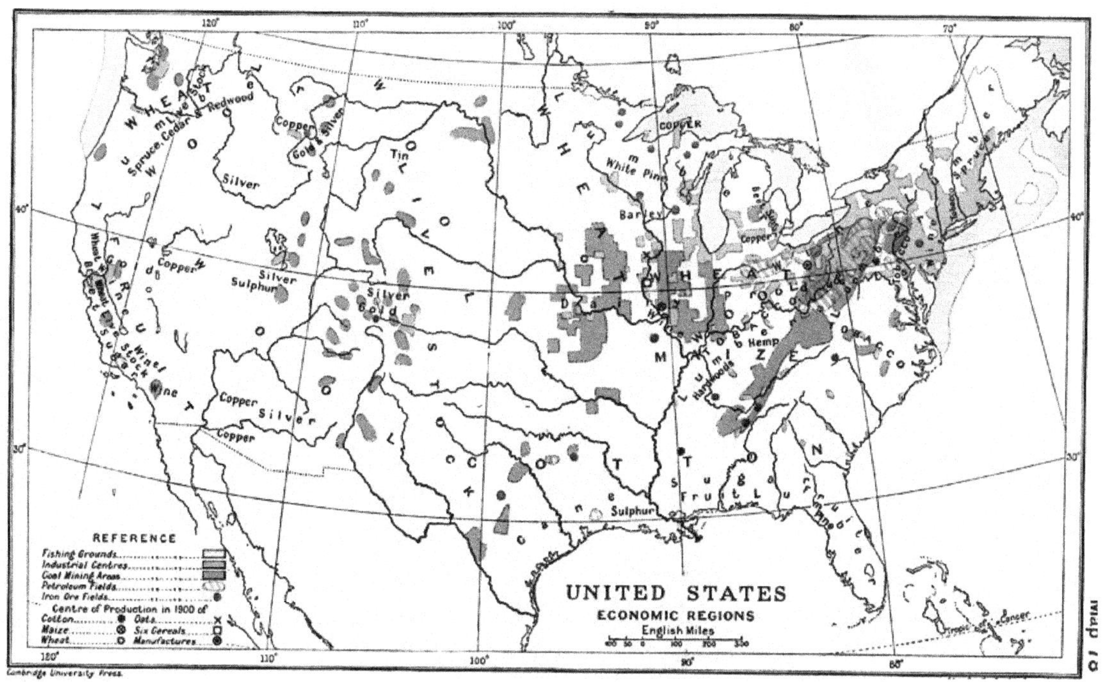

United States Economic Regions 1900

Chapter Forty-six

Conversion to Urban Industrialism

The United States became industrial champion of the world in the Gilded Age. It was not a Golden Age. Industrial output was growing at double the rate of population, notwithstanding the continuously heavy immigration and, indeed, because of it. "The Gilded Age" was the happy title of a novel by Mark Twain and C.D. Warner that dealt with the ludicrous contradictions of the times. It might well be applied to a country of desperate aspiration and clumsy achievement, whose needs and problems festered under the rich wrappings of an extravagant and ostentatious barbarous elite.

It was the age between the fateful withdrawal of federal troops from the South and the turning of the country into an urban industrial civilization, roughly then between 1877 and 1907. It was evident, if not admitted, in the end that the urban areas would be largely Catholic and preponderantly descended from nineteenth century immigrants.

Abraham Lincoln was mindful of how the North and West were developing even while the Civil War was being fought, and pridefully told the country in 1863 that he was proclaiming the last Thursday in November to be Thanksgiving Day and that the prospering condition of the country was a miracle evidencing the Divine regard for America.

"Needful diversions of wealth and of strength from the fields of peaceful industry to the national defense have not arrested the plow or the shuttle, or the ship; the ax has enlarged the borders of our settlements, and the mines, as well of iron and coal as of the precious metals, have yielded even more abundantly than heretofore".

In every foreign war in which it engaged, America's economy has expanded briskly. It is arguable that the Civil War was no exception. On the one hand women and Blacks had to work harder, and the economy was on a war footing; on the other hand, after the war, the South recovered slowly except in the Southwest and Border States. Likewise in the North, people worked harder, and no slackening or recession could occur in wartime.

The cities and industries grew apace, agriculture, too. Much of American agriculture and industry modernized and developed to huge proportions outside of the cities. Most of the cities would have grown large even if they had been deprived of most of the new industry.
In world history and in poor countries and rich, cities have grown large because, in addition to seating new and old industries,

they have been centers of trading and communications, of government, and of the arts and sciences, not to mention being a place where hordes of people with nothing else to do or nowhere else to go preferred to live.

The pace of urban growth speeded up. In the 1880's 100 cities more than doubled their populations. And most of these acquired suburbs, too. For the outfitting and management of their new cities, Americans drew heavily upon European inventions and experience - in sanitation, public health measures, road and drains construction, plumbing, in everything having to do with the arts - hardly in government, unfortunately.

The grand growth of cities and industry in America was accompanied by a continual dismal chanting against the cities and in praise of the countryside. The "authorities" of political science and sociology lent their baritones to the rural buffoons of politics. Just as the urban came to outnumber the rural population, the chant reached its fortissimo, at the turn of the century. A vein of ethnic prejudice lined the doleful music, implying that the urban-dweller was racially as well as environmentally inferior to the mythical countryfolk.

The vast peopling occurred largely without inside toilets and running water, without municipal sewers, in fact with hardly anything that came to be regarded a few years later as the vital public services. The largest cities emptied their sewage into private cesspools, with 70,000 privies in Baltimore alone at the end of the century. They paved their streets first not at all, some then with planks, then with macadam, then cobblestones, then in some cases granite blocks, sometimes with brick, then after the eighties with asphalt, the whole transition taking about one political generation. Often then, the streets had to be torn up to lay drains and pipes.

Muddy boots became as much a part of the American city as of the rural areas. Filth and crime were commonly encountered on the streets. From their very beginnings American cities were unfit to walk in and have persisted so until the present. They had not aspired until the end of the century to have parks. President Eliot of Harvard was as close to a Renaissance man as the age produced; he proposed plans for cities of parks and walks, of decentralized housing and industry; his effect was a spit in the ocean of pain and ugliness.

High achievements in engineering were registered. The skyscraper was invented and realized, a creature of iron and steel to begin with; concrete came much later. Although William Le Baron achieved the first skyscraper of Chicago in 1885, it was Louis Sullivan, also of Chicago, who was the prime architect of the new structures. The electric building elevator replaced the mechanical elevator in tall buildings after 1889. Marvels were accomplished in steel: Brooklyn bridge was completed in 1883.

The Chicago River was reversed so as not to dump its wastes into Lake Michigan, laid so beautiful along its edge, but the River turned into a canal that ended in the Mississippi River (hopefully with its polluting material dropped to the bottom en route).

Horse-drawn street cars were brought in; steam railways were tried, some on elevated tracks, but were too awkward and dangerous. Cable cars worked well, though cumbersome. The solution was the electric trolley car of the 1890's. Meanwhile New York, Philadelphia and Boston were tunneling subways for electric trains.
The rapid spread of the eminently useful bicycle after 1888 pressured for better streets.

No major invention came about after the turn of the century to save the cities from themselves. Many small steps occurred, usually to correct some growing fault, sometimes causing more of a problem than existed before, like water purification to replace the old pure natural water, asphalt instead of brick streets, more street lighting by gas and then electricity, electric traffic signals, buses in place of trolley cars on tracks, fill-ins of wetlands in and around the cities.

Houses were erected slapdash for the most part in the fast early stages of growth. Buildings rose in height. Families were squeezed into small flats and smaller houses and lots. But the excellent returns on renting to workers and clerks encouraged more substantial buildings; brick tenements and row houses became common. They quickly became slums; it was as if a decree had once been promulgated that every American must have had an ancestor who had lived in a slum, rural or urban. Surprisingly, about a third of the families in America owned their shelters. Most of these were in the country, of course, but many were in the city, where, given a little time and family members at work or bringing in a wage, a stick house could be erected and quickly filled with family and tenants. Mortgage and loan associations enticed many to borrow and be plagued thereafter by the threat of eviction for defaulting on payments.

Yet we speak of averages, and are likely to overlook the considerable number of people who, given a higher than average wage or salary, could hire excellent immigrant workers to put up a house, paying them very little. Before the age was out, suburbs had grown up, usually beginning as independent nearby villages and then becoming bedroom communities, obtaining richer neighbors, fresher air, and quiet, in exchange for a long commuting time.

Cities were vile places. Neighborhoods stank of the particular industries sheltered by them. Sewage was sniffable practically everywhere. Public health was continuously menaced. Typhoid fever, tuberculosis, yellow fever, cholera, smallpox were endemic and often epidemic. (Still, the idea that rural areas were healthy, long a myth, has been discharged by numerous studies, the earliest of them beginning in this period; the primeval forest was bad enough, but the remade rural environment gave a worse account of itself, lagging far behind in the application of preventive medicine, hygiene, diet, and medical care.)

People did not have strong convictions about cleanliness nor could they keep clean if they wanted to in many circumstances. Other diseases came from pollution and occupational poisons; hundreds of thousands of miners suffered from lung disease, usually called "black lung" in the coal mining areas. The poverty of the workers, the inadequacy of urban facilities, and the lack of a tradition of cleanliness in cities such as Dublin, Glasgow and London, whence came many immigrants, did not foster sanitary personal and family habits.

Diet was miserable. A penchant for bits of meat, pancakes, potatoes and sweets - skip the vegetables and fruit - led to frequent rickets and shorter lives. Milk was becoming abundant but germ-ridden often; only late in the century did the cows get chased out of town, along with the chickens and pigs, and with them went some of the sophistication and amusement of children from coming to know animals - including the terrors of their slaughter a few yards down the street. Pasteurization of milk (a French invention) came along with several other important controls based upon discoveries in micro-biology; these spread quickly everywhere.

Families were usually large and included several children. A sample of several thousand urban households of the 1880's gives us useful data. Border-state natives were the largest, and had the largest number of children, with about 30% having five or more children. Foreign-stock families came next in size and about 28% held over five children, then came Southern natives, and finally Northern native-born families, with considerably fewer members to a household and less children. German and Irish families in Philadelphia in1900 averaged seven children, Southern whites and blacks, six.

Indian household heads of the North brought in the highest median earnings, $485.
British husbands took in $453 (a difference, one writer stresses, worth 200 pounds of beef).
Continental men took in $383, Irish $367, French Canadians $358, and Anglo-Canadians $345. The differences relate to the skills and locations of work, and the kind of industry worked in. The native husbands of the Border State households (presumed all Caucasians) earned $343, and Southerners only $250.

These same families (not a random or even highly valid sample, but much more reliable than the guesses or journal accounts) spent a total of $605.60 on the average per year - 42% for food, 20% on the household, 15% on clothing, 4% on sickness and death costs, 6% on discretionary and 6% on all other costs. (Cato, writing 2200 years ago, tells us that the marginal laborer of the Roman Republic spent 52% for food, 8% for clothing, and 40% for rent and other costs of living. Generally his family ate wheat puddings, vegetables, rarely meat, and drank wine. Bread and circuses later were provided free.)

The 25% with the lowest income ($110 - 457 for the year) got their money 76.7% from the husband, 12.9% from working children, 5.2% from working wives, 3.3% from boarders, and 1.9% from other sources. The most affluent workers' families ($800-$2,777) got three times as much of their income from the labor of their children. Child labor operated under appalling conditions, but it kept most American working-class families surviving, solvent, and secure.

Butter and eggs were used in place of meat. Still, fresh and salt meat came to $75.00 of a total food expenditure of $223.00 for a family of seven in a year's time, according to a remarkable accounting by one worker's wife. Total wages of the household came to $576.00 for the year, rent to $84.00 and a small surplus was claimed.

She warns us, however, that when the factory shut down, as it did the past year for six weeks, everyone felt the necessary sacrifices. Illness was, of course, not compensated for in any way. Nor accidents; there were more than half a million serious industrial accidents per year. (Employer's liability was negligible).

Such a family could be and often was ruined by the next year's events. It could also be pushed into the next higher category of the poor owing to a child coming of an age, twelve or older, when he or she might find work or tend the other children while the mother worked. In any event, the portrayal here is of a well-organized, healthy family with a full "breadwinner". Chances are good, in fact, that the story was a concoction of government propagandists. Most farmers, Black and White, most laborers Black or White, most Blacks, did not come near to this state of affairs.

Infant mortality in 1900 was 162 per thousand births, lower than the average of the previous century; the rate declined to 100 in 1915; and halved to 77 in 1923. The figures were not reliable, inasmuch as in rural areas infant deaths went unreported, not to mention abortions and miscarriages, especially among the poor and the Blacks.
A third of all pregnancies of Michigan women in 1898
were artificially terminated, that is, aborted.

The crude death rate betrayed the same unreliability, but it seems to have declined between the early 1800's and the early 1900's, perhaps by nearly 50%. At 24 per thousand and 14 per thousand, the rate was still high, but so it was around the world. For men and women, life expectancy increased by seven years between 1789 and 1855, a memorial generation. In the next 40 years, until 1897, there occurred a 14-year increase in life expectancy. Industrialization and urbanization were accompanied, that is to say, by an increase in longevity.

In the Gilded Age, half the booming country's assets
were owned by 1% of the families.
Most people could not save. They could only
do a little better or worse from year to year.
National production rose steeply between the
Civil War and 1914. In consequence
prices declined over the same period. Real wages
did double between 1860 and 1914.
In 1890 the average national wage per year
amounted to $439 for all manufacturing workers,
with a low of $302 in cotton textiles and
a high of $630 in soft drinks and beer.

Salaried workers received more (including the honor of being paid a salary rather than a daily wage, and a presumption that lay-offs would be rare); clerks received $848 (this was the age when the social superiority of clerks over manual workers was advertised and believed), but railroad clerks earned only $635; postal employees averaged $878; schoolteachers, almost entirely female, brought in a mere $256.

Farm wages were considerably less. In 1900 the average annual wage was $490.00, requiring a work-week of 69 hours on a six or seven-day stint. Per capita income for the whole population, for all incomes and all gainfully employed in industry, commerce, governments, and agriculture, amounted to about $190 in 1890.

Still the cities were more attractive than the country, never mind the lovely myths about country life that the urban and small-town middle classes foisted on the schoolchildren and themselves. When Judge Gary, infamous head of New York Steel, giver of the name of Gary, Indiana, which name, unlike Stalingrad, has never been changed, to Laborville, say, testified before a Congressional committee about working conditions at the plants of the largest company in the country, possibly in the world, where men had to labor practically all of their waking hours all the week long, he compared them with country labor as getting a favorable deal.

But the country worker, the farmer at least, could call for his own respites, watch the sky and scene roundabout from time to time, and usually set his own pace, nor was he likely to be observed and bullied by bosses and what a century later came to be called security guards, who were then mere thugs, backed by the company managers and these by the local sheriffs and police departments.

Englishmen make poor workers, complained a Carnegie executive in 1875, because they brought to American notions of unions, conditions of work, and wages from the Old Country; give us instead, he said, the Germans, Swedes, the Irish (sic), the fresh lad from the American farm, who are more willing.

In Europe at the same time, the worker might observe a number of holidays without penalty, mostly religious in origin. Bare-bones Protestantism had shed most of these before the factory system began in America. Whatever his condition otherwise, the peasant of

Britain, Ireland, Germany, and the other European counterparts of Americans could often be found discussing the state of the world and heaven with others, or even at a cafe or bar.

The lads were leaving the farms as fast as they could - Americans then, as ever, were not happy at farming: for every man who left the city for the country, twenty left the country for the city. These native Americans were no less exploited than the immigrant or minority member. They could, however, escape a little easier into higher positions, where still they were worked very hard and had almost none of the perquisites of middle management today.

There were three major phases of the so-called industrial revolution that took early America to the end of the twentieth century. The first was the crafts phase, when small businesses were commencing to spread into a large variety of manufactures and transportation modes, prompted by many inventions, both mechanical and psycho-social; the second can be called the smoke-stack phase; and third and present phase the electro-chemical.

In the latter half of the nineteenth century, we are observing the smoke-stacks - water power and steam engines greatly magnified, the multiplication of inventions (and the prototypes of twentieth century major industries, such as electricity and diesel engines working upon oil). Coal and iron mines, and to a lesser degree petroleum wells, provided fuel and heavy construction material.

A new lexicon came into being; what men were doing now had to be described by new terms for the new processes, even beyond the new terminology of the materials and machines. Increased specialization brought many new job descriptions to go with the new kinds of work. Accounting practices were heavily revised. With increased functions and personnel, bureaucracy came to large business and government. The factory system took over everywhere, covering large acreages, attracting or building its worker communities. A new class of clerks came into being; these would for most of a century feel themselves superior to the manual workers and imagined themselves as ready to take over management roles as soon as their worth was recognized.

Before the crafts industrial revolution, the cottager, the printer, the work unit tended to be complete: the raw material came out ready for consumption. In the beginning of the industrial revolution, the movement of work processes was toward specialization of the company, that would deal with distant companies, agents, middlemen; there was neither horizontal nor vertical integration.

It was typical to receive an already begun thing and pass it along before it was ready for the consumer. But now the new captains of industry sought economies, controls over people and processes and prices, and smoother, quicker coordination of the total process of their industry.

Where they succeeded, as did John D. Rockefeller for some time in the petroleum industry - drilling, pumping, storage, transportation, refining, distribution, sales - the profits were huge. His key achievement was to gain control of 95% of the refining capacity of the country, which he achieved by efficient organization, astute bargaining with the parties on all sides, by making secret deals with the railroads, buying out competitors, undercutting others, refusing services to others, in short, employing whatever tactics might prove effective.

Later on, J.P. Morgan did the same for the steel industry with the formation of the United States Steel Corporation, which began with iron ore quarries and extended to the customers for finished steel. The list of giant industries that sprang up is long. They all went through the stages of discovery, initiation, scrambling for capital, fighting competition at every stage, mutually destructive pricing, voluntary or compelled amalgamation, and controlled raw material sources, production quotas, and pricing.

Most major industries came to be monopolized by one or at most several firms. They numbered in the scores; their annual product exceeded that of many countries of the world, and if the rest of the country's gross domestic product were to have been measured and added, it would have exceeded that of any nation in the world by the end of the century. Its industrial production surpassed that of united Imperial Germany. To the great corporate names already mentioned could be added three score others, that the American citizen was coming to know as well as he did the names of the individual States, names like American Can, Pullman Car, Dupont in explosives, and Singer Manufacturing Company in sewing machines.

Societies tend to move in a coordinated, transacting fashion, we should remember, and agriculture in cheap-land mobile America was as revolutionary as urban industry. As early as the seventies small farmers were barely holding their own, while giant farms were bringing about a new agro-industry. Wheat farms and cattle ranches of thousands of acres were working the soils of the Near Northwest down to the Near Southwest, from Canada to the Rio Grande.

German discoveries and practices in chemical fertilizers were enthusiastically adopted, and taught to students of the expanded agricultural and mechanical colleges that had been funded everywhere by the federal government (under the 1862 Morrill Act). The coincidence of heavy German immigration to Northwestern farms and the prompt dissemination of German scientific advances is notable. Environmentalism, more in philosophy than in practice, a kindness to the landscape, came into being in the Gilded Age. (Ernst Haeckel coined the term "ecology" in 1866.)

The Constitution was user-friendly to businessmen. Especially as interpreted by the courts. Governments continued to help the capitalist and the entrepreneur, the good ones and the bad ones, and to persecute the complaining workers and their representatives, whether good or bad. Expectedly, there is argument over the qualities of those who emerged top dog during the Gilded Age. Some say that there was no special way. No special genius. No morality that one would find unambiguously recommended in the Gospel, in the Constitution, in Shakespeare, in a writer of consequence, in poets.

The general formula for great success was, first of all, settling upon the strategically correct business - new enough for new men; vast potential for growth; a technology that had gone through the invention and pioneering stage. Then came choosing reliable and competent partners and employees and clients; working hard; lucking in; and arranging, sooner rather than later, banking and financing connections. Getting all of this together required a lot of talent and a steadfast character.

The tycoons knew how to make deals and seize opportunities, how the future was shaping up. Like politicians watching the polls, they scrutinized the faces and fates of the unsuccessful, learned how the mob was heading, paid as little attention as possible to legal forms and restraining laws. They let neither politicians, nor lawyers, nor media criticism, nor reformers stand in their way - and there were all too few of these last types anyway in the Gilded Age.

In one way or another, most of the new achievers came out of the old possessors, not John D. Rockefeller or Andrew Carnegie to be sure - they had been poor boys - but J.P.Morgan, for instance. Long after the myth of "from rags to riches" became part of folklore, sociologists and economists dug up family records on the oligopolists, and even as Roberto Michels found among the early Bolsheviki, the successful commissars disproportionately came from successful families, and tried usually to hide their origins. They did not emerge from bitter poverty and ignorance.

Sympathy for the businessmen who were displaced, edged out, or ruined by the monopolists, would be misplaced. They shared all of the vices of the monopolists, and gnashed their teeth only at not being able to exploit the worker and the environment as greatly and profitably as the triumphant barons of industry and commerce. If Rockefeller had not forced out of business most of his competitors, the whole group of speculators and producers, refiners and distributors of petroleum would have battled continuously, raising and lowering prices to the consternation of the business community, the financial institutions and the public.

Rivers of petroleum would have been wasted. As it was, Pennsylvania oil reserves did disappear quickly and the industry went West to repeat the act. Furthermore, the weak individual industrialists would have been victimized by the railroad directors, for they had little bargaining power in their individual capacity.

Not until 1890, after the horse had escaped from the barn, did Congress attempt, half-heartedly, a restraint upon the monopolists.

Then it was that a bill of Senator John Sherman of Ohio, ably reworked and conducted through the toils of the legislative process by Senator George Hoar, declared unlawful all trusts and combinations in restraint of trade and manufacturing. However, this was window-dressing. It did little more than reiterate what the common law had said for centuries about monopolies, that they were unlawful conspiracies against the public and the realm.

In reality, the syndicates, secret pacts, trusts, interlocking directorates, and holding companies that were the substances causing protest and attempts at legal controls, might thank Congress for a vague and unenforceable and lackadaisical law, that the economic oligarch waved at in overtaking and passing. Many more trusts were formed and the new phase could be hardly countered by the Sherman Act or any act thought of to this day, the use of simple investment banking techniques to see that all the controls of an aggregate of concerns controlling an aggregate of production were in the proper hands to count on the results of their activities. J.P.Morgan brought this upon the American Republic.

Exceptional men invented and pioneered and rode the roller-coaster at least part of the ways. Alexander Graham Bell patented a variety of telephone that after many design changes entered the inventory of the American Telephone and Telegraph Company in 1885. Thomas Alva Edison not only invented numerous devices - the phonograph (1877), the incandescent light bulb (1879), a storage battery, a copying machine, and the motion picture (all of these with competitors in Europe who claimed credit, too), but he set up an "institute of invention", an avant-garde conception of how things ought to be developed in the modern world, the first R & D establishment, that brought him in lucrative contracts and produced profitable innovations. His lamp bulb fed on direct current, that unfortunately could not be carried long distances along a wire.

Nicholas Tesla, an engineer who immigrated from Croatia in 1884, espoused alternating current, and was fought by Edison, and sold out to Westinghouse. He invented the electric dynamo still basic to electric power and set up the Niagara Falls power system. He ran a fantastic experiment station in the Rocky Mountains to pass currents through the Earth and obtain charges therefrom of the potency of lightning, and died in an unpaid Manhattan hotel room, his only friends the pigeons he fed from his window. Frank Westinghouse carried on most successfully with the AC system.

Charles Proteus Steinmetz was another immigrant, from Breslau, who fled in 1888 when his socialist convictions got him into trouble. He became a professor at Union College and a General Electric Company consultant, worked like Tesla on lightning, transmission lines, and generators, to the tune of over 200 patents.

Few believed that man could ever fly by motor until he did so fly. Balloon flights were old by a century when Wilbur and Orville Wright began a lifetime of experiment and construction at Dayton, Ohio, encouraged by their father, who was an itinerant preacher on the road half the time, but also by their mechanically gifted mother. The sons never married, their sister married at 52. They were upstanding, abstemious, determined bicycle repairmen, absolutely determined to fly a machine and doing so definitively in 1903, assiduous afterwards in seeking patents, contracts, payments, and credits. Orville, the surviving brother, sold their business for a million dollars. Like Charles Lindbergh, who was to fly the Atlantic Ocean solo two decades later, the Wrights were the rage of Paris.

With all this industry on top of trade and transportation, and the millions of workers entailed, there had to be an enlarging middle class. Some of its elements were old, meaning that they descended usually from middle or upper class parents, but the majority were new, coming out of the new or greatly expanded occupations of the smoke-stack age. The older types were heavily represented, for example, among teachers, among professionals such as doctors and bankers, among writers and publishers, and among ministers (but not priests, these being newly minted from generation to generation by the Catholic Church).

The civil servants were new except in the upper realms where politicians could obtain support for election from the old middle class gentlemen and ladies. Also included here would be the prosperous independent farmers, and large land-owners and rentiers of country and city. All of these increasingly sent their children to increasingly exclusive private schools, boarding them there often, so that a kind of national upper-middle class began to develop, sometimes in this manner keeping in touch with the scions of the truly and permanently rich.

The overwhelming number of the middle niches were filled by new types. Here were most civil servants, technicians and machinists, suppliers of mechanical goods, smaller independent farmers, retailers and wholesalers, artists and entertainers, and the great American salesman. Ladies were still absent in all occupational categories of the middle class, except as landladies. The potential wave of women in middle-level jobs of industry and business and politics was imperceptibly forming far out at sea. It would take a hundred years for it to come crashing in.

Good ladies were concerned with welfare, particularly with the innumerable depressed, but here they were forced almost entirely into a certain decorum. They had to propel and stand behind their menfolk. They could, if they would, read some of the reports of the absolutely foul conditions of life in the city for most of its inhabitants. They might not only derive a lubricious satisfaction from these, but also truly learn what life was like just down the street from them.

They could be shocked by hearing how many women were prostitutes (never mind the mistresses, call girls, loose women of their circles), as many as they and many more. These hung around and lent a promising air to dance halls, saloons, hotel lobbies, vaudeville shows, theaters, magazine stands, amusement parks, Turkish baths, restaurant back rooms, state fairs, barber shops, excursion boats whether on the Hudson, the Ohio, the Mississippi, Lake Michigan, or wherever, lonely wharves by the thousands, and - need we say - the streets, and the scores and hundreds, and in Chicago and New York, the thousands of brothels themselves, plain and plush. One can think of all of this as part of the Gilt or part of the Problem of the grossly enlarging city. And think, too, that the automobile back seat had hardly been dreamed of.

We shall probably not be able to ascertain the number of women, or men for that matter, who were onto drugs in the Gilded Age. Neurasthenia and hysteria were common. In fact, one observer after another tells us that the typical American countenance in this period was strained and anxious, among women as well as men. It evidenced the social climber's and survivors' diseases.

Fatigue was as common among the leisure classes as among the laborers, among "unoccupied" women, lying among their chocolates and cats, as among their menfolk. Depression was common, too. And the fits of hysteria that practically imaged the Victorian Age, the fits that allowed Freud to build a theory of psychoanalysis at the end of the period. Cocaine was the drug of choice, after alcohol, of course. Cocaine was used in some cases to break the alcohol or heroin habit. It was easily obtainable. Some mixed it with tobacco and smoked it or chewed it. Some took their cocaine in wine or whiskey. It was certainly a stroke of genius but also a promise of what was really therein to call it - whatever it was - a few years later, "Coca Cola".

Electricity had its domestic side. The sewing machine was electrified, then the room fan, the toaster and teakettle, and, in the 1880's, the vulvular vibrator, followed, a decade later, by the vacuum cleaner and electric iron. Numbers of women had long since suffered the illness called hysteria (from the ancient Greek word for uterus and early referred to as "womb furie".) Physicians treated it variously, by hypnosis, by psychoanalysis, by sleeping potions, and by digital manipulation of the genitals. But the vibrator was to be cheaper and more patient than the doctors, and its electrified manifestations were manifold, with an enormous market nudged along by advertisements and scientific arguments in respectable magazines.

American males, who were too obtuse to comprehend and

too ashamed to admit it, were convicted of amorous incapacity and put in their place by, ironically, a mechanical device. (Spas, to which women resorted, also lent douche hoses, which were used for vaginal play.)

Farmers and workers organized rapidly on occasion, but just as rapidly their organizations dispersed. They treated the hard tasks of the organization of unions, of cooperatives, and of socialism as they had the sporadic revival movements of the century before–chiliastically, enthusiastically, ready to win their demands tomorrow, but not to wait for the day after.

One of the longest-lived of farmer-worker organizations was the Grange, or Patrons of Husbandry, founded by farmers in 1867. It counted a million members within a few years, and collected a million votes when its candidates ran under the Greenback Party label in 1878. (But the Greenbacks disappeared after 1884.) Besides running candidates, Grange lodges set up producers' and consumers' cooperatives - aimed at the unpopular middlemen who owned silos and wholesale stores and bought and sold grain. They conducted themselves as social clubs as well in a great many farming communities.

Another group, less affluent on the whole, the Farmers' Alliances, was developed during the period in many states; they were not a political party but hoped for social legislation, were friendly to women's rights, and sought to form cooperatives in order to eliminate the middlemen, who, we may recall, were the bane of poor Whites and Blacks in the South and were nearly as oppressive in the North: or so it seemed to the unsuccessful farmer, that is, most farmers. The Alliances numbered a million-and-a-half Whites plus, separately organized, a million Blacks in 1890.

For two decades around then, with the founding of the Knights of Labor, nearly a million workers were brought together to demand shorter hours, elimination of children from the work force, cooperatives, cheap money, and from time to time the exclusion of Chinese and other immigrants, although immigrants among them were numerous.

The Noble Order of Knights were a confused lot, reaching out as a fraternal organization and secret society, a political movement, a political party, a resettlement group, an egalitarian and yet discriminatory congeries. Often they organized both men and women, Blacks and Whites, and skilled and unskilled workers. After earlier railroad strikes succeeded, the ever-guileful Jay Gould sucked them into a strike for which he prepared an ambush by violent strikebreakers.
(There had been terrible depressions in 1873 and 1877, each with heavy wage cuts and unemployment that ruined hundreds of thousands of poor families.)

The 1877 strike of the railroads showed the nation what a more radical aggregate of migrant workers, radical immigrants, miners, lumberjacks and sundry other groups fully organized labor movement might achieve.
The militia of several states had to be called out and finally federal troops descended upon the scene.
As usual, the "forces of law and order" suppressed the strike supporters, to the benefit of the companies.

The Industrial Workers of the World, the IWW or "Wobblies", were a more radical aggregate of migrant workers, radical immigrants, miners, lumberjacks and sundry other groups. "Big Bill" Heywood led and inspired them. They won an important strike in Massachusetts but lost more often, usually in bloody combat with the authorities and owners. The movement slipped after 1912, and was persecuted in World War I by the Federal Government for its pacifist and socialist principles.

A more sober socialist party was led initially by Daniel de Leon, a Dutch West Indian, who was replaced in 1901 by Eugene Debs, of Alsatian ancestry, America's greatest socialist.
He had led the railroad union workers in the Pullman strike of 1894.
Despite support from around the country, the strike collapsed in the face of determined onslaughts by

outside strikebreakers and federal troops ordered in by President Grover Cleveland. As candidate for President, Debs won nearly a million votes in 1912. He went to jail for his pacifism in World War I. When he was visited in jail by affectionate friends, the *New York Times* said, "Why all the kissing, Mr. Debs? "

Widespread violence had attended also the Homestead, Pittsburgh, steel strike two years earlier. In this, perhaps the most violent of strikes, workers destroyed much company property and fought against hundreds of strikebreakers brought in from outside the area by the companies, and ultimately were mowed down by the state militia. This was the year after the founding of the Populist Party in 1891; Ignatius Donnelly, whose books on ancient catastrophes were mentioned in *Chapter One*, drew up its party platform.

Besides proposing the usual social welfare programs that were in vogue, the Populists wanted to increase the silver and paper money in circulation to $50 per capita; over the generation past this figure had gone down greatly. The farmers were the hopeful ones behind the demand; its enactment would cheapen money, thus making more of it available for the repayment of debt and the purchase of necessities. Another Populist or People's Party demand was for an income tax, still another the popular election of U.S. Senators. They also hoped for the nationalization of the railroads. In 1892 the Party picked up a million votes for its Presidential candidate. They practically forced the candidacy of William Jennings Bryan upon the Democratic Party in 1896, and he lost the election narrowly, scaring high business and finance. He lost twice more as the Democratic candidate.

Bryan's oratory was the culmination of the traditional evangelical style. For opposing reasons, both populists and banking circles went hysterical over his Democratic Convention speech of 1996 in which he implored the voters not to let America be crucified upon a cross of gold.

Silver mining interests applauded as vigorously as the Populist Democrats, for they, too, wanted to cheapen the currency, increase the money supply, give the poor man something to clink in his overall pockets. Presumably America could not be crucified on a cross of silver.

Bryan later became Secretary of State under Woodrow Wilson, resigning when the anti-German policies of the government became apparent to him. When last in the public eye, he was debating Clarence Darrow in a Tennessee court of law over the guilt or innocence of a schoolteacher named Stokes, whose offense was to teach, contrary to a State statute, that man was formed by long periods of evolution from lower forms of life – an anti-Judeo-Christian idea that Bryan disliked. Although Stokes was convicted, his case was later dismissed on appeal, for technical reasons.

Among the immigrants were numerous anarchists, who believed private property was basically theft, that capitalists were to be eliminated in favor of workers' cooperatives, and that violence had to be used to bring down the social system. In Chicago, a largely Germanic anarchist group met at Haymarket Square, 4 May 1886 to protest the killing of a striking worker at the International Harvester Plant. When police descended upon the meeting violently, a bomb was thrown among them killing one officer and wounding others. Retribution was visited upon the agitators; four were hanged, on doubtful evidence of complicity in the crime, while others were handed long prison sentences.

The Haymarket bombing initiated the first major "red scare" - as distinguished from customary violence against agitators for workers' causes. All labor problems could be sloganized to justify root and branch extermination. Radicals, communists, socialists, anarchists, and all who sympathized with them fell prey to police, vigilantes, zealous prosecutors, and a persecutory press.

Foreigners, in this case Irish nationalist workers, were also involved in the "Molly McGuires", most prominently active in the coal mining areas. They were a secretive group, operating as a combined international anti-British conspiracy, anti-employer organization, secret labor union within the labor unions, an association to bring preferment to Irish Catholics, and in all of these aspects committed hundreds of killings and beatings. Managers and uncooperative workers were often their victims. Their decline was associated with the achievement of minor objectives in the mines, with the assimilation of many members to the larger society, and with the arrest of key members by Pinkerton private detectives and state police, followed by convictions.

Some immigrants were easier to unionize
than Indians. The latter had been profoundly
individualistic all along and
had little impulse to give up their regularly
enjoyed liberty of decision and action in order to
fight against the owners of industry and their thousands
of minions and private police, certainly not
to join with "foreigners" against the native-born elite.
Immigrants, by contrast, came already aware of the
great strides that labor movements were taking in
Europe, of the gains that they had won. England and
Germany, for instance, had much social welfare
legislation on the books a good political
generation before the United States acted.

But blacks were humble, poor southern whites
bewildered, and immigrants of halting speech:
actually all shared all three traits that
combined with their rawness and newness
and rural backgrounds to render them near to hopeless
prospects for unionization.

With an ideological breach between native and foreigner,
there could be no enduring union. Worse,
the several ethnic groups were prey to division and betrayal.
One could be employed to crack another.
Moreover, only a hundred years earlier,
there still existed indentured servants, those who had
been so much a part of the settlement of the country,
so that employers, consonant with American habit and culture,
could see in the worker not much beyond the status of the

indentured servant. (We may hope that the reader does not hold the notion that a man who has risen from the ranks is usually a more benign boss than a person given an entitlement to command others straightaway.)

For these reasons, the American labor movement never really got off the ground, though on several occasions it went roaring down the runway. It was anti-socialistic, individualistic, atomistic, permeated by bucolic ideology and utopian visions. Americans who agonized over the condition of the working class could not arrive at an effective formula for winning a respectable permanent place in the hugest of industrial societies. Indeed, they made their intransigence and defeat into a virtue and victory, claiming that unions were an evil and foreign influence on the true-blue worker.

The American Federation of Labor was the exception. This assembly of autonomous crafts unions was set up in 1886 under the leadership of Samuel Gompers, a Dutch Jew who learned social science by reading to his fellow workers in a tobacco shop in Florida while they spit on and rolled the leaves. Separate unions were set up, locally autonomous but each having a national headquarters and affiliations and thus capable of calling upon their fellows everywhere to join in strikes and boycotts. Carpenters, Pullman Car porters, masons, numerous other trades, even professional musicians, soon had their unions. The scheme proved more effective, especially when it was executed in collaboration with local politicians needing personal and financial support.

But it overlooked the mass of industrial workers. As for the clerical workers, they were hopeless so far as the union movement was concerned. Sitting below the bosses admiring, they would watch their advantageous position and initial superiority in pay diminish with time. They were self-respecting but proletarianized without knowing it, which meant that they were poor but unorganizable, and without class-consciousness.

The American tradition of corruption and violence naturally characterized labor relations. The crafts union leaders were often involved in bribery, pay-offs and racketeering; they could usually call upon thugs to threaten or injure non-union scabs and recalcitrant employers. The largest demonstrations of the violent tenor of America occurred, however, in connection with the efforts of the true class movements and mass movements of labor, such as were described fleetingly above..

When all efforts to organize a working-class mass movement failed, the workers and farmers could exclaim,
"We have met the enemy and they are us".

Politics of the city and nation in these years left much to be desired: the Presidents were mediocrities, wrote Lord Bryce, a careful and systematic authority on American government. (He is not so brilliant, nor so celebrated today, as Alexis de Toqueville who wrote a half century earlier - but then de Toqueville was more moved by populist democracy.) Not only were the Presidents unimpressive, said Bryce, but the cities were the most conspicuous failure of American democracy.

It is easy and correct to generalize here. Both the cities and the nation were dominated by the moneyed interest, as Hamilton and Madison would put it. But now we were talking about veritable dinosaurs crunching about the country. National politics operated usually without giving much trouble to the industrial captains. The Senate was "a rich man's club", said everybody, peaking perhaps in 1900 with 25 millionaires in residence. Considering that the club was elected by the state legislatures, still, this fact casts the state legislatures in a lurid light: indeed they were rings of corruption.

A persuasive case can be made that the most scientific concept to be applied to modeling the American political system for some fifty years here was a set of interlocking rings of corruption. We have already advanced the thesis, without fear of slander, that the Presidents of the post-Civil War period were worse than mediocrities, and contributed on the whole to the defeat of racial and industrial and social harmony in general.

At least, in the Congress, voices could be heard denouncing one unholy alliance after another. The Sherman Anti-Trust Act, for all its weaknesses, was intended sincerely to call a halt to monopolization of all the industries of America. Not without representations by the National Labor Union, a predecessor of the major workers' groups named above, Congress decreed an eight-hour day for all federal government employees; this was well ahead of private industry, which seemed to take no note of the fact. Washington was dominated by business interests. The place, still hot, humid, and culturally a negative, was relatively inactive, bereft of knowledge regarding planning, administration, and late technology, except in a few departments insulated from politics. The opinion still prevailed, that the best government did little or nothing.

From 1888 onwards, Senator James Blaine was in charge in the Senate and Washington and lent his brokerage services to monumental deals around the capital and country. Senator Nelson W. Aldrich of Rhode Island might be termed the perennial Crown Prince of the Republic. It was their group and its ring upon ring, interlocking networks we would say today, that crushed in a panic the labor movements, the reform movements, the Democratic Party when it fell under the influence of cheap money advocates such as William Jennings Bryan - who, let it be said in favor of his opposition, that no man had a freer voice in trying to upset the American plutocracy over so many years.

The United States was still a developing country, although its adolescent girth was huge. The government's continuous struggles over the relation of gold to silver content, in backing up bonds and currency, helped cause one and then another economic panic and depression. President Cleveland, for instance, found the country's gold reserves "low" at one point, and decided that Congress had better stop backing government bonds with gold, and repeal the fixed relation between the price of gold and silver in dollars.

What should have been a plausible idea, little better or worse than the next man's, caused many silver mines promptly to fail, credit generally to collapse, unemployment to rise to 20%, riots to break out, industrial production to diminish, imports to lessen, and

European investors to begin to sell out their American interests. In the next elections, of 1894, the Republicans regained control of Congress. Financiers August Belmont and J.P. Morgan lent the government the credit facilities it needed to reassure the anxious and baffled sheep of the financial community, the media, the politicians and the foreign bankers.

Not only does our lack of space forbid an explanation of all this here now, but there was really no explanation: it was one more depression such as had continually occurred from the beginning of the Republic, once or twice per decade, each time inflicting increased anxiety and hardship for a couple of years on most Americans. Still, as wars killed and wounded their myriads, but the population increased, so depressions brought their compounded and confounded miseries while, underneath, the generative forces of the next phase of economic expansion readied themselves to leap forward.

The cities were going their own way. Their political leaders - in rings, fiefdoms, and gangs - learned how to negotiate and compromise with the leaders of industry and yet persuade the denizens of the city that they were respected and even dominating the government. Connections between the cities and the State and national governments were many, and more a network of corrupt arrangements than they were of *"planned scientific and administrative benefits for the whole of the city in relation to the state and nation"*. Such latter expressions could inspire ironic laughter.

The phenomenon of the boss was nationwide, from Boston to San Francisco. The boss signified the combination that worked, the myriad minor precinct captains, the money streaming in from all quarters, the pathetic endlessly suffering dependent poor gratefully putting on the role of a supporter, not a beggar, the clamoring business elements who were ready to fulfill civic needs if only they were given the contracts to do so.

The cities had to do very much, but how to do it was the question.

State legislatures, usually fully corrupt, gave the cities hostile and inefficient, but extremely detailed, instructions on how they must do everything, until a city home rule movement in Illinois and a few other places reduced the dictatorship of the yokels. But this did not help the situation, because the city slickers ran everything corruptly too. The difference was that cities had to be constructively corrupt, whereas the legislators were usually purposeless in their grafting.

It was like the situation in the world of the late twentieth century, when some progressive governments did much of their work with the grease of corruption, like Italy and France; the corruption found its way to formidable progress; but in others, like the Soviet Union, corruption was only personal, could not be invested in enterprise or to carry on political debates, and made matters worse.

The conclusion is obvious: capitalist corruption is much less damaging and more constructive over a wide range of effects than socialist or communist or militarist or, for that matter, civil service corruption.

Legislatures - Congress among them - became the seats of the bucolic imagery of America that proved itself destructive over the next century, keeping the cities from doing anything, applauding the labor relations philosophy of business, despising the incoming immigrants, keeping the educational systems in thrall to the rural imagery.

The Gilded Age was also the age that brought the glamorized cowboy, whose ragged outfits became highly styled by city folk, "saddle-set" tourists, dudes from the East and abroad whose coming engendered a false folk culture that fixed itself on the minds of the next century of Americans and the whole world via the media. They came to hunt and fish and ride the range, doing their bit to exterminate the buffalo and the fowl. They liked rugged landscapes and the presence, even when hostile, of Indians. A few bought huge cattle and sheep ranches and stayed a while.

Physical mobility remained high during the Gilded Age. Over 50% of the persons registered in the city of Rochester's Directory in 1864 were gone by 1869. Middle and working classes, not to mention the large migrant element, shared the penchant for moving.

Stabilizing factors did begin to appear. Many members of the new middle classes slowed their movements with their investments in jobs; industrial workers with families had their moves encumbered; the newer waves of immigrants were more and more inclined to be embraced by family life. As work and therefore skills became specialized, one could less easily expect to find employment elsewhere.

There may also have been a slowing of the eagerness to buy land: a paucity of land opportunities was noised about, but land was still cheap as dirt, and perhaps the reluctance to go onto the land came from realizing that one would buy land now from a failure, not the government or a primary promoter in most instances - a scary thought; the potential settlers felt like soldiers marching to the front past uniformed blasted bodies and wrecked equipment. Better to take up city jobs.

A final question disturbs us. Could the country have developed industrially as fast by treating workers, whether foreign or native, well? Much of Germany, the Netherlands, Northern Italy, Northern France, and England, after all, developed about as fast, while giving the worker a better deal. Still - probably not. Because the United States had other costs to pay: the general backwardness of the population that included Southern Whites, Blacks, frontier simplists, footloose myriads, and an unassimilated work force: there were heavy communication costs incident to the mixture of types presented to businessmen to organize, train, and direct. Hardheartedness beat out sympathy in human relations generally.

www.ingramcontent.com/pod-product-compliance
Lightning Source LLC
LaVergne TN
LVHW061217100826
845148LV00004B/783

9781603770811